**Ireland at the Polls
1981, 1982, and 1987**

Ireland at the Polls

1981, 1982, and 1987

A Study of Four General Elections

HOWARD R. PENNIMAN AND
BRIAN FARRELL, EDITORS

An American Enterprise Institute Book
Published by Duke University Press
1987

© 1987 AEI (American Enterprise Institute
for Public Policy Research)
All rights reserved
Printed in the United States of America
on acid-free paper ∞
Library of Congress Cataloging-in-Publication Data
Ireland at the polls, 1981, 1982, and 1987.
(At the polls)
"An American Enterprise Institute book."
Includes bibliographies and index.
1. Elections—Ireland.   2. Political parties—Ireland.
3. Ireland—Politics and government—1949-
I. Penniman, Howard Rae, 1916-   .   II. Farrell, Brian.
III. American Enterprise Institute for Public Policy
Research.   IV. Series.
JN1541.I72   1987   324.9417'0824   87-13513
ISBN 0-8223-0754-5 (alk. paper)
ISBN 0-8223-0786-3 (pbk. : alk. paper)

Contents

Tables and Figures

Tables

Figures

Preface

──────Ireland at the Polls, 1981, 1982, and 1987: A Study of four General Elections is another in the series of national election studies prepared by the American Enterprise Institute for Public Policy Research (AEI). Books in the series include volumes on some thirty national democratic elections around the world. Distinguished foreign and American scholars have contributed to the studies.

An annual volume has recently been added to the series that will devote a chapter to each competitive national election held in a given calendar year in countries with populations of two million or more. The first volume will be The World at the Polls, 1983: Competitive National Elections. Books in the series are published jointly by Duke University Press and AEI.

A Note on the Single Transferable Vote System

Today Ireland is the only major country where members of both houses of the national legislature are chosen by what the Irish constitution calls "'the system of proportional representation by means of the single transferable vote,' but what most Irish people refer to as simply PR."[1]

The single transferable vote (STV) system was invented quite independently in the mid-nineteenth century by Carl Christopher Georg Andrae, a Dane, and Thomas Hare, an Englishman. Andrae's version of STV was used in Danish national elections for the decade beginning in 1856. Thereafter, for a period, it was used only to elect some members of the Danish upper chamber. Later it was abandoned entirely.

In Britain STV received strong support after 1850 from John Stuart Mill who wrote that its advantages "place Mr. Hare's plan among the very greatest improvements yet made in the theory and practice of government."[2] Mill also argued for adoption of STV in the House of Commons. In spite of more than a century of diligent effort, STV supporters have never been able to win serious parliamentary consideration for the system. Members of Parliament have preferred to stay with the country's traditional plurality system by which they have been selected. Today a small reform society continues an apparently futile effort to develop support for STV in Britain.

While Parliament never adopted STV at home, it prescribed the system for the Irish in the Government of Ireland Act of 1914. That law, however, became effective only after World War I. The first Irish national legislature was elected under the new rule in 1923. It continues to be the Irish electoral system to this day.

Outside of Ireland, considerably modified forms of STV are used to elect members of parliament in the tiny Mediterranean island country of Malta and in Australia where it is used to select twelve senators from each of six states plus two from each of two territories. The STV systems in each of these countries so differ from STV as initially conceived that neither would meet the expectations of traditional STV proponents.

In Malta there are now only two parties and a handful of independents. The election of 1981 went to the minority Labour party aided by carefully gerrymandered districts that gave Labour seven of the thirteen districts with a vote of 109,990 while the Nationalist party's 114,132 votes carried only six districts. The twenty-nine independent votes had no influence on the outcome. The Labour party had welcomed the presence of Soviet personnel and agreed to send Maltese troops to Libya for military training. These developments have done little to increase the confidence of the Maltese majority in either its electoral system or its government.

A law enacted in Australia after the 1983 national elections provides that a voter may, as in the past, number the names of all the candidates seeking senatorial office in his or her state. Not long ago that meant that the voter in New South Wales was forced to number seventy-two names in an election. Failure to number each name (except one) made the ballot "informal" or void. The new law, however, allows the voter simply to place the number "1" in a box above the name of one party and that automatically endorses every candidate on the ballot in the order recommended by that party's leaders. In the 1984 elections this meant that the number of spoiled ballots was significantly reduced, but it also nullified a key goal of many STV advocates who support the system precisely because they wish to free voters from what they view as the excessive influence of parties.

Irish Politics

The 1977 Irish elections witnessed a spectacular victory for Fianna Fáil, the largest of the country's parties, which won 84 of 148 seats then in the Dáil. It was the greatest margin of victory in half a century. The outcome was interesting not only because the elections were conducted under STV which, like other PR systems, may be expected to fragment the vote thus making it difficult for a single party to win even a bare majority, but also because the incumbent Fine Gael-Labour party coalition had redrawn constituency boundaries with an expectation that the new districts would considerably enhance the coalition's prospects for reelection. The very large Fianna Fáil vote actually reversed the anticipated impact of the gerrymandered districts, increasing the magnitude of the Fianna Fáil landslide. To avoid future gerrymandering, a new law has assigned the task of redistricting to an independent commission.

Four years after Fianna Fáil's overwhelming victory, Ireland's political mood changed again. The three elections in 1981 and 1982 ended what Brian Farrell called "an enviable degree of political stability" that had marked Irish politics for nearly sixty years—a record almost unmatched elsewhere in Western Europe. The elections in June 1981 produced a vulnerable government composed of Fine Gael, Labour, and some independents. The election in February 1982 brought to power a comparably weak government that included Fianna Fáil, small parties, and independents. Finally, the November 1982 election provided a clear-cut victory for the Fine Gael-Labour party coalition. Perhaps more important for the future of Irish politics was the fact that Fine Gael by itself came within five seats of matching Fianna Fáil's seat total in the Dáil. It was the closest race between the country's two largest parties since the 1920s. Labour's sixteen seats assured the coalition of a working, if not overwhelming, majority in the Dáil.

For many years Irish parties, candidates, and voters have generally been described as district-oriented rather than nation-oriented. Even recently, nearly half the voters responding to a survey research question have said they chose a "candidate to look after the constituency." Peter Mair states that some candidates perceived their role as brokers on behalf of constituency interests. He contends, nevertheless, that "regardless of the undoubted emphasis on personality appeals . . . Irish voters appear to be party voters." He further argues that the increased power of the national party leaders is based on "a major increase in the organizational resources and activities of the parties at the national level." And Brian Farrell says that "there has been a significant shift toward elevating the role of the Taoiseach" (prime minister) in policy formation. Most of the other contributors to this volume agree with these assessments. Some might add that this recent development has affected Fine Gael's constituents and officeholders more than comparable persons associated with Fianna Fáil. Certainly Fine Gael headquarters have aggressively sought to control more of the party's campaign and policy decisions.

The first nine chapters in this volume cover in some detail virtually every aspect of the 1981 and 1982 elections, including the campaigns, the parties, the voters, and postelection problems. In chapter 9, Basil Chubb summarizes much of this information and then turns his attention to the future and the problems that he expects the Irish government to face. His very thoughtful essay is informed by years of service with and study of the government. The essay is of special importance because many of the problems that face Ireland confront some, perhaps most, other democracies. "Effectiveness suffers when governments become overloaded, whether in financial matters or in their ability to cope with their public services." Some scholars and politicians, Chubb says, "would argue that most democracies are clearly overloaded, with public expenditures and public sector wage costs, outstripping available resources and with clear signs of overcomplex, overstrained political and administrative organizations failing to administer or enforce the law in some areas." They also "recognize that electorates [special interests] long used to rising levels of prosperity will not tolerate lower levels of services or lower living standards." Even as the state becomes less able to foot the current bill, the interest groups demand more government services.

Chubb concludes by saying that "while Ireland is still a democracy, its democratic institutions are not working well." Perceptive observers in some other democracies may recognize symptoms of a comparable nature that exist at home.

Eight authors who have taught in Irish universities have contributed to this volume. Brian Farrell, in addition to coediting this book, wrote the introductory chapter that describes the context in which the first three elections were held, a second chapter that discusses the office of the Taoiseach and the selection of his cabinet ministers, and the final chapter that covers the 1987 elections. Joseph O'Malley describes party manifestos and the financing of political campaigns. Richard Sinnott reports on the findings of opinion surveys, the issues in the campaigns, the relationship of the parties to the electorate, and possible changes in the status of political parties that may develop as a consequence of the elections. Peter Mair describes the organization of Irish parties and the increasing centralization of their campaign strategies. Maurice Manning traces the changing place of women in Irish politics. John Bowman examines the role of the media in campaigns and their relations with the parties. John Coakley describes the unusual process by which senatorial candidates are nominated and elected to the Seanad or senate. As noted, Basil Chubb looks at the possible future of democratic politics and its problems in Ireland.

I wish to thank Randa Murphy for her many contributions to the final manuscript and especially for her careful preparation of the index.

Brian Farrell has earned my deepest gratitude for writing three chapters, for his work in planning the volume, and for his great contribution as coeditor.

Howard Penniman, general editor
At the Polls Series

Notes

1. Basil Chubb, "The Electoral System," in Howard Penniman, ed., *Ireland at the Polls: The Dáil Elections of 1977* (Washington, D.C.: American Enterprise Institute, 1978), p. 21.
2. John Stuart Mill, *Considerations on Representative Government* (New York: Forum Books, 1958), p. 111, reprinted from 1861 edition.

1   The Context of Three Elections

BRIAN FARRELL

In sixty years of self-government the Irish system created and developed an enviable degree of political stability that was virtually unique among the new nation-states that emerged in the twentieth century.[1] At the beginning of the 1980s that stability was shaken. On three occasions in the brief period between June 1981 and November 1982 general elections were held. (The February 1987 election is discussed in chapter 10.) Two of these contests produced short-lived minority governments defeated by adverse parliamentary votes. None resolved the issues of credibility, equity, and economic management that were central to the campaigns. Public opinion polls throughout 1983 registered a marked dissatisfaction with government; despite three rapid changes in government, a majority, when questioned from early summer on, favored another change.[2] The old molds of Irish politics set more than half a century earlier, the established patterns for registering electoral choice, and the narrowing range of policy options being offered were no longer adequate to secure a mandate. The Irish political system was creaking under its governmental overload.

In many ways the uncertainty of the early 1980s was less remarkable than the long-term stability that had preceded it. The Irish state that emerged in the 1920s faced formidable political problems. In part the product of an armed struggle for independence, it was born into a civil war that fractured a centrist-nationalist consensus into two uneven but ideologically almost indistinguishable wings (subsequently the two major parties, Fianna Fáil and Fine Gael) and limited the small Labour party to a peripheral role.[3] The new state was prey to the tensions created by a disputed border and was challenged by a militant minority denying its legitimacy; its developing constitutionalism was weakened by the regular needs to invoke special powers against subversives. Committed to an electoral form of proportional representation that seemed likely to encourage a high level of party fragmentation and political individualism,[4] the Irish Free State of 1922 might have been destined for that collapse into excessive factionalism, internal anarchy, or military regime that has been the common experience of so many new postcolonial states.

Instead, building on an already established and firmly democratic tradition, it settled into an orderly series of electoral contests between the few major parties. Within ten years of the civil war, parties alternated in government with minimal disruption of the existing administrative machine. A few years later a new constitution, adopted by popular referendum, largely confirmed the status quo; a decade later the declaration of the Republic of Ireland reinforced the geographical framework and settled political conventions of this small European democracy.

For the greater part of sixty years successive Irish governments were not subject to any insupportable social or economic demands. Ireland was a compact, rural, relatively underdeveloped society with modest economic expectations, marginal and manageable internal social divisions, and a narrowly defined partisan cleavage. A traditional habit of emigration produced a distorted demography: a population pattern that combined high marriage age, low marriage rate, and high fertility rate and was heavily weighted toward the very young and the old, in which young adults were a subdued and self-conscious minority. A basic conservatism, reinforced by a powerful and popular Catholic church, was protected from pressure. Educational opportunity was limited and controlled. Sexual discrimination reflected accepted social norms. Radical ideas were easily dismissed or suppressed by formal and informal censorship. The tendency toward self-absorption and isolation, so common among new states, was enhanced by Irish neutrality during World War II. A stability that bordered on stagnation was sustained by the persistent predominance of the first generation of Irish political leaders into the 1960s. Throughout the 1970s, while Northern Ireland continued to be wracked by an internal upheaval that challenged the basic framework of an orderly society, the Republic of Ireland appeared set to continue in its staid, even stuffy, mode of politics.

The 1977 Election

That cosy expectation was only marginally upset by the unexpected outcome of the general election in June 1977.[5] The incumbent coalition government of Fine Gael and Labour, led by Liam Cosgrave, could face the contest optimistically, despite earlier political embarrassments (which included an unprecedented vote by the Taoiseach [prime minister] against his own government's Family Planning Bill and the resignation of President Cearbhall Ó Dálaigh) and inflation of almost 100 percent over the previous years. The coalition had introduced a popular budget, had been successful in recent by-elections, and had engineered an apparent bonus of six extra seats in the Electoral Amendment Act of 1974 contrived by Minister James Tully. In the event it was precisely this "Tullymander" that told against them. Fianna Fáil fulfilled the trend indicated in the public opinion polls (which had been dismissed by commentators) and captured more than half the first preference vote. The constituency revision now converted this victory into a record majority for Fianna Fáil with 84 of the Dáil's 148 seats. Although, on the night of the count, party leader Jack Lynch predicted that the size of the victory would cause problems, the initial analysis suggested that little had changed in Irish politics. There were some indications that Fianna Fáil had successfully wooed a higher proportion of younger voters, a clear indication that Fine Gael had lost ground among the traditionally loyal farmers with large holdings, and the reassurance that Labour maintained support against a weak challenge from the left. But none of this was a guarantee that Fianna Fáil could sustain future electoral success.

The emphasis on "consumer politics," which had been a significant feature of the 1977 campaign, seemed likely to displace the old rhetoric of nationalist politics and the newer invocation of expansive but vague economic promises. Traditional party loyalties still dominated, but that had been diluted by a more calculated approach to voting. Self-interest and a demand for tangible results would be more likely to determine future election results. Irish society was already changing; the face of Irish politics could not remain static.

Quickly both Fine Gael and Labour changed party leaders. Garret Fitz-Gerald replaced Liam Cosgrave as the leader of Fine Gael. He promised a new professionalism to his party and began by moving the party headquarters, recruiting an expert staff, and reviewing the constituency organization. He established a research service, selected a new front bench, and set out on a detailed tour of the party's branches. A specially commissioned poll probed the reasons for the election defeat and provided data for securing and regaining traditional sources of support and encouraging the recruitment of new and younger supporters. The small Labour parliamentary party divided almost equally between two contenders for the leadership. Elected after a second ballot, Frank Cluskey appointed his rival, Michael O'Leary, as deputy leader. But the strained relations between the two men remained and did nothing to raise the party's sagging morale.

When the Twenty-first Dáil met, Jack Lynch nominated new senior and junior ministers and announced a strong commitment to public service reform and a reallocation of ministerial functions. In office the new team began implementing the promises made in the Fianna Fáil election manifesto. Significantly, Charles Haughey (who had been dismissed from office by Lynch and subsequently charged in connection with importation of arms) was included in the cabinet;[6] he was known as a rival and critic of the Taoiseach and as an opponent of the extravagant promises made in the manifesto. Nevertheless, Fianna Fáil, an essentially pragmatic party carefully seeking to expand support by balancing benefits to all sections of the community, was secure with its parliamentary majority and its renewed wide social and regional base and seemed set for a comfortable period in office.

Things soon went wrong. Economic difficulties were magnified by the accumulating social pressures of an accelerated rise and radical restructuring of the Irish population.[7] The decision to postpone the regular census due in 1976 had obscured the extent of the change. The 1979 results revealed a rise of 13 percent over the 1971 figures. Ireland had become the youngest and fastest-growing population in Western Europe. The increase, which reversed the century-old decline, had first appeared in the 1960s in the more developed and urbanized eastern and southern regions; by the 1970s it was manifest in all areas. Combined with a marked decline in emigration, it was transforming Irish demography and putting new burdens on a developing economy.

Ireland's economic growth, initially stimulated by state-led attempts at economic planning and expansion and encouraged by membership of the European Economic Community, was not maintained. The worldwide recession of the later 1970s was particularly damaging to a small, open economy. Government revenue, agricultural prices, and personal incomes could not keep pace with an inflation that was intensified by the international oil crisis, by handsome pay settlements to both public- and private-sector employees, and by an acceleration of rising expectations that had been encouraged by the politicians' promises. The official statistics confirmed the widespread recognition that full employment—long a goal of policy—was increasingly remote from reality. They also revealed the as-yet-unappreciated trend of government expenditure, both on current and capital account, to rely on incrementally more expensive foreign borrowing. From the mid-1970s governments had regular recourse to annual budget deficits as a means of evading difficult decisions. The electorate soon expressed its dissatisfaction.

On 7 June 1979 the local elections coincided with the first direct elections to the European Parliament. The results revealed a remarkable narrowing of the gap between the two major parties.[8] In the direct elections, Fianna Fáil polled only 34.68 percent of the vote and secured five of the fifteen seats while Fine Gael won four seats with a vote of 33.13 percent. Labour also secured four seats with 14.48 percent, and the remaining two seats went to independents (one, T. J. Maher, was strongly identified with the farming lobby; the other, Neil Blaney, was a former Fianna Fáil minister). In the local elections, Fianna Fáil, with 38.2 percent of the vote, was down from its 1974 performance and only 4 points ahead of Fine Gael. In the major urban constituencies (Dublin, Cork, Limerick, and Waterford) the two parties were equal with an average vote of 30.1 percent; in 1974 Fianna Fáil had been 5 points ahead of Fine Gael.

The Haughey Succession

The results gave substance to those who argued that the Lynch government had failed to offer decisive and effective leadership in the face of Ireland's economic difficulties. Further complaints, this time on the sensitive issue of security, were provoked when on 27 August 1979 Lord Louis Mountbatten and some of his party were assassinated while on a fishing holiday in County Sligo on the same day that eighteen British soldiers were killed in Northern Ireland. There was controversy about Lynch's initial response to the assassination and further criticism when a British announcement expressing satisfaction about cross-border security cooperation was interpreted as indicating that some concession had been made to Britain permitting incursions into Irish airspace. This topic was especially divisive within the government party. Newly elected Dáil representative and Eurodeputy Sile de Valera (granddaughter of the party's founder) emerged as the most outspoken voice of militant republicanism within Fianna Fáil. The continuing controversy was seen (although without any apparent evidence) as part of an orchestrated campaign to replace Jack Lynch with Charles Haughey as leader of the government and the party.

Lynch, who had served as leader since 1966, had already decided to retire early in 1980, leaving his successor ample time to become entrenched before the next general election. Events were now to force the pace. The first two by-elections in the life of the Twenty-first Dáil were held on 7 November 1979. Both were held in Cork, one in Cork City—the home constituency dominated by Jack Lynch for two decades; both seats were won by Fine Gael candidates.[9] A change of leader was now imminent, and two contenders appeared: George Colley, Tanaiste (deputy prime minister), and minister for finance, Charles Haughey. Both had contested the leadership in 1966 and had come to represent distinct elements within Fianna Fáil. Haughey, who had developed strong ties with party activists throughout the country, appealed to those who spoke of the country's republican traditions and offered new horizons for backbenchers fearful of the continuing decline. Colley was strongest among senior ministers, the nonmilitant center of the party associated with Lynch, and the moderates who hoped for continuity. The contest was sharp and extremely divisive. The overwhelming majority of the cabinet supported Colley, but when the votes of the whole parliamentary party were counted, Haughey won by 44 to 38. Colley was able to demand concessions in cabinet appointments in return for continuing to serve as Tanaiste and publicly defined his loyalty to the Taoiseach in terms that clearly signaled future troubles for the party. A bitter speech by

FitzGerald, leader of the opposition, on the formal nomination of Haughey in the Dáil sharply distinguished between the acceptable face of Fianna Fáil and its unacceptable new leader. The pace of partisan politics was accelerating.

In part, Haughey, a former minister for finance, had been chosen in the hope that he could restore confidence in the government's capacity to manage the economy. He began by arguing in a special ministerial broadcast on television the case for reducing the level of public-sector borrowing and the budget deficit, but the subsequent budgets avoided effective corrective action. Inflation, unemployment, public-service pay, and public-sector borrowing all continued to rise—the last reaching 14.6 percent of GNP in early 1981. Clearly, early action would have to be taken; equally clearly, Haughey, who had inherited a twenty-seat Dáil majority, would first seek a personal mandate from the electorate.

Donegal By-election. The death of the Ceann Comhairle provided a first test. Joseph Brennan, former minister, had been a Fianna Fáil deputy for Donegal since 1951. The country had normally been divided with occasional variations in boundaries into two three-seat constituencies, and Fianna Fáil had obtained two seats in each.[10] Following the arms crisis and the breakaway of Neil Blaney, standing as "Independent Fianna Fáil," this hegemony had been broken. The county was constituted into a five-seat constituency in 1977, and because of Blaney's intervention, Fianna Fáil and Fine Gael drew level in votes (respectively 36.40 percent and 36.34 percent) and obtained two seats each.

The close result encouraged speculation that Fine Gael could win the by-election because of the intervention of a Blaney-sponsored candidate. Haughey conducted a vigorous, high-profile campaign in Donegal. On 6 November when the votes were counted, a gap of nearly six points had opened between the two main parties, and Fianna Fáil won the seat. This result encouraged the still new Taoiseach to plan an early general election.

It may well have encouraged a growing hesitancy and even contradiction in government decision making. As the run-up to the election became extended, there was a tendency to defer difficult choices; if good news could not be provided in the harsh economic climate, at least bad news could be withheld. Also, personal interventions by the Taoiseach in matters that might be customarily left to ministerial colleagues noticeably increased. These disturbed the normal, formal, orderly processes of administration for senior officials.

Given the continuing problems of economic management in a period of recession, the Northern Ireland crisis might have provided an alternative electoral platform for Haughey. His appeal to the traditional republican elements had contributed to the successful bid to become leader. But two meetings with the British prime minister, Mrs. Thatcher, in May and December 1980—

although characterized as a historic breakthrough and publicized as precursors to possible new constitutional structures—had achieved only the promise of joint Anglo-Irish studies of "possible new institutional structures" as part of an overall review of "the totality of relationships between these islands." Moreover, the protest by republican prisoners in the H-blocks, which had dragged on since 1967, was hardening into a determination to seek a final solution by resorting to a hunger strike.[11] If the North was to be the cornerstone of Haughey's campaign, he had to call an election as soon as practicable after the January budget before further pressures developed.

The 1981 Election

The Campaign. There is good reason to believe that the campaign was to be launched at the Fianna Fáil Árd-Fheis (annual party conference) on 14 February 1981.[12] Haughey's presidential address stressed his commitment to resolving the Northern issue. But the speech was never delivered. In the early hours of the morning, forty-eight young people were killed in a tragic fire at the Stardust entertainment center in Dublin. The Árd-Fheis and the election were both postponed. The initiation of the H-block hunger strike on 1 March and subsequent deaths of prisoners (including that of Bobby Sands, who had won a Westminster seat in a Northern Ireland by-election) further delayed decision. It was not until 21 May that the Dáil was dissolved; on the same day two more H-block hunger strikers died.

These deaths were not a happy augury and did nothing to sustain Haughey's claim to have called the election "because of the grave and tragic situation in Northern Ireland." Fianna Fáil began this campaign deprived of the customary tactical government advantage of choosing its own time; it was also unable to determine the strategic issues on which the election would be fought. The discipline, organization, and unity that had contributed to its success in 1977 had dissipated in the intervening years. Fianna Fáil was forced into a defensive posture, justifying its efforts to create jobs for the rapidly expanding young population and claiming to have reined in inflation. The party leader, in an extensive countrywide tour, sought a personal mandate, which was not being endorsed by senior colleagues, and warned the electorate against the danger of entrusting its fortunes to the inherent instability of an unknown coalition.

Fine Gael was better prepared to enter the contest. FitzGerald had revitalized the constituency organizations, accumulated substantial campaign funds, geared up the headquarters staff, and built up a useful cadre of new candidates (developed in part from the European Parliament campaign). The day after the election was called, Fine Gael unveiled an elaborate and carefully tailored package of policies that balanced promised benefits against novel tax proposals. While looking forward to a not-too-distant prospect of governing on its own, the party was pledged to coalition as a realistic alternative to Fianna Fáil. FitzGerald was presented in a highly personalized presidential style campaign as the alternative Taoiseach. Labour's policy document also stressed the economic issues in the election and, while committed not to enter any preelection pact and required to submit any subsequent negotiated program for government to a special delegate conference, clearly favored Fitz-Gerald to Haughey as a national leader.

In addition, three other sets of candidates were to play a significant role. Sinn Féin the Workers' party (SFWP) put forward fifteen candidates, mainly well-established and active local-authority representatives in their own constituencies.[13] The "National H-Blocks Committee," the coordinating body for the campaign to achieve political status for republican prisoners, arranged the nomination of twelve protesting prisoners in Britain and Northern Ireland: four were already on hunger strike, and all were selected for sensitive border areas and other republican strongholds. Finally, this first election based on constituency boundaries drawn up by an independent, nonpartisan commission encouraged an unusually large number of candidates broadly described as "others." These candidates included seven from the Socialist Labour party, two from the Communist party of Ireland, two from the Socialist party, and fifty-three independents.

Throughout the campaign, public opinion polls monitored response to the parties' performances. They also revealed that the emphasis on economic issues injected by Fine Gael and Labour more accurately reflected the real concerns of the electorate than the attempted invocation of the Northern troubles by Fianna Fáil; the rhetoric of Irish electoral politics was responding to the perceived interests of its citizens. In the course of three weeks the gap between the alternative government teams of Fianna Fáil and Fine Gael-Labour narrowed. Calculated as a swing of 6 percentage points, the change indicated that the outcome between these two blocs would be very close. The destabilizing effects of the H-block interventions were recognized as a challenge, in particular, to the hegemony of Fianna Fáil in republican areas, and the intervention of SFWP and other socialist candidates was seen as damaging to the Labour party. Analysis of the polls suggested that a few deputies outside the main parties would play a critical part in ensuring the formation of a government. The results confirmed these prognoses.

The Results. Eight of the 166 seats in the enlarged Twenty-second Dáil were held by the "others." H-block prisoners secured two seats in border areas; SFWP and the Socialist Labour party took one each. Former Fianna Fáil minister Neil Blaney and former Labour deputy Dr. John O'Connell (both also Eurodeputies) held their seats. Independents in Dublin and Limerick gained the other two seats. These interventions deprived the major blocs of an overall parliamentary majority, even though the absence of the two H-block deputies reduced the target figure of eighty-three.

Fianna Fáil's first-preference vote slipped 5.37 points from its 1977 level. With seventy-eight seats it was five short of an effective overall majority. Fine Gael's 36.46 percent of the vote was unprecedented and translated into sixty-five seats, a record in both absolute and relative terms. But even combined with Labour's fifteen seats, the putative coalition was left three short of an effective majority. For a fortnight after polling, until the Twenty-second Dáil assembled on 30 June 1981, there was uncertainty about who would form the next government.

Labour clarified its position. For the first time since 1932 the party leader had lost his seat in a general election. In a disagreement with Cluskey about nominations in the newly drawn constituencies, Dr. John O'Connell had resigned the party and, standing as an independent, defeated his former party leader. The parliamentary party quickly elected Michael O'Leary, a minister in the former national coalition, as leader on 11 June. He had little difficulty concluding an outlined common program for government in private consultations with FitzGerald.

The Coalition Agreement. This package proposed alloting Labour four of the fifteen seats in a new coalition cabinet (including the appointment of O'Leary as Tanaiste and minister of energy). The program provided for a National Development Corporation to be involved as shareholder in existing state corporations and in new growth industries. The issue of wealth tax, a bone of contention between the two parties, was converted into a pledge of higher taxation for those with "substantial productive capacity." The reformist impulse in both parties was reflected in the undertaking to establish an all-party parliamentary committee and in contentious issues of family law. Overall the program was designed to be acceptable to the moderate center of the Labour party and the newly dominant liberal FitzGerald wing of Fine Gael.

Within both parties residual doubts and hesitations remained. They surfaced most openly at the special delegate conference of the Labour party, held in the Gaiety Theatre (hence "The Gaiety Agreement") on Sunday, 28 June. There was considerable vocal opposition to the prospects of a further coalition, most noticeably from party chairman Michael D. Higgins (who had secured a seat for Labour in Galway West) and from party secretary Brendan Halligan (who had failed to win in Dublin North-West). Nevertheless, the agreement was endorsed by a 737 to 477 vote. On the same day FitzGerald's parliamentary colleagues happily accepted the same coalition arrangement. The stage was now set for the Dáil to meet and nominate a government.

After the formal reading of the writs and results of the election, the first business of a new Dáil is the election of a Ceann Comhairle (presiding officer). Under Irish law the deputy appointed is returned automatically in the subsequent general election. The Ceann Comhairle does not participate in most Dáil divisions but, by convention, in a tied Dáil casts a decisive vote in favor of the status quo, that is, the government of the day.[14] Typically the majority side of the House has secured the position for one of its own senior deputies; in the particular circumstances of 1981, Dr. John O'Connell was persuaded to accept election to the chair and was unopposed.

In the first division on the subsequent nomination of the Taoiseach, Haughey received the support of his own party and of Blaney (a total of seventy-nine votes). He was opposed by eighty-three other deputies, and a single independent (Loftus) abstained. On the second ballot, FitzGerald was supported by one independent (Kemmy) in addition to Fine Gael and Labour (a total of eighty-one votes); the other three deputies (Browne, Loftus, and SFWP's Sherlock) abstained. So the new coalition's government was formed on a parliamentary knife edge, particularly risky since the two H-block seats might, under normal circumstances, be expected to revert to Fianna Fáil and since Kiernan Doherty (Cavan-Monaghan) was on the twenty-first day of a hunger strike when elected.

In the considered view of one political journalist, "It was not a satisfactory election. It was not a satisfactory result. It made the birth and early days of the administration extremely difficult."[15] The precarious position of the new administration was soon illustrated when, because of the illness of a minister and the accidental absence of a backbencher, it failed to secure the renomination of a government deputy as Leas-Cheann Comhairle (deputy speaker). Fianna Fáil captured this part-time but paid position without sacrificing a valuable vote in the lobbies. This result was an early warning signal of difficult parliamentary divisions ahead. The coalition's parliamentary supporters soon had even more unpalatable news to digest.

The First FitzGerald Coalition

Barely in office, the coalition government announced that the critical condition of the public finances had been concealed by the previous administration. The level of public expenditure and the rate of inflation were both higher than had been revealed. A supplementary budget would be necessary and would be difficult to frame in the light of the agreed coalition program for government and of the uncertain parliamentary situation.

The new minister for finance, John Bruton, unveiled his emergency budget proposals on 21 July 1981. The package included sanction for increased charges on various services (including postal, electricity, telephone, transport, and mortgage interest rates) that had been postponed in the later stages of the

Haughey administration. Increases in excise duties (on alcohol, tobacco, and oil products) and in value-added tax (VAT) were announced. The only ameliorations offered in fulfillment of the government's agreed program were a 5 percent increase in social-welfare pensions and similar benefits, the implementation from the following April of a weekly tax credit to housewives (part of the Fine Gael election manifesto), and a youth employment fund to be financed by a 1 percent levy on all incomes. There was doubt about whether these measures could gain sufficient support (a government backbencher was brought by ambulance to vote in the various divisions). The measures were carried, however, and on 23 July the Dáil adjourned for a long summer recess until October.

But the government's problems were not easily postponed. The tension created by the H-block hunger strikes continued to mount. There were clashes between police and demonstrators on both sides of the border through July and August as prisoners were allowed to die. Following the death of Kiernan Doherty (elected for Cavan-Monaghan) on 2 August and the threat of fellow H-block deputy Paddy Agnew to resign his seat, the sense of political instability was heightened. Some of the tension was reduced when the hunger strike was settled in October, but the uncertainty remained.

Given the need for even sterner corrective financial measures and the fragility of the government's parliamentary position, there were persistent rumors that the Taoiseach might seek an early dissolution and a clear mandate to govern. There were ample precedents for such a course. On four previous occasions (1927, 1933, 1938, and 1944) a minority government had sought, and successfully obtained, an electoral majority.[16] In autumn 1981 there was evidence that such an appeal might succeed. An awareness that corrective budgetary measures were needed was growing, although it was coupled with a residual resistance to accepting the harsh consequences. The public opinion polls registered approval for FitzGerald's performance as Taoiseach. There was even the tempting possibility that Fine Gael might become the majority party.

Certainly Fianna Fáil had been slow to accept the outcome of the general election and to settle into the role of effective opposition. The strategically placed independent deputies were criticized instead of cultivated. Haughey, conscious of dissension in the senior ranks and disappointment among backbenchers, deferred naming a formal front bench. The whips could not always muster a full turnout for divisions. Only belated disciplinary action was taken when an individual deputy delivered speeches accepting the coalition's critique of the state of the public finances inherited from the Haughey administration.

A general consensus on the central thrust of policy seemed to be emerging inside and outside the Dáil. There was widespread support from the media, the economic interests, and academic economists for an analysis that linked three critical factors: the need to curtail public expenditures, to reduce foreign borrowing, and to phase out the current budget deficit. As the Taoiseach and his senior ministers concentrated on devising a budget strategy that would achieve these aims without losing parliamentary support, there was less inclination to listen to those who advised an early dissolution in pursuit of a majority.

The "Constitutional Crusade." Moreover, FitzGerald himself had introduced into political life a new theme that seemed to rule out a general election.[17] He had long been a critic of the sectarian ethos in the Irish constitution and in his book *Towards a New Ireland* (1972) had urged the case for a pluralist emphasis. He had also acknowledged that no substantial revision of the constitution was possible without Fianna Fáil assistance. A little-publicized newspaper interview and informal background briefing session with political correspondents preceded a radio interview on 27 September. In the interview, in an apparently unguarded response, FitzGerald spoke of his ambition to lead a "republican crusade" and said "If I were a Northern Protestant today, I cannot see how I could be attracted to being involved with a state which is itself sectarian. . . . The fact is that our laws and our Constitution, our practices and attitudes reflect those of a majority ethos and are not acceptable to Protestants in Northern Ireland." It was a remarkably outspoken and controversially phrased statement from any Taoiseach, let alone for the leader of a minority coalition. It was a challenge to conservative elements as much within his own party as anywhere else. The generally positive media response and a flow of supportive messages directly into his office persuaded FitzGerald that what was quickly termed "the constitutional crusade" would gain majority acceptance. Apart from substituting "denominational" for the more objectionable term "sectarian," he made no effort to tone down the remarks to achieve that wider consensus. He seemed equally unyielding in pursuing economic policy.

In some measure this intransigence reflected the extent to which Labour had become locked into the coalition. There was considerable criticism among party supporters and activists as the government's policies took effect. Among senior party officials and some parliamentarians was an unease about O'Leary's capacity or even concern to maintain any distinct Labour presence rather than become a junior partner to Fine Gael. Their worries became more acute as the main lines of future economic strategy were revealed in the weeks preceding the budget.

The Bruton Budget. On 27 January 1982 the minister of finance, John Bruton, unveiled his budget package. Committing the government to eliminate the current budget deficit in four years, he announced a series of increased direct and indirect taxes and severe expenditure cuts. These changes included an adjusted removal of food subsidies and the imposition of VAT on all footwear and clothing; they were justified on the grounds that such blanket subsidies and exemptions were disproportionately beneficial to those with the highest incomes. But politically they were too sensitive, and it became clear that most of the independent deputies would not support the proposals. At a theoretical level the case could be made that the changes marked a shift from regressive to progressive taxation. In practical political terms the independent deputies were closer to popular response than the coalition ministers who were isolated by office. In particular, independent socialist, Jim Kemmy, had told a television reporter as he entered the Dáil on budget day that he would not vote for such measures.

Kemmy's decision was critical. Of all the independents he had been most consistent in fulfilling his promise to support the government for a reasonable period of time. A critic of Haughey, he had enthusiastically endorsed Fitz-Gerald's so-called constitutional crusade to achieve a more pluralist Ireland. Since entering the Dáil he had often agreed with Socialist Labour party deputy Noel Browne who was prepared to support the Bruton budget if only to keep Haughey out of office. As the division bells rang, the Taoiseach could be seen in the chamber attempting to convince Kemmy to sustain the coalition. But it was too late. The Taoiseach was to pay the price for putting the technical advice of the Department of Finance ahead of considered political judgment and parliamentary management.

Traditionally, the first vote on the budget is the technical parliamentary sanction required to give immediate effect to excise increases. These, though severe, were broadly recognized as necessary. In reality, the division was a test of confidence in the whole budgetary strategy. Dutifully, Fine Gael and Labour deputies, many of whom had considerable reservations, obeyed the party whips and voted in favor: Browne was the only other deputy to join them. The other four independents went into the other lobby with Fianna Fáil and voted against. Defeated by eighty-two to eighty-one on budgetary matters, Fitz-Gerald had no choice. He sought a dissolution, and 18 February 1982 was fixed as the date for a new general election.

The February 1982 Election

The Campaign. Initially a simple choice seemed to face the electorate.[18] The two leaders began by articulating the alternatives. On one side, there was the known, detailed, harsh, and apparently unchangeable budget strategy proposed by Fine Gael and Labour; on the other, the promise of a less severe but vague alternative approach to economic management by the Fianna Fáil leader. The leaders of both sides spoke on the night of the dissolution.

FitzGerald, undoubtedly shaken by the collapse but determined, announced that he would fight the election on the budget as presented. He refused to make concessions on either food subsidies or VAT on clothing and footwear. Pressed on the grounds that at least children's wear could and should be exempted, FitzGerald replied that such an exemption would create administrative problems and might even be unfair: women with smaller feet would pay less for shoes than their children with larger feet. The budget, he argued, was necessary, fair, and carefully constructed. There would be no deviations.

Haughey rejected not only the detail but also the whole economic strategy of the budget. That night and on the following day at his first press conference (accompanied by only one front-bench spokesman and the party secretary) he dismissed what he called the "obsession" with foreign borrowing; repeatedly he spoke of government and commentators "hypnotized" with the subject. He listed unemployment and inflation as the main issues and declared, "I believe that the election will be fought very largely for and against yesterday's budget."[19] Replying to a question, he said Fianna Fáil would be foolish to sketch out an alternative budget; "only a Government in office can form and put forward a budget." There would be no details.

Undoubtedly budgetary prospects did become central to the campaign. But this early simple distinction between the two sides was not maintained. Both sides soon shifted their ground. Under Labour pressure, the coalition agreed to the VAT concession on children's wear but balanced the costs by specific tax increases. It was an extraordinary reversal by FitzGerald, who had allowed the government to fall by his intransigence on the issue. Under pressure from party colleagues, Haughey committed his party to the same levels of borrowing and the same budget deficit as the coalition. The early strategic policy gap on the economy was narrowing down.

When FitzGerald offered his opponents the services and resources of the civil service machine in the Department of Finance to cost any alternative budget proposals, Fianna Fáil accepted. It was clear that the detail rather than the broad sweep of public financial management would be the issues of the campaign. Since the Fianna Fáil alternative budget (largely the work of Dr. Martin O'Donoghue, a Lynch confidant dropped from government by Haughey and only recently restored to the front bench) took time to prepare and cost, the focus turned to other topics.

In particular, allied to the budget controversy was the question of credibility. Credibility, often a code word for a discussion of Haughey's suitability as a leader, underlined the presidential style of the campaign and gave additional interest to the unprecedented television debate between the two leaders broadcast two days before the election. At the end of the campaign, as at the outset, published polls indicated a close contest. A report on the latest findings, taken after the Fianna Fáil alternative budget had been published, cautiously indicated "FF support edging up but outcome still uncertain."

The Results. For the second time a general election delivered an indecisive verdict. Turnout was marginally down: at 73.8 percent it was the lowest since the 1961 election. None of the major parties could claim a victory.

Fianna Fáil gained an extra two points from 1981 with 47.26 percent of the vote. It won three extra seats (including the two border areas that had elected H-block candidates) but was still three short of an overall majority. Since 1932 the party had never lost two general elections in succession. The outcome, which compared unfavorably with Lynch's twenty-seat majority in 1977, renewed doubts about Haughey's leadership. Fine Gael gained an extra 8 percent of the vote but lost two seats. Labour continued the slide in its popular vote evident since 1969 and fell back to 9.1 percent, its lowest level in twenty-five years. Sinn Féin the Workers' party ran two extra candidates, increased its share of the national vote by 0.6 percentage points, and jumped from one to three seats. Only four independents were returned: Tony Gregory, a left-of-center "community" deputy from Dublin's inner city, joining Blaney, Kemmy, and O'Connell (who, as Ceann Comhairle, was automatically returned). The radical republican vote that had emerged in the previous election collapsed: candidates standing for Provisional Sinn Féin and the Irish Republican Socialist party achieved 1.2 percent of the vote nationally compared with the 2.5 percent H-block candidates received in 1981.

Once again the margin of seats between the outgoing government and the opposition was narrow; once again the votes of the "others" were critical. It was generally accepted that O'Connell would be chosen as Ceann Comhairle and that Blaney would and Kemmy would not support Haughey. In particular, the support of the three sfwp deputies and of the newly elected Gregory was solicited. But two other developments added to the postelectoral uncertainty even as the leaders negotiated for support.

Haughey is challenged. Since his election as leader in 1979, Haughey had failed to win the wholehearted support of the parliamentary party. His stated goal had been to bind the party together and he had not achieved that. The original choice of cabinet and the belated appointment of a front bench had done nothing to reduce internal tension. Discontent had barely been contained during the campaign. Only under pressure did he change the initial electoral strategy and use the talents of known critics (in particular, Dr. Martin O'Donoghue) to present the Fianna Fáil's alternative policies persuasively. Party canvassers on the doorsteps confirmed the public dissatisfaction with Haughey already revealed in the opinion polls. The inconclusive election results, attributed in part to this "Haughey factor," stiffened the resolve of rivals and critics to take immediate action before the Dáil resumed.

Traditionally the parliamentary party meets to select the party's parliamentary nominees to the five panels for the ensuing contest to fill seats in the new Senate. In a break with custom it was announced that the Fianna Fáil deputies would elect their leader at a meeting on 25 February (normally there is no question of renewing the leadership between parliaments). Active canvassing by influential deputies, including former Tanaiste George Colley and former party general secretary Seamus Brennan among others, led to a formal declaration by another former minister, Desmond O'Malley, that he would stand for the leadership "in response to demands from many people." O'Malley was known to be the favored choice of Jack Lynch, the Taoiseach who had originally appointed him as chief whip and elevated him to the cabinet at the time of the arms crisis. He had strong support from those who had earlier preferred Colley to Haughey as leader, and he was known to be attracting other deputies to his side. Involved in the pressure of an intricate campaign, O'Donoghue believed that a broad-based consensus could be achieved to replace Haughey. When it became clear that such a consensus would not be achieved, O'Donoghue made a strong plea at the parliamentary meeting for party unity. O'Malley withdrew his nomination, and Haughey was unanimously reelected.

Haughey had faced down the challenge; he had not united the party. Suspicions of deceit and rumors of ugly pressures to keep deputies in line had hardened internal rivalries. Haughey had again proved his superiority over other contenders as a tactical professional politician; he had managed to confirm his leadership of the party. He had yet to resume leadership of government.

Labour has doubts. In the Labour party, too, the three-week period between election day and the convening of the Twenty-third Dáil was marked by dissension. There had been trouble at the beginning of the campaign. Michael O'Leary, as leader, committed the party to continuing in coalition. Others disagreed, including the party chairman, Michael D. Higgins (who retained his seat in Galway), and the party secretary, Brendan Halligan (who ostensibly refused to stand on a coalition ticket). Higgins insisted that a majority of the party's ruling administrative council was opposed to maintaining the coalition.

After the election O'Leary planned once again to hold a special delegate conference on the question. On the basis of published public opinion polls, the known views of the overwhelming majority of the parliamentary party, and the perceived attitudes of most supporters, he could be confident of success. But, in an unexpected procedural ruling, the administrative council instructed him to conduct negotiations with all other parties and report back before the new Dáil sitting. O'Leary secured a new agreement with FitzGerald. This—in a remarkable reversal of policy after such a dogged election campaign— excluded the most unpopular provisions of the proposed budget on food subsidies and VAT on clothing. Nevertheless, although supported by all but two of the Labour deputies voting at the administrative council, O'Leary's plan for a further period of coalition was not carried: on the casting vote of the chairman, Higgins, the administrative council decided that Labour should not participate in any new government. There was considerable argument about whether the parliamentary party was bound by this ruling. The decision intensified existing divisions within the party between pragmatists who argued that only in government could they serve their constituents and hope to implement Labour policy and those committed to the view that participation in coalition had always weakened the party's ideology, effectiveness, and support. That internal debate would continue to absorb Labour energies. But the issue was not put to the test when the Twenty-third Dáil assembled on 8 March 1982.

The Gregory Deal. Although uncertainty prevailed until the last moment, two hidden choices had already determined the formation of the next government. The Árd-Chomhairle (ruling council) of sfwp had decided not to negotiate support for either side but to vote for Haughey for tactical reasons. Since there was no deal, there was no commitment to continue that backing; it was enough to say that voters seemed to prefer a Fianna Fáil government. By not announcing their intention until the Dáil met, the sfwp deputies had encouraged uncertainty and had helped to enhance the value of the vote of independent deputy Tony Gregory. This situation led to "the Gregory deal."[20]

A schoolteacher involved in radical politics since his student days, Gregory stood as a community representative for the deprived inner city of central Dublin in the 1981 election. The outcome of the 1982 election cast him in a pivotal role, and he tried unsuccessfully to forge a socialist alliance with Kemmy and sfwp. In addition, all three major party leaders held discussions with Gregory and his associates. Only Haughey impressed the young deputy. After further negotiation, Gregory undertook to vote for Haughey as Taoiseach in return for wide-ranging, specific concessions designed to meet the needs of the inner city. The full details of the deal were cobbled into a thirty-page document signed by both men and "witnessed" by the general secretary of the Irish Transport and General Workers' Union, the largest trade union in Ireland. The minimum cost to the Exchequer was variously estimated between £80 million and £175 million. The deal was an unprecedented testimony to the influence of a single deputy and an incentive for voters to demand that their representatives, irrespective of party, exercise similar muscle. It was further evidence of the pressures exposing the vulnerability of the political system in the 1980s.

The Second Haughey Government

When the Twenty-third Dáil assembled on 8–9 March 1982, Dr. John O'Connell was reelected Ceann Comhairle, the sfwp decision and Gregory deal were revealed, and the nomination of Haughey as Taoiseach was carried by 86 to 79 votes. The nomination did not remove the underlying instability. A switch by the three SFWP deputies combined with any parliamentary accident could wipe out Haughey's majority. Haughey began his second term in office with a fragile power base, and his position was not helped by continuing internal tensions with Fianna Fáil that affected the formation of government.

Nevertheless, Haughey resumed government in a buoyant mood and with a decisive air. He had chosen his own team for government, manufactured a parliamentary majority, and brushed aside the internal threat to his leadership. He was now ready to pick up the role of Taoiseach and to take full advantage of a brief mid-March tour of the United States already arranged for his predecessor. Speaking to the Economic Club of New York, he pressed the advantages of investment in Ireland and impressed his audience with an easy and confident response to questions. He used the occasion of a St. Patrick's Day lunch at the White House and a meeting with the congressional Friends of Ireland group to reiterate forcefully his view that a solution to the Northern Ireland problem required action by the two sovereign governments in Dublin and London.

Dublin West By-election. He also acted to improve the narrow parliamentary balance. In 1981 Haughey had chosen Michael O'Kennedy (one of the small minority of Lynch ministers to have switched to his side in the leadership contest with Colley) to succeed Dick Burke of Fine Gael as Irish nominee to the European Commission. In the February election O'Kennedy returned to win his old Dáil seat, at the expense of a party colleague. Haughey now proposed to nominate Burke, who had been reelected to the Dáil, with the clear expectation that Fianna Fáil could be favored to capture his Fine Gael seat in the subsequent by-election. Despite strong opposition from his party and after some hesitation, Burke accepted.

Dublin West, the site of the contest, was a new five-seat constituency, geographically the largest in the Dublin region, socially very mixed, politically almost equally divided between the two major parties. Labour, heavily pressed by SFWP (since 24 April named simply the Workers' party), barely counted. Fianna Fáil had reduced Fine Gael's 3.4 point lead in 1981 to only 0.8 percent in February 1982. Burke's decision seemed certain to damage Fine Gael, which was forced to select a new and almost unknown candidate, Liam Skelly. Fianna Fáil had three advantages: they could draw on their full cabinet team for the campaign, they could ask for support to resolve the parliamentary instability, and they had a well-established candidate. Eileen Lemass, Haughey's widowed sister-in-law, had been deputy for the area, and her defeat in 1982 had drawn sympathetic media and political comment.

Voting turnout on 25 May 1982 was down to 61.7 percent. Skelly maintained a 0.7 point lead over Lemass on the first count and accumulated the required extra preferences in the two subsequent counts (including a significantly higher proportion from the Workers' party leader, Tomas MacGiolla). The maneuver to secure a parliamentary advantage had failed, Fine Gael retained the seat. The Workers' party was given cause to reconsider its support for the Haughey government. In Dáil divisions the political arithmetic remained precarious and uncertain.

So did the government's approach to economic management. Ray Mc-Sharry, Haughey's newly appointed Tanaiste and minister for finance, had begun his period in finance by insisting that the "doom and gloom" of the coalition's economic analysis would be converted to "boom and bloom" under Fianna Fáil. The rhetoric was easier to manage than the public finances. The budget was accepted with no difficulty on 25 March. But, although there was a growing consensus among the politicians about the need for harsh measures, there was still resistance among sectional interests.

A month before the by-election, the government announced an "adjustment" costed at £45 million in the Pay Related Social Insurance (PRSI) scheme in an effort to meet protests from some workers. Despite this announcement and further concessions in the finance bill revealed at the beginning of June, pressure was growing. The death of John Callinan, a government backbencher from Galway East, increased the tension already created by the Dublin West result. The three Workers' party deputies abstained in the vote on two amendments at the committee stage of the finance bill on 24 June. On both occasions only the casting vote of the Ceann Comhairle saved the government from defeat.

A week later a new crisis was precipitated when the government was defeated on a motion concerning a factory closure. Although the Workers' party deputies and Gregory supported Haughey on the subsequent confidence motion, they had clearly signaled dissatisfaction with economic policies. With such a tight Dáil margin the vacancy in Galway East deprived government of a vital vote. It was decided to proceed immediately to a by-election, timed for 21 July, only days after the Dáil recess.

Galway East By-election. An overwhelmingly rural constituency, Galway East belongs to the western heartland of Fianna Fáil. The boundaries have been changed in various revisions, but the area has invariably given Fianna Fáil a clear majority of its votes and seats. An unusual exception occurred in December 1964. The sitting deputy and founder-member of Clann na Talmhan died during the all-Ireland football final; his son, John Donnellan, captain of the successful Galway team in the match, won the seat for Fine Gael in the subsequent by-election. In the February 1982 general election Fianna Fáil gained 2.2 points on its previous vote to win 55.1 percent of the vote. Although doubts about the future of the Sugar Company factory in Tuam (the only substantial industry in the constituency) created some problems, the government was set to win. Nevertheless, Haughey played an active part in a vigorous campaign in which the whole cabinet participated and Fianna Fáil retained the seat.

Ten days later, on 30 July, with the Dáil recessed, the government announced a pay freeze for those in the public service and a series of cuts in public spending that indicated new health charges and reductions in educational grants. Clearly, the optimism of the "boom and bloom" period was well over. The gap on the management of public finances between Fianna Fáil and Fine Gael had, in essence, narrowed down to the fact that one party was still in government and the other in opposition. How long that situation would remain was problematic, for adding to Haughey's problems was an unexpected scandal that erupted in mid-August.

GUBU. Malcolm MacArthur, who was wanted in connection with two much-publicized murders, had been arrested in the apartment of the attorney general where he had been living. Haughey reacted to the news by calling it "grotesque, unprecedented, bizarre, and unbelievable."[21] A longtime critic of Haughey (and former Labour minister in the Cosgrave coalition), Conor Cruise O'Brien, seized the phrase and coined a new term to describe a serious political embarrassment: GUBU. The label stuck, in some measure because Haughey ineptly handled the affair and in some part because it was the latest in a series of political inconveniences.

In March there had been the unnecessarily extravagant wooing of Gregory. In April Haughey's personal solicitor and election agent had been charged with voting at two separate polling stations. In May the Dublin West by-election had destroyed the value of Burke's appointment to the European Commission. In June there were allegations that telephone equipment installed in Haughey's Dáil office had an override capacity that could be used to eavesdrop on conversations. Now, in August, the attorney general was initially allowed to leave Ireland almost immediately after the MacArthur arrest; then he was called back from the United States and asked to resign. That sequence seemed to reflect a serious error of judgment and decision. Taken in conjunction with a catalog of earlier events and with rumors about aspects of the Taoiseach's private life, GUBU seemed to suggest a politician prone to accident. It fed a general sense of unease and uncertainty in and about Irish public life that was not limited to any one party.

There were divisions in Fine Gael. An older conservative element had never trusted the more liberal, secular thrust given to party policy by Fitz-Gerald. Some newer deputies were suspicious of his willingness to make concessions after the February election to gain office; in particular, they opposed the suggestion of any deal with the Workers' party. A former minister, John Kelly, declined to serve on the front bench to be freer to speak out openly in public affairs; he had already suggested a temporary alliance of Fine Gael and Fianna Fáil to cope with the economic crisis. Labour was still locked at many levels of the party in an internal debate on the question of coalition. The Workers' party was reconsidering its tactics in the light of developments. But, above all, it was in Fianna Fáil—traditionally the most disciplined and united, as well as the largest, political party—that dissension surfaced most damagingly.

Haughey's Second Challenge. In a surprise move at the beginning of October, Fianna Fáil backbencher Charles McCreevy put down a motion of no-confidence in the leader of the parliamentary party. McCreevy, an accountant by profession, had supported Haughey in the 1979 succession vote but had been disappointed by the failure to control the public finances. Provocative public statements by McCreevy had led to his resignation from the parliamentary party in January 1982. He had secured renomination and reelection and had supported O'Malley's later challenge to Haughey.

Now he was prepared to provoke a new move against Haughey; his action created a crisis. Under pressure, the Taoiseach sought but failed to obtain the unanimous support of the ministers of state and the members of the government. Both Desmond O'Malley and Martin O'Donoghue resigned from the cabinet. Adding to stories about deputies being harassed and threatened was a procedural wrangle about whether this internal confidence motion should be by secret ballot or by roll-call vote. In the event, the latter mode was chosen. Nevertheless, twenty-two of the eighty deputies voted against Haughey. No incumbent Fianna Fáil Taoiseach had ever faced such a naked threat to his leadership. A fortnight later his parliamentary position was further eroded by the death of one Fianna Fáil deputy followed by the severe illness of another.

Against this background, the unveiling of a new policy document, *The Way Forward*, was unconvincing. It was presented, in the presence of senior civil servants as well as ministers, as a blueprint for recovery. It detailed ambitious targets for growth but gave little indication of how they could be achieved. Importantly, it now committed Fianna Fáil to phase out the current budget deficit over a period of four years; this was the yardstick of fiscal rectitude originally proposed by the coalition.

Labour's Division on Coalition. But the prospect of another coalition seemed less likely after the Labour party's annual conference at the end of October. By tradition and structure the Labour party has been less deferential than the two major parties to either its leader or its parliamentary party. The tension between ideologically inclined activists and the pragmatic parliamentarians had often revolved around the issue of coalition. One side argued that Labour had bought access to government at the cost of socialist principle, had sacrificed its own identity in becoming a "Fine Gael Mark II," and had suffered a corresponding decline in support since its 1969 historic high, 17 percent of the national vote. Others responded that Labour needed transfers from Fine Gael to secure seats, that no socialist policies could be implemented from the opposition benches, and that electoral support had declined because of the confusion about whether Labour would have an effective say in forming government.

At a packed four-hour debate at the annual conference in Galway on 23 October, all the arguments were rehearsed. All participants were agreed that Labour should fight as an independent party on its own program in any future election. Then various proposals were largely subsumed in three composite motions. One motion urged that Labour should neither enter coalition nor support a minority government; another recommended postelectoral backing for either major party forming a minority government; the third—strongly pressed by Labour leader Michael O'Leary—proposed to allow "the Administrative Council and the Parliamentary Labour Party to jointly decide on electoral strategy and the formation of government." Not one of these motions was found acceptable. Instead, a combination of moderate constituency delegates and union bloc votes accepted the strategy of 1981: that a special postelection delegate conference should hear a report from the party leader, after consultation with other parties and deputies, and then "decide whether or not the Labour Party shall enter into government, support a minority government, or enter into opposition."

A week later, his advice spurned, O'Leary resigned not only from the leadership but from the Labour party and almost immediately joined the Fine Gael parliamentary party. The fourteen remaining Labour deputies quickly agreed on a thirty-two-year-old barrister, Dick Spring, as party leader. An international rugby player, Spring had become deputy for North Kerry in 1981, replacing his father who had served there since 1943. He was soon to be tested.

On 3 November a new motion of confidence brought the Twenty-third Dáil to an end. The Workers' party, buoyed up by improved showing in the opinion polls and hoping to secure the election of its leaders after the Dublin West by-election, was ready to change. On 4 November the division yielded a vote of eighty for and eighty-two against the Haughey government. The Dáil was dissolved, and a general election was called for 24 November.

The November 1982 Election

The Campaign. Summoned to a general election for the third time in eighteen months, the voters did not relish another hectic campaign.[22] The parties, with funds depleted, could not afford to mount it. Reduced to the minimum three weeks required by law and suffering the inevitable sense of déjà vu, it was not an exciting campaign.

The general question of how the economy should be managed, although remaining central, was largely translated into the question of who could best be trusted to direct broadly similar strategies. Fianna Fáil had difficulty promoting *The Way Forward*. It was evident from the course of events during 1982 that little separated the actual immediate aims of either Fianna Fáil or Fine Gael when in government. Both were now committed to controlling public expenditure, restraining public service pay, and eliminating the current budget deficit over the next four years. Sharing fiscal goals, constrained by the same set of circumstances, rehearsing arguments from the earlier campaign, the two main parties were forced to concentrate on and develop other themes. Credibility and stability in government were again issues. Only in these general terms was national economic management an issue in the campaign.

The Referendum on Abortion. Another potentially explosive issue—abortion—was defused at the outset of the campaign.[23] Several organizations, mainly Catholic, had begun to cooperate in 1980 to strengthen the existing legislation that made the procuring of an abortion a criminal offense in Ireland. The method chosen to strengthen the legislation was to secure support from the major parties for an amendment to the Irish constitution stating: "The State recognises the absolute right to life of every unborn child from conception and accordingly guarantees to respect and protect such right by law." In the spring of 1981, with a general election in the offing, both FitzGerald and Haughey agreed in principle, and in the June election a commitment to hold a referendum preventing "the legislation of abortion" was included in the Fianna Fáil and Fine Gael manifestos.

Despite prompting from the pro-life amendment campaign (PLAC), no action was taken during the first FitzGerald coalition. In the February 1982 campaign, however, the organization again received commitments from Fianna Fáil and Fine Gael. Haughey promised to initiate a referendum during 1982; FitzGerald, during the life of the next Dáil. In government, Haughey invited PLAC to submit suggested wording for an amendment to the attorney general's office.

By now it was evident that the issue was more complex than had originally appeared. Medical, legal, and moral arguments were advanced about whether every termination was necessarily an abortion. The divergence between the Catholic teaching on specific exceptions and the views of other religious groups was invoked to suggest that the proposal was inherently sectarian. There was disagreement about whether such an amendment would affect existing practice in Irish hospitals and prejudice the legal use of certain contraceptives. There was uncertainty about whether any form of words could be drafted to cover the many objections being raised.

Just three days before the election was called the Fianna Fáil government published the text it would be proposing. This text appears to have been the outcome of further discussions with PLAC. It read "The State acknowledges the right to life of the unborn and, with due regard to the equal right to life of the mother, guarantees in its laws to respect, and, as far as practicable, by its laws, to defend and vindicate that right." Within two days FitzGerald not only accepted this formula as the best available but promised that Fine Gael in government would hold a referendum by March 1983.

Haughey responded by charging that FitzGerald could not be trusted to fulfill this promise; he had not done so in his first term. The Fianna Fáil leader also claimed that Labour had demanded the abandonment of the amendment as a condition of entering coalition. This claim was denied by Spring, who had sufficient problems maintaining a nonaligned attitude to coalition. More importantly, PLAC issued a public statement accepting FitzGerald's undertaking. From that time the question of the constitutional referendum on abortion was no longer a national campaign issue, although it surfaced in regard to some individual campaigns and was influential in Limerick where independent Jim Kemmy lost his seat.

Irish Security and the British Dimension. In the latter part of the campaign several topics related to Anglo-Irish affairs, Northern policy, and Irish security were raised. Some effort was made to suggest that FitzGerald had been involved in persuading a senior British peer to support plans for devolution in Northern Ireland. It was alleged that the Duke of Norfolk was a "spymaster." Haughey warned the British establishment and media not to interfere in an Irish election by backing FitzGerald. FitzGerald added fuel to these fading embers by suggesting an all-Ireland court and police force as a solution to security problems on both sides of the border.

This imprudently timed repetition of a controversial policy provoked a predictably hostile Fianna Fáil response. The known antipathy between Haughey and FitzGerald was now being tinged with a political rhetoric reminiscent of the Irish civil war. FitzGerald's claim to keep the Northern issue out of the campaign by following his precedent in earlier elections and limiting himself to a single speech on the topic seemed to have backfired. The two main parties had not appeared so divided on their approach to the North since the time of the arms crisis.

Whether the heightened and heated discussion influenced the outcome is difficult to judge. There is evidence that it was pursued with particular vehemence in some constituencies where republican sympathies might be expected to respond. The discussion came too late and was a tangle of too many strands to be monitored in published public opinion polls. It did, however, add a steely note to the hour-long television debate between Haughey and Fitz-Gerald at the end of the campaign.

The Results. Once again turnout was down; the 73 percent figure was the lowest since 1961. But the result was decisive. Fianna Fáil, with 45.2 percent of the first-preference vote, lost 2 points that translated into a loss of six seats. Fine Gael gained nearly 2 points, a record 39.22 percent of the vote. Mainly because of its superior vote management and candidate selection in key constituencies, Fine Gael gained seven extra seats. That seventy-seat total was a new record for Fine Gael; for the first time since the election of September 1927 only five seats separated the two main parties. That gap was easily bridgeable by Labour, which with a tiny increase in votes had gained an extra seat. The Workers' party had run four extra candidates, had picked up an extra 1 point in votes, and had been reduced from three to two seats. Apart from Dr. O'Connell (as outgoing Ceann Comhairle he was automatically returned to the Dáil), the only independents to gain seats were Blaney and Gregory.

Program for Government. The Fine Gael and Labour party leaders lost no time settling down to negotiate an outline agreement for coalition. Spring was adamant that Labour's options remain open; the party would accept coalition only in return for at least some policy input. FitzGerald was as prepared to make concessions in November as he had been in February; virtually unchallenged in his own party, he was conscious of Spring's dilemmas. Both men understood the advantage of leaking indications of difficulties in negotiation and of timing the revelation of any understanding so as to facilitate acceptance.

Eventually a thirty-page printed document put forward the proposed *Fine Gael/Labour Programme for Government.* This document balanced an insistence on improved competitiveness and productivity with the establishment of an employment task force working with a new national planning board. Another Labour-inspired input was a national development corporation, and there was an undertaking to introduce "a fundamental reform of the taxation and social welfare . . . within the lifetime of the Government." But primary importance was still attached to curtailing the budget deficit. In another concession to Labour this proposal was now couched in more conciliatory language and given a slightly longer period for implementation: "The phasing of the elimination of the current Budget deficit between now and 1987 will have to be undertaken with due regard to prevailing economic conditions, and in particular, to the importance of achieving economic growth and dealing with unemployment."

This statement was enough to convince the special delegate conference of the Labour party in Limerick on 12 December 1982. Anticoalitionists, including the party chairman Higgins and the former general secretary Halligan, had failed to win seats. The party was ready to trust its new leader and gave an increased endorsement, by 846 votes to 522, in favor of the proposal. On the same day, with only a single dissident voice, the Fine Gael parliamentary party accepted the program.

When the Twenty-fourth Dáil assembled on 14 December, the two parties combined to elect a Fine Gael deputy, Tom Fitzpatrick, as Ceann Comhairle. The former minister was elected for the five-seat constituency of Cavan-Monaghan, which traditionally had returned three Fianna Fáil deputies; the balance could now be expected to swing to Fine Gael. On the nomination of the Taoiseach, Haughey was defeated by a vote of 77 to 88, and FitzGerald returned with 85 votes to 79 (with Dr. O'Connell abstaining).

Postelection Developments

The Second FitzGerald Coalition. Major changes in personnel and in the distribution of portfolios gave a distinctly new look to the second FitzGerald coalition. Those changes also intensified the problems of ministers learning to cope with new portfolios, new colleagues, and new relations with former colleagues. They further emphasized the authority and the responsibility of the Taoiseach.

FitzGerald could not escape criticism when the new minister of education at first announced significant economies in the free school-bus system and was then forced to make concessions. Similarly, FitzGerald had to intervene when speeches by the new minister for finance seemed to be forcing unnecessarily harsh measures on government colleagues. Luckily the new minister for justice seemed well able to handle yet another twist in the much-publicized wrangling within Fianna Fáil.

The Third Challenge to Haughey. This challenge arose with the disclosure that Haughey's minister for justice, Sean Doherty, had instigated tapping the telephones of two political journalists who had been writing well-informed and critical reports on previous upheavals in Fianna Fáil. It was also revealed that Ray McSharry, who was then minister for finance, had been supplied with police assistance to tape and transcribe a conversation with a fellow minister, Martin O'Donoghue. In three carefully worded statements, the Fine Gael minister for justice, Michael Noonan, gave an outline of these events and announced the resignation of both the commissioner and the deputy commissioner of the Garda (police). Coming on top of other allegations about Doherty's actions as minister for justice, this situation provoked another attempt to remove Haughey as leader.

On Saturday, 23 January 1983, at a lengthy special meeting of the Fianna

Fáil parliamentary party, former Haughey supporters spoke against his continuing as leader. Nothing was resolved then nor on the following Wednesday when he made an ambiguous statement that he would go in his own time and would consult his parliamentary colleagues. A special committee of the party was to investigate the various aspects of the bugging and tapping allegations. There was a growing belief that Haughey would offer his resignation, and there was active canvassing for several alternative leaders including O'Malley, O'Kennedy, and Collins.

The next parliamentary party meeting, on 2 February, was to be decisive. The tragic death of Donegal Deputy Clem Coughlan on 1 February, however, postponed action. A statement from Haughey was interpreted by his spokesman as a willingness to carry the leadership issue from the parliamentary party to the Árd-Fheis. This interpretation provoked further intemperate reaction by opponents, but it was denied by Haughey in a radio interview on Sunday, 6 February. At the end of a protracted meeting throughout the following day Haughey survived yet another leadership vote and shortly afterward named a broadly based front bench. If this vote signified a remarkable feat of survival in political leadership, it scarcely healed the damage already done to party unity.

Nevertheless, Fianna Fáil easily retained its seat in the Donegal Southwest by-election fought on 13 May. The victory owed much to the recurrent tendency of Irish elections to favor relatives of recently deceased deputies: Cathal Coughlan was elected to succeed his brother. The result suggested a return to normalcy. In the fifth election in a series in Donegal the party had again increased its share of the vote.

The New Ireland Forum. The inauguration of the New Ireland Forum on 30 May 1983 revealed a continuing divergence, begun during the election campaign, of emphasis between and within the parties on attitudes toward Northern Ireland. Proposed as a meeting place in which democratically elected politicians from North and South could deliberate, the forum had effectively become an alternative for the SDLP to the Northern Ireland Assembly (launched by Secretary of State Jim Prior), which the SDLP had decided to boycott. In turn, none of the Northern Unionist parties nor Alliance were prepared to take up places in the forum. There was a noticeable difference in emphasis between FitzGerald's stress on the primary need to bring all sections of opinion in Ireland, North and South, closer together and Haughey's insistence that only agreement between two sovereign governments in Dublin and London could achieve a breakthrough. The forum, like the election campaign, seemed unlikely to integrate these divergent views, resting on differing analyses of the Northern Ireland situation. It could all too easily become another partisan arena for the parties in the republic, despite evidence from internal documents that all main parties recognize that considerable, and unpopular, reforms will be required in many areas of Irish life.

Developments in the campaign to achieve a constitutional referendum relating to abortion also proved divisive and partisan. Back in office FitzGerald discovered what he declared to be serious flaws in the formula proposed by Fianna Fáil and accepted by him in October. The attorney general issued a lengthy opinion giving the grounds for this adverse view. The director of public prosecutions (an independent law officer) concurred with a statement that the formula might facilitate rather than prevent the introduction of abortion. After considerable controversy, delay, and open disagreement within the Fine Gael parliamentary party, FitzGerald's government put forward a revised form of wording, which was rejected by the Dáil in favor of the original Fianna Fáil version. A further delay ensued, and the referendum was not held until 7 September 1983.

The campaign provoked much bitterness and confusion as pressure group representatives on both sides argued for and against the proposal. The eventual outcome was substantial ratification: 66.5 percent voted for the amendment and 32.9 percent voted against. Despite the intensity of the campaign and canvass (which included a formal appeal by the Catholic hierarchy for voters to participate in what was seen as a major test of public morality), however, 46.3 percent of the electorate did not vote.

That result was one confirmation of the extent to which Irish society was changing. Another confirmation was supplied in a poll issued in spring 1983 by the Market Research Bureau of Ireland to mark its twenty-first year in operation.[24] This poll charted some developments in Irish attitudes, values, interests, and influences. If some of the differences reflected trends visible in other Western countries, others were more specifically related to peculiarly Irish circumstances. Principal among these were the continuing growth of population, the effects of the long-term Northern troubles, and the perceived reshaping of traditional authority.

The challenge for the political parties is to recognize and evaluate these changes, to come to terms with them, and to accommodate both the structures and processes of government to demands of change. The events of the early 1980s revealed just how difficult balancing new needs and older demands was in a society that had been encouraged to aspire to high expectations. In particular, the three elections in 1981 and 1982 showed the problem of creating and maintaining a stable parliamentary majority for government within the constraints imposed by the single transferable vote system of proportional representation.

That task requires considerable subtlety, a sense of timing, and a delicacy as well as firmness in political leadership. It demands loyalty and discipline, as well as the customary alertness to constituency pressures, from parliamentary representatives. It posits some willingness to temper personal and sectional interests to a larger sense of the public good on the part of the electorate. Over its first sixty years of independence the Irish system—leaders, parliamentarians, voters—has managed, with varying degrees of success, to achieve that combination. Failures on the part of all three sets of political actors in the early 1980s exposed the fragility of the system. But after three general elections and a period of evident political instability, the fundamental durability of the Irish constitutional and parliamentary tradition was vindicated.

Notes

1. The standard text is Basil Chubb, *The Government and Politics of Ireland*, 2d ed. (London: Longman, 1982), which discusses inter alia the general, political, social, and economic background. For a convenient summary see also Howard R. Penniman, ed., *Ireland at the Polls: The Dáil Election of 1977* (Washington, D.C.: American Enterprise Institute, 1978). There is an analysis of Irish political stability in Brian Farrell, ed., *The Irish Parliamentary Tradition* (Dublin: Gill and Macmillan, 1973). See also R. Kenneth Carty, *Party and Parish Pump: Electoral Politics in Ireland* (Waterloo, Ontario: Wilfrid Laurier University Press, 1981).

2. For a convenient summary of Irish public opinion, see the series *IMS Poll*, vols. 1–6 (Dublin: Irish Marketing Surveys [IMS], 1982–83). See also the report on attitudes in Market Research Bureau of Ireland (MRBI), *21st Anniversary Poll* (Dublin: MRBI, 1983): "The People of Ireland—a Tribute."

3. The origins and development of the party system are conveniently summarized in Maurice Manning, "The Political Parties," in Penniman, *Ireland at the Polls*, pp. 69–95.

4. On the single transferable vote system of proportional representation practiced in Ireland, see Appendix A. See Paul McKee, "The Republic of Ireland," in Vernon Bogdanor and David Butler, eds., *Democracy and Elections: Electoral Systems and Their Political Consequences* (Cambridge: Cambridge University Press, 1983), pp. 167ff.

5. For a full discussion, see Penniman, *Ireland at the Polls*; Ted Nealon, ed., *Nealon's Guide to the 21st Dáil and Seanad '77* (Dublin: Platform Press, 1977).

6. For a brief account, see Maurice Manning, "The Political Parties," pp. 76–77. For an extremely critical account of Haughey's career, see Joe Joyce and Peter Murtagh, *The Boss: Charles J. Haughey in Government* (Dublin: Poolbeg Press, 1983).

7. See John Blackwell, "Economic Aspects of Changing Population Trends and the Implications for Social Policy," Twelfth Regional Symposium of the International Council on Social Welfare, TDC Ireland, 12–22 July 1983 (unpublished).

8. Department of the Environment, *Local Elections, 1979: Election Results and Transfer Votes* (Dublin: Stationery Office, 1980) (Prl. 9322); Department of Local Government, *Local Elections 1974: Results and Statistics* (Dublin: Stationery Office, 1975); and European Parliament Information Office, Dublin, *Election Results: Ireland, June 1979* (Dublin: Stationery Office, 1980).

9. By-election results in Ted Nealon and Seamus Brennan, eds., *Nealon's Guide to the 22nd Dáil and Seanad Election '81* (Dublin: Platform Press, 1981), p. 187.

10. On the constituency background, see Paul Sachs, *The Donegal Mafia: An Irish Political Machine* (New Haven, Conn.: Yale University Press, 1976).

11. See Tim Pat Googan, *On the Blanket* (Dublin: Ward River Press, 1980). Later developments reported in *Magill* magazine.

12. For accounts of this election, see *Nealon's Guide '81*; Vincent Browne, ed., *The Magill Book

of Irish Politics (Dublin: Magill Publications, 1981); Michael A. Busteed, "The 1981 Irish General Election," *Parliamentary Affairs* 35, no. 1 (Winter 1982): 39–58; and Cornelius O'Leary, "The Irish General Election of 1981 and 1982," *Electoral Studies* 1, no. 3 (December 1982): 363–74.

13. On the origins and development of SFWP, seé Vincent Browne, "The Secret World of SFWP," *Magill*, April 1982.

14. The precedent was stated on formal terms by Michael Hayes, Ceann Comhairle, when a motion of no-confidence resulted in a tied vote on 16 August 1927: "The vote of the Chair should, I think, always be given in such a way as to provide, if possible, that the House would have an opportunity for reviewing the decision arrived at. Secondly, the status quo should, if possible, be preserved." *Dáil Debates*, vol. 20, cols. 1749–50. For an earlier case on a money matter, see *Dáil Debates*, vol. 3, col. 1331, 30 May 1923.

15. Bruce Arnold, "The Campaign," in *Nealon's Guide '81*, p. 156.

16. For discussion, see Brian Farrell, "Government Formation and Ministerial Selection," chap. 5 of this volume.

17. The constitutional crusade began with an interview in the *Cork Examiner*, 22 September 1981, reprinted in the *Irish Times*, 24 September. The text of the radio interview is in *Irish Times*, 28 September 1981.

18. For information on this election, see Ted Nealon, ed., *Nealon's Guide to the 23rd Dáil and Seanad Election '82* (Dublin: Platform Press, 1982); Vincent Browne, ed., *The Magill Guide to Election '82* (Dublin: Magill Publications, 1982); and Cornelius O'Leary, "The Irish General Elections."

19. For a detailed account of this press conference, see Vincent Browne, "Learning to Cook at Donoghue's Ball," *Magill*, February 1982, 25–26.

20. See Gene Kerrigan, "Pushing on the Open Door: How Haughey Came to Terms with the Gregory Team," *Magill*, March 1982; Pat Brennan, "The Gregory Deal: A Short Measure," *Magill*, November 1982, 15–16.

21. Cf. Vincent Browne, "The GUBU Factor."

22. For accounts of this election see, Ted Nealon, ed., *Nealon's Guide to the 24th Dáil and Seanad 2nd Election '82* (Dublin: Platform Press, 1983); Brian Trench, ed., *Magill Book of Irish Politics, 1982* (Dublin: Magill Publications, 1983); Cornelius O'Leary, "The Irish General Election (November 1982)," *Electoral Studies* 2, no. 2 (August 1983).

23. On the background to the amendment controversy, see Emily O'Reilly, "The Current Political Objective Is the Defeat of the Amendment," *Sunday Tribune*, 15 May 1983, and Pat Brennan, "Abortion: Backlash and Blackmail," *Magill*, July 1983.

24. Market Research Bureau of Ireland, *21st Anniversary Poll*.

2 Campaigns, Manifestoes, and Party Finances
JOSEPH O'MALLEY

The three Irish general elections in eighteen months may be seen as three battles in a long electoral war dominated by the contrasting personalities of two men, Charles Haughey and Garret FitzGerald, and fought around a single issue, the economy.

The November 1982 campaign yielded a decisive victory: a majority coalition (Fine Gael and Labour) government with the parliamentary means to survive a full five-year term in office. The three results affirmed a pattern established since 1973, where no incumbent government has been reelected.

Economic Background

All three elections took place against the background of an economy moving deeper into recession. The three years (1980–82) saw real incomes decline annually, while inflation fluctuated between 17 percent and 20 percent.[1] Unemployment rose to record levels; in the eighteen months between the first and the final elections, the two minority governments watched monthly out-of-work totals rise by 46,400 to 169,900 — 13.2 percent of the country's labor force.[2] At the root of the economic problem was a world recession compounding the difficulties of Irish governments, which since 1979 had tried unsuccessfully to check the growth in public spending and restore balance to public finances.

From 1979 to 1982 total public spending (current and capital budgets) rose from 54 percent of gross national product (GNP) to 66 percent. Every year budget deficit targets were greatly exceeded, with borrowing (increasingly foreign) used to bridge an ever-widening gap between spending and revenue.[3]

Between January 1980 and December 1982 the country's national debt almost doubled (95.96 percent) to £12,816 million, with the foreign debt component soaring 243 percent to £5,290 million.[4] Where in 1979 foreign borrowing accounted for 23.5 percent of total national debt, by 1982 this had risen to 41.2 percent. In that year the real burden of governments' past borrowing profligacy became fully apparent; interest payment to service the huge foreign debt reached £515 million, just half of the balance of payments deficit on current account and representing a net outflow from the economy of some 4.4 percent of national output.[5]

One consequence of the country's growing foreign indebtedness was a drop in Ireland's credit rating in international capital markets in 1982.[6] It followed a year when foreign borrowing reached £1,255 million, or 73 percent of total Exchequer borrowing.

After its surprise by-election defeat (Dublin West), Fianna Fáil belatedly came to realize that free spending policies no longer produced electoral dividends. That, allied to an urgent necessity to convince international financial opinion that the government had a coherent and planned approach to the intractable problems of public finances, produced *The Way Forward*. Published in October as the government's economic plan, within weeks it became Fianna Fáil's election program.

By November 1982 and the final election, a new consensus had emerged between Fianna Fáil and Fine Gael, neutralizing the economy as a political issue between the parties. The plan proposed a four-year phasing out of the current budget deficit by reductions in public spending and tight controls on public sector pay. Politically, the move was a vindication of the coalition government's tough line on public finances that led to its budget defeat in January and general election defeat in February 1982.

For Fianna Fáil and Charles Haughey, *The Way Forward* was a step backward to the readoption of an economic policy first outlined by the Fianna Fáil leader in January 1980 but never implemented. This was a second conversion to the politics of austerity and fiscal rectitude that raised major questions of credibility for the party and its leader.

How and why Charles Haughey came to readopt policies he had first proposed and later abandoned represents a major part of the story of the three elections in eighteen months and why the Fianna Fáil leader lost the crucial final battle in the country's longest electoral war.

Haughey's Dilemma — A Problem of Timing

When Charles Haughey succeeded Jack Lynch as Fianna Fáil leader and Taoiseach in December 1979, he took over a party bitterly divided by his own narrow victory. All but one of his cabinet colleagues, Michael O'Kennedy, had voted against him. The seventeen-seat parliamentary majority he inherited was a legacy from his predecessor. However, a leadership change at the midterm of a government that had been elected by the largest majority ever provided no basis for Charles Haughey to seek the personal mandate he wanted from the voters. That would have to wait.

His defeated opponent, George Colley, retained his position as Tanaiste (deputy prime minister) but secured a veto on some key ministerial appointments. Later he was to make a careful public distinction between his loyalty to Haughey as Taoiseach and his qualified loyalty to him as leader of Fianna Fáil. Clearly, Charles Haughey faced major difficulties in imposing his authority on the party without first securing that personal mandate.

Early in January 1980 in a major television address, Haughey spelled out his economic priorities: to reduce government overspending and, thereby, the borrowing needed to finance it. "As a community we are living away beyond our means," he said. "We have been borrowing enormous amounts of money, borrowing at a rate which just cannot continue."[7]

The politics of the economic strategy implied a leader prepared to take a medium-term view, ready to subordinate political considerations as unpopular but necessary decisions were taken. By August signs indicated that the new Taoiseach was having second political thoughts about the primacy of his economic strategy. In a major speech in Ennis he announced dramatically: "Because of the success achieved by the budgetary strategy in correcting the deterioration in our public finances and in our balance of payments," there now was scope for limited expansion.[8]

The Permanent Campaign. The evidence for the claim was tenuous, but the announcement foreshadowed a series of actions that indicated a reversal in economic policy and signaled a slow buildup to an early general election. The Taoiseach assumed a higher public profile and took a more public, interventionist role in economic affairs.

In September came a one-sided mediation effort to break the deadlock in national pay talks, where Haughey pressed an expensive wage settlement on reluctant employers. In October the government set aside the pay recommendation of the review body it had established to examine teacher's pay. Unilaterally, the government raised the cash terms, and the review body resigned in protest.[9] The end year (1980) Exchequer figures showed the budget deficit outturn some 55 percent above the January target—in part because public service pay rose 34 percent.

For Charles Haughey the political gamble in this economic turnaround now lay in whether he could get to the country and win a new mandate before the costs and consequences of the series of U-turns became fully apparent. An earlier (November 1980) by-election success in Donegal offered every encouragement.

The single action with the most serious implications for the economy and for Haughey's own credibility was his government's preparation of the spending estimates for the 1981 budget. Minimum increases in spending were proposed, for example, a projected 3 percent rise in nonpay services at a time of 18 percent inflation; this appeared to reduce borrowing without any need to raise taxes dramatically. It was an exercise in creative accounting, which, given the previous failure to control public finances, now required the suspension of disbelief, not least in what was clearly an election year.

In his first year as Taoiseach, Charles Haughey had moved from dramatizing the problems of the economy to understating and underestimating them as electoral considerations became the increasingly predominant concern.

If the U-turn on economic strategy represented one part of the permanent campaign, the other key element was Northern Ireland, which when he became Taoiseach, he had declared as his top political priority. Northern Ireland as a political entity had failed, he claimed, and only a joint initiative by the Irish and British governments could offer new hope. In December 1980 after the Anglo-Irish summit in Dublin where he met British Prime Minister Margaret Thatcher, the Taoiseach spoke of a "historic breakthrough."[10] The Irish question, he considered, had been raised to a new plane, with the two governments agreeing to joint studies covering "the totality of relationships within these islands." The impact of the meeting and the subsequent interpretations placed on the joint communiqué raised nationalist expectations that the talks were opening the way to progress toward Irish unity and that the phrase "totality of relationships" held out the prospect that new constitutional forms would be discussed.

The economy and the North were now the key elements in the permanent campaign, but maximizing their political advantage meant choosing the optimum time for the election. The clear intention was that the party's Árd-Fheis (annual party conference) should serve as a rallying point for supporters waiting the call to electoral battle. It never came. On 14 February (St. Valentine's night) as the Árd-Fheis opened, a fire in a Dublin disco in Charles Haughey's own constituency blazed uncontrollably, killing forty-eight young people. The Árd-Fheis was cancelled: the general election plans, suspended.

For the Taoiseach, his peak electoral opportunity had passed. Over the next three months, under the pressure of events, the economy and the North became diminishing political assets, increasingly difficult to convert into votes the longer polling was delayed. In March the government, which for three months had refused to clarify whether constitutional or institutional structures were under discussion in the joint studies, finally relented.

Minister of Foreign Affairs Brian Lenihan spelled it out: "There's no question of constitutional—it is institutional structures we are talking about."[11] The British Secretary for Northern Ireland Humphrey Atkins was even more specific and, from Fianna Fáil's electoral viewpoint, damning: "The studies have nothing to do with, nor have they touched on, nor will they touch on, the internal government of Northern Ireland or its constitutional position." [12]

The historic breakthrough was now much more prosaic. For Charles Haughey a new challenge loomed, one that haunted and preoccupied him over the next three months and right through the election campaign. From 1 March the series of hunger strikes by Provisional IRA members seeking political status at the North's Maze prison got under way. All efforts at mediation by the Taoiseach, either with relatives of the hunger strikers or with Mrs. Thatcher, proved fruitless.

On the economy the first-quarter Exchequer figures provided dispiriting reading. In the first three months 40 percent of the projected full-year budget deficit figure had been reached; public finances were drifting further out of control. The optimum time for holding a general election had passed, and events, both in the North and on the economy, passed more and more outside the influence of the man who months earlier, through the Anglo-Irish summit and budget, had closely shaped them.

"Irresolutely, reluctantly, it seems, Mr. Haughey has been drawn into the vortex of a general election"—that was how the *Irish Times* viewed the Taoiseach's announcement on 21 May, naming 11 June as polling day. He had lost the tactical advantage of surprise. His move, he explained, was to dispel the uncertainty that had made governing difficult. His aim was to win the voters' endorsement for the government's economic and social policies.

Manifestoes

Fianna Fáil: Our Programme for the 80s. If the title suggested a preview of the future, the content was much more a review of the past and of the party's achievements in office. It identified Northern Ireland as "the most urgent political problem" and Irish unity as the party's "first political priority." The economic scenario presented was a benign one: the economy was coming out of recession, unemployment had begun to stabilize, and inflation was falling and running at an annualized 10 to 12 percent. Over the past four years the annual average growth rate, 3.7 percent, was the highest in the EEC. On borrowing, given the country's export-earning capacity and the exceptional rate of growth, the level was not excessive. By contrast with the party's 1977 manifesto, this program made no promises, partly because previous weeks had seen a number of electoral sweeteners dispensed by the government: for farmers, abolition of a resource tax, with smaller farmers (under £50 ratable valuation) exempted from payment of rates; for consumers, increased food subsidies with transport and energy price rises held back; for home buyers, a

new £3,000 mortgage interest subsidy to first-time purchasers and significant
increases in the state's provision for local authority housing finance.

Fine Gael: A Better Future. Within twenty-four hours Fine Gael had responded to the opening Fianna Fáil challenge. The party program identified
the "grave economic crisis" as the central issue in the election. Under the slogan
"Let the Country Win," Fine Gael proposed to phase out the current budget
deficit over four years, thus bringing public finances back into balance and
minimizing the risk of currency devaluation, and to reduce prices and costs
through an eighteen-month anti-inflation program. At the same time through
a combination of selective spending increases and tax cuts, the investment
climate would be transformed. Politically, Fine Gael hoped to tackle the problems without alienating the voters. For the voters, the program offered a
reduction in standard-rate income tax—from 35 percent to 25 percent—
financed by a once-off increase in indirect taxes; the introduction of new
housing, energy, and conservation grants; a low-cost mortgage scheme; and a
£1,000 tax credit for those in rented accommodation. For wives and mothers
working in the home, no less than three different kinds of financial support
were proposed: increased child benefit allowances; the payment of all welfare
dependency allowances to the dependent spouse, normally the mother; and the
payment of half the married person's tax credit (£500) directly to the spouse
working at home.

In costing these proposals, the £101 million in extra spending was to be
matched by balancing additional revenue from five different sources. The net
cost of the tax reform program was estimated at £263 million, after allowing
for increased health contribution charges (at 2.5 percent of all income) and a
special 3.75 percent levy on all income over £8,500. The essence of the Fine
Gael program was its tax reform package, designed in the words of a party
advertisement "to give you more of your money to spend as you choose."

Labour. On 25 May, the fifth day of campaigning, Labour presented its election program, identifying unemployment as the main problem in an economy
in crisis. The solution was a planned economy, with a three-year economic and
social plan administered by a National Planning Board. The plan would cover
incomes, prices, employment, taxation, and growth. Central to its operation
would be a state-owned Development Corporation investing in the potential
growth sectors. An unemployment scheme for young unemployed—more than
a quarter of the out-of-work total—would be financed through a 1 percent
income levy on all at work. On taxation, Labour proposed "a comprehensive
and properly structured system of capital taxation, including a wealth tax."
On public finances, the party committed itself to a phased reduction of the
current budget deficit on a planned basis but without any time scale.

The First Campaign: June 1981

Throughout, the election was like a scaled-down and less flamboyant version of the 1977 contest. The parallels were very obvious, even if roles were now reversed as Fine Gael, the challenger, sought to apply some of the political lessons learned from Fianna Fáil's greatest electoral success. Reflecting on that victory four years earlier, Jack Lynch then warned that if the unemployed —then 105,804—numbered over 100,000 come the next election, Fianna Fáil would not deserve to be returned.[13] By May 1981 unemployment had reached 123,500. The economic crisis remained; only the dimensions had changed.

The response from the politicians on opposite sides of the argument raised echoes of the tone, sentiment, and style invoked four years earlier. Liam Cosgrave's assurances that the National Coalition would not get involved in a "Dutch auction" for votes was echoed in Charles Haughey's promise that this time the party would make no promises.[14]

Electoral Strategy. Fine Gael's approach was to present itself boldly as a single-party alternative to Fianna Fáil and to seek support primarily on that basis. That strategy helps to explain both the content of its election program and the tactical manner adopted in fighting the campaign. It was a strategy derived partly from political necessity, partly from political opportunity.

If Labour's 1979 decision to rule out a preelection coalition pact created the necessity, then Fianna Fáil's leadership change in December provided the electoral opportunity. Private Fine Gael surveys in early 1980 pinpointed a clear potential for movement of support between Fianna Fáil and Fine Gael, following Charles Haughey's accession. The party's general secretary, Peter Prendergast, concluded from this and other reasons that Fine Gael, standing on its own, could beat Fianna Fáil. So the challenge facing Fine Gael was to maximize its vote without jeopardizing its relations with Labour, whose future support, passive or active, it would certainly need, at best in a minority government or more likely as a future coalition partner. For Labour, campaigning on its own independent policies, the electoral need was to maximize its own vote, both to increase representation in the new Dáil and to give the party more leverage in any postelection talks on the formation of a government.

Opening Stages of the Campaign. When Charles Haughey finally called the election, the government had already lost the tactical advantage of surprise; the date had been well anticipated by the opposition parties. Fine Gael and Labour had held conventions and selected candidates. So, over the first weekend as Fianna Fáil hurriedly followed suit, the initiative quickly passed to Fine Gael, which set the election agenda on the economic issues raised by its own program. On its contents, Garret FitzGerald had cautioned: "There are no give-aways, we are not pretending this has not to be paid for." Fianna Fáil's reaction was dismissive, claiming that the Fine Gael program contained some two hundred proposals to increase spending and that it was spendthrift, monetarist, and wholly unprincipled.

Fianna Fáil's opening gambit was to try to drive a wedge between Fine Gael and Labour, reducing the credibility of any governing alternative to itself. From the outset of the campaign, however, Garret FitzGerald and Frank Cluskey had called on their own supporters to use transfers against the government, thus mobilizing an effective voting pact. Fianna Fáil's best opportunity for attack came with the publication of Labour's program. While the Fine Gael and Labour manifestoes shared points in common—like the commitment to planning—there were also clear differences, notably on job creation, public finances, and capital taxation. To Fianna Fáil these policy differences were proof that the aims of Fine Gael and Labour were contradictory and that their ideologies were incompatible, making a postelection coalition deal impossible. Labour refuted this presumption, with Frank Cluskey claiming that the divisions within Fianna Fáil were greater than those between Fine Gael and Labour.

From Fine Gael's campaign-opening press conference, the party's new professionalism and organizational thoroughness were visibly apparent: they showed in the overnight speed with which election posters appeared countrywide; it was reflected in the keen electoral appeal of its program; it was expressed in the flair and imagination shown in opening the leader's national tour by chartering a train and packing it with journalists. All symbolized the internal transformation Fine Gael had undergone in just four years. The most significant change was at the top, where the party, with FitzGerald, at last had a leader to rival Fianna Fáil and one whose support transcended party allegiance.

As the Fianna Fáil and Fine Gael leaders opened the traditional national tour, their path was repeatedly obstructed by H-block protesters, and often in dramatic fashion.[15] In Dublin the Taoiseach ducked a can of paint thrown at him; in County Donegal, an egg duly struck its target; and in County Monaghan a bomb was found in the party office hours before he was due to visit. On the H-block issue itself, the Taoiseach rejected any idea of confrontation with Britain, while the Fine Gael leader agreed that Haughey's handling was the best in the circumstances.

On tour, the men cut contrasting figures. Haughey clearly relishing the crowd contact and confessing: "It's the kind of electioneering I enjoy most."[16] FitzGerald reacted uneasily but dutifully to the presidential role he had been cast to play by party managers. One headline summed up the performance, "Garret tries hard to be a man of the people."[17]

Campaign at Midpoint. Approaching the halfway stage, the second in the series of *Irish Times*/Irish Marketing Surveys (IMS) polls showed a sharp swing from Fianna Fáil. Published on 2 June, the survey indicated that the government's earlier 9-point lead over the combined (Fine Gael-Labour) opposition was reduced to 3. As in 1977 the government had been forced to contest the election on terms dictated by the opposition—namely, Fine Gael's tax reform proposals. These had clearly emerged as the central economic and political issue of the campaign. To the Taoiseach the Fine Gael program was an "incredible fantasy," while the £9.60 weekly payment to stay-at-home wives was a cruel trick on the housewives of the country. The real cost of the program was not £263 million but £800 million. Fianna Fáil, by ministerial speech and party advertisement, was highlighting its claim that between 1977 and 1980, some 80,000 more people were at work. The economic debate was a dialogue of the deaf, with disputes unresolved on costs, achievements, and claims.

Only a major television debate between the alternative leaders of a new government seemed likely to reconcile some of these differences. Early in the campaign the Fine Gael leader issued just such a challenge, and the Taoiseach took it up. Agreement in principle ended without agreement in practice; after two weeks of fruitless discussions on program format, the debate had to be abandoned.

Fianna Fáil was forced to reassess its campaign strategy. Its response was twofold: to increase advertising spending to counter the key selling points of the tax package (particularly the £9.60 payment) and to center the political debate on the cost and credibility of Fine Gael's overall program. Challenged by a resurgent Fine Gael party now dominating the campaign, Fianna Fáil also faced another electoral threat that it was badly placed to withstand. On 29 May the H-block committee announced the candidacy of nine prisoners, mainly Provisional IRA members, four of whom were on hunger strike. This dramatic intervention threatened to break Fianna Fáil's monopoly of republican support—particularly in border constituencies—and, by splitting the vote, put key marginal seats in jeopardy. The party was fighting a battle for survival on two fronts.

The final week of the campaign posed difficult tactical choices for Fianna Fáil and Fine Gael. With the government party losing ground, would it make any last minute bid for support through some major voter concession and at great risk to its own credibility? Would Fine Gael, with clear signs of a movement in its favor, try to boost that support by highlighting its claim as the alternative government, thus virtually excluding all other options? The hope, and gamble, of maximizing its electoral gains had to be measured against the risk of conflict with Labour.

On 4 June, a week before polling, Garret FitzGerald signaled his party's intentions. In a speech he opened the way for postelectoral talks with Labour, but without compromise on "fundamental issues." Although FitzGerald was convinced that Fine Gael would emerge as the largest single party, he tempered his enthusiasm, adding cautiously, "Should this assessment be incorrect and should we require additional support in the Dáil, we are prepared to discuss with the Labour party the formation of a strong alternative government on the basis of our programme."[18]

Fianna Fáil raised the level of its attack on the Fine Gael program, mainly through extensive advertising that identified "the cruel deception of Fine Gael" and set out the "hidden facts of the Fine Gael tax promises." The claims were that the £9.60 payment was really an income transfer from husband to wife (which it was) and not a net benefit from the state. It insisted that over half the eligible wives (600,000) would not qualify, while husbands earning more than £8,500 annually would be no better off under the new proposals.

On the final Sunday before polling (7 June), on radio Charles Haughey declared credibility was the central election issue, thus ruling out any last-minute bid to woo the wavering voter. To Fine Gael, in the words of the advertising copy surrounding the full-page, life-sized picture of Garret Fitz-Gerald, "Honesty has become the real question in this election." On the state of the economy and on tackling the problems of the nation, Fine Gael presented itself as the honest party nailing Fianna Fáil's "six big lies."[19]

On 11 June a rather bemused electorate decided between credibility and honesty and gave an inconclusive answer in the ballot box. In the concluding stages Fianna Fáil had arrested, but not reversed, the drift of support. In the course of the campaign, Garret FitzGerald with one baleful eye on the scale and complexity of the problems awaiting the new government, joked, "Whoever wins this election should have first choice on going into opposition." This election provided a result, but no winners.

The voters denied victory to all the parties: Fianna Fáil with seventy-eight seats was five short of an overall majority; Fine Gael with sixty-five seats had never done better, while Labour with fifteen seats was two down on its 1977 position. That left six independents (including two H-block candidates) and one Sine Féin the Workers' party (SFWP) deputy as political kingmakers in the formation of the new government. With eighty seats Fine Gael and Labour together had a two-vote margin over Fianna Fáil. However, not until 30 June, when the Dáil met to elect a new government, was the outcome assured. Then, the independents by and large abstained, leaving the new coalition with a three-vote majority, and a very qualified endorsement.

The Second Campaign: February 1982

The life of the Twenty-second Dáil ended dramatically on 27 January 1982, making the coalition the shortest-lived government in half a century and the first to fall on a budget vote. The snap parliamentary defeat left Fine Gael and Labour contesting a general election in the most adverse electoral circumstances.

The previous June, when Fine Gael had won its highest vote ever, the party's tax reform proposals were central to its success. On budget day, Fine Gael Finance Minister John Bruton confirmed that the key proposal, reducing the standard rate of income tax, would have to be deferred. In opposition Fine Gael had underestimated the cost by some £156 million, and Fine Gael in government had found public finances far worse than feared.[20] In office the new coalition priority became tackling the crisis in public finances through a phased four-year reduction in the current budget deficit. So Bruton, though cutting the deficit by less than £100 million, proposed to raise an extra £1,000 million in taxation. The sheer scale and extent of those tax increases, in the second budget in seven months, precipitated the coalition's downfall. For the minority government, defeat was a serious failure in parliamentary management.

Six weeks earlier, Charles Haughey had prophesied that the coalition would be "annihilated at any election or by-election they dare to face."[21] As the Dáil was dissolved and the campaign opened, few would have dissented. For the government parties, by supporting a budget rejected by the Dáil, were standing on an election platform of reduced food subsidies, higher taxes on footwear, clothes, and drink, and the taxation of social welfare benefits. That night Fine Gael and Labour members looked like condemned men on whom sentence had just been passed, but with a three-week stay of execution granted —until polling day on 18 February.

The Campaign. Fianna Fáil was caught as much off guard by its own Dáil victory as the coalition by its defeat. The election meant that all parties were equally unprepared, either in financial, organizational, or policy terms. Throughout the country, discolored posters of the party leaders still hung from lampposts, reminders of the extensive and hard-fought June campaign.

This, however, was a general election with a one-dimensional aspect; more like a referendum on economic policy, with budgetary strategy as the specific issue. The instinctive reaction of the Taoiseach, Garret FitzGerald, was to fight the campaign on an unchanged budget; Charles Haughey's was to dismiss it as "savage and anti-social" with a promise to dispose of most of its provisions.[22] Haughey, to whom the government seemed "hypnotized" by borrowing, rejected the strategy and the detail of its budget. Accepting the budget as the central economic issue, he fudged the economic alternative, claiming that only a government in office could put forward a budget.[23] Labour consulted with its ruling administrative council and, after six hours of debate, backed the budget proposals and the necessity to phase out the current budget deficit. On electoral strategy, circumstance forced the party to adopt a compromise stance. Defending its minority role in government, Labour sought to maintain separate identity and distinct policies, while the administrative council reserved the right to call a special delegate conference, after the election, to decide Labour's future role in any government.

After reflection, each party moved from its opening position. The government, to help secure a formal electoral alliance between the coalition partners, agreed to one minor change. Value-added tax (VAT) on clothing and footwear would not apply to children under ten. Within Fianna Fáil the shift was more profound. The newly appointed finance spokesman, Dr. Martin O'Donoghue, annoyed by his leader's failure to consult or involve him, won front-bench support for a reversal of positions. The party would not oppose the coalition measure outright and would accept its proposed current deficit figure. On 31 January, four days into the campaign, Charles Haughey conceded that it would not be "sensible, wise or prudent" to depart too much from that target.[24] Later, by accepting civil service help on costing and framing a budget alternative, Fianna Fáil was committed to producing its own. Tactically, Fianna Fáil still held the advantage. As Garret FitzGerald remarked: "The Government's cards are face up on the table."[25] The problem Fianna Fáil faced was how to trump the coalition's hand.

Over the first week of the campaign Fianna Fáil had moved from opposition to qualified endorsement and acceptance of the broad outline of the coalition's proposals. On 2 February Fianna Fáil published a ten-point program that sought to "cancel out the harshest effects" of the budget by "maintaining food subsidies at existing levels and eliminating the new 18 percent VAT on clothing and footwear while fully implementing the social welfare provisions."[26] Fianna Fáil's aim in accepting the stipulations of the coalition budget was to try to neutralize the major issue of public finances and contain the debate within the narrow area of disagreement (alternative revenue sources) where the party had the greatest advantage. On public finances, Fianna Fáil was clearly vulnerable, a situation that became readily apparent with the publication in *Magill* magazine of an article based on a leaked Department of Finance document, which purported to show that Fianna Fáil had seriously underestimated spending in its January 1981 budget. The magazine charged that the figures had been effectively falsified to justify a "preelection splurge" by the party, causing a "serious crisis in the nation's public finances."[27]

Confirming the documents' authenticity, Finance Minister John Bruton, while reluctant to accuse Fianna Fáil of deliberate falsification, said on 1 February, "In this instance the figures speak for themselves."[28] The government of the day, he claimed, had acted with total irresponsibility in presenting wholly unrealistic estimates. Charles Haughey accused the magazine of "gutter journalism" and the government of "national sabotage" for allegedly leaking it, claiming that in 1975 an earlier coalition government similarly overshot its budget targets.[29] An important difference, however, was that 1975—unlike 1981—was not an election year.

As the campaign approached midpoint, the first opinion polls contained two major surprises: both the coalition and Fianna Fáil were level while Garret FitzGerald held a 20-point lead over Charles Haughey—compared to a 1-point advantage the previous June. Haughey's poor showing bore out canvass reports of marked resistance to his leadership on the doorstep. For the remainder of the campaign the Fianna Fáil leader assumed a lower public profile, while the image of collective leadership was increasingly projected by the front bench.

The polls, however, held some consolation for the opposition. On the three key budgetary measures proposed by the coalition, the voters clearly signaled their rejection. A *Sunday Independent*/Market Research Bureau of Ireland survey, published on 7 February, showed 74 percent opposed VAT on clothing and footwear, even in its amended form, while 73 percent rejected lower milk and butter subsidies, with 49 percent against taxing short-term social welfare benefits. Fianna Fáil, committed to repealing all three, was well placed to exploit its electoral unpopularity while delaying announcement of its tax alternatives. What was at issue between the parties was how £119 million in tax revenue—just over one-third of 1 percent of total taxes—should be raised. The exaggeration of these minor differences of detail obscured the very real convergence of fiscal policy that had taken place. On a broader level the parties presented distinct images of themselves: Fine Gael claimed to be the party in government that had told the truth about the country's economic problems and provided the harsh but necessary remedies; Fianna Fáil presented itself as the party of stability, the only one that could secure an overall majority, and therefore provide stable government.

If Fianna Fáil was stable, given its performance on the economy, it had a major credibility problem; if Fine Gael and Labour were credible on public finances, questions remained about their stability. The previous seven months had seen a number of disagreements between Fine Gael and Labour ministers on aspects of economic policy—notably the implementation of Fine Gael's tax package. Throughout the campaign there was continuing public uncertainty on just where Labour stood on the coalition question. Party leader Michael O'Leary had no doubt that a Fine Gael-Labour majority would make the party's participation in government "certain," while party chairman Michael D. Higgins rejected this notion, insisting that no electoral alliance existed.[30] There was little doubt, however, that Labour was actually campaigning as part of a government still in office and clearly reluctant to give up power.

The closeness of the working relationship between the governing parties was reflected in the clear instruction on the bottom of Fine Gael advertising: "Vote Fine Gael and continue your preferences for Labour." Electorally,

Labour faced a challenge from the right from Fine Gael, as it broadened its base to become more a social democratic party, and from the left from Sinn Féin the Workers' party, a Marxist-oriented party with growing support in Dublin. SFWP opposed the key tax measures in the budget and called on Labour not to enter government after the election but to join a workers' opposition.

The February election could not have been more different from its June counterpart: here was an election with a clear focus that the June campaign had lacked, with the time of year and financial penury of the parties limiting the scale of the campaign, curtailing the extent of the national tours of party leaders. In consequence, the campaign was centralized in Dublin on a narrow range of relatively esoteric economic issues—levels of borrowing, size of budget deficit, and the like—via press conferences and television debates before a far-from-deferential press corps.

When just under a week before polling Fianna Fáil presented its budget alternative, the choice was between a budget as tough in its direct impact on taxpayers, but avoiding the harshness of the coalition formula, and a soft-option measure that raised the revenue needed but inflicted minimal cost on taxpayers. On 12 February, six days before polling, Fianna Fáil chose the soft option, raising over three-fourths of the revenue needed from the corporate sector through advance payments of existing direct (corporation tax) and indirect (VAT) taxes, which would give the Exchequer a once-off, nonrecurring, benefit. Finance spokesman, Dr. O'Donoghue, argued that it would prove not only fairer than the coalition budget but also that it would help increase employment by some four to five thousand in 1982.

Minister of Finance John Bruton warned that the Fianna Fáil proposals merely postponed solving the country's problems until 1983. Fianna Fáil, he claimed, had again employed "the use of funny money from the same accountancy stable as produced the 1981 budget."[31] Labour leader Michael O'Leary dismissed them as a confidence trick that could lead to devaluation and make 1983 the year of financial collapse.

The campaign ended on much the same note on which it had begun, the intervening period serving only to reinforce the prejudices government and opposition held about each other. To Fianna Fáil, the coalition approach was inhuman, one that put accountancy and figures before people. To Fine Gael and Labour, Fianna Fáil's preference for the soft option was a potential return to the same profligate course followed in 1981. On 16 February, just two days before polling, the final *Irish Times*/IMS survey provided a pointer to the outcome, showing that Fianna Fáil had surged ahead on the basis of its budget proposals. Fianna Fáil, in the words of a party spokesman, was now certain of election success; it had shown how taxes could be raised without hurting the poor. To many, the choice was between living now and paying later, or paying now and living later. On 18 February they chose the former.

The Final Campaign: November 1982

The country's second election in nine months, on 24 November, was precipitated in the same way as the first, but this time by a Dáil defeat on a government motion of confidence and by a two-vote margin. Unlike the coalition's downfall on the January budget, however, this was much more clearly signaled in advance. Over the summer recess Fianna Fáil saw its Dáil voting strength reduced through death (Dr. Bill Loughnane) and illness (Jim Gibbons) from eighty-one to seventy-nine, just as the government dramatically reversed policy in a bid to regain control over public finances. On 30 July a pay freeze in the public service was announced as part of a £120 million package of government spending cuts, followed on 21 October by its economic plan *The Way Forward*, which committed the government to eliminating the current budget deficit over four years.

Ever since Fianna Fáil had taken office in March as a minority government, its survival in the Dáil hinged on voting support from the three Workers' party members. But Fianna Fáil's sudden adoption of deflationary policies jeopardized that voting alliance. That, allied to the consistently high level of support for the Workers' party in the polls and the sudden leadership crisis in Labour, provided it with a number of different reasons for withdrawing support from the government and causing a general election.

At Labour's annual conference (22–24 October), party leader Michael O'Leary found his advice on electoral strategy supported by a majority of his parliamentary party colleagues but rejected narrowly by the delegates. Within days he resigned as leader, before quitting the party altogether to join Fine Gael. O'Leary's departure left Labour electing a successor, thirty-two-year-old barrister Dick Spring with eighteen-months parliamentary experience, just three days before the election was called. Within Fianna Fáil, just a month earlier, Charles Haughey had survived a second leadership challenge in nine months as twenty-two members of the parliamentary party publicly voted no confidence in him.

So as the Twenty-third Dáil faced dissolution, the latest IMS poll (22 October) showed Fine Gael at an all-time high (41 percent) and within two points of the government. Fianna Fáil (43 percent) had hit its lowest polling point since 1979. Dissatisfaction with government (72 percent) was never higher; satisfaction with Charles Haughey as Taoiseach (32 percent) never lower.

The Campaign. The third and decisive battle in the country's longest electoral war opened on 4 November. As the incumbent, Fianna Fáil was badly placed to exploit potential electoral advantages. Internal divisions arising from the latest leadership bid now raised questions about Fianna Fáil's traditional claim as the party of stability. Morale was low throughout all levels of the organization, while financially it was in poor shape to contest a snap election. In adopting the government's economic plan as its election program, the party had, through its title *The Way Forward*, borrowed a slogan favored by Fine Gael in the February campaign and, in its contents, borrowed the economic strategy pursued by the coalition since June 1981. While the move neutralized the economy as a major electoral issue between Fianna Fáil and Fine Gael, it revived questions about the party's credibility on economic matters. For Charles Haughey, it was the latest in a series of policy somersaults, which saw the Fianna Fáil leader advocating the politics of austerity, returning to the position he had first clearly set out as Taoiseach in January 1980 but failed to implement.

If in February the coalition was forced to contest the election with its cards face up on the table, this time it was Fianna Fáil's turn. Through its plan, the government was proposing to eliminate the budget deficit in four years, helped by reductions in public service numbers, tight controls on its pay, and a 5 percent volume fall in the level of government services. In addition, proposed changes in the welfare code would set a new and lower ceiling on the maximum benefit levels of those out of work.

Fine Gael based its election program on an abridged version of the party's *Policy of Economic Recovery*, published in October, which identified unemployment as the central concern. The party renewed its commitment to a four-year phasing out of the budget deficit and to a continuation of the constitutional review begun as part of FitzGerald's constitutional crusade. On its own Labour again contested independent policies, proposing increased levels of capital taxation, a strong national development corporation, and greater economic democracy through worker participation. The Workers' party, now with three seats, set full employment by 1991 as its main priority.

The broad consensus between Fianna Fáil and the opposition parties on the economy meant that for the first time in three elections it was not the major campaign issue and the main focus of debate. All parties accepted, to a greater or lesser degree, that this election would be won or lost by success or failure at the constituency rather than at the national level. The team with the best candidates, strategically positioned in the constituency and backed by a party organization skilled in the delicate techniques of vote management—splitting the vote evenly among candidates to maximize seat gains—would have the edge. The two earlier elections gave the parties all the electoral data needed to identify opponents' strengths and weaknesses in all forty-one constituencies.

At the national level, however, it was a campaign where themes—credibility, trust, stability of government, and the like—seemed to matter more than issues. The party differences on the specific issues (after both sides had short-lived experiences in minority governments) were, invariably, more apparent than real. Abortion, the first issue of the campaign, illustrates this point. Fianna Fáil raised the issue to challenge Fine Gael's claim as the party of trust and credibility. Since the June 1981 election, both major parties had an unmet commitment to introduce a constitutional amendment outlawing abortion (already illegal under statute law) by asserting a right to life of the unborn. Three days before the election was called, Fianna Fáil published its proposed amendment, the wording of which was quickly welcomed by the Fine Gael leader as being "about as good a formula as you could get."[32]

Charles Haughey did not trust Fine Gael to proceed with it claiming that Labour had made the dropping of the referendum a precondition for any coalition with Fine Gael. Labour's new leader refuted this, insisting his party was unequivocally opposed to abortion, though he had legal reservations about the wording. The pro-life group that sponsored the amendment, accepted Fitz-Gerald's assurance that there would be no delay, thus defusing the controversy.

The pattern of the first half of the campaign was uneven, reflecting Fine Gael's tactical decision not to take the initiative and Fianna Fáil's failure to command public attention with its austere election program. Fine Gael's approach was two-phased. In the first half of the campaign the party highlighted the degree of consensus on major policy matters, later concentrating on the policies that distinguished the parties from each other. As the campaign moved toward the halfway stage, the first opinion polls from IMS and the Market Research Bureau of Ireland (MRBI) showed no significant movement on the pre-election trend. If Fine Gael's concern was peaking too soon, Fianna Fáil —trailing between 6 and 8 points behind Fine Gael and Labour combined— had little time to make up lost ground and limited scope on the issues.

Fianna Fáil's reaction was to switch the focus of attention away from its party program and onto Anglo-Irish relations and affairs of Northern Ireland, where the main thrust on the party's attack was on the Fine Gael leader's strongest point, his credibility. Neither issue had figured prominently in earlier campaigns, while among voters they did not register as priority concerns. On matters Anglo-Irish the blunt political charge from Minister of Foreign Affairs Gerry Collins was that FitzGerald had allowed himself to be used as an instrument of British policy in Ireland. The minister claimed on the basis of a report in *The Times* (London) of 9 November that Northern Secretary James Prior had used the Fine Gael leader to lobby the duke of Norfolk (a Catholic peer in the House of Lords) in favor of his devolution proposals.

Rejecting the allegation as false, FitzGerald said his informal conversation with the duke was an attempt to seek an amendment in the legislation setting up the Northern Ireland Assembly that proposed to debar a nationalist

(Social Democratic and Labour party member Seamus Mallon) on the grounds of his membership in the Irish Senate. Throughout the second half of the campaign, Fianna Fáil's dominant, if not exclusive, theme centered on allegations about FitzGerald's role in Anglo-Irish relations and charges of British interference in the election itself. Boldly stated, the Fianna Fáil thesis maintained the Fine Gael leader was an instrument of British policy, in collusion and collaboration with the British government and that both the British government and the media were interfering in the election because they wanted Charles Haughey out. It was something of a political conspiracy theory, rationalized out of circumstantial rather than factual evidence and relying on minor political figures like the duke of Norfolk.

The charge of collusion arose from remarks attributed to James Prior in the United States, where he suggested that Garret FitzGerald would shortly make proposals for an all-Ireland court and police force. Prior denied the remarks—implying some foreknowledge of FitzGerald's intentions—but said that he was aware of newspaper reports indicating proposals that might be made. On 18 November, when FitzGerald maintained precedent by making one major speech on the North, he fulfilled that earlier newspaper speculation. In doing so, despite major misgivings inside his own party, he made Fine Gael's security proposals a central campaign issue and one that gave new impetus to a flagging controversy conducted in a histrionic manner by the Fianna Fáil leader.

The security proposals, in fact, were not new. They had first been raised with the British government during the coalition's earlier tenure in office and were later publicly advocated by FitzGerald when he gave the 1982 Dimbleby lecture on BBC television. Indeed the principle of the all-Ireland court had been favored by Fianna Fáil since the mid-1970s and supported again months earlier in the senate by the Minister of Agriculture Brian Lenihan. The Taoiseach, however, bluntly repudiated that line, claiming it was no longer Fianna Fáil policy. Fine Gael proposed a federal solution to the problem of cross-border security. These included the establishment of an all-Ireland security council and court and prison system with a new police force separate from both the Gárda (police force of the Republic) and the Royal Ulster Constabulary that could operate on either side of the border.

Charles Haughey claimed that the proposals terrified him. Therefore, over the final days of the campaign, the election took on a bitter and hostile note as relations between the two leaders deteriorated and angry words were exchanged. Garret FitzGerald claimed that the Taoiseach was waging a campaign of lies and vilification against him by attempts to smear him on the abortion question, through the false charge of collaboration with the British government, and by the Fianna Fáil leader's misrepresentation of the party's proposal on joint policing.

Rejecting these charges, the Taoiseach insisted he had told no lies, adding, "I have only made attacks on his policies and his actions."[33] To add the final twist to the by now Machiavellian plot linking FitzGerald and the duke of Norfolk, however, the Taoiseach boldly insisted that in meeting the duke, FitzGerald "had lunch with a trained British spy."[34] The duke's curriculum vitae, identifying him as head of intelligence at the British Ministry of Defence until 1967, was offered as evidence. And there Charles Haughey finally rested his case.

Over the final weekend the full impact of Fianna Fáil's Green-card tactics, designed largely to raise morale among traditional supporters and check voting abstention, became publicly apparent as leaflets were distributed in some constituencies asking the question: "Do you want the R.U.C. policing our streets?"[35]

Three days before polling saw the sudden and unexpected intervention by Attorney General John Murray into the campaign debate, claiming that the Fine Gael proposals on security were vague, improbable, and likely to undermine the effectiveness and independence of the forces of law and order.

The campaign ended as it has begun, still centered on the personalities of Haughey and FitzGerald — with the voters required to adjudicate, after three weeks of intemperate debate on marginal issues, the candidates' respective claims to credibility, trust, and public confidence.

Campaign Finances

The three general elections in eighteen months cost the three main parties an estimated £4 million just to finance their national campaigns.[36] The June 1981 election proved as costly as both 1982 campaigns together. Fianna Fáil, which in 1981 outspent Fine Gael by a two-to-one margin (£1.2 million to £600,000) met increasing financing problems as the series progressed. By November 1982 party spending was just over one-fourth its 1981 level and, for the first time ever, almost matched by Fine Gael.

For the two major parties the cumulative loss on the election series was substantial, leaving Fianna Fáil, traditionally best able to fund its campaigns, with a major cash crisis. Total estimated debt, according to a party source, was £1 million, of which three quarters was accounted for by the deficit on campaign spending.[37] Fine Gael ended with a £420,000 overall shortfall. Only Labour, which started in a weak financial position, avoided major deterioration through minimal national spending, an estimated £213,000.

The parties maintained strict secrecy about all aspects of their election fund-raising efforts, with Fianna Fáil relying exclusively on business contributions to fund national campaign costs. Fine Gael balanced revenue from business and individual donors with an election levy raised from the constituency organizations. Labour relied on election grants from the political funds of affiliated trade unions as the main basis of support.

Election costs at the local level were difficult to calculate, varying with the constituency size and organizational strength of the parties and the extent of their financial reserves. Fianna Fáil, by rebating 40 percent of the annual national collection to the constituency organization that raised it, helped provide a local campaign fund.[38] In 1981–82 that came to £287,828. Fine Gael levies the local party annually to finance the operating costs of its national organization. Any money raised in excess of both the annual and the election levies provides reserves for local funding in a general election. With a local party organization more independent of central control, Labour pays an annual levy to party headquarters. At election time the constituency party relies less on national support than either Fianna Fáil or Fine Gael does.

Campaign contributions are sought confidentially: companies face no legal obligations on disclosure, the parties are under no restraints on the amounts raised, and the parties have no obligation for public accountability on the campaign funds or how they are disbursed. The parties view the subject as their private business. The attitude is well illustrated by the reply from Charles Haughey when asked whether, as had been reported, Fianna Fáil owed over a £1 million. He said, "I wouldn't attempt to answer you that question because this is our private business. We are in a position to carry on as a political party. We have financial problems and what we owe, or don't owe, what our assets are, what our reserves are, that's our own business."[39]

Clearly, the spending and revenue-raising capacities of the three main parties differ considerably, with an estimated 1981–82 total election spending for Fianna Fáil of £2.3 million, with Fine Gael at £1.4 million and Labour at £213,000. On the expenditure side, among the main parties an estimated half of total spending is accounted for by national press advertising. No paid political advertising is allowed on the state radio or television. The balance is divided among three items: printing and posters (party programs, election leaflets, stickers, and the poster of the party leader); the organizational costs of the leader's national tour; and the production costs of the parties' political broadcasts for radio and television, which are transmitted free.

Fianna Fáil. The party that before June 1981 seemed least likely to have financial difficulties funding its campaign costs ended that election with a major overrun on spending. At the midpoint of the campaign, when the polls showed a narrowing of the Fianna Fáil lead, the party hastily revised its strategy, leading to substantial extra advertising spending. An election budgeted to cost £650,000 ended costing nearly twice that amount. The party's outstanding debt problems were then compounded in February 1982 when revenue raised to fund a £750,000 campaign partly failed to be collected in the postelection period after an internal row. Only in the November election did revenue collected actually exceed the party's greatly reduced current campaign costs.[40] At £350,000, Fianna Fáil's spending was just 29 percent of the June 1981 level. Overall the party spent an estimated £2.3 million in the three elections, representing some 59 percent of the total spending by the main parties. On press advertising, as measured by column inches in the national press— not including provincial papers or magazines—the party in 1981 accounted for 58 percent of the total political advertising, dropping to 50 percent and 35 percent in February and November 1982.[41]

Fine Gael. Nowhere was the contrast between the old Fine Gael—1977 vintage —and its new 1981 style more apparent than in the transformation of the party organization at the central level. It was expressed in its capacity to fund and carry through a major election campaign that certainly matched and, in some respects, surpassed Fianna Fáil. The party came through the three elections with the least difficulty in financing its campaigns, ending with an outstanding debt of £420,000, less than half the Fianna Fáil total. For the 1981 campaign, Fine Gael hoped to raise half the cost from within the organization —by a special election levy on the constituency party—with the rest from business and individual contributions. The levy was fixed at £2,000 per Dáil seat.

On total campaign spending of £600,000, some 60 percent came from outside the party (business sources) and 40 percent from within. For the two elections in 1982, the special constituency levy was reduced by half, resulting in a much greater dependence by the party on business donations for campaign funding. At the end of the three elections, the overall balance between external and internal sources of funding suggests a very heavy reliance on business sources for election finance. According to one article in *Magill* magazine, a breakdown of the level of contributions suggests that most ranged between £50 and £300 with three donations over £10,000 and some 100 over £1,000.[42] With money raised from the business sector, contributions were invariably made to both Fianna Fáil and Fine Gael; political preference expressing itself far more in the relative size of the donation to each party.

Fine Gael's total spending for the 1981–82 elections came to £1.4 million —some 60 percent of the Fianna Fáil outlay. Outspent in 1981 by a two-to-one margin, in February Fine Gael had narrowed the gap (£500,000 to Fianna Fáil's £750,000) and by November had virtually closed it (£300,000 to Fianna Fáil's £350,000).

Labour. By the time of the 1981 election, the party still had not recovered from the huge cost overrun in Labour's budget for the 1979 European Parliament elections. In consequence, it raised a £50,000 interest-free loan from the

Socialist group in the European Parliament to ease its financial problems. In 1979 and 1980 the party showed operating losses of £34,313 and £28,982, respectively. At its annual conference in 1980 the party took drastic action to bring day-to-day spending at headquarters back into balance and to raise funds for the imminent general election. Delegates voted to triple individual membership charges and to double affiliation fees from trade unions. In 1981 national campaign costs came to £93,258, with income of £76,224 coming from trade union grants and business contributions. The latest party accounts (1981) give details of the global cost of the campaign and the total revenue raised, but provide no further breakdown.

The mainstay of Labour's trade union support has been the Irish Transport and General Workers Union (ITGWU) and the Federated Workers Union of Ireland (FWUI), which together account for about half the country's 474,292 union members. Both remain dominant influences in Irish trade unionism and, through their affiliation with the Labour party, in its affairs also. In 1981 the ITGWU paid out £51,386 in affiliation fees and grants out of its political fund, with the FWUI contributing £25,334. In 1982 the ITGWU figure rose to £56,000, while that of the FWUI dropped to £16,078.[43] Not all money paid out of the political fund of the affiliated unions is forwarded directly to the party and reflected in national campaign spending. In 1982 some money from the ITGWU's political fund also helped union-sponsored Social Democratic and Labour party (SDLP) candidates contesting the Northern Ireland Assembly election. Likewise in the general elections in the Republic, individual grants have ranged from £500 to £1,500, depending on the candidate's chance of success. The party has also actively, if discreetly, sought support from business sources. By comparison with the flow of funds to Fianna Fáil and Fine Gael from that quarter, the response is negligible, but in the context of Labour's own small level of national spending it still represents a very significant contribution, varying with the party's stance on coalition.

Even allowing for a £17,034 deficit on election spending, Labour managed an overall £8,633 surplus in 1981. In the February 1982 election the party faced its greatest financial strain. Relations with the trade unions—largely hostile to Labour in coalition—had deteriorated. Election grants were slower in coming to the party, and one affiliated union, the Amalgamated Transport and General Workers Union, turned down an appeal for funds.[44] At the annual conferences of the ITGWU and FWUI in June 1982, Labour faced a strong attack from delegates, but motions seeking union disaffiliation were rejected. By November the circumstances of the dramatic election of the third Labour leader in eighteen months, Dick Spring, helped ease strained relations between the party and the unions and increased the flow of funds for Labour's campaign. Total spending on all three elections came to £213,000, with £93,000 spent in 1981 and £60,000 in each of the two subsequent elections. In June

1981 the party took 5.6 percent of total political advertising space in the national press, dropping to 3.8 percent in February and rising to 5.7 percent in November 1982.

Conclusion

Three general elections, which in normal times might have been spread over ten to twelve years, were crowded into the year and a half from June 1981 to November 1982. Over that time, two minority governments survived equally short periods in office before falling in similar fashion—on a Dáil vote. The electoral volatility was matched by a similar instability within the parties. Fianna Fáil leader Charles Haughey faced two challenges to his leadership and survived; Labour contested all three elections under different leaders; only Fine Gael, which had increased its vote at successive elections, remained untroubled. For deputies of all parties the three elections accelerated change by increasing the rate of turnover among members. By November 1982 some 71 (43 percent) of the 166 deputies in the Twenty-fourth Dáil had first been elected in the 1981–82 period.[45]

Fianna Fáil's failure in three consecutive elections to win an overall majority was without precedent but explained by a number of factors. The challenge was a formidable one: for the first time, the constituencies had been drawn by an independent commission. By creating a large number of five-seat constituencies (containing 45 percent of all seats), the commission had ensured a stricter proportionality between votes gained and seats won. For Fianna Fáil, this meant the end of the bonus it had traditionally secured as the largest party, where seats gained in excess of its proportionate share of the vote had previously enabled it to form governments. In 1969 with 44.66 percent of the vote, it took power as a majority government; in February 1982 with 47.26 percent, it was still a minority government.

Winning the vote share, therefore, required about 48.5 percent to secure an overall majority and an above-average electoral performance. The party, any party, also needed luck, and Fianna Fáil in early 1981 was unlucky that a series of circumstances frustrated the holding of a spring election at a time of maximum electoral opportunity. It needed credibility, but after April 1981 Fianna Fáil's credibility on economic policy was progressively eroded as the policy somersaults of Charles Haughey took place against the background of an economy moving deeper into recession. Fianna Fáil needed unity to sustain its claim as the single-party, stable, alternative government, but the palpable divisions apparent, even before the two leadership challenges, clearly indicated a lack of unity.

Fine Gael, which in 1977 dropped to its lowest level of support in twenty years, was (along with the Workers' party) the only one to come through the series of elections with support rising at each, to end in November 1982 with its highest national vote ever (39.22 percent) and just five seats short of Fianna Fáil. In doing this, Fine Gael showed it had a party organization that could campaign with a professionalism and efficiency that more than matched Fianna Fáil. The key to the party's success was Garret FitzGerald, who in five years had transformed the party at every level, taking it close to becoming the largest single party and to a position where it could challenge Fianna Fáil's monopoly role as the natural party of government.

The nature and extent of the economic crisis, allied to the convergence of the policy responses from Fianna Fáil and Fine Gael, might have laid the basis for a significant electoral advance on the left. But Labour—which fought all its elections on independent policies and without preelection commitment on coalition—found throughout its support under attack from right and left: on the right, from a revitalized Fine Gael with a broader social democratic appeal; on the left, for a socialist alternative, the Workers' party, which had steadily increased its support from 1.72 percent in June 1981 to 3.25 percent in November 1982. Only in that last election did Labour manage to halt a steady decline, but with under 10 percent of the vote throughout the election series, the party had returned to the same level of support it had enjoyed in the mid-1950s. These were elections held in circumstances that should have favored the smaller parties, but the total two-party dominance of Fianna Fáil and Fine Gael was reflected in their capacity to win eight out of every ten voters.

Notes

1. Department of Finance, *Economic Review and Outlook, Summer 1983*, Pl. 1593 (Dublin: Stationery Office, 1983), pp. 33, 45.
2. Ibid., pp. 42–43.
3. Organization for Economic Cooperation and Development (OECD), *Ireland, Economic Surveys 1983–1984* (Paris: OECD, 1983), p. 68.
4. Department of Finance, *Finance Accounts 1980 and 1982*, Prl. 9309, Pl. 1163 (Dublin: Stationery Office, 1981, 1983), pp. 54–55 (1981), pp. 56–57 (1983).
5. *Economic Review*, Summer 1983, p. 19.
6. *Irish Times*, 14 September 1982.
7. Ibid., 10 January 1980. Mr. Haughey said: "As a community we are living away beyond our means. I do not mean that everyone in the community is living too well. Clearly many are not and have barely enough to get by. But taking us all together, we have been living at a rate which is simply not justified by the amount of goods and services we are producing. To make up the difference, we have been borrowing enormous amounts of money, borrowing at a rate which just cannot continue."
8. Ibid., 18 August 1980.
9. *Dáil Debates*, vol. 326, cols. 902–11, 3 February 1981.
10. *Irish Times*, 9 December 1980. Report of press conference by Mr. Haughey: When asked to comment on that portion of the joint communiqué that referred to the talks as being "extremely constructive and significant," the Taoiseach commented that he was hopeful that

they were "in the middle of an historic break-through" and that the problems facing the two governments had been placed "firmly on a new plane."

11. Ibid., 19 March 1981. Mr. Lenihan's clarification came on the RTE television program "Today Tonight," the day before. He had been asked by the Labour leader, Mr. Cluskey, if both the British Prime Minister Thatcher and her Northern Ireland Secretary Atkins were lying, when they denied the constitutional position of Northern Ireland was under discussion.

12. Ibid., 23 March 1981. The paper reported: The statement issued by the secretary of state was described by British government sources as carrying "the full authority and approval" of Mrs. Thatcher. Mr. Atkins said: "The joint studies commissioned by Mrs. Thatcher and Mr. Haughey are intended to examine matters of common interest between the United Kingdom and Republic and to improve relations between the two countries. The studies have nothing to do with, nor have they touched on, nor will they touch on, the internal government of Northern Ireland or its constitutional position. The Government and Mrs. Thatcher have repeatedly made this clear."

13. RTE Radio, "This Week," 8 January 1978.

14. Brian Farrell and Maurice Manning, "The Election," in Howard R. Penniman, ed., *Ireland at the Polls: The Dáil Election of 1977*, (Washington, D.C.: American Enterprise Institute, 1978), p. 141.

15. H-block took its name from the shape of the cell block formation in the Maze prison in Northern Ireland, the site of the mass hunger strike by republican prisoners that resulted in ten deaths in 1981. Since 1978, both Provisional IRA and Irish National Liberation Army prisoners there had campaigned for the return of political or special category status, withdrawn by the British government in 1976. The protesting prisoners at first refused to wear any clothing, except a blanket, later refusing to wash or use the toilet facilities. The hunger strike, a dramatic extension of the campaign, accelerated in May 1981, following the death of Bobby Sands, within weeks of his election to the House of Commons as a member of parliament.

16. *Irish Times*, 1 June 1981.

17. Ibid., 30 May 1981.

18. Ibid., 5 June 1981.

19. Ibid., 9 June 1981. The advertisement was headed: "Fine Gael the big lies." It set out claim and counterclaim on six areas where Fianna Fáil had attacked its program:

> Lie: Huge increases on petrol, beer and spirits.
> Fine Gael will strictly control the price of these items.
> Lie: All housewives will not gain from the Fine Gael proposals for women.
> The Fine Gael package will benefit nine out of ten housewives.
> Lie: Everybody will pay more tax.
> With Fine Gael ALL taxpayers with incomes under £50,000 will have MORE take home pay.
> Lie: VAT will be put on clothing and footwear.
> Fine Gael will not put VAT on clothing and footwear.
> Lie: Fine Gael policies would cost £1,000 million.
> All the experts accept the Fine Gael costings as accurate.
> Lie: Rates will be reintroduced. You will lose tax allowance on your mortgage and other reliefs.
> Fine Gael will not reintroduce rates. Mortgages and other reliefs will still be allowed at your top rates.
> Vote Fine Gael. We'll put it right.

20. Ibid., 14 December 1981.

21. *Dáil Debates*, vol. 331, col. 2848, 18 December 1981.

22. Ibid., vol. 332, col. 388, 27 January 1982.

23. *Irish Times*, 29 January 1982.

24. Ibid., 1 February 1982.

25. Ibid., 1 February 1982.

26. Ibid., 3 February 1982.

27. Vincent Browne, "How Haughey Cooked the Books in 1981," *Magill*, February 1982, 22–27.

28. *Irish Times*, 2 February 1982.

29. Ibid., 2 and 3 February 1982.

30. Ibid., 5 February 1982.

31. Ibid., 13 February 1982.

32. RTE Television, "Today Tonight," 4 November 1982.

33. *Sunday Independent*, 21 November 1982.

34. Ibid., 21 November 1982.

35. A reference to Fianna Fáil's emotive exploitation of nationalist feeling on the Northern Ireland question for electoral gain, notably in the latter half of the campaign, and reflected in loose charges that Dr. FitzGerald had collaborated with the British government. The phrase originates in Northern Ireland when in 1886, Lord Randolph Churchill, a leading Conservative, played what he described as the Orange card. He wanted to use Ulster unionist opposition to Home Rule as a means of advancing Conservative support in Britain. At an anti-Home Rule rally in Belfast he championed the cause of Ulster unionism and played the Orange card with his famous rallying cry "Ulster will fight and Ulster will be right."

36. Estimate based on author's interviews with Frank Wall, general secretary, Fianna Fáil; Finbarr FitzPatrick, general secretary, Fine Gael; Senator Tim Conway, financial secretary, Labour; and from published sources. These include: Labour party, *Annual Report of the Administrative Council and Parliamentary Party, 1980–82* (Dublin, 1982), pp. 22–23; Brian Trench, "The Price of Votes," *Magill*, June 1981, 34–37; "Fianna Fáil's Financial Ills," *Aspect*, 17 June 1982, pp. 12–14; Des Crowley, "Who Pays for the Party . . . ," *Success*, April 1983, pp. 28–32; Geraldine Kennedy, "The Men in Room 547 of the Burlington," *Sunday Tribune*, 9 May 1982; and Geraldine Kennedy, "How They're Bringing in the Money," *Sunday Press*, 22 May 1983.

37. Private memorandum circulated to all members of the Fianna Fáil parliamentary party on 23 March 1983, by Paul W. MacKay. A joint auditor for the Dublin North Central constituency (represented by Charles J. Haughey), he was later expelled from the party for "conduct unbecoming a member"—drawing attention to Fianna Fáil's precarious financial state.

38. See Fianna Fáil, *Árd-Fheis Clar, 1983* (Agenda for party conference), p. 22, for auditors' report on party receipts and expenditure in 1981–82, other than general elections.

39. RTE Radio, "This Week," 1 May 1982.

40. Geraldine Kennedy, "The Men in Room 547 of the Burlington," *Sunday Tribune*, 9 May 1982; Geraldine Kennedy, "How They're Bringing in the Money," *Sunday Press*, 22 May 1983, provide a detailed background on Fianna Fáil fund raising methods.

41. F. X. Carty, *Elections '82: What the Papers Said* (Dublin: Able Press, 1983), p. 16.

42. Vincent Browne, "The Whizz Kids Who Won the Election for Fine Gael," *Magill*, December 1982, 6.

43. Annual reports, ITGWU and FWUI, 1981 and 1982.

44. "ATGWU Joins Attack on Labour Party," *Irish Times*, 18 June 1982.

45. Ted Nealon and Seamus Brennan, eds., *Nealon's Guide to the 24th Dáil and 2nd Seanad Election* (Dublin: Platform Press, 1983), p. 161.

3 The Voters, the Issues, and the Party System

RICHARD SINNOTT

Party systems operate at several levels—parliamentary, national headquarters, constituency, and what has come to be called the party-in-the-electorate. The last is the focus of this chapter. The three elections of 1981–82 raised very large questions about the current state of the Irish party system and about its role in the wider political system. There were suggestions that fundamental changes were in train, hints of these being found in the unprecedented three successive failures of Fianna Fáil to win a majority of seats, in Fine Gael's climb to an all-time high in both share of votes and share of seats, and in the continued gradual decline of Labour party support. There were also indications of a chipping away at the edges of the established party system in the surprisingly strong performance of H-block candidates in June 1981 and the eruption onto the Dáil scene of the Workers' party and several ideologically minded independent deputies. Beyond the question of gains and losses, there was some speculation about the failure of the parties to cope with economic and social challenges. Alleged instances were the response to the crisis in public expenditure and the vulnerability of the parties to the importunities of single-issue pressure groups. In the light of all this, the old chestnuts of breaking the political party mold and realigning the party system on left-right lines assumed greater currency and even, for a time, some greater credibility.

Not only were the questions raised by the three elections large ones; the actual issues were of unusual intricacy. Questions of high finance were very much to the fore and were further complicated by the oscillation of the parties between the politics of promise and the politics of austerity. The only apparently simplifying factor was a prime ministerial contest of unprecedented explicitness and intensity, but even its effect on voting behavior was not as straightforward as it might, at first sight, have seemed to have been.

The analytical problems do not end with these complexities, not at least if we accept Donald E. Stokes's recent strictures on electoral analysis: "Indeed, it might also be said that the frameworks by which we understand the influence of leaders and issues on electoral politics are still in remarkable disrepair."[1] In other words, the already difficult task of interpreting Irish electoral behavior in 1981 and 1982 is rendered more difficult by the inadequacy of the available analytical tools. This is not the place to attempt to make good the flaws of the general paradigm of electoral research. It may help, however, before launching into a detailed analysis of the three elections, to examine the current state of theoretical and comparative understanding of the Irish party system.[2]

The Irish Party System: Basic Features and Implications

There is broad agreement on one aspect of the party system: it has institutionalized or is the embodiment of a conflict that occurred in the past. This view goes considerably further than the conventional wisdom about the historical origins of the two main Irish parties in two ways. First, it emphasizes that this institutionalization of past divisions is by no means unique to the Irish party system. As Seymour Martin Lipset and Stein Rokkan put it, in what has almost become a dictum of the literature on party systems, "The party systems of the 1960s reflect, with few but significant exceptions, the cleavage structures of the 1920s."[3] Second, this perspective on the Irish party system differs from purely historical accounts in that, going beyond the labels protreaty and antitreaty, it addresses the nature of the conflict that has been enshrined in the party system. Moreover, it does so in a comparative framework, seeking to determine whether the underlying conflict can be described in terms similar to those used to account for conflicts in other party systems.

The comparative yardstick most frequently resorted to in the study of European party systems is that suggested by Lipset and Rokkan. As we have already seen, this emphasizes the longevity of party systems. Party systems are frozen as a result of the political mobilization that accompanied the extension of the right to vote to the mass of the people. The conflicts embedded in the party system reflect the cleavages dominant at the time of mobilization and, according to the theory, are likely to comprise one or more of the following fundamental sources of division in society: center versus periphery; state versus church; land versus industry; owner versus worker.[4] Given the general agreement that Irish parties have been molded by conflicts that occurred in the past, a considerable part of the debate about the nature of the party system boils down to the question whether the particular conflicts that were the basis of mobilization and institutionalization in Ireland can be described in Lipset and Rokkan's terms.

R. K. Carty comes down emphatically in favor of the view that the cleavage in Irish politics is unique. Referring specifically to Lipset and Rokkan's theory, he concludes: "The Irish party system deviates from the cleavage model, which has so far provided a powerful accounting of the other causes of democratic political competition in Europe."[5] Rather than being based on social structural cleavages, the Irish party system, according to Carty, is based on a "purely partisan cleavage" built around issues "defined and created" by the political elite at the time.[6] This interpretation attributes almost total autonomy to political elites. The fact that they are described as "choosing to mobilize electoral support on the basis of these political differences" implies that they could equally well have chosen other issues and that they were acting without significant constraint.

Two assumptions, one explicit and the other implicit, are crucial to Carty's interpretation. The first relates to the date of origin of the party system, which he identifies as the period 1922 to 1932. In a footnote he is even more explicit on this issue, saying, "I do not think the period from 1918 to 1922 was crucial to the structure of the new party system."[7] Related to this is a second, implicit, but equally important assumption: that the only way the Lipset and Rokkan categories can be applied to the Irish party system is in terms of an internal center-periphery conflict between Dublin and the West.[8] By combining these two assumptions with a convincing demonstration that "the parties in the new bipolar system of electoral competition did not reflect a center periphery cleavage within Irish society,"[9] Carty is able to conclude that the Lipset and Rokkan cleavage framework cannot account for the Irish case. The problem is that neither of the two assumptions is tenable.

In regard to the first assumption, Brian Farrell has shown that the modern Irish party system originated in 1918 when the combination of electoral mobilization, the dominance of nationalism, and the abstention of the Labour party "permitted the shaping of a basic cleavage in Irish political life that ran along a constitutional axis and cut across other potential sources of political disagreement."[10] Acceptance of 1918 as the starting point of the system also undermines Carty's second assumption because it suggests a radically different application of the Lipset and Rokkan categories not just to the situation in 1918 but to the development of the party system over the period from 1918 to 1932.

In the first place Farrell's insight can readily be incorporated into a Lipset and Rokkan perspective, as the following outline will suggest. The 1918 election was a mobilizing election with a clear and overriding issue: the conflict between the periphery (southern Ireland) and the center (England). The party that was dedicated to the secession of the periphery (Sinn Féin) swept the electoral board.[11] Insofar as the mobilization of the electorate in the periphery is concerned, the consequence was the creation of a nationalist or secessionist consensus. The domination of this consensus over the other potential source of division in the periphery—the owner-worker cleavage—was sealed by the abstention of the Labour party in that critical contest.

The second point to note in applying the Lipset and Rokkan theory to the genesis of the Irish party system is that because the secession of the periphery was incomplete both in form and in extent, the conflict between Ireland as periphery and England as center remained the major issue in the politics of the newly independent state. It formed the basis, initially, of a short and bloody civil war and, subsequently, of party conflict. In summary, the bulk of the electorate in the periphery was mobilized in two related phases: first, in 1918, into identification with the periphery against the center and, second, between 1922 and 1932, into two camps within this peripheralist or nationalist consensus. The two sides of this internal division represented, on the one hand, an uncompromising commitment to the periphery and, on the other, a willingness to accept, at least on an interim basis, something less than total autonomy from the center. In short, the two parties stood for a more peripheralist versus a less peripheralist position, or a more nationalist versus a less nationalist position. The crucial point to note is that the same center-periphery conflict underlay *both* phases of mobilization, the implication being that the party system does reflect a classic structural cleavage that cannot be written off as the invention of politicians.

A third aspect of this particular sequence of mobilization and secession is also usefully highlighted by application of the remaining categories of cleavage suggested in the model—the church-state cleavage and the land-industry cleavage. The periphery virtually coincided with one pole of each conflict. In the church-state cleavage, the periphery was overwhelmingly and loyally Catholic in a state (the United Kingdom) in which church-state conflict mostly took the form of conflict between the Catholic church and the Protestant and secularizing state. In the land-industry conflict, the economy of the periphery was predominantly agrarian, and its interests had for long been subordinated to those of its industrializing neighbor. Thus when the periphery broke off to form its own state, what emerged initially was a society characterized by the virtual absence of these two major sources of political division.[12] This strengthened the grip of the center-periphery issue on the emerging party system.

The implications of this theory of the Irish party system are manifold. The theory postulates an entrenched party system that revolves mainly around differences in the degree of the parties' commitments to nationalism. The center of gravity of the system is toward the strongly nationalist side. As a result, the party that was most representative of an untrammeled nationalism quickly achieved and for long maintained the status of a predominant party. A related feature of the system is the absence of any clear-cut class basis to the support of the major parties, particularly that of Fianna Fáil. The theory does, however, also posit a left-right cleavage that differentiates the two major, nationalist parties from a third, minor party. The subordinate status of this cleavage and the consequent minority status of the left-wing party are structural features of the system.

Obviously the theory imputes a considerable degree of stability to the party system. Stability is not, however, to be equated with immutability. Realigning elections can occur, or the original alignment may be gradually eroded without being replaced by anything as clear-cut. Adopting the Lipset and Rokkan perspective obliges us to search constantly for signs of realignment or erosion. Neither does stability imply immobility. Parties do attempt to respond to new problems and issues, and their success or failure in doing so affects their electoral support. As Hans Daalder, in a comprehensive review of the literature on party systems, has put it, "Even if one regards with Rokkan the party systems of the 1960s as mainly a reflection of cleavage structures of another era, this does not gainsay their evident ability to handle a host of new issues and changes." [13] The effect of a particular cleavage or cleavages embedded in the party system is not to cause parties to ignore contemporary problems but to affect the way in which they respond to such problems. This may be seen in the existence of areas of constraint and lack of constraint.

In the Irish party system the prevailing alignment means that the parties are highly constrained in relation to nationalist issues. The relative positions of the two major parties are predetermined: Fianna Fáil as more nationalist and Fine Gael as less nationalist, with the proviso that, if Fine Gael is to challenge Fianna Fáil's predominant status, it must not stray too far from the nationalist "center."

By contrast, in the socioeconomic realm the two major parties square up to each other largely unencumbered by long-standing or deeply rooted commitments. It is true that in the past, especially in the late 1920s and 1930s, both parties had somewhat more clearly defined images in this respect— Fianna Fáil as the radical party, Cumann na nGaedheal/Fine Gael as the conservative party. Both have had very little difficulty, however, in shedding or at least shelving that side of their inheritance as circumstances required. It is also true that both are free enterprise parties. Since this feature distinguishes the two of them from what is only a minor party, however, it does not have to be made explicit or emphasized, and it has little bearing on the competition between the two large parties. Thus, in relation to a whole range of socioeconomic issues, among them the basic question of the appropriate level of public expenditure, the two major parties move in an environment characterized by flexibility rather than constraint; in political science terms they are nonprogrammatic. Lacking the twin buffers of a long-standing commitment to a program *and* a constituency that can be relied upon to support that program, parties are severely exposed to short-run demands and the clamor of the most vocal pressure group. As a result, policy in these areas, especially in time of recession, is more likely than it would otherwise be to consist of ad hoc responses to whichever pressures are most immediate. If, instead of the virtual programmatic vacuum on this issue, the party system had had a more substantial and more salient left-right dimension, then, at the very least, debate and decision rather than drift might have characterized the growth of public expenditure in Ireland. In this sense it could be argued that, if the lack of a substantial left-right cleavage in the party system needs to be assessed, this should be not, as is most often the case, just in terms of the weakness of "voice" from the left but also in terms of the virtual inaudibility of "voice" from the other side of the political spectrum.[14]

Finally, the parties are constrained by the consensus on church-state issues, a consensus that arose because the periphery that broke away to form its own state was virtually identical with the (Catholic) church side of the church-state conflict within a larger arena. Thus, church-state conflict did not become entrenched in the party system. But neither could the emerging parties be indifferent. They were implicitly—indeed, it could be argued, inevitably—on the pro-church side. While there is some evidence that this consensus is beginning to fragment, events throughout the antiabortion constitutional amendment saga and the results of the referendum itself suggest that it still conditions the behavior of both the parties and the electorate.

It should be emphasized that what has been described so far is no more than the background against which electoral competition occurs and no more than the starting point from which analysis of electoral behavior must begin. It does not by any means tell us all we need to know about particular elections. It does not even ordain what the dominant issue in successive elections will be. This last point is particularly important in view of one possible objection to the theory: that, since the Northern Ireland issue has scarcely figured in an overt way in recent elections, nationalism can no longer be regarded as a major dimension of the party system. The fact is, however, that before a problem, no matter how grave, can become an electoral issue, political parties must fulfill one of two conditions. The first is for the parties to adopt conflicting goals or objectives in regard to the problem. In the case of Northern Ireland this is precluded by the overriding consensus in the society on nationalist goals, a consensus that is part and parcel of the entrenched party system. When goals are agreed on, the only way for a problem to become an electoral issue is for one of the parties to be seen to be putting forward a more effective strategy, that is, that it be seen to have made or to be about to make significant progress toward attainment of the goal. The deep and obvious intractability of the Northern Ireland problem makes fulfillment of this condition extremely difficult.[15] The net result is the neutralization of the problem as an overt electoral issue. Far from being incompatible with the theory outlined, this electoral stalemate on the issue is, to a considerable extent, a result of the fact that nationalism has been and remains fundamental to the structure of the party system.

What might be regarded as a stronger objection to the theory focuses on its prediction of considerable electoral stability, a prediction that at first sight might seem to be contradicted by the apparent volatility manifested in recent Irish elections. The system, after all, experienced an electoral landslide in 1977 and has witnessed changes of government at five successive elections. Electoral volatility in Ireland is, however, more apparent than real. Having conducted a detailed and comprehensive examination of the evidence through the election of November 1982, Michael Marsh concludes:

> In general then there is little evidence of volatility. Rather there is con-siderable stability. Small inter-election changes have been to the long term benefit of Fine Gael but massive shifts between major parties, or the rapid growth of new parties have not occurred in recent times. Some case for there being some potential for more dramatic change could be made. . . . However, the case for stability is more easily made and stability rather than change is what must be explained.[16]

Lipset and Rokkan's theory goes a long way toward providing just such an explanation. As has already been emphasized, however, no party system is immutable, and we must therefore tackle the question whether we are wit-nessing the onset of fundamental change. Equally important, electoral swings and changes of fortune do occur within an overall pattern of party system stability, and it is to the beginnings of such change in the 1977–79 period that we now turn.

The Erosion of a Landslide:
Fianna Fáil, 1977–1979

In discussing the potential long-term effects of the remarkable results of the 1977 election, the first volume of *Ireland at the Polls* adverted to the possibility of a new electoral alignment, with Fianna Fáil bidding for the position of the party of economic recovery and progress.[17] It emphasized, however, that such an outcome required that Fianna Fáil fulfill its major promises and that no other issue emerge as the basis of the electorate's verdict. Within the first two years of taking office Fianna Fáil had carried out its immediate material promises (virtual abolition of the road tax, abolition of domestic rates, £1,000 grants to first-time purchasers of new houses). It could not, at that stage (mid-1979), be fairly judged on its more fundamental promise of economic recovery —the commitment that was the real basis of its victory in 1977. The economic strategy was a four- to five-year one, and, accordingly, the date of redemption

Figure 3.1   Satisfaction with government, and
voting intentions, January 1978–June 1981

Percent

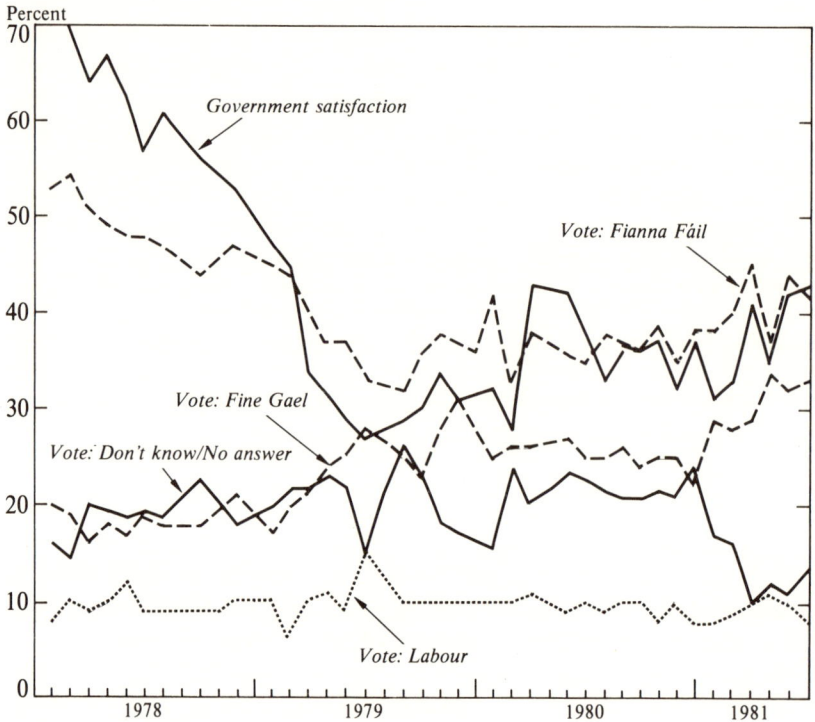

Source: IMS poll data (Dublin, Irish Marketing Surveys).

of that crucial promise was still a considerable way off in 1979. Yet, within that
first two-year period, it was clear that Fianna Fáil had failed to cement its
1977 support.

Beginning in September 1978 the quite astonishingly high support for
Fianna Fáil began to slip. This slip was first registered as a fall in the percentage of the electorate expressing general satisfaction with government performance, from an average of 64 percent for the first seven months of 1978 to 56
percent in September and 53 percent in November (see figure 3.1). This decline
and even the subsequent fall to 47 percent in January and 45 percent in February might be regarded as no more than the ending of a long honeymoon
period, particularly as the falloff in Fianna Fáil voting intentions was not
nearly as marked. (In February 1979, for example, the percentage intending to
vote for Fianna Fáil, at 44 percent, was 17 percentage points ahead of the
combined Fine Gael and Labour support.) In March 1979, however, the slide
became precipitous. Satisfaction plummeted to 34 percent within a single

month and continued downward—April, 31 percent; May, 29 percent; June, 27 percent. Much more seriously, Fianna Fáil support slipped to the lowest ever recorded in opinion polls—March, 40 percent; April and May, 37 percent; June, 33 percent.

Although Fianna Fáil's economic strategy in 1977 was a high-risk one that could be, and indeed was, criticized from the outset from a purely economic point of view, its eventual failure was not apparent in early 1979. The rate of unemployment was actually falling and continued to do so until virtually the end of 1979. Although the rate of inflation had begun to rise again, it was, by the standards of the mid-1970s, still moderate. In February 1979 the year-to-year figure was 10.8 percent and in May it was 12.3 percent.[18] In March and April 1979, then, did the voters prejudge the government's economic performance? Or were they sufficiently prescient that they could anticipate the economic difficulties that lay ahead? Or was the electorate so well attuned to the prognostications of professional economists that it understood the real situation? Or, the alternative to all these explanations, had another issue or other issues intervened to undermine the electorate's confidence in the Fianna Fáil government? The evidence points to the last explanation.

In the first place, the period of the slide coincided with a prolonged strike in the postal service, a strike that had a highly disruptive and widespread effect throughout the society.[19] That it had a considerable adverse effect on the government's popularity is strongly suggested by a comparison of the public's ratings of government performance on three issues—unemployment, inflation, and industrial relations—in 1976 and 1979. In 1976 the National Coalition (Fine Gael-Labour) government was thoroughly unpopular, having a satisfaction rating of only 32 to 33 percent. In its ratings on these three issues, its deficit in relation to unemployment was 56 percentage points and on inflation 58 points, while its deficit on the industrial relations issue was only half that, 22 points (see table 3.1). In addition, the electorate was more polarized on the unemployment and inflation issues, in relation to which only 22 to 28 percent

Table 3.1 Assessment of government performance on unemployment, inflation, and industrial relations, 1976 and 1979 (percent and percentage points)

Assessment	Unemployment		Prices / inflation		Industrial relations	
	1976	1979	1976	1979	1976	1979
Well	11	24	7	13	20	5
Badly	67	49	65	59	42	78
Don't know	22	27	28	28	38	17
Deficit	−56	−25	−58	−46	−22	−73

Sources: 1976: *RTE/IMS Survey Politics*, Irish Marketing Surveys, September 1976 (*N* = 1,004; weighted base = 2,038); 1979: IMS poll, Irish Marketing Surveys, April 1979 (*N* = 1,308).

Table 3.2 Assessment of ministerial performance,
1979 (percent and percentage points)

Assessment	Colley	Faulkener	Fitzgerald	O'Donoghue	O'Malley
Good	22	8	25	31	27
Poor	47	65	27	28	30
Don't know	31	27	48	41	43
Surplus Deficit	−25	−57	−2	+3	−3

Source: IMS poll, Irish Marketing Surveys, April 1979 (*N* = 1,308).

had no opinion, while 38 percent had no view on government performance on industrial relations. In 1979 the Fianna Fáil government had fallen to almost exactly the same level of unpopularity as the coalition government in 1976, but its relative performance on these issues was almost reversed. The deficit in the government's public opinion rating on industrial relations had zoomed to 73 percentage points, and only 17 percent had no opinion, whereas on the unemployment issue the deficit was now only 25 points. The government's rating on inflation had not improved as much as on unemployment, but even with a deficit of 46 points it was considerably less unpopular on this issue than on industrial relations.

Further evidence in the April 1979 survey indicates that the postal strike in particular rather than industrial relations in general was a major source of public disquiet. A question on the performance of ministers that specified which government department a minister headed allowed us to calculate ministerial popularity surpluses and deficits (table 3.2). Gene Fitzgerald, as minister for labour, was responsible for industrial relations. Almost half the respondents had no opinion on the merits of his performance; among those who had an opinion, he was running a deficit of only 2 percentage points. By contrast, the minister directly responsible for the postal service, Padraig Faulkener, minister for posts and telegraphs, was in the red to the tune of 57 points, and only 27 percent had no view about his performance. Other aspects of the data underline the fact that government unpopularity was related to specific problems rather than to general economic performance. Thus Martin O'Donoghue, minister for economic planning and development and architect of the Fianna Fáil economic strategy, had a marginally positive rating (+3 percentage points), and another minister with fairly direct responsibility for both jobs and prices, Desmond O'Malley, minister for industry and commerce, was only just on the other side of the line. Among ministers with general responsibility for government economic policy, only Minister for Finance George Colley was at a significant deficit (25 points), a deficit that was, however, less than half that of Faulkener. The dissatisfaction with Colley may have been simply the unfortunate lot of any minister of finance, or it may have been directly related to another specific issue to which events suggest we should look for the source of Fianna Fáil's 1979 losses—the tax revolt that culminated in mass demonstrations in March 1979.[20]

In the wake of the demonstrations the government's rating on the taxation issue was predictably low—a mere 12 percent approved of its performance, 64 percent disapproved, and only 24 percent had no opinion. Thus, with a satisfaction deficit of 52 percentage points, the government was doing as badly on this issue as on industrial relations. Unfortunately, there are no precisely comparable data from an earlier period against which to measure change in public opinion on this issue. Focusing not on absolute good-bad judgments, however, but on the relative capacity of Fianna Fáil on the one hand and Fine Gael and Labour on the other to handle the taxation issue provides some sense of the shift in public opinion. Table 3.3 shows that in the run-up to the 1977 general election Fianna Fáil had a lead of 27 points on the taxation issue (43 percent of the voters did not take a view one way or the other). Within two years of gaining office that lead had been wiped out, to be replaced by a 13-point deficit, and the proportion of the electorate with no view had been almost halved. On the unemployment and inflation issues, Fianna Fáil had had a similar lead in 1977 (25 to 26 points). Its lead on unemployment had shrunk in the first two years of office, but only marginally compared with the reversal that had occurred on the taxation issue; in April 1979 Fianna Fáil still led the Fine Gael and Labour parties on ability to deal with unemployment by 13 points. Its reputation had suffered more on the inflation issue, but with a deficit of 3 points, the damage was by no means as serious as on the issue of taxation.

Table 3.3 Assessment of relative competence of parties on unemployment, inflation, and taxation, 1977 and 1979 (percent and percentage points)

Assessment	Unemployment		Prices/inflation		Taxation	
	1977	1979	1977	1979	1977	1979
Fianna Fáil best	44	47	43	32	42	31
Fine Gael and Labour best[a]	19	34	17	35	15	44
Both equal/neither/ don't know	36	19	40	34	43	24
Fianna Fáil lead deficit	+25	+13	+26	−3	+27	−13

Sources: 1977: *Irish Times*/NOP election surveys, first survey, 27–28 May 1977 (*N* = 611); 1979: MRBI political survey—1848179, conducted for Fine Gael, April 1979 (*N* = 497).

Note: Percentages may not add to 100 because of rounding.

a. In 1977 this alternative was listed as "Coalition Best"; in 1979 it was listed under two separate categories: "Fine Gael Best" and "Labour Best."

These storms might have been weathered, and the decline in Fianna Fáil support in the first half of 1979 might have been no more than a blip on the opinion pollsters' charts had it not been crystallized in the European elections of 1979, in which the Fianna Fáil national vote tumbled from its 1977 high of 50 percent to 36 percent. This public reversal for Fianna Fáil and its even more devastating confirmation in the Cork by-election defeats of November 1979 hastened Lynch's retirement as leader of Fianna Fáil. A bitter and divisive leadership contest ensued, the reverberations of which were felt throughout the three elections of 1981–82.[21] From an analytical perspective, however, it may seem tempting to argue that the 1979 European election result has few, if any, implications for basic trends in party support and that it can be dismissed as the product of considerations of personality, the intervention of independents, and the fact that governmental power was not at stake.[22] These factors undoubtedly played a role, and some aspects of the result can be dismissed as due to special circumstances—for example, the Fianna Fáil loss in Connacht-Ulster and the Fine Gael loss in Munster. When the combined evidence of the opinion polls, the European elections, the local elections, and the November by-elections is taken into account, however, the Fianna Fáil loss cannot be explained away. This is particularly true of Fianna Fáil's disastrous performance in Dublin. Its 28-percent vote in the European election in Dublin placed it behind both Fine Gael and Labour. That this was not related solely to the European election is demonstrated by the decline of Fianna Fáil support in Dublin, as measured by general election voting intentions, to virtually that level (28 percent) in the previous April. The significance of the 1979 results lies, therefore, not just in their immediate internal party consequences but also in their long-term electoral implications. Fianna Fáil had lost the ground it had gained in 1977 and had done so on mundane domestic issues about which something could have been done. The 1977 victory had proved ephemeral, and Fianna Fáil faced the recession induced by the second oil crisis, a recession that inevitably undermined its already high-risk economic strategy, with no reserves of electoral support to draw on.

A New Politics with Social Bases?

With the single exception of January 1980, Fianna Fáil support did not reach even 40 percent again until the spring of 1981. In February 1981 it was 40 percent, in March 45 percent (see figure 3.1). The spring election that everyone expected did not take place, however, and when the election came in June, both the political situation and the electoral situation were greatly complicated by the H-block hunger strike and by the decision of the National H-Block Committee to run H-block prisoners as candidates. So began what can best be described as the 1981–82 election series.

That the three elections were fought in unchanged constituencies and occurred so close in time suggests that analysis of the changes constituency by constituency might be useful. What such an analysis highlights, initially at any rate, is the effect of a host of special factors. In comparing June 1981 and February 1982, for example, it is apparent that Fianna Fáil's overall modest increase (2 percentage points) was boosted by dramatic gains in individual constituencies. A significant number of those gains can be explained by what might be called the absent-friends syndrome: that is, a number of opposing candidates who were notable because of personality, long service, or particular issues had dropped out. The most obvious example is the absence of the National H-Block Committee candidates with their highly charged single-issue campaign. Fianna Fáil's vote increased by over 3 percentage points in six of the nine constituencies concerned, and in three of these (Cavan-Monaghan, Louth, and Sligo-Leitrim) the increase contributed to the party's acquisition of an extra seat.[23] Fianna Fáil also benefited in seats from the absence of major Labour party personalities in Meath and Wexford and benefited significantly in first preferences from the absences of T. J. Maher in Tipperary South and Dr. John O'Connell in Dublin South-Central. Likewise, constituency-by-constituency comparisons of the results for February and November 1982 seem at first sight to be interesting for the special factors they bring to light, such as the performance of the Fianna Fáil dissidents and the effect of vote-management strategies implemented especially by Fine Gael.[24]

If, however, we focus on the Dublin area, and there are good reasons for doing so in that it was the area that registered most change over the three elections, culminating in the displacement of Fianna Fáil by Fine Gael as the leading party in the region, a suggestion of a coherent pattern emerges.[25] Among those Dublin constituencies in which either Fianna Fáil or Fine Gael made significant gains in February 1982 and in which the analysis is not excessively complicated by the comings and goings of successful independent candidates, Fianna Fáil's gains were in areas with concentrations of high-density and relatively low-cost housing, that is, Dublin North-West, Dublin South-West, and Dublin West. By contrast, Fine Gael's February gains were in constituencies with concentrations of older, established middle-class housing (Dublin South, Dublin South-East, and Dun Laoghaire).[26] The other and very important difference between the gains made by the two major parties in these different areas is that the Fine Gael gains were consolidated in the third election of the series (November 1982) whereas the gains by Fianna Fáil in February 1982 had faded away by November—mainly to the net benefit of the Workers' party. All of this suggests, without of course proving, the existence of a social class factor in these elections, with a sustained middle-class swing to Fine Gael and a temporary working-class swing to Fianna Fáil, a swing that seems to have redounded ultimately to the benefit of the Workers' party. Two

Table 3.4 Voting intention by occupational class, 1969–1982 (percent)

Party and year	All classes	Middle class	Skilled working class	Unskilled working class	Farmers (fifty acres or more)[a]	Farmers (less than fifty acres)[a]
Fianna Fáil						
1969	43	45	40	43	38	53
1977	49	46	54	47	48	48
1981	44	43	46	45	35	49
February 1982	47	42	45	52	35	59
November 1982	40	37	42	40	37	51
Fine Gael						
1969	25	28	21	14	46	26
1977	28	30	20	22	42	38
1981	33	37	29	24	53	36
February 1982	35	42	36	25	54	28
November 1982	37	46	31	28	54	35
Labour						
1969	18	14	27	28	2	5
1977	9	7	11	16	1	5
1981	10	10	10	16	4	2
February 1982	7	6	6	10	3	4
November 1982	9	7	11	14	6	1
Sinn Féin the Workers' party / Workers' party						
1969	—	—	—	—	—	—
1977	—	—	—	—	—	—
1981	2	—	2	4	1	—
February 1982	2	—	3	4	—	—
November 1982	4	2	5	6	1	2
Other / don't know / no answer						
1969	14	13	12	15	14	16
1977	14	16	14	15	8	8
1981	11	10	14	9	6	12
February 1982	7	10	10	10	8	9
November 1982	9	8	11	12	2	12

Sources: 1969: Whyte, "Ireland: Politics without Social bases," tables 2 and 3, pp. 631–32; 1977: *Irish Times* / NOP election surveys, 27–28 May, 3 June, 9 June 1977 (figures based on amalgamated results of all three surveys) (N = 1,788); 1981: *Irish Times* / IMS political opinion poll, 7–8 June 1981 (N = 1,050); February 1982: *Irish Times* / IMS poll: election 1982, poll no. 2 (N = 1,051); November 1982: *Irish Independent-Sunday Independent* / IMS poll, 9–10 November 1982 (N = 1,049).

Note: Percentages may not add to 100 because of rounding.

a. In the 1969 Gallup poll survey, the categories of farm size were thirty acres or more and less than thirty acres.

points should be made about these observations. First, they are tentative, one might even say speculative. Second, if such a class factor was at work, it was at work in a party system notable above all for its lack of a class basis. Both of these points indicate that any hypothesized class factor in the 1981–82 elections should be examined in the light of evidence from opinion polls and over a longer time span.

Table 3.4 presents preelection voting intentions by occupational class from 1969 to 1982.[27] The basis of Whyte's conclusion that Irish party politics could be characterized as "politics without social bases"[28] is evident in the figures for 1969, particularly in the remarkably even spread of Fianna Fáil support across the nonagricultural occupational spectrum. Examination of Fianna Fáil support over time reveals remarkably little change. The exceptional nature of the 1977 gains—made mainly among the skilled working class and among large farmers—stands out clearly. The next election (June 1981) saw a return to the normal size and shape of the Fianna Fáil vote. By the last election of the series (November 1982) Fianna Fáil support was, with one important exception, about the same as it had been in 1969. That exception was its support among middle-class voters, which had dropped from 45 percent in 1969 to 37 percent in November 1982. It is noteworthy that the decline became significant only at the very end of the period, that is, between the February 1982 and the November 1982 elections. That decline was not, however, the only class factor affecting Fianna Fáil support in the 1981–82 election series. In line with the February 1982 increase in the Fianna Fáil vote in the more working-class Dublin constituencies, Fianna Fáil voting intentions among the unskilled working class rose 7 percentage points between June 1981 and February 1982. The table also reveals an aspect of this swing to Fianna Fáil that was not evident from looking at the results at constituency level; that is, it occurred among the less well-off in the agricultural sector as well—Fianna Fáil support among small farmers in February 1982 was up 10 points (to 59 percent) from what it had been in June 1981.

Although the intention to vote for Fine Gael rose in the electorate as a whole by 8 points between 1969 and 1981, the actual vote for Fine Gael in the June 1981 election was only just over 2 points higher than its 1969 vote (36.5 percent in 1981, 34.1 percent in 1969).[29] It has been argued that this underrepresentation of Fine Gael support in opinion polls in the earlier period was caused by the presence of a higher proportion of transient voters as opposed to party identifiers in the Fine Gael and that this could be traced to the electoral alignment that had taken root between 1918 and 1927–32.[30] That declared Fine Gael voting intentions and the actual Fine Gael vote have come to approximate each other suggests that this weakness in Fine Gael support has been eradicated. It is arguable, indeed, that this solidification of Fine Gael support in the elections of 1981 and 1982 is as significant as the actual increase in its share of the vote. While these gains by Fine Gael in declared voting intentions between 1969 and 1982 were made across the occupational spectrum, they were more pronounced in some sectors than in others. Thus Fine Gael support increased by 18 points in the middle class, by 14 points among unskilled workers, by 10 points among skilled workers, and by 9 points among small farmers. Although these variations are relatively small, their effect was to add further weight to the already existing middle-class bias in Fine Gael support. And whereas in 1969 that imbalance was offset by the strength of Fianna Fáil in the middle class, in November 1982 it was reinforced by the fact that Fine Gael had overtaken Fianna Fáil among middle-class voters and was within striking distance of majority support in that sector of the population (46 percent).

The 1977 election was but a temporary setback for Fine Gael; for the Labour party it was a stage in a steady decline from the high points of the middle and late 1960s. The decline is documented in appendix B, and its social class components can be examined in table 3.4, which highlights the dilemma underlying Labour's declining support. In 1969 Labour, in addition to its working-class constituency (28 percent), had significant middle-class support (14 percent); by 1982 it had lost substantially on both fronts. It must now decide whether to seek to reconstruct the broad appeal of the late 1960s or to rebuild its strength on the basis of a more exclusive working-class appeal. The dilemma is all the more acute since its recovery of support among middle-class voters must meet the challenge of the social democratic and liberal appeal of the FitzGerald-led Fine Gael and it must contend with the continued strength of Fianna Fáil among the working class and with the still small but evidently growing support for the Workers' party. On the other hand, the picture of the Workers' party making substantial gains, apparently as a result of Fianna Fáil decline, in several working-class constituencies exaggerates the threat to the Labour party because the observations were made on the basis of a very small number of constituencies, which are not necessarily representative. In fact the Labour party increased its working-class vote by considerably greater amounts than did the Workers' party. The data also show a steady growth of the Workers' party among working-class voters to the point where it can claim the support of almost half as many such voters as the Labour party. A greater concentration of votes and superior organization might ensure more effective conversion of this support into seats in coming elections. All of this points to a qualified conclusion: the Labour party faces a real threat, but on present evidence it would be premature to predict its displacement as the third largest party in the state.

At this point it must be asked whether all this discussion of class factors does not fundamentally alter the traditional picture of Irish party politics as "politics without social bases." The answer seems to be a qualified no. First, the changes in the voting behavior of the various occupational classes, though significant, were relatively small. Second, the line of demarcation in the election most affected by class contrasts (February 1982) is not consistent with the usual class interpretations of politics. The Fianna Fáil gains in that election were made among the lowest groups on the occupational spectrum (the unskilled working class and small farmers). In that election, however, Fine Gael consolidated its position not only among the middle class but also among the skilled working class. That in February 1982 one section of the working class tended to switch to Fianna Fáil and the other to Fine Gael and that both sections showed a tendency to desert the Labour party belie any notion that the election marked the emergence of what would normally be thought of as class-based politics. Finally, the pattern evident in February 1982 was not stable. A major aspect of that pattern—Fianna Fáil's gains among the unskilled working class—had disappeared by November. That particular swing to Fianna Fáil appears to have been due to the special circumstances of the February election. A few qualifications of the "politics without social bases" account appear to be in order, however. In November 1982 Fianna Fáil support had slightly less of that cross-class character that had been so remarkable a feature of the party for so long. The corollary of this was that Fine Gael, from being merely a somewhat middle-class party, edged toward becoming the party of the middle class. At the same time, however, Fine Gael increased its working-class support. Finally, the evidence of a growing struggle for the role of representation of that section of working-class voters that is not attached to either of the "bourgeois" parties suggests that, in that limited arena, the salience of class politics will continue and perhaps increase.

The foregoing description of vote movements and swings in different occupational strata raises more questions than it answers. That is particularly so given the complexity of the changes that occurred and the lack of a straightforward class explanation of what was happening. In pursuit of a fuller understanding, therefore, it is necessary to turn to an examination of the issues and the parties' ratings on them as these were seen by the electorate.

The Issues: Party Performance and Capacity

From the mid-1970s economic recession had dictated what were to be the main issues—prices/inflation and unemployment. These constituted the single "most important issue in the election" for some 40 and 30 percent of the electorate, respectively, in the 1977 election, and each was mentioned by roughly 75 percent of the electorate as one of a set of important issues.[31] Four to five years later they continued to preoccupy almost the same proportion of the electorate—the only major change being that in 1981–82 unemployment began to be cited as most important more often than inflation. In the first *Irish*

Times/Irish Marketing Surveys (IMS) poll in the 1981 campaign, for example, "unemployment/jobs for young people" was the most important issue for 41 percent, and "prices/inflation/food prices" was the most important for 25 percent. This order of precedence continued through the three elections of the series.

The only other major change in the electorate's agenda between 1977 and June 1981 was an increase in concern with Northern Ireland and the related problem of security. In 1977 this pair of issues was rated as most important by 4 percent; at the outset of the May–June 1981 campaign this proportion had risen to 14 percent, and 41 percent rated the combined issue of "Northern Ireland/security" as among the important issues in the election. The increase in concern was presumably due to the H-block hunger strike and the events associated with it. On the day before the opinion poll just cited was taken, two more deaths had occurred among the hunger strikers, and at that stage the National H-Block Committee had clearly indicated its intention of running an unspecified number of candidates in the forthcoming election. Apparently, the fears of many voters were quickly assuaged because, even within the short space of the election campaign, the perceived importance of the issue fell sharply; with three to four days to go to polling day the problem was rated as the most important issue by only 6 percent, and the proportion of those including it among a range of important issues fell from 41 percent to 25 percent. For a small but significant number of voters, however, the H-block question continued to be of overriding importance, ultimately determining their first-preference votes.[32]

By February 1982 the H-block issue had disappeared, and with it went the salience of Northern Ireland as an electoral issue. At the same time, purely domestic political events—the collapse of the Fine Gael-Labour minority government—brought new issues to the fore. While unemployment and inflation remained the leading issues, accounting for 59 percent of "most important issue" identifications, three issues closely related to the prevailing political crisis were identified as most important by 31 percent of the voters. The issues were "reducing government spending/foreign borrowing/national debt" (12 percent), "the Coalition Budget" (11 percent), and "stable government" (8 percent). Interestingly, although much of the campaign rhetoric dealt with these issues, concern with them among the electorate declined slightly (to 26 percent) as the February 1982 campaign developed.

By definition the budget issue was specific to the February 1982 election. Some of those whose concern in February focused on this issue might have been expected, once that election was over, to switch their primary attention to the underlying problem of government expenditure; in fact, concern with the "government spending/foreign borrowing/national debt" issue had declined further. By November 1982 the two major parties had adopted virtually identical positions on public expenditure and government borrowing. The other issue that had arisen in February could not be so easily neutralized. In fact the events of 1982, including as they did the collapse of two minority governments, ensured increasing concern with stable government. Identification of this as the most important issue rose from 7 percent in the middle of the February campaign to 17 percent one week after the calling of the November election. At 17 percent stable government vied with prices/inflation (16 percent) for the position of second most important issue on the electorate's agenda.

Perhaps as significant were the issues that did not make it onto that agenda or did not figure on it as prominently as might have been expected. Despite a considerable increase in crime, the perception of the problem as an electoral issue did not increase correspondingly. In 1977 "security" had been seen as the most important issue by 2 percent of the electorate and as an important issue by 20 percent. In the 1981–82 opinion polls the problem was coded more specifically as "crime" or "crime/law and order," but its rating as an issue remained much the same and even declined somewhat in 1982: 3 percent most important and 26 percent important in June 1981; 0 percent most important and 10 percent important in February 1982; 2 percent and 11 percent in November 1982.[33]

In discussing the dramatic decline of Fianna Fáil support in early 1979, it was argued that the issues of industrial relations and taxation had contributed substantially to the government's unpopularity but that, if the European elections of June 1979 had not intervened, the situation, from the government's point of view, might have been retrieved. The evidence of the extent to which industrial relations and taxation were perceived as election issues in 1981–82 tends to bear out this view. In June 1981 the salience of industrial relations was only marginally greater than in June 1977—the proportions being 4 percent as the most important issue and 23 percent as an important issue in 1981 compared with 0.6 percent and 16 percent in 1977. Not only was the issue not particularly prominent, Fianna Fáil had actually made up considerable ground on it since the debacle of early 1979, when 78 percent of the electorate felt the government was handling industrial disputes badly. At that stage a poll conducted by the Market Research Bureau of Ireland (MRBI) showed Fianna Fáil trailing Fine Gael and Labour by 17 points on this issue;[34] in June 1981 Fianna Fáil was ahead by 5 points. This may mean either that the public has a short memory on specific issues or that, given time, a government can redeem itself in the public eye by subsequent successful action. Some evidence in support of the latter interpretation can be found in a 1980 opinion poll taken immediately after the government's use of the army to keep supplies moving in the face of a strike by petrol tanker drivers. Public opinion on the handling of this particular strike was the reverse of what it had been on industrial relations eighteen months earlier: in October 1980 some 72 percent thought the government had handled the petrol tanker drivers' strike well, 22 percent thought it had handled it badly, and 7 percent had no opinion.[35]

The issue of taxation appears to have declined in electoral salience between 1977 and 1981, a decline that is surprising in view of the agitation on the issue in the intervening period and the extent of government unpopularity in this area in 1979. Between 1977 and 1981 the salience of the issue had just about halved—from 10 percent to 4 percent as the most important issue and from 52 percent to 28 percent as an important issue. Nor did its salience increase in subsequent contests: at the outset of the February 1982 campaign, 3 percent saw it as the most important issue, and 26 percent rated it as an important issue; in November 1982, 4 percent said it was the most important issue, and 13 percent included it among the four most important issues.[36] What is remarkable about all this is the apparent failure of an incipient tax revolt to penetrate the electoral arena substantially, even though both opposition parties made tax reform a part of their 1981 campaign manifestoes. It is difficult to find an explanation of the relatively low salience of the tax issue in the mind of the electorate; perhaps there is after all something in the time-worn government ploy of appointing a commission as a means of defusing an issue.[37]

Probably the most surprising nonissue of the 1981–82 elections was the proposal to hold a referendum to insert a specific antiabortion, or "right to life of the unborn," clause into the constitution. This was a nonissue in a rather complicated way, however. Clearly, once the proposal was put by the "pro-life" pressure groups, it was an issue, sometimes an excruciating one, for party leaders and party strategists. Equally clearly, there was a broad antiabortion majority in the electorate.[38] By the November 1982 campaign the issue might have been expected to have registered in the public consciousness, if only because of the Fianna Fáil leader's explicit reference to it in the opening shots of the campaign. A mere 1 percent of the electorate ranked it as the most important issue of the campaign, however, and a miniscule 2 percent included it among their four most important issues.[39] It was not that the public did not have a view on the question of holding a referendum nor that its view was entirely one-sided. Toward the end of the November 1982 campaign, an *Irish Times*/MRBI poll put the following question: "It is proposed to hold a referendum on the Abortion issue after the new government is elected. Do you think this referendum should or should not be held?" Some 54 percent thought it should be held, 35 percent thought it should not, and a mere 12 percent had no opinion. That this divergence of opinion was not reflected in electoral terms suggests that parties can, albeit perhaps at considerable cost in policy commitments, effectively neutralize an issue by adopting identical positions on it.

Ultimately, of course, it is the electorate's ratings of the parties on the issues that matter. In June 1981 unemployment was almost 10 percent, and

Table 3.5 Fianna Fáil's lead or deficit in assessment of relative competence of alternative governments on issues, 1981–1982 (percentage points)

Issues	1981 Campaign		February 1982 Campaign		November 1982 Campaign
	22 May	7–8 June	2–3 February	1–14 February	9–10 November
Unemployment	0	−6	+9	+12	−7
Prices/inflation	+1	−2	+3	+10	−12
Taxation	+4	−8	+2	+5	−7
Northern Ireland	+10	+9	−6	−3	−2
Crime	+6	+4	+1	+1	−15
Budget	a	a	−1	+5	a
Government borrowing/spending	a	a	−26	−22	−24
Stable government	a	a	+10	+21	−5

Sources: 1981: *Irish Times*/IMS political opinion poll, 22 May 1981 ($N = 1,048$), 7–8 June 1981 ($N = 1,050$); February 1982: *Irish Times*/IMS poll: election 1982, poll no. 1, 2–3 February 1982 ($N = 1,049$), and poll no. 2, 13–14 February 1982 ($N = 1,051$); November 1982: *Irish Independent-Sunday Independent*/IMS poll, 9–10 November 1982 ($N = 1,049$).
Note: + means lead; − means deficit.
a. Not an issue in the election.

inflation was running at 17 percent. There was also widespread concern among commentators regarding the level of government borrowing and the general state of the nation's finances. At this stage the economic verdict was in, and Fianna Fáil, for whatever reason, had failed to fulfill its 1977 promise of recovery. It could not, in the circumstances, have hoped to be in the lead on the key issues of employment and inflation. What is in fact remarkable about the figures on voters' assessments of the parties' abilities to handle these issues (table 3.5) is that in June 1981 Fianna Fáil was not at a huge deficit. At the beginning of the campaign and admittedly before the opposition parties had launched their manifestoes, the two sides were level on the issue of employment and virtually level on inflation. Fianna Fáil was marginally ahead on a number of other issues, including the issue of taxation, in regard to which it had expeienced such unpopularity in 1979. Insofar as there was any movement of opinion on the issues during the campaign, it was in favor of the Fine Gael-Labour alternative, but such movement was slight and could be regarded as significant only on the issue of taxation (12 percentage points in favor of Fine Gael-Labour). Tax reform proposals were, indeed, a major part of the Fine Gael electoral package. The favorable response would appear to have been due more to the promise of an overall cut in taxation than to the more specific and probably most distinctive aspect of the proposals—the £9.60 weekly payment to wives working in the home. At least this seems to be the implication of the greater increase in support for the coalition alternative on the tax question among men (up 13 points) than among women (up 7 points). Whatever the precise source of the coalition's gains on the issue, the problem remained that there was no corresponding increase in the salience of the issue, taxation being much less salient in 1981 than it had been in 1977. It is, therefore, not possible to isolate any single issue as responsible for the gains by the coalition parties (principally by Fine Gael) during the campaign. The effects of the changes of opinion on issues that did occur appear to have been cumulative, and intentions to vote for Fine Gael rose by 5 points between the opening and closing days. This made the two opposing sides virtually level and set the stage for the indecisive outcome of 11 June.

Preoccupied in the economic realm with public expenditure and government borrowing and devoting most of its attention to budgetary policy (a supplementary budget in July 1981 and preparation of the 1982 policy), the coalition government that took office in July 1981 was able to offer little hope on employment. As a result it trailed 9 points behind Fianna Fáil at the opening of the shock February 1982 election. It also trailed marginally on inflation and taxation, the narrowness of the Fianna Fáil lead in the latter area being somewhat surprising given the coalition's confessed failure to implement its 1981 tax reform program. Interestingly, the coalition was ahead on Northern Ireland policy, whereas in the previous June its rating on this issue had been at a deficit of 9 points. This change could be variously attributed to Taoiseach Garret FitzGerald's tough stand on the H-block issue, to his subsequent smoothing out of Anglo-Irish relations in talks with Margaret Thatcher in late 1981, or to the most prominent aspect of the coalition's Northern Ireland policy—the Taoiseach's "crusade" for constitutional reform as the prerequisite of any move toward Irish unity.

While unemployment and inflation were still regarded as the two most important issues in February 1982, and it was undoubtedly useful to Fianna Fáil to have even a marginal lead on them, they were not the issues that might be regarded as characteristic of that election, and they did not dominate public debate. Moreover, as we have seen, 31 percent of the electorate cited one or another of the new themes—the budget, government borrowing, stable government—as the most important issue. On the issue of the budget, which had occasioned the election, only 1 point separated the two sides. Moreover, on the issue that lay behind the controversial budget strategy—the issue of government borrowing—the coalition was streets ahead of the opposition (coalition best, 47 percent; Fianna Fáil best, 21 percent; both equal/not much any government can do, 31 percent). All of this was a remarkable initial public response to the harshest budgetary proposals in living memory, and opinion on these issues seems not to have shifted appreciably in the course of the campaign. Why then did the coalition not win? There was, of course, the other "new" issue—really an old one given a new lease on life by the dramatic Dáil vote of January 27—the issue of providing stable government. Fianna Fáil's lead in this matter was 10 points at the outset of the campaign and 21 points with four days to go. Like the taxation issue in 1981, however, this was not on its own sufficiently salient to have a major effect on the outcome. The real explanation is that the apparently static situation in regard to the electorate's assessment of party performance on issues during the February campaign hides considerable movement within particular sections of the electorate.

First, the concerns of the various sections of the electorate changed as the campaign wore on. The most important changes were a rise in concern with prices and inflation among the unskilled working class (from 19 to 28 percent) and a falling off of concern with government borrowing as the priority (from 23 to 14 percent) among the middle class. The situation resulting from these changes was still marked by considerable class contrasts. For example, 28 percent of the unskilled working class but only 11 percent of the middle class were concerned about prices/inflation as a priority. Similarly, government borrowing was seen as the primary problem by a mere 5 percent of the unskilled working class but by 14 percent of the middle class—a figure that rises to 22 percent if we focus on the professional and managerial groups within that class.

Second, there was considerably more movement in attitudes on various issues than is apparent in table 3.5. The coalition did in fact advance during the campaign but arguably on the wrong issue and only within a limited segment of the social spectrum. For instance, it increased its lead in ability to handle the government spending/borrowing problem by 16 points among skilled workers and by 9 points among the middle class (see table 3.6). This issue was of declining concern to the middle class, however, and of virtually no concern among the unskilled working class. By contrast, Fianna Fáil increased its lead among most social groups on the issues of unemployment and prices/inflation. This increase was especially noticeable in the unskilled working class, among whom Fianna Fáil ended up with a lead of 20 points on the unemployment issue and a lead of 18 points on prices/inflation. The latter issue was of increasing importance to this particular group as the campaign wore on.

The most interesting contrasts occurred on the budget issue. As detailed in chapter 2, Fianna Fáil's initial strategy in this area was to focus on the specific question of alternative revenue sources and on its proposal to drop the most controversial proposals of the Bruton budget. Later in the campaign (February 12), having availed itself of the government's offer of civil service assistance, Fianna Fáil announced its alternative, described in chapter 2 as "a soft option measure that raised the revenue needed but inflicted minimal cost on taxpayers."[40] The data show the state of public opinion close to the begin-

Table 3.6 Fianna Fáil's lead or deficit in assessment of relative competence of alternative governments on issues, by occupational class, 1982 (percentage points)

Issue and date	All classes	Middle class	Skilled working class	Unskilled working class	Farmers (fifty acres or more)	Farmers (less than fifty acres)
Unemployment						
2, 3 February 1982	+9	+4	+19	+9	−1	+13
13, 14 February 1982	+12	+8	+9	+20	−11	+26
Prices / inflation						
2, 3 February 1982	+3	−7	+12	+6	−13	+14
13, 14 February 1982	+10	+2	+11	+18	−22	+31
Budget						
2, 3 February 1982	−1	−14	+15	+6	−16	−6
13, 14 February 1982	+5	−8	+3	+21	−21	+24
Reducing government spending / foreign borrowing						
2, 3 February 1982	−26	−38	−19	−21	−43	−9
13, 14 February 1982	−32	−47	−35	−16	−39	−18

Source: *Irish Times* / IMS poll: election 1982, poll no. 1, 2–3 February 1982 ($N = 1,049$), and poll no. 2, 13–14 February 1982 ($N = 1,051$).
Note: + means lead; − means deficit.

ning of the campaign and then immediately after the unveiling of the Fianna Fáil alternative budget. They make it apparent that, on the budget issue, considerable movement had taken place. At the outset two groups in particular—the middle class and large farmers—were clearly in favor of the coalition budget. Small farmers were somewhat in favor, and the working class as a whole was opposed. By the time the Fianna Fáil alternative proposals had become known, the middle class had wavered somewhat but remained supportive, while support among large farmers had strengthened still further. At the other end of the occupational spectrum, opinion moved decisively against the coalition. On this issue Fianna Fáil moved from a deficit of 6 percentage points to a lead of 24 points among small farmers and from a lead of 6 points to one of 21 points among the unskilled working class. The appeal of the Fianna Fáil budget appears to have been almost exclusively to the least well-off: opinion within the skilled working class moved in favor of the coalition on this issue, Fianna Fáil's lead in this group being cut from 15 points to 3. One must enter a caveat at this point. It is not possible to be definitive in tracing cause and effect on the basis of the analysis above. Certain groups of voters may have decided for entirely different reasons to switch to Fianna Fáil and then have brought their opinion on issues into line with their voting intentions.

It is significant, however, that the social class movements in opinions on issues indicated by the data in the table are consistent with the role social class appears to have played in relation to changes in voting intentions between the elections of 1981 and February 1982. It is also significant that the movements in opinion that occurred were more substantial on some issues (especially the budget issue) than on others. The most plausible conclusion seems to be that in the February election a shift of opinion in favor of Fianna Fáil, most notably on the budget issue, occurred in the lower socioeconomic groups and contributed to a swing to Fianna Fáil within those groups and thereby to the pattern of class voting that characterized that election.

The coalition's problem in February 1982 was that it was forced to campaign on unfavorable ground. Fine Gael strategists were determined not to allow such a situation to recur in November, and at that stage, of course, they had the freedom of maneuver. In any event, given Fianna Fáil's adoption of *The Way Forward* as its election program, conservative fiscal policy was no longer a Fine Gael monopoly and hence no longer an electoral encumbrance.[41] The Fine Gael approach to the November campaign was low-key and seemed designed to avoid losing support rather than aggressively to seek it out. In light of the party's standing in the polls before the election was called, this was an understandable strategy. After its February victory Fianna Fáil had enjoyed only the outward formalities, as it were, of an electoral honeymoon. The first postelection poll (May 1982) gave the party 48 percent in voting intentions but also showed that those who were dissatisfied with the government outnumbered the satisfied by 20 points. This gap increased in July to 27 points, in August to 36 points, in September to 40 points, and in October to a staggering 49 points (23 percent satisfied, 72 percent dissatisfied, 5 percent don't know).[42] Levels of voting support for the two major parties in that October poll were also closer than they had ever been in the IMS opinion poll series (Fianna Fáil 38 percent, Fine Gael 36 percent).

This decline in Fianna Fáil support is confirmed by an across-the-board worsening of its rating on issues (see table 3.5). This included a notable shift of opinion for the first time on the issue of ability to handle the crime problem, with Fianna Fáil falling 15 points behind the coalition. The sole exception to the decline in Fianna Fáil's rating was on the Northern Ireland issue. The biggest and most important change was on the issue of stable government. Fianna Fáil had led on this issue by 10 points at the beginning of the February campaign and by 21 points before the campaign closed. In the following November, that lead had been replaced by a 5-point deficit after a week of campaigning. The reversal is made all the more significant by the rise in the proportion of those mentioning this as the most important issue in the election from 7 percent in February to 17 percent in November. That Fianna Fáil managed to close the gap during the campaign, ending just 1 point behind the coalition on the issue, could not disguise the party's loss of what many had long regarded as its trump card—its perceived ability to provide stable government.[43] Moreover, the evidence suggest that the electorate was not simply reacting to the collapse of a Fianna Fáil minority government that it had just witnessed, just as in January it had seen a similar collapse of a minority coalition. In the first place, an October *Irish Times*/MRBI poll taken before Fianna Fáil's Dáil defeat showed Fianna Fáil only 1 point ahead on stability of government. Second, in the *Irish Independent/Sunday Independent*/IMS poll taken during the campaign, 61 percent of respondents agreed with the statement "Fianna Fáil is so divided that it cannot provide effective government," and 29 percent disagreed. In contrast, the balance of opinion in that same poll was on the side of the viability of coalition governments—48 percent agreed with the statement "Our experience in recent years proves that coalition governments can work well for the country," and 42 percent disagreed. Although the two statements are not exactly comparable, the responses do suggest that the traditional Fianna Fáil image of unity, discipline, and capacity to provide stable government had taken quite a beating. The focus of Fianna Fáil's difficulties in this area was the question of party leadership, a question that inevitably arose as an electoral issue.[44]

The Leadership Issue

The battle lines on the leadership issue were drawn in the Dáil debate on the nomination of Charles J. Haughey as Taoiseach on 11 December 1979. A marked feature of that debate was the claim by opposition speakers that, in their bitter denunciation of Haughey's nomination, they were speaking for a majority of the electorate. A related claim was that the selection of Haughey would have a negative effect on Fianna Fáil support—"an uncovenanted bonus to Fine Gael," as Garret FitzGerald put it.[45] There is little or no evidence in the opinion poll data that these claims accurately portrayed the state of public opinion *at that time.* By the end of the period we are dealing with, however, there was considerable evidence of the unpopularity of Haughey's leadership. When and how did this occur, and what were its effects on voting behavior?

Let us begin with the state of public opinion on this issue at the time of the leadership change in Fianna Fáil. A clear majority of the electorate were satisfied with Haughey's performance as Taoiseach in his first six months in office. His average satisfaction rating of 54 percent was only marginally less than that of Jack Lynch during the last six months of 1979 (Lynch average: 59 percent). The only significant difference between the ratings of the two in these periods was the larger number of "don't knows" in the Haughey case (Haughey, first three-month average: 24 percent; Lynch, last three-month average: 9 percent). The consequence of this suspension of judgment on the part of a sizable proportion of the electorate was that Haughey's dissatisfaction rating at the outset was actually less than that of Lynch in the period immediately before his resignation. As the proportion of Haughey "don't knows" declined, the rate of dissatisfaction increased. Throughout the period to June 1981, however, Haughey maintained a significant surplus of satisfaction over dissatisfaction, and this at a time when the Fianna Fáil government's rating was at a sizable deficit. Thus, although Haughey never attained the heights of popularity as Taoiseach enjoyed in the immediate post-1977 period by Lynch, neither did he, in that first period of office, alienate the voters in the manner suggested by the opposition. The subsidiary prediction of the opposition—that he would alienate Fianna Fáil support—is likewise not borne out by the data up to June 1981. Although Fianna Fáil support did not suddenly expand as Haughey's backers hoped it would, there was no evidence of an immediate bonus for Fine Gael. Having made its first significant advances in the last year of the Lynch administration, Fine Gael did not show further gains until more than a year after Haughey's accession, and at that stage (early 1981) the Fianna Fáil vote was also picking up in what was obviously the run-up to an election. The first poll of the 1981 election campaign showed that the proportion of Fianna Fáil supporters satisfied with Haughey as Taoiseach (80 percent) was virtually identical with the proportion of Fine Gael supporters satisfied with FitzGerald as leader of Fine Gael.

The story of FitzGerald's satisfaction rating, from the time he assumed the Fine Gael leadership to the 1981 election, is easily told—it fluctuated in the middle to high 60s, occasionally going over 70 percent, rarely falling below 60. By this measure, then, FitzGerald was well ahead of Haughey; he had indeed, been ahead of Lynch from April to December 1979. The problem here, however, is that like is not being compared with like: one is being assessed as Taoiseach, the other as leader of a party in opposition. The contest is more even when the question asked related to preference for Taoiseach.[46] Haughey and FitzGerald were first matched in this way in March 1980, and the outcome was a 4-point lead for Haughey: Haughey, 40 percent; FitzGerald, 36 percent; don't know, 24 percent. Thereafter FitzGerald led in the majority of polls taken until the election was called in May 1981. His lead was, however, neither stable nor commanding—an average of 3 points between March 1980 and May 1981. In the first *Irish Times*/IMS poll of the 1981 campaign, Haughey was 3 points ahead, and three weeks' campaigning produced little change in the final preelection poll. FitzGerald had edged in front, but by only 1 point. This stalemate on the leadership issue in 1981 masks an interesting class difference. FitzGerald's appeal at that stage was mainly to those at the upper end of the occupational spectrum; he had a 12-point lead among the middle class and an 18-point lead among large farmers. In contrast, Haughey was consistently, though less substantially, ahead at the other end (the skilled working class, +4; the unskilled working class and small farmers, +8). It appears then that, in the overall balance of public opinion, the "Haughey factor" was not significant until after the June 1981 election and that in 1981 it had a positive effect in one stratum of the society and a negative effect in another.

Both leaders' satisfaction ratings suffered in the aftermath of the 1981 election. In the wake of electoral defeat, Haughey's satisfaction rating was down a few points to just under 50 percent. Judged by the more exacting standards of being Taoiseach, FitzGerald's satisfaction rating fell substantially: in opposition it had been in the middle to high 60s; in government it was, in the latter half of 1981, in the low 50s. In preference for Taoiseach, however, FitzGerald maintained a consistent and somewhat more substantial lead (9-point average) over Haughey in this period.

The real change in the leadership stakes occurred in early 1982, before anyone had an inkling that an election was about to take place. In a January IMS opinion poll, fieldwork for which was carried out between January 20 and January 27, the proportion of the electorate dissatisfied with Haughey was, for the first time, greater than the proportion satisfied. The deficit was not large (satisfied, 42 percent; dissatisfied, 46 percent) but the change was significant because before that Haughey had enjoyed a surplus that was rarely less than 10 points. In the same opinion poll, FitzGerald went 15 points ahead in preference for Taoiseach (FitzGerald, 49 percent; Haughey, 34 percent; don't know, 17 percent). The dates during which the fieldwork for this poll was carried out are important because they establish that the poll measures public opinion after the McCreevy affair.[47] While arguments of the post hoc, ergo propter hoc form must always remain speculative, it is tempting to suggest that Haughey's popularity problems in January were due to criticism of his leadership from within his own party. The argument would be that the public expects swinging attacks by one party on the leadership or policies of another and discounts them accordingly. When, however, serious dissent and criticism surface within a party, public opinion takes the matter much more seriously and is more likely to be affected by it. Whatever the explanation, when the fall of the government and the chance Haughey had been waiting for came on 27 January, he was, in personal popularity, ill prepared to take advantage of it. In the first *Irish Times*/IMS opinion poll of the campaign, his satisfaction rating had slipped to a deficit of 19 points, and he was 20 points behind FitzGerald in preference for Taoiseach (FitzGerald, 51 percent; Haughey, 31 percent). Toward the end of the campaign the gap in preference for Taoiseach was 23 points. Yet Fianna Fáil won the election. It is true that its Dáil majority was an artifact of parliamentary maneuvering, but it did win more first-preference votes than Fine Gael and Labour combined and had a larger share of the first-preference vote than at any time since 1965 except for the 1977 election. Obviously, leadership was neither the only nor the decisive factor in the election. Before looking in detail at the effect of the issue on voting, it is necessary to trace the course of the issue through to the third round in November 1982.

On resuming office, Haughey did not return to the positive satisfaction levels he had enjoyed before June 1981, but he did close the gap between the satisfied (47 percent) and the dissatisfied (46 percent) and came within three points of FitzGerald in preference for Taoiseach. These figures relate to the first half of May 1982 and could be seen as a considerable improvement on his poor showing in January and February. This was, however, just before the Dublin West by-election, when it appeared likely that Haughey's stratagem for securing his Dáil majority was likely to pay off. Against the odds, Fianna Fáil lost the by-election, and an opinion poll taken immediately after that defeat showed Haughey at a 6-point deficit in satisfaction and trailing Fitz-Gerald by 8 points in preference for Taoiseach. July 1982 marked the beginning of a downward spiral in the popularity of the Fianna Fáil government. The same can be said for Haughey's popularity as Taoiseach, although it must be added that the government's rating was consistently 8 to 9 points lower than that of its leader. Since the outstanding political event of that period was the resignation of the attorney general,[48] it is important to emphasize that the slide, first in the government's popularity and then in the Taoiseach's popularity, began in July and August and that the August poll was conducted before the resignation. It is not that that controversy had no effect—it is entirely probable that it had, since the deficit in Haughey's satisfaction rating increased another 10 points in September and he dropped 10 points further in preference for Taoiseach. Matters worsened further in October;[49] in the first opinion poll of the November 1982 campaign, 64 percent of the electorate were dissatisfied with Haughey, 30 percent were satisfied, and he was 25 points behind FitzGerald in preference for Taoiseach. The latter gap closed somewhat during the campaign—an MRBI poll taken on 19 and 20 November showed Haughey only 15 points behind FitzGerald. This improvement in Haughey's position must be qualified by the fact that his satisfaction deficit remained in the mid-thirties, or almost twice what it had been in February. The discrepancy between the very large deficit in Haughey's satisfaction rating and the relatively small gap between him and FitzGerald in preference for Taoiseach suggests that FitzGerald was not able to capitalize fully on Haughey's increased unpopularity and that the electoral potential of the issue may not have increased between February and November 1982.

This brings us directly to the question, How much did the leadership issue affect voting behavior? In the first place, the effect of the issue is likely to have been reduced by the social class bias in the reactions it elicited. This was detectable beneath the apparent stalemate on the issue in June 1981. When

Table 3.7 FitzGerald lead or deficit in relation to Haughey in preference
for Taoiseach, by occupational class, 1981–1982 (percentage points)

Date	All classes	Middle class	Skilled working class	Unskilled working class	Farmers (fifty acres or more)	Farmers (less than fifty acres)
7–8 June 1981	+1	+12	−4	−8	+18	−8
2–3 February 1982	+20	+31	+20	+11	+32	+7
13–14 February 1982	+23	+42	+33	+3	+38	+5
9–10 November 1982	+25	+33	+24	+11	+51	+25
19–20 November 1982	+15	+26	+1[a]		+44	+7

Sources: 1981: *Irish Times*/IMS political opinion poll, 7–8 June 1981 ($N = 1,050$); February 1982: *Irish Times*/IMS poll: election 1982, poll no. 1, 2–3 February 1982 ($N = 1,049$), and poll no. 2, 13–14 February 1982 ($N = 1,051$); November 1982: *Irish Independent-Sunday Independent*/IMS poll, 9–10 November 1982 ($N = 1,049$), and *Irish Times*/MRBI poll, 19–20 November 1982 ($N = 1,026$).
a. A breakdown of the working class into skilled and unskilled subcategories is not available in the *Irish Times*/MRBI poll for 19–20 November 1982.

aggregate opinion on the issue shifted in February 1982, considerable class contrasts remained: in the second *Irish Times*/IMS opinion poll in the February campaign, Haughey and FitzGerald were virtually even among the unskilled working class and among small farmers, whereas FitzGerald enjoyed a lead of 42 points among the middle class, a 38-point lead among large farmers, and a 33-point lead among the skilled working class (see table 3.7). In the November election these class contrasts appeared to wane somewhat at first, but closer to the election they reasserted themselves, so that in the last opinion poll of the campaign (an *Irish Times*/MRBI poll) FitzGerald was streets ahead among large farmers (44 points), very substantially ahead among the middle class (26 points), just barely ahead among small farmers (7 points), and virtually even (1 point ahead) in the working class as a whole.[50] The problem for Fine Gael is that the appeal of its leader was clearest to those sections of society already predisposed to vote Fine Gael. Accordingly, although the leadership issue undoubtedly played a role, it may not have brought as large a bonus to that party as predicted.

A second reason for concluding that the issue may have had a relatively slight effect on voting behavior is that selecting the Taoiseach is the first criterion of only a small proportion of voters. Although the proportion of voters who professed to employ this criterion increased, in 1982 it still amounted to only one-fifth of the electorate, whereas a fairly constant two-fifths adhered to the priority of "choosing a candidate to look after the needs of the constituency" (see table 3.8). Between February and November 1982 the proportion of voters who concentrated on choice of Taoiseach did not increase at all, despite the controversies surrounding Haughey's leadership and the two attempts to unseat him that had occurred in the interim.

This measure of the criterion voters employed is limited in two respects: it is what voters say that guides their choice, and it is only their most important criterion. There is a high probability that more than one factor was at work; indeed, the system of the single transferable vote in multimember constituencies encourages this by making the constituency-service criterion compatible with other criteria. Despite these limitations, it is worth looking at the strength of the main parties within each of the four groups of voters as defined by their use of the four criteria listed.[51] For convenience, I refer to them as choice-of-Taoiseach voters, cabinet-composition voters, policy voters, and constituency-service voters (see figure 3.2). In June 1981 Fianna Fáil scored equally strongly in voting intentions among three of the groups: choice-of-Taoiseach voters, cabinet-composition voters, and constituency-service voters. It was noticeably less strong among policy voters. Quite remarkably, in view of the data on the

Table 3.8 Voters' perceptions of most important criterion determining their vote, 1977–1982 (percent)

	Election			
Criterion	1977	1981	February 1982	November 1982
Choosing the Taoiseach	8	16	20	19
Choosing the set of ministers who will form the government	18	16	17	15
Choosing between the policies as set out by the parties	21	24	27	25
Choosing a candidate to look to the needs of the constituency	46	42	35	41
Don't know	7	3	1	0
Total	100	100	100	100
N	(597)	(1,050)	(1,051)	(1,049)

Sources: 1977: *Irish Times*/NOP election surveys, third survey, 9 June 1977; 1981: *Irish Times*/IMS political opinion poll, 7–8 June 1981; February 1982: *Irish Times*/IMS poll: election 1982, poll no. 2; November 1982: *Irish Independent-Sunday Independent*/IMS poll, 9–10 November 1982.
Note: In each poll those interviewed were handed a card with these response categories on it and asked, "Which of these will be most important to you in making up your mind how to vote?" Percentages may not add to 100 because of rounding.

Figure 3.2   Party support by most important voter criterion, 1981–1982

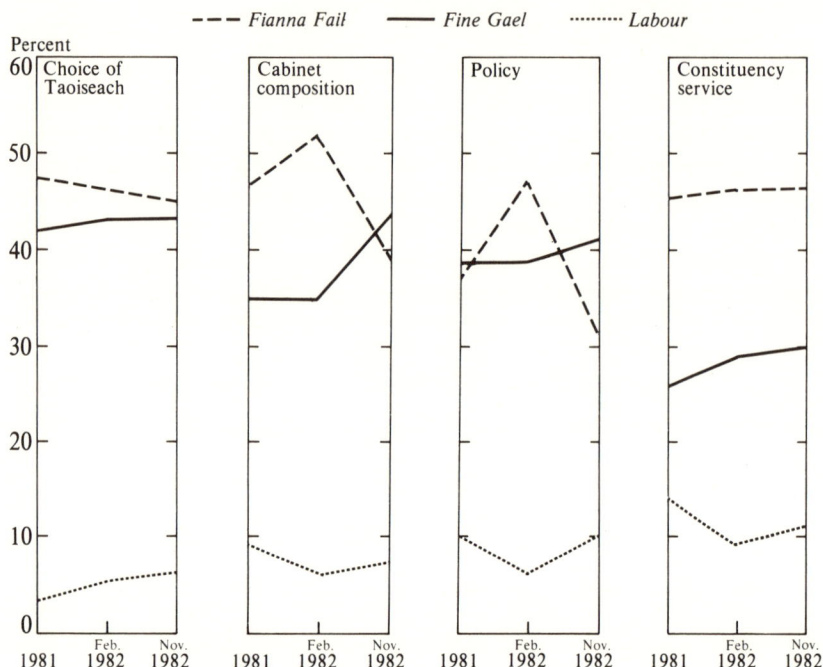

Sources: 1981: *Irish Times*/IMS political opinion poll, 7–8 June 1981 (*N* = 1,050); February 1982: *Irish Times*/IMS political opinion poll: election 1982, poll no. 2, 13–14 February 1982 (*N* = 1,051); November 1982: *Irish Independent*/*Sunday Independent*/IMS political opinion poll, 9–10 November 1982 (*N* = 1,049).

leadership issue, Fianna Fáil strength among choice-of-Taoiseach voters held virtually steady in the three elections, slipping only a single point in February 1982 and in November 1982. Fianna Fáil also held steady among constituency-service voters—consistently the largest block of voters. Fianna Fáil won and lost the elections of 1982 among cabinet-composition voters and policy voters. It made sizable gains in both these groups of electors in February 1982. Its problem was that, for whatever reason—controversies surrounding individual ministers, acute party divisions, ministerial resignations, or policy U-turns— these gains did not withstand the test of office. Not only were the February gains lost, but in November 1982 Fianna Fáil had considerably less support among cabinet-composition voters and policy voters than it had in June 1981. While it can legitimately be argued that policy failures and ministerial or cabinet failures must ultimately be laid at the door of the incumbent Taoiseach, the evidence suggests that, in the electorate's eyes, Fianna Fáil's problems in

November 1982 were far wider than can be encompassed in the phrase "the Haughey factor."

In analyzing reactions to the leadership issue above, it was noted that the tide of public opinion as a whole did not turn substantially in favor of Fitz-Gerald until early 1982 and that in June 1981 a Fine Gael advantage was discernible on this matter only in the better-off sections of society. The data in figure 3.2 indicate that the issue had some limited effect on Fine Gael support in June 1981: the party's strongest support was among choice-of-Taoiseach voters (42 percent). The boost to Fine Gael fortunes from this source was not overwhelming, however, in that support among policy voters was not far behind (38 percent) and support among cabinet-composition voters also quite strong at 35 percent. Of far greater significance in assessing the contribution of the leadership issue to the growth of Fine Gael is the fact that the party's support among choice-of-Taoiseach voters did not increase in either of the elections of 1982. For Fine Gael, February 1982 was a holding operation on the three fronts of Taoiseach, cabinet, and policy, and this must be seen as a remarkable achievement in the circumstances. The election marked a marginal increase in Fine Gael's weakest sector (constituency service). The significant point in this context is that the gap on the leadership issue, which occurred in January-February 1982, does not appear to have affected Fine Gael support in February among the section of the electorate most susceptible to such an appeal. By November 1982, however, with increased dissatisfaction with Haughey and a still substantial FitzGerald lead in choice of Taoiseach, Fine Gael support among such voters might have been expected to increase significantly. The evidence is, however, that Fine Gael's gains in November were made not among choice-of-Taoiseach voters but among cabinet-composition voters and, more marginally, among policy voters. When the latter small gain is added to Fianna Fáil's considerable loss in the same sector, Fine Gael emerges with a substantial lead over Fianna Fáil among policy voters. The Fine Gael vote was, with the notable exception of the constituency-service sector, very evenly spread; it was not a presidential vote.

Analysis of the changes in Labour party support among these four voter categories offers something for both procoalitionists and anticoalitionists. Anticoalitionists could point to a decline in Labour support among policy voters after a spell of participation in coalition government and the recovery of that support after a period in opposition and after a campaign that placed more emphasis on "Labour's independent socialist policies." Procoalitionists could point to a very marginal growth in Labour support among choice-of-Taoiseach voters—a growth that presumably derived from Labour's continued association with Fine Gael. The other point to note is the slight reduction in the Labour party's traditionally strong support among constituency-service voters.

The leadership issue does not appear, then, to have had a major effect on

Table 3.9 Party solidarity, 1977–1982 (percent)

Election	Fianna Fáil	Fine Gael	Labour
1977	75.9	72.1	66.7
1981	78.3	77.5	61.1
February 1982	80.4	79.5	58.7
November 1982	80.2	79.7	64.3

Sources: Calculations based on data in *Election Results and Transfer of Votes* (Dublin: Stationery Office), various issues.
Note: The entries in the table are estimates of the proportion of a party's vote that are transferable to a candidate of the same party when at least one such candidate remains in contention. In deriving this estimate, surpluses yielding a zero nontransferable vote are omitted (see note 53).

electoral outcomes in 1981 and 1982. There is evidence that it produced some advantage for Fine Gael in June 1981 but that as the gap in satisfaction rating and in preference for Taoiseach between Haughey and FitzGerald widened, there was no corresponding increase in Fine Gael support or decline in Fianna Fáil support among voters who professed to be most concerned with the choice of Taoiseach. Another somewhat surprising finding is that, despite all the controversy surrounding the leadership of Fianna Fáil in 1982, the proportion of the electorate giving priority to the choice of Taoiseach increased only marginally in the elections of that year. This would, of course, minimize the electoral effect of changes in the ratings of the party leaders. That effect was further attenuated by the class bias in leadership preferences—FitzGerald was most popular in those strata of the electorate where Fine Gael was already strong and where, accordingly, there was less electoral advantage to be reaped.

Transfer Patterns and the Party System

The Irish electoral system of proportional representation by means of the single transferable vote yields information on aspects of the parties that, under other electoral regimes, can only be guessed at or measured indirectly through survey research.[52] The characteristics in question relate to the ways in which a party's supporters react not just to their own party but to other parties in the system. They have been categorized by Michael Gallagher as party solidarity, party exclusivity, and interparty relationships.[53] In addition to these general characteristics, the evidence of transfers can be used to explore particular voting phenomena, the obvious case in point being the nature of the H-block vote in June 1981.

A major objective of parties in the Irish system must be to ensure that those who cast a first-preference vote for a candidate of the party and who are therefore in a sense party supporters transfer their vote on second and subsequent preferences to the party's other candidates. If supporters do so, they exhibit party solidarity, and the party effect of their vote is maximized. Their failure to do so leads to a direct loss of votes for the party. Table 3.9 presents estimates of solidarity for the three main parties from 1977 to November 1982. In 1977 Fine Gael solidarity (72 percent) was almost 4 percentage points lower than that of Fianna Fáil (76 percent), and Labour was considerably lower again (at 67 percent). In 1981 Fine Gael solidarity improved considerably (from 72 to 77 percent) and it added an additional point in February 1982. In that election, however, Fianna Fáil solidarity went up to the remarkably high level of 85 percent, and it was not until the November election that the two major parties were effectively equal on this score—Fianna Fáil 83 percent, Fine Gael 82 percent. We have seen that Labour solidarity was noticeably lower than that of the other two parties in 1977. It fell back further in 1981 (62 percent) and reached a low point of 55 percent in February 1982. The implications of the February 1982 figure are not as alarming as might, at first sight, appear. This is because the impact of the lower level of solidarity was offset by a nomination strategy that minimized the number of votes affected by leakage. In the election in question (February 1982) Labour cut its number of candidates by almost one-third (from sixty to forty-one). In doing so, it cut the number of occasions on which leakage could occur from twenty-six in 1981 to five in February 1982. This change is reflected in the *numbers* of voters recorded in the Labour column of table 3.9. In 1981 Labour lost, through leakage, 38 percent of 36,627 votes; in February 1982 it lost a higher percentage (45 percent) but of a much smaller quantity of votes (6,347). The reduction in the number of nominations was maintained in November 1982 (forty candidates) and, just as one must discount the significance of the fall in Labour solidarity in February 1982, so one must discount the impact of the recovery in solidarity (to 64 percent) in November.

The two other characteristics that can be inferred from transfer patterns (exclusivity and interparty relationships) are opposite sides of one coin. A party is exclusive to the extent that, when there are no more of its candidates in contention, its votes do not transfer to candidates of other parties. If, however, a party cultivates a relationship with another party by means of an implicit or explicit alliance, its terminal transfers will be affected, and its exclusiveness will be minimized. Data for both exclusivity and interparty relations are contained in table 3.10. The exclusivity figures are to be found in the column marked "Nontransferable." It is difficult to arrive at absolutely reliable estimates of Fianna Fáil exclusivity because of the small number of votes. Accordingly, the drop in Fianna Fáil exclusivity between 1977 and 1981 should not be overinterpreted. Such fluctuations aside, however, it is clear that Fianna Fáil is a highly exclusive party, with an average exclusivity over the three elections of 1981–82 of almost 60 percent, in situations in which *both* the other main parties were available to receive transfers.

Table 3.10 Party exclusivity and interparty transfers, 1977–1982

Source of transfers and election	Fianna Fáil	Fine Gael	Labour	Other	Nontransferable	Number of votes
Fianna Fáil						
1977	—	4.4	20.0	0.0	75.6	4,030
1981	—	16.9	24.4	0.0	58.6	5,291
February 1982	—	11.9	14.8	14.0	59.3	5,505
November 1982	—	20.5	26.7	0.0	52.9	4,931
Fine Gael						
1977	9.2	—	67.6	0.0	23.2	14,766
1981	a	—	a	a	a	a
February 1982	13.9	—	69.1	0.0	17.0	15,647
November 1982	12.5	—	69.4	0.0	18.5	14,828
Labour						
1977	13.2	56.4	—	15.0	15.3	26,056
1981	18.9	55.1	—	7.4	18.5	42,742
February 1982	18.3	59.5	—	8.6	13.6	32,651
November 1982	18.8	59.9	—	10.9	10.4	36,983

The table header spans: Destination of terminal transfers (percent) over Fianna Fáil, Fine Gael, Labour, Other, Nontransferable.

Sources: Same as for table 3.9.
Note: Percentages may not add to 100 because of rounding.
a. Because the transfers in this category consist exclusively of surpluses that yield a reported nontransferable rate of zero, it is not possible to estimate actual transfer rates (see note 53).

Although coalition arrangements between Fine Gael and Labour were less solid in the elections of 1981–82 than they had been in 1977 or in 1973, in general, the Fine Gael to Labour level of terminal transfers was the higher of the two, though it fell to 61 percent in February 1982 and then recovered again in November to 69 percent. Unfortunately, it is impossible to estimate the Fine Gael to Labour transfer ratio for 1981—indeed the attempt to do so illustrates the problem of taking transfer results at face value. Such an attempt would yield a figure of 86.8 percent, which would indicate a considerable increase in the enthusiasm of Fine Gael voters for coalition. There is, however, no evidence for such a conclusion, because the 86.8 percent figure is based on two cases, both of which involved the transfer of surplus votes. As explained in note 53, the process by which surplus votes are redistributed leads to an understatement of the actual number of nontransferable votes. The reported nontransferable rate in the two cases in question was zero. All that can be validly inferred from the published results, however, is that the actual rate of nontransferability was between zero and 61 percent in one case and between zero and 75 percent in the other—clearly an extremely imprecise and not very useful inference.[54] Accordingly, no reliance can be placed on the 86.8 percent figure as an estimate of the actual rate of transfers from Fine Gael to Labour in 1981.

In the 1973 election, the first for over a decade and a half in which there were explicit coalition arrangements, the supporters of Fine Gael and Labour had, as it were, honored the coalition pact with equal percentages of terminal transfers to the coalition partner.[55] In 1977, after four years of coalition government, transfers from Labour to Fine Gael had fallen substantially from the 1973 level of 73 percent to 56 percent. This lower level continued in June 1981 and, despite a slight rise in the elections of 1982, it remained below 60 percent throughout the 1981–82 period.

From this brief review of the evidence of transfer patterns, we can identify certain features of the party system in the period between 1977 and 1982. Fine Gael solidarity increased steadily until, at the close of the period, it rivaled that of Fianna Fáil. Even for these two parties, however, solidarity is not absolute, and both must still be concerned about vote leakage. Lack of solidarity poses a much more severe problem for the Labour party, a problem that has been circumvented rather than solved by the strategy of nominating fewer candidates. Not only is Fianna Fáil a party with a high degree of solidarity, it is also a highly exclusive party, with a clear majority of its supporters plumping for the party rather than transferring to the other parties. With the exception of February 1982, the Fine Gael-Labour partnership was endorsed somewhat more substantially by Fine Gael votes than by Labour voters. It is clear, moreover, that Labour voters throughout 1981–82 were less enthusiastic about coalition than they have been at the outset of the present arrangement in 1973. Nonetheless, majorities in both parties did transfer their votes within the coalition and these rates of transfer seem to be unaffected by subtle variations in electoral and coalition strategy at the elite level.

A remarkable aspect of the 1981 election was the size of the first-preference vote for H-block candidates—10 percent in the constituencies in which they stood. The significance of this vote for the party system as a whole depends on whether it should be seen as arising from a humanitarian response to the plight of the hunger strikers or from extreme republican sympathies. If the former, it can be dismissed as a one-time phenomenon related to the particular circumstances. If the latter interpretation is correct, the same vote could presumably be mobilized in the situation of another acute crisis in Northern Ireland. While it is not possible to give a definitive answer to this question, there are some clues. The failure of Provisional Sinn Féin to reproduce the same level of support in February 1982 might point in the direction of the humanitarian interpretation. There are also pointers in the other direction, however. Analysis of the H-block first preferences shows that the vote was much higher in the border region—15 percent in three border constituencies as against 7.5 percent in six nonborder constituencies. Analysis of H-block transfers shows a relation between H-block voting and party affiliation. Six of the seven H-block eliminations can be divided into three categories: (1) where all major parties were still in contention, (2) where Fianna Fáil and Fine Gael were still in contention, and (3) where a Fianna Fáil candidate alone remained.[56] In each of these situations, upward of 45 percent of the H-block votes transferred to Fianna Fáil. When Labour was in contention, its candidates received 22 percent of the transfers. The transfer to Fine Gael candidates by H-block voters was relatively low—it amounted to 13 percent in situation (1) and 30 percent in situation (2). What is significant is that the Fianna Fáil and Labour shares of the H-block transfers tended to reflect their usual shares of the overall vote. Fine Gael's share of the H-block transfers, by contrast, tended to be noticeably less than its usual share of the vote. This suggests that H-block voters were more likely to be former Fianna Fáil and Labour voters than Fine Gael voters.

With this information on the regional and party affiliation characteristics of the H-block vote, we can return to the question of choosing between a humanitarian and an extreme republican interpretation of that vote. Survey research has shown that extreme republican attitudes show the same relationships to region and party affiliation as does the H-block vote.[57] If we assume that it is improbable that humanitarian concern would also show just these same relationships, we have grounds for accepting the interpretation that the H-block vote contained a significant extreme republican component. Accordingly, we can conclude that the H-block vote does have implications for the party system. The implications are that, given a situation of acute crisis in Northern Ireland, the party system could come under pressure from an extreme nationalist quarter. The possibility may be remote, but the evidence suggests that it cannot be dismissed altogether. The significance of such a development would lie not so much in the number of seats that might be won by what would probably be abstentionist candidates as in the use of such electoral support to give a veneer of pseudodemocratic legitimacy to a campaign of terror.

Conclusion

Setting the Irish party system in comparative perspective suggests that its main features—the division within a nationalist consensus; the subordinate status of the left-right issue; the virtual absence of other axes of interparty difference; the lack of clear-cut class bases of party support—are not to be dismissed as fast-disappearing residues of the past. Rather, in a process that has parallels throughout Europe, they have been built into the structure of the party system. I have argued that, because the party system imposes constraints on the actions of politicians in some areas and is notable for the lack of constraint in others, it has far-reaching policy implications. This is not to say that politicians cannot break through the limits set by the system. In fact, developments at this level are one possible source of the transformation of the system. The other possible source of change and the one that concerns us directly here is the behavior of the electorate. The party system can be thought of as the context within which electoral behavior takes place and in terms of which it must be understood, with the proviso that one should be always on the lookout for signs that what the voters do is about to alter the system radically.

The elections of 1981 and 1982 did not portend change on this scale. First, the elections established that 1977 had been a hiccup rather than a watershed. Indeed, the ephemeral nature of the 1977 Fianna Fáil victory was already apparent by 1979. Second, the elections of 1981–82 did not themselves signal a new pattern. The Fianna Fáil vote was not significantly lower than in 1969 and 1973. The Fine Gael gains were made in piecemeal rather than breakthrough fashion, and even their cumulative effect was modest enough— in November 1982 the Fine Gael vote was 39.2 percent, up from 35.1 percent in 1973. At the same time it is evident that within an overall pattern of stability, changes were occurring: in class patterns of voting, in issue concerns, in the electorate's assessments of the parties and their leaders, and in the strength and position of the parties.

Social class played a complex role in the elections of 1981 and 1982, showing up in substantial but temporary gains for Fianna Fáil in February 1982 and in sustained middle-class gains by Fine Gael. The latter culminated in Fine Gael's outstripping Fianna Fáil among middle-class voters by the end of the period. Although these developments do not invalidate the established picture of Irish party politics as "politics without social bases," they do suggest some qualifications. In opinion on issues, the electorate came closest to a form of class politics in February 1982. In that election there were considerable class contrasts in the degree of interest in certain issues, notably in the issue of government borrowing, a decisive swing to Fianna Fáil among unskilled workers and small farmers on the issue of each side's budgetary proposals. June 1981 had been a lackluster election on issues—opinion was either so finely balanced as to be in stalemate or the issues on which there was an imbalance lacked salience. The main change on issues in November 1982 was on the question of stable government. Not only did the salience of this issue grow substantially between February and November of 1982, but party fortunes on the issue were significantly reversed: Fianna Fáil lost what many had long regarded as its trump card, at a time when the electorate's concern with the issue increased. Perhaps the most talked-about issue of the 1981–82 election series was that of party and governmental leadership. It must be emphasized that the available evidence does not permit a definitive conclusion in regard to the effect of this issue on voting behavior. Close inspection of opinion poll evidence suggests, however, that its impact was not at all a simple matter of direct translation of leadership preference into voting preference. What is interesting is that several distinct pieces of information tend to point in the same direction, that is, toward the conclusion that the effect of the issue on voting was a good deal less than might at first have appeared. Although the issue made some contribution to Fine Gael strength in June 1981, the gap between Haughey and FitzGerald did not become substantial until January–February 1982. Second, the choice of Taoiseach was the primary concern of at most one-fifth of the electorate. Third, this proportion did not increase in the course of 1982 despite two leadership challenges within Fianna Fáil during that year. Furthermore, the opening up of a gap between the two leaders in preferences and rates of satisfaction was not accompanied by any decline in Fianna Fáil support or growth in Fine Gael support among voters who professed to be guided by the choice of Taoiseach criterion. The situation was further complicated by a class bias in the electorate's preferences in this matter: the gap was very much less and at times nonexistent among voters of the unskilled working class and small farmer occupational groups.

Despite its failure to win a clear victory in any of the three elections of 1981–82, Fianna Fáil's support appeared, on the surface, to have remained remarkably steady. At its lowest (November 1982), Fianna Fáil's first-preference vote was only a fraction of a percentage point less than in 1969 (45.2 percent compared with 45.7). In the transfer of votes its solidarity was as high as ever and higher than it had been in 1977. The problem for Fianna Fáil is its isolation. It tends neither to give nor to receive transfers. Accordingly, when faced with an alliance of other parties, it must outperform itself to win. It is in this context that certain weaknesses in its vote become particularly significant. It has ceded first place to Fine Gael among a number of crucial categories of voters: policy voters, middle-class voters, Dublin voters, and an especially significant category not so far mentioned—young voters. It is appropriate to consider the question of age and voting in this concluding section, since doing so may suggest likely future developments. In 1977 Fianna Fáil enjoyed a remarkably even spread of support across the age spectrum while Fine Gael's support came disproportionately from the older age groups (table 3.11). By November 1982 this situation had been reversed, Fine Gael having attained an even spread of support among the different generations and Fianna Fáil suffering an imbalance. The reversal is particularly striking among those under twenty-five: Fianna Fáil support in this age group was 49 percent in 1977 and 33 percent in November 1982; Fine Gael's support moved up from 19 percent to 38 percent. A smaller-scale but similar reversal occurred among those aged twenty-five to thirty-four. Two things make these figures potentially significant. The first is that the younger generations constitute such a large proportion of the population. The second is the possibility that those in the youngest age bracket will continue to vote as they did in 1982, that that vote will form the

Table 3.11 Voting intention by age group, 1977 and 1982 (percent)

Party and election	Age group			
	18–24	25–34	35–64	65 or more
Fianna Fáil				
1977	49	49	50	45
November 1982	33	37	44	45
Fine Gael				
1977	19	24	31	32
November 1982	38	35	38	37
Labour				
1977	13	12	7	12
November 1982	10	11	8	6
Sinn Féin the Workers' party / Workers' party[a]				
1977	—	—	—	—
November 1982	7	8	1	1
Others				
1977[a]	4	4	1	2
November 1982	3	3	1	2
Don't know / will not vote / no answer				
1977	14	11	11	10
November 1982	8	6	8	8

Sources: 1977: *Irish Times*/NOP election surveys, 27–28 May, 3 June, 9 June 1977 (figures based on amalgamated results of all three surveys) ($N = 1,788$); November 1982: *Irish Independent–Sunday Independent*/IMS poll, 9–10 November 1982 ($N = 1,049$).
Note: Percentages may not add to 100 because of rounding.
a. In the 1977 polls voting intentions for Sinn Féin the Workers' party were included under the heading "Others."

basis of a habit, as it were. Given that assumption, the figures would indeed be distressing to Fianna Fáil and comforting in varying degrees to the other parties. Experience since 1977, however, cautions against too easy an acceptance of the assumption. Predictions of the fate of Fine Gael made by application of that assumption to 1977 data would have been wide of the mark indeed. Leaving all predictions aside, however, the age imbalance and the other weaknesses identified must give Fianna Fáil considerable cause for concern.

Fine Gael's electoral strengths are in many respects the other side of the coin of Fianna Fáil's weak points. Fine Gael has improved its position most clearly and most consistently among Dublin voters, middle-class voters, and young voters. I have discussed the potential that lies in Fine Gael's advantage over Fianna Fáil among younger people. The other notable sources of current strength (Dublin and the middle class) could prove disadvantageous in the long run, if they foster an image that prevents the party from making inroads on Fianna Fáil's support in other areas and other sectors of the population. Fine Gael's most significant weak spot is among constituency-service voters, and its greatest source of strength is *not* the appeal of its leader. Paradoxically, that the belief in the electoral potency of the Fine Gael leader is considerably exaggerated may ultimately be to the party's advantage. In a parliamentary system, it is in a party's interest not to depend too much on a highly personalized, quasi-presidential vote. Another improvement in Fine Gael support in the elections of 1981–82 was a small but significant increase in party solidarity. This increase was evident in 1981, it was sustained over the next two elections, and it put Fine Gael on a par with Fianna Fáil in what had traditionally been an area of Fianna Fáil advantage. Appearances in June 1981 notwithstanding, the rate of transfer from Fine Gael to Labour did not increase but was maintained at its existing level. Fine Gael transfers marginally more to Labour than it gets; but, of course, it still benefits disproportionately from the arrangement since there are more Fine Gael candidates to receive terminal Labour transfers than there are Labour candidates to receive such transfers from Fine Gael. This relation with the Labour party highlights a fundamental problem for Fine Gael. The size of the Fine Gael vote leaves the party dependent on Labour to achieve power while at the same time tempting it to strike for power on its own. On the one hand, its perceived dependence on Labour is an obstacle to its achieving power on its own; on the other, any attempt to cast off that dependence undermines the alliance on which its present enjoyment of power and future most realistic prospects of retaining it rest. An outright go-it-alone strategy would be a very high-risk one for Fine Gael.

There is some small comfort for the Labour party in the results of the last election of the 1981–82 series. Its first-preference vote showed an increase, admittedly a minute one: its position among working-class voters improved sufficiently to keep it substantially ahead of the Workers' party in that sector of the population, and the solidarity of its vote improved slightly. At best, however, these developments have only halted what has been a remarkable slide. Recovery for Labour involves two possibilities—one a winning back of the small but significant block of middle-class support enjoyed by the party in the late 1960s, the other a building on the incipient signs of a recovery of its support in the working class. Both will be resisted, the first by a social-democratic-leaning Fine Gael and the second by the Workers' party, and both will be contested by Fianna Fáil. The Labour party must be particularly concerned about the concentration of Workers' party support among the younger generations and by the fact that only 3 percentage points separate the two parties among those aged under twenty-five and those aged twenty-five to thirty-four. If, however, the Workers' party competes only with Labour, its position will always remain weak, and if it wins, it will merely inherit the minority position that has been Labour's lot. Clearly, what it must hope to do is to draw off working-class support from the two major parties, particularly from Fianna Fáil. This challenge to Fianna Fáil's leading position is a possible source of fundamental change in the party system. At present, however, the major challenge to Fianna Fáil lies elsewhere, and that challenge implies considerably less change in the party system. That Fine Gael is evidently intent on, and may, in the long run, be capable of, achieving power on its own intensifies the competition between it and Fianna Fáil and thus reinforces rather than undermines the existing party system.

Notes

1. Donald E. Stokes, "What Decides Elections?" in David Butler, Howard R. Penniman, and Austin Ranney, eds., *Democracy at the Polls: A Comparative Study of Competitive National Elections* (Washington, D.C.: American Enterprise Institute, 1981), p. 292.
2. For a detailed account of the debate on the nature of the Irish party system, see Richard Sinnott, "Interpretations of the Irish Party System," *European Journal of Political Research* 12 (1984): 289–307.
3. Seymour Martin Lipset and Stein Rokkan, "Cleavage Structures, Party Systems, and Voter Alignments: An Introduction," in Lipset and Rokkan, eds., *Party Systems and Voter Alignments* (New York: Free Press, 1967), p. 50.
4. Ibid., pp. 14, 47.
5. R. K. Carty, *Party and Parish Pump* (Waterloo, Ontario: Wilfrid Laurier University Press, 1981), p. 6.
6. Ibid., p. 90.
7. Ibid., p. 86.
8. The most complete exposition of an internal center-periphery interpretation of the post-independence Irish party system is to be found in several works by Tom Garvin: "Political Cleavages, Party Politics and Urbanization in Ireland: The Case of the Periphery-dominated Centre," *European Journal of Political Research* 2 (1974): 307–27; "Nationalist Elites, Irish Voters and Irish Political Development: A Comparative Perspective," *Economic and Social Review* 8, no. 3: 161–86; and "The Destiny of the Soldiers: Tradition and Modernity in the Politics of de Valera's Ireland," *Political Studies* 26, no. 3 (September 1978): 328–47. It should be noted, however, that some role, albeit a minor one, has always been accorded to the larger conflict between Ireland as periphery and England as center; see, for instance, Garvin, "Political Cleavages," p. 316. The relevance of the wider arena is more explicitly endorsed in Tom Garvin, *The Evolution of Irish Nationalist Politics* (Dublin: Gill and Macmillan, 1981), p. 217.
9. Carty, *Party and Parish Pump*, p. 97.
10. Brian Farrell, "Labour and the Irish Political Party System: A Suggested Approach to Analysis," *Economic and Social Review* 1, no. 4 (1970): 489.
11. The extent of the Sinn Féin landslide must be qualified by reference to the number of uncontested seats. This does not, however, nullify the long-term mobilizing implications of the 1918 contest. See the discussion of this point in Sinnott, "Interpretations of the Irish Party System," p. 301.
12. This aspect of the application of Lipset and Rokkan to the Irish case was first suggested by

John Whyte, "Ireland: Politics without Social Bases," in Richard Rose, ed., *Electoral Behaviour: A Comparative Handbook* (New York: Free Press, 1973), pp. 647–48. Obviously, as time went on, conflicts on both the church-state and the land-industry dimensions arose and the parties responded to them in varying ways. The point, however, is that these issues were not, as they had been in many other countries, among the building blocks of the party system.

13. Hans Daalder, "The Comparative Study of European Parties and Party Systems: An Overview," in Hans Daalder and Peter Mair, eds., *Western European Party Systems: Continuity and Change* (London: Sage Publications, 1983), p. 18.

14. On the notion of "voice," see Albert O. Hirschman, *Exit, Voice, and Loyalty: Responses to Decline in Firms, Organizations, and States* (Cambridge, Mass.: Harvard University Press, 1970).

15. For evidence of interparty differences on this issue at the parliamentary party level, see Richard Sinnott, "Party Differences and Spatial Representation: The Irish Case," *British Journal of Political Science* 15 (1985): 295–319. The implications for party competition of the intractability of the Northern Ireland problem are discussed in Peter Mair, "Issues, Dimensions, and Party Manifestos," *EUI Working Paper No. 41* (Florence: European University Institute, 1982), pp. 10–11.

16. Michael Marsh, "Electoral Volatility in the Republic of Ireland, 1948–83," in Ivor Crewe, ed., *Electoral Change in Western Democracies: Patterns and Sources of Electoral Volatility* (London: Croom Helm, 1985), p. 198.

17. Richard Sinnott, "The Electorate," in Howard R. Penniman, ed., *Ireland at the Polls: The Dáil Elections of 1977* (Washington, D.C.: American Enterprise Institute, 1978), pp. 65–66.

18. These and subsequent figures for the rate of inflation are based on data published in *Economic Review and Outlook Summer 1983* (Dublin: Stationery Office, 1983). Unemployment figures are from the same source.

19. The postal strike lasted from 19 February 1979 to 25 June 1979, and involved 13,841 workers. It accounted for 1.2 million man-days lost, or 83 percent of days lost for the entire year (I am grateful to Tom Murphy of the Department of Industrial Relations, University College, Dublin, for these figures).

20. On Sunday, 11 March 1979, 50,000 people took part in a tax protest demonstration in Dublin, and lesser but still substantial numbers participated in similar events at various centers throughout the country. A follow-up demonstration just over a week later, on Tuesday, 20 March, attracted upwards of 150,000 in Dublin and correspondingly increased numbers at other centers.

21. The two Cork by-elections were held on the same day (7 November 1979), one in an urban constituency (Cork City), the other in a rural constituency that had, however, a number of medium-sized towns (Cork North-East). On turnouts that were relatively high, the results for the government were devastating. The turnout in Cork City was 55 percent, and the Fianna Fáil vote was down from 58.6 percent in 1977 to 35.9 percent. In Cork North-East, the turnout was 69 percent, and the Fianna Fáil vote dropped from 48.2 percent in 1977 to 36.3 percent. (Results taken from Ted Nealon and Seamus Brennan, eds., *Nealon's Guide to the 22nd Dáil and Seanad Election '81* [Dublin: Platform Press, 1981], p. 187.)

22. The importance of personality and "quality of candidate" considerations had been identified in preelection research carried out on behalf of the Fine Gael and Labour parties. See Market Research Bureau of Ireland, "European Election Research Programme, July 1978– April 1979" (Dublin: MRBI, 1979).

23. For constituency results, see appendix B.

24. On the performance of the Fianna Fáil dissidents, see Joseph O'Malley, "Analysis of the Election," in Ted Nealon and Seamus Brennan, eds., *Nealon's Guide to the 24th Dáil and*

Seanad 2nd Election '82 (Dublin: Platform Press, 1983), p. 152. On the subject of vote management, see Peter Mair, "Party Organization, Vote Management and Candidate Selection: Toward the Nationalization of Electoral Strategy in Ireland," chapter 4 of this volume.

25. Fianna Fáil's vote in the Dublin region increased slightly between June 1981 and February 1982 (from 41.4 to 42.4 percent) but fell back substantially in November 1982 (to 38.3 percent). In November 1982 it was almost three percentage points behind Fine Gael in the Dublin region, Fine Gael's vote having increased from 36.2 percent in June 1981 to 38.9 percent in February 1982 and 41.1 percent in November 1982. (Figures taken from Nealon and Brennan, eds., *Nealon's Guide to the 22nd Dáil and Seanad Election '81*, p. 10; *Nealon's Guide to the 23rd Dáil and Seanad Election '82*, p. 8; and *Nealon's Guide to the 24th Dáil and Seanad 2nd Election '82*, p. 10 [Dublin: Platform Press, 1983].)

26. For constituency results, see appendix B.

27. The proximity of the date of the opinion poll to the date of the election varies somewhat. The polls used for June 1981 and February 1982 were taken within a few days of polling day. For 1969 it is necessary to go outside the campaign period—to April 1969—for data. In 1977 the results of all three waves of the *Irish Times*/NOP (National Opinion Polls) surveys taken at intervals throughout the campaign are amalgamated because of the relatively small sample size (approximately 600) of each individual survey. For November 1982 I have used a poll taken two weeks before election day (the *Irish Independent-Sunday Independent*/IMS poll) rather than one taken with only four or five days to go, because the former poll uses a question on voting intentions that is comparable to the one used in earlier polls and because it provides a fuller breakdown of voting intentions by occupational class.

28. Whyte, "Ireland."

29. For general election results, see appendix B.

30. Sinnott, "The Electorate," pp. 44–45.

31. These and all subsequent figures on opinions on issues are based on IMS poll data unless otherwise noted.

32. Because the most useful evidence on the H-block vote comes from an analysis of the transfer of votes, the question of the nature of that vote will be taken up below in dealing with transfer patterns in general.

33. The second figure for November 1982 (11 percent) is taken from the *Irish Times*/MRBI poll of 11–12 November 1982, because the IMS poll for that election measured only respondents' single most important issue. Because of differences in question wording, the IMS and MRBI figures are only roughly comparable.

34. Private poll conducted for Fine Gael by MRBI, April 1979.

35. The *Irish Times*/IMS poll, October 1980.

36. The 13 percent figure is from an MRBI poll—see note 33.

37. On 28 March 1980, Minister for Finance Michael O'Kennedy announced the appointment of a commission "to enquire generally into the present system of taxation and to recommend such changes as appear desirable and practicable so as to achieve an equitable incidence of taxation, due attention being paid to the need to encourage development of the national economy and to maintain an adequate revenue yield." *First Report of the Commission on Taxation: Direct Taxation July 1982* (Dublin: Stationery Office, 1982), p. 25.

38. In a survey carried out for the European Value Systems Study Group, opposition to abortion in the Republic of Ireland ranged from 49 percent to 87 percent depending on the circumstances specified in the question. The percentage disapproval/approval figures were 49/43 where the mother's health is at risk; 68/23 where it is likely that the child will be born handicapped; 86/6 where the woman is not married; and 87/5 where a married couple do not want any more children. For full details of question wording and responses, see Michael Fogarty, *Irish Values and Attitudes* (Dublin: Dominican Publications, 1984).

102 Voters, Issues, and the Party System

39. The 2 percent figure is from an MRBI poll—see note 33.
40. Joseph O'Malley, "Campaigns and Party Finances," chapter 2 of this volume.
41. *The Way Forward: National Economic Plan 1983–1987* (Dublin: Stationery Office, 1982).
42. For an account of events during this period, see Brian Farrell, "The Context of Three Elections," chapter 1 of this volume.
43. The *Irish Times*/MRBI poll, 19–20 November 1982. The overall results of this poll suggest that the Fine Gael low-profile strategy was not without its risks. The poll shows a small move in favor of Fianna Fáil on almost all issues in the latter half of the campaign. These shifts were not, however, sufficient to wipe out the deficit with which Fianna Fáil had set out.
44. On the subject of the Fianna Fáil leadership struggle, see Brian Farrell, "Government Formation and Ministerial Selection," chapter 5 of this volume.
45. *Dáil Debates*, vol. 317, col. 1332, 11 December 1979.
46. Both measures—satisfaction rating and preference for Taoiseach—must be considered. One could, for example, be quite dissatisfied with an incumbent Taoiseach and yet not prefer the alternative candidate on offer. Equally, one might have a preference for the challenger over the incumbent without being dissatisfied with the incumbent and without, therefore, one's preference having any great implications as to how one should vote.
47. See Farrell, "Context of Three Elections."
48. Ibid.
49. The fieldwork for the October 1982 poll commenced on 27 September and was completed on 8 October. Thus a substantial amount of the fieldwork would have been completed before the onset of the second explicit challenge to Haughey (1 October), and some would have been carried out after Haughey had successfully fended off that challenge (6 October). As a result, it is impossible to use the published poll data to draw any inferences regarding the precise effect of those events on public opinion.
50. The *Irish Times*/MRBI poll of 19–20 November 1982 does not give a breakdown of voting intentions in the skilled and unskilled subgroups of the working class.
51. This is an extension of an analysis carried out by Byrne for the Fianna Fáil vote for the two elections of 1982. See Des Byrne, "Election Polls in Ireland—1982" (Dublin: Irish Marketing Surveys, 1982).
52. For details of the electoral system, see Basil Chubb, "The Electoral System," in Penniman, *Ireland at the Polls*, pp. 21–34.
53. Michael Gallagher, "Party Exclusivity, Party Solidarity, and Inter-Party Relationships," *Economic and Social Review* 10, no. 1 (October 1978): 1–22. A problem arises in estimating these characteristics, however, because for this purpose the published results cannot be taken at face value. In the transfer of surplus votes there is a difference between the actual proportion of the elected candidate's votes that are nontransferable and the reported nontransferable vote for that count. This difference arises because nontransferable votes are set aside before calculating the proportions according to which surplus votes are to be redistributed. They are, therefore, reported only if the number of surplus votes is greater than the number of transferable votes in the set of votes examined and some nontransferable votes are needed to make up a number equal to the surplus. Thus, taking the reported nontransferable vote for distributions of surplus votes at face value inevitably underestimates the aggregate nontransferability. This leads to an overestimation of party solidarity and an underestimation of party exclusivity. The greater the number of surpluses involved in any particular process of estimation, the greater the margin of over- or understatement. Estimation of rates of terminal transfer between parties involved in electoral alliances tends to be less affected, with the notable exception of transferability from Fine Gael to Labour in the election of June 1981 — a case discussed below in the text.

For details of the counting and reporting procedures that give rise to the problem above, see rule 6(3) and rule 6(4) of the "Proportional Representation Election Rules," *Third Schedule to the Electoral Act of 1923, as Amended by Sections 36 to 40 of Act of 1963* (Dublin: Stationery Office, 1964). These rules are reproduced in all editions of the official publications of election results; for example, *Election Results and Transfer of Votes in General Election (June 1981) for Twenty-Second Dáil and By-Elections to Twenty-First Dáil (1977–1981)* (Dublin: Stationery Office, 1982), pp. 59–64.

54. These are the proportions of the sets of votes examined that are left with the elected candidate (that is, the last parcel of votes received minus the surplus). Obviously, with zero nontransferable votes reported in each case, the proportion of nontransferable votes cannot exceed these percentages. In all probability, the proportion of nontransferable votes is much lower, but we have no way of knowing how much. In the nearest elections in which one can accurately calculate transferability from Fine Gael to Labour, the figures were, for Wexford, 59.2 percent transferable to Labour with 21.8 percent nontransferable (February 1982) and, for Carlow-Kilkenny, 59.0 percent transferable with 38.5 percent nontransferable.

55. For 1973 coalition transfers, see Sinnott, "The Electorate," pp. 62–63.

56. In the seventh case (Waterford) comparison of the relative proportions of H-block transfers going to the main parties is obscured by the fact that a candidate of Sinn Féin the Workers' party was still in contention when the H-block candidate was eliminated.

57. E. E. Davis and Richard Sinnott, *Attitudes in the Republic of Ireland Relevant to the Northern Ireland Problem* (Dublin: Economic and Social Research Institute, 1979), pp. 110–15, 123–25.

4 Party Organization, Vote Management, and Candidate Selection: Toward the Nationalization of Electoral Strategy in Ireland

PETER MAIR

Are Irish Voters Party Voters?

One of the major concerns of this paper is the electoral strategies of Irish political *parties*. One of the major assumptions, therefore, is that Irish voters are party voters, an assumption that requires some justification. As the now quite extensive literature on Irish voting behavior testifies, personalist and candidate-centered cues figure prominently in the attitudes of electors. One recent survey, for instance, reported that 43 percent of respondents felt that "choosing a candidate to look after the constituency" was the most important factor in their decisions on how to vote, whereas 25 percent identified policies as the most important factor, 17 percent mentioned choosing between alternative Taoisigh, and a further 17 percent mentioned choosing between alternative sets of government ministers.[1] Moreover, the TDS (or deputies) themselves often seem to place more weight on their role as "brokers" of constituency interests rather than on their legislative roles and spend much of their time "going about persecuting civil servants."[2] To emphasize party, therefore, may be to miss the central dynamic of Irish electoral behavior.

Yet despite the evident personalism in Irish politics and despite the obvious importance of candidate-centered electoral cues, a strong case can be made for the role of party and for the presence of pervasive and deep-rooted party loyalties among Irish voters. As R. K. Carty has suggested,

> two distinct interpretations of the behaviour of the Irish electorate are available. The first, emphasising the parochial and particularistic character of electoral competition, argues that voters are mobilised by the personalised appeals of local notables. . . . The second . . . contends that the electorate has a highly developed set of partisan allegiances, so that individual voting choices reflect a voter's party identification.[3]

Carty's own conclusion, that "Irish electors are party voters," can certainly be supported by a substantial body of data, albeit indirectly.[4]

In the first place, on the basis of research findings in other countries, one can argue that the very conditions in which Irish voters find themselves are conducive to the development of stable and long-term affective ties toward parties. The traditional appeals to nationalism, which have played such an important role in the rhetoric of Irish politics since the foundation of the state and which are essentially symbolic in character, are precisely the sort of appeals associated with the development of affective rather than pragmatic motivations for voting.[5] In addition, the relative longevity of the contemporary political alternatives and the long history of uninterrupted electoral competition are characteristics also associated with the development of a strong sense of party identification.[6]

In the second place, contemporary survey evidence points to a quite widespread sense of party loyalty. Two surveys, in 1976 and 1977, asked respondents if they normally thought of themselves as Fianna Fáil, Fine Gael, Labour, or whatever and, if so, how strongly they felt about the party in question. In both surveys, only 20 percent of the respondents replied that they did not think of themselves in party terms, while of the vast majority who did identify themselves with a party, 22 percent in 1976 and 18 percent in 1977 felt "very strongly" about their party, and 39 percent in both years felt "fairly strongly" about their party.[7]

In the third place, empirical analyses of aggregate voting data suggest that party cues are of crucial importance. A recent study of voting patterns in referendums, for instance, has shown that the constituency-by-constituency outcome is closely associated with the partisan breakdown in preceding or succeeding general elections to the extent that "the crude electoral support for or opposition to a proposal may be estimated in terms of support for parties coming down on either side.[8] Similar evidence of the importance of party cues can be seen in the distribution of lower-preference votes at general elections, as the transfer patterns for all three major parties show quite low levels of vote "leakage" or ticket splitting. Between 1948 and 1977 an average of 82 percent of votes transferring from Fianna Fáil candidates passed on to other Fianna Fáil candidates, while the comparable figures for Fine Gael and Labour were 74 percent and 67 percent, respectively.[9] Thus even in the case of Labour, only one vote in three transferred to another party or candidate rather than staying within the Labour list, with Fine Gael losing only one vote in four and Fianna Fáil only one vote in five. Regardless of the undoubted emphasis on personalistic appeals, therefore, Irish voters appear to be party voters.

The main point, to be emphasized here, and which takes us right to the center of the problem of vote management at the constituency level, is that there is no necessary contradiction between personalism and partisanship (here, a willingness to vote for an entire party ticket). Particularistic concerns can be accommodated by the parties. In other words, a party voter need not necessarily eschew personalist considerations in deciding to support his or her preferred party, nor does a personalist voter need to eschew partisan considerations. Because the STV (single transferable vote) electoral system necessitates a ranking of *candidates* and the major parties (with the recent exception of Labour) will normally nominate more than one candidate in each constituency, even the most staunchly partisan voter is obliged to rank individuals within a party list. As Carty points out, "Elections involve appeals for partisan support, but in responding, the electorate must give their support to individual candidates."[10] Voters therefore act as partisans (by voting for all the party's candidates) and for specific personalist reasons (by ranking the party's candidates) *at one and the same time.* Problems will only arise then when these interests conflict as when, for instance, the preferred party does not include on its list a candidate who satisfies particularistic interests.

As far as the parties are concerned, the ultimate aim of effective vote management is to avoid such potential conflicts of interest by use of judicious nomination strategies. Since most particularistic concerns are primarily territorial, in that voters prefer to see a locally based candidate elected in the constituency, the parties tend to favor the nomination of a list of candidates embracing the major territorial units within any given constituency.[11] Such a nomination strategy, however, is not always possible because of factional fighting within the local party, rivalries between incumbent TDs and potential candidates, and the simple fact that by nominating too many candidates the party runs the risk of dispersing its vote so widely that it ceases to be effective.[12] Therefore, the interests of different territorial units in any given constituency may not be represented in any given party's list of nominees. Hence the voter's potential conflict of interests: if his preferred party does not nominate a local candidate, but another party does, how does he vote? Does he opt for a particularistic solution, thereby necessitating a vote for a favored individual but not for a favored party, or does he opt for a partisan solution, voting for the favored party even at the possible cost of sacrificing particularistic interests?

It is impossible to know which element is uppermost in voters' minds when casting their first preferences. Certainly, as Anthony Parker has demonstrated, any given candidate for a party records his highest level of electoral support in his own immediate locality.[13] What cannot properly be ascertained, though, is whether these votes would have gone to the same party—albeit to a different candidate—if the local nominee had not been standing for election. In other words, at least at first-preference level, it is impossible to know whether the votes for candidate A of party X are primarily the candidate's votes or the party's votes. As such, whatever assumptions party strategists may make when drawing up their list of candidates, in the end they remain simply assumptions.

The picture is much clearer at the lower preference level, because the distribution of transfers between the candidates offers a reasonably valid indication of the importance of locality vis-à-vis party. One useful example is that afforded by the count in the constituency of Carlow-Kilkenny in the November 1982 election. As its name suggests, this constituency comprises two separate administrative counties, and hence is characterized by particularly heightened localistic concerns. To the extent that locality predominates over party, therefore, one would have expected lower-preference transfers to remain "within county" rather than "within party." In fact, the opposite proved to be the case. Following the elimination of Joseph Manning, a Fine Gael candidate from the smaller county of Carlow, five candidates remained in the running. Four of these were based in Kilkenny, two Fine Gael candidates, one Fianna Fáil and one Labour; and one was Carlow-based, a Fianna Fáil candidate. To remain "within county," therefore, Manning's transfers would have to cross party lines; to remain "within party," on the other hand, they would have to cross county lines. As it turned out, 81 percent of Manning's transfers passed to his Fine Gael running mates in Kilkenny, with only 8 percent crossing party lines to the Fianna Fáil candidate from Carlow. Nor is this example exceptional: a recent study that sought to isolate the impact of locality in the 1977 general election concluded that "as a factor in electoral decisions, locality is at best second to party."[14]

This appears to suggest a paradox. On the one hand, party strategists, believing locality to be important, stress the need for a geographically balanced set of candidates in any given constituency. Empirical evidence of the distribution of first-preference votes within constituencies also supports this view, because the vote for individual candidates quite clearly peaks in their own localities. On the other hand, the example of Carlow-Kilkenny, where county loyalties are reckoned to play an important role, Michael Marsh's evidence of the impact of locality in the 1977 election and Michael Gallagher's evidence of the high levels of intraparty transfers all suggest that party rather than locality is of primary importance.

One possible way out of the paradox is to suggest that party voting *is important—but as party voting mediated through candidate preference*. In other words, a supporter of party X will vote for the entire party ticket *if* that ticket includes a locally based nominee. If party X fails to include a local nominee, however, and party Y does, then the otherwise loyal supporter of party X will vote for party Y and will also give his lower preferences to the other candidates of party Y. This is party voting. The party in question, however, is chosen according to the locality of its candidate(s) rather than for policy or affective reasons.

This is, of course, an extreme case. However important locality may be, each party must perforce command the allegiance of a certain number of voters who will loyally support the party ticket regardless of the individual candidates nominated. It does suggest, though, a crude typology of voters that, moreover, permits a more useful understanding of the targets that party strategists have in mind when devising nomination strategies. If we assume, all else remaining the same, that a number of voters will normally prefer one party to another, and if we further assume that in any given constituency the preferred party fails to nominate a local candidate while an alternative party does so, then the otherwise loyal supporters of that party may respond in three ways. First, they may support the party regardless, partisanship being significantly more important for them than particularistic concerns. Second, they may give their first-preference vote to the local candidate of the alternative party, returning to the preferred party with their subsequent preferences. Third, they may give not only their first-preference, but also their lower-preference votes to the alternative party. Voters taking the first option may be defined as *pure partisans*, those taking the second as *deviating voters*, and those taking the third as *conditional partisans*.

The evidence of high transfer-retention rates within parties suggests that very few voters are deviating voters. Moreover, as far as vote management and electoral strategy are concerned, the parties need do little to win the support of voters in the first category—the pure partisans are guaranteed party voters. To the extent, therefore, that nomination strategies play a part in vote management, they are aimed at the third type of voter, the conditional partisan. In effect, according to this assumption, party voting exists, but it is to some extent mediated through candidate appeal. Party X is supported by certain voters because it is the party of candidate A rather than vice versa.

How valid is this assumption? The consistency of voting patterns over time, though less marked than in some other countries,[15] is high enough to suggest the presence of a substantial partisan tradition over and above the appeals of individual candidates. Moreover, a regional breakdown of aggregate voting patterns over the postwar period suggests that much of the volatility over time is a feature of the eastern and more developed part of Ireland, while the peripheral and poorer areas along the western seaboard, where particularistic interests are normally reckoned to be most important, show remarkably high levels of consistency from one election to the next.[16] This consistency seems at odds with the notion that party voting is mediated through candidate appeal.

One way to test this notion is, therefore, to examine the record of candidates who left their parties or were expelled and who subsequently stood as independents in the same or equivalent constituencies in the election immediately following their departure. To the extent that their support was candidate

Table 4.1 Electoral record of party candidates turned Independents, 1948–1982

Prior party affiliation	Fianna Fáil	Fine Gael	Labour
Number of cases of increased personal vote	1	2	1
Number of cases of decreased personal vote	7	2	1
Total personal vote at last election as party candidate	43,127	12,341	4,846
Total personal vote at first election as independent following departure from party	26,652	9,853	6,245
Change in personal vote	−38%	−20%	+29%
Change in personal vote as proportion of turnout	−7%	−1%	+1%
Total *N*	8	4	2

Source: Calculated from information in Vincent Browne, ed., *The Magill Book of Irish Politics* (Dublin: Magill, 1981); Vincent Browne, ed., *The Magill Guide to Election '82* (Dublin: Magill, 1982); and Brian Trench, ed., *Magill Book of Irish Politics 1983* (Dublin: Magill, 1984).
Note: These data concern only those candidates who stand for one of the three parties at any election and who then stand as Independent candidates in the same or equivalent constituency in the subsequent election.

centered, we should expect them to retain a substantial proportion of the first preferences that they had previously won as party nominees. To the extent that their vote is a party vote, we should expect to see a significant drop in their support. Table 4.1 reports these data for candidates from the three major parties in the period 1948 to November 1982. Because there are very few cases—eight in Fianna Fáil, four in Fine Gael, and two in Labour—we should treat the results cautiously. Nevertheless, a pattern does emerge, albeit entirely a function of the Fianna Fáil figures. Of the fourteen candidates who left their parties and stood at the next election as independents, ten experienced a drop in their personal vote. In the Fianna Fáil case, only one of the eight dissidents managed to increase his vote (Noel Browne in 1957), while the overall vote won by the dissidents declined from 43,127 in the election immediately preceding their leaving the party to 26,652 in the election immediately after their departure when they stood as independents. This represents a decline of 38 percent. The comparable figures for Fine Gael and Labour are 12,341 to 9,853 (−20 percent) and 4,846 to 6,245 (+29 percent), respectively. Controlling for differences in turnout as well as minor changes in constituency boundaries, we can see that the share of the poll won by the average Fianna Fáil dissident declined by 7.1 percent (from 18.4 to 11.3) and that of the Fine Gael dissidents fell by an average of 1.1 percent (7.9 to 6.8), while the average Labour dissident increased by 0.8 percent (from 5.9 to 6.7).

Although the number of party candidates turned Independents is very small, the data in table 4.1 do support the contention that many Irish voters are indeed party voters. Although a significant section of the electorate is probably quite indifferent to party, judging from the 1976 and 1978 surveys already cited, it is unlikely that these latter account for much more than 20 or 25 percent of the electorate. Moreover, these electors are arguably less likely to turn out to vote and, if they do so, are probably also more likely to split their preferences between candidates of different parties.

If we accept that the remainder and large majority of the electorate is composed of either partisans or potential partisans in the sense defined earlier, that is, they are willing to vote an entire party ticket, and if we also extend the earlier notion of the conditional partisan to include those voters concerned with general issues as well as those motivated simply by localistic concerns, then we can broaden the original definition of partisans by classifying them into three basic types. First, there is the pure partisan whose support is more or less guaranteed—that is, the hard-and-fast party identifier. Second is the *particularistic* conditional partisan whose support for the party ticket depends on the candidates nominated at the constituency level. Third is the *issue-oriented* conditional partisan whose support for the entire ticket depends on the policies or records of the contending parties.

In conclusion, then, it has been argued that Irish voters are primarily party voters and that their willingness to vote party derives in some cases from long-term affective ties, in other cases from a concern with particular issues or policies, and in other cases from their support for individual candidates nominated by the party. Moreover, the relevant arena of vote management varies, it seems, according to the motivations of the target group to which party activities are directed. As such, those responsible for vote management will work at the national party level in one case—the party leaders, policymakers, election headquarters staff, and so on—and at the local party level in another case—local directors of election, party activists, and so on. Based on this background, the remainder of this chapter will assess the changing role of the parties' central offices or national executives in the elaboration of party strategy and will further argue that among the most significant recent developments in Irish politics has been the trend toward the fusion of national and local strategies in a newly centralized and coordinated party organizational structure.

The Growth of National Election Campaigning

For much of the postwar period Irish parties appear to have regarded election outcomes as either foregone conclusions, in which the national election campaign itself counted for little, or dependent upon the local election campaigns, the costs and management of which were left largely in the hands of the local constituency parties. Irish voters seemed fairly stable in their preferences, tied to specific parties or candidates in such a way that efforts to change their minds appeared largely a waste of resources. Although there was substantial electoral volatility—Ireland ranks fourth in a list of fourteen Western European nations in terms of its average postwar volatility[17]—the apparent inevitability of Fianna Fáil government suggested that Irish politics was immobilist in the extreme.

As such, none of the parties ran full-blooded and intensive electoral campaigns in the 1950s and 1960s. Fianna Fáil itself, for instance, did not issue a formal election manifesto at any election between 1948 and 1973, preferring to rely on the combination of undeviating party loyalists and a record of "good government." Thus its decision to publish a full, comprehensive statement of policy at the beginning of the 1977 campaign—replete as it was with promises to abolish car tax, award grants to first-time house buyers, and other more substantial commitments on economic growth and unemployment—marked a radical change in the party's otherwise complacent approach to vote management at the national level. Although the suddenness of the change resulted from its 1973 defeat by the Fine Gael-Labour coalition and the fear that the coalition would again emerge victorious in 1977, it also represented Fianna Fáil's first real response to what it saw as the demands of an increasingly urban and middle-class electorate. These voters would be less easily convinced by traditional appeals and the tapping of familial loyalties. The survey cited earlier, which reported that 25 percent of respondents emphasized choosing among policies as the way to decide how to vote, also reported that the equivalent figure for city areas was 31 percent and for the ABC1 social group (that is, upper middle class and professionals) 33 percent. Irish voters had changed; rather than taking their loyalty for granted, the parties now had to woo their support actively and, in the process, to develop new organizational and campaigning techniques.[18]

The new attitude toward campaigning contrasted sharply with that prevailing during the 1950s and 1960s and, indeed, for a good part of the 1970s. Explaining why Fianna Fáil had not issued a formal manifesto until the election of 1977, Jack Lynch, leader of the party from 1967 to 1979, stated that "in the old days you were either pro-de Valera or anti-de Valera or pro-Lemass or anti-Lemass, or neither, and then you supported Labour."[19] The same fatalism was evident in the practices of the other parties. Although both Fine Gael and Labour regularly issued manifestoes and elaborated alternative policies to those pursued by the Fianna Fáil government, they seemed to do so more in a pro forma sense than in any real hope of winning widespread support. The *Just Society* program issued by Fine Gael in 1965 provides a case in point:

even though it is now believed that this program represented a major watershed in the party's ideological development, it appears to have played but a minor role in the campaign of that year. One local party worker at the time has been quoted as saying that "there was not always a clear Fine Gael position on some issues, so in writing speeches we would simply try to hammer out our own policy. When the belatedly issued copies of the *Just Society* reached us, we sometimes found that statements in it were in contradiction to positions our candidate, or other party candidates, had taken." [20] Indeed, it can be argued that throughout the 1950s and 1960s and even up to the period of revitalization that followed the coalition's 1977 defeat, Fine Gael lacked a central organization. Headquarters maintained a minimal full-time staff, most party branches regularly failed to affiliate with the national party organization, and no membership register was maintained. Even as late as 1977, when Fine Gael was contesting the election as the major partner in the outgoing coalition government, press relations in party headquarters were the responsibility of a university academic with little or no media experience who was recruited as a volunteer at virtually the last moment.

Labour was in a comparable position—at least before the 1969 election. Although shortages of funds accounted for the persistently inadequate staffing at party headquarters, even those organizational resources that did exist were rarely used to full effect. In the 1965 campaign, for instance, an internal memorandum complained that

> the full campaign committee met only briefly after the joint meeting of the Administrative Council and the Parliamentary Party. Details of the number of candidates were conflicting and the list of candidates notified was vague until late in the campaign; apart from press handouts, liaison with the press seemed poor; the servicing of key constituencies with speakers for their meetings almost completely broke down; no prior panel of campaign speakers was arranged and circulated to branches; key marginals were not given special attention when it became obvious that they were in serious danger . . . ; the general election campaign fund was opened too late to accumulate and enable decisions to be taken on expenditure; the single telephone line at Head Office was constantly engaged and no extra clerical staff was employed for the campaign; only the bare minimum of the Election Manifesto was duplicated and no special election posters were produced. [21]

More generally, Labour campaigns appear largely to have been simply the sum of a host of local campaigns that bore little relation to one another and that appeared to emphasize Labour per se as opposed to the individual candidates only in a very formal sense. [22] Faced with a lackluster opposition, Fianna

Figure 4.1   The relationship between economic well-being and the
electoral performance of incumbent parties, 1948–1982

Change in vote of incumbent parties (%)[a]

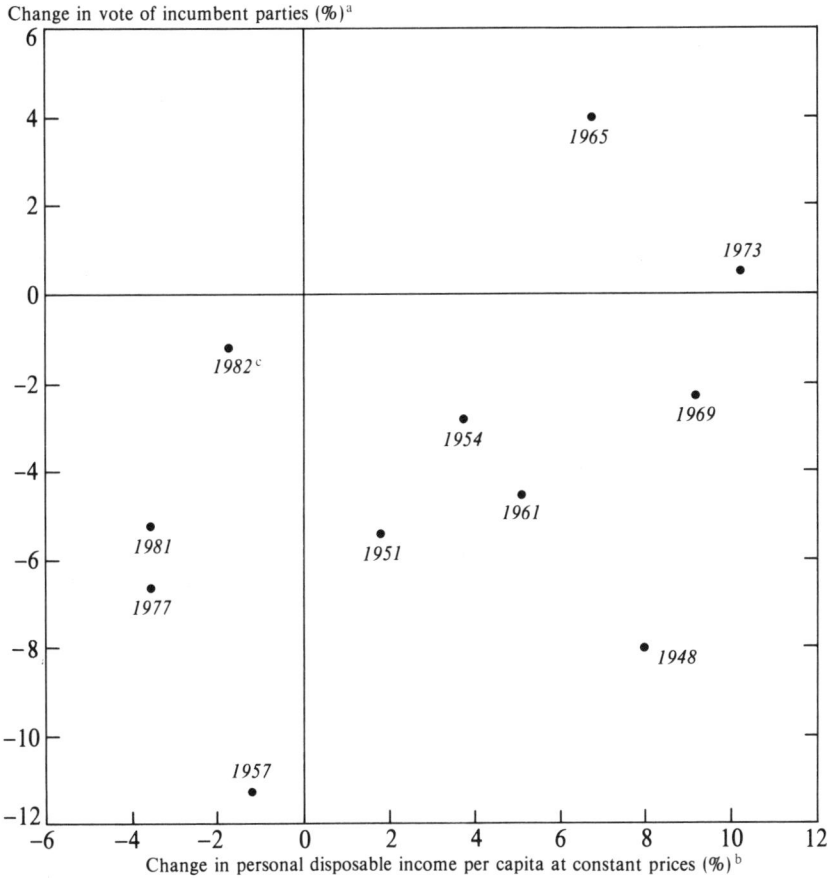

Source: Economic data provided by the Central Statistics Office.
a. Change in the vote of incumbent parties is the percentage change from their vote at the immediately preceding election.
b. Change in per capita disposable income refers to the change in the year immediately preceding
the election relative to the previous year.
c. For the purposes of this figure, the 1982 election data represent the average for the February
and November elections.

Fáil felt sufficiently secure in office to rely simply on long-standing loyalties
and the appeal of its record in government.

   Indeed, in the absence of major electoral campaigns and of an emphasis
on competing sets of policy, Irish voters seem to have relied heavily on the
record of the outgoing government as a way of deciding how to vote. Figure 4.1

charts the relationship between changes in per capita personal disposable income, which is a useful summary of changes in economic well-being, and changes in the support for incumbent parties. As is evident from the figure, the relationship is reasonably strong (r = .49), with changes in the economic index explaining some 25 percent of the change in the vote of the incumbent parties. Although these parties rarely improve their level of support in the wake of a period in office (the exceptions are in 1965 and 1973), they tend to lose a smaller percentage of votes in periods of increasing economic prosperity.

Fine-tuning the economy with a view toward the next election could be interpreted as a macro form of vote management. In this sense the parties did not take their support for granted in the period before the 1970s. Indeed, two other techniques were also favored by the parties in this period, though these were less concerned with actually winning new votes than with a better and more effective use of existing support. The first of these techniques involved variations on gerrymandering, which in some cases required minor changes of constituency boundaries to gain more value from local pockets of partisan support. In other cases these changes caused the adoption of completely new constituency configurations; in these instances the judicious distribution of three-, four-, and five-seat constituencies led to a maximization of a party's gains in areas of strong support and a minimization of losses in areas where another party was strongly supported.[23]

The specific practices need not concern us here. What is relevant, however, is that the redistricting technique has been used by all three parties at different stages and that, following the 1977 election when a major coalition gerrymander backfired and actually facilitated the return of Fianna Fáil to office with its largest ever Dáil majority, a nonpartisan, independent boundary commission took over responsibility for redistricting.

The second technique was the encouragement of partisan voting among one's supporters, in other words, an emphasis on support for the entire party ticket, rather than for just one or two of the party's candidates. More recently, this sort of campaign was used to even more effect on an interparty basis by the Fine Gael-Labour coalition in 1973. During that campaign both parties urged their supporters to transfer within the coalition, so that Fine Gael supporters would give their lower-preference votes to Labour candidates and vice versa. The result was a greatly increased "used" or effective vote,[24] which gave the coalition parties 51 percent of the seats with 49 percent of the vote, as against a combined Fine Gael-Labour total of 47 percent of seats and 51 percent of the votes in 1969. Largely as a result of the intracoalition transfer-retention rate, Fianna Fáil lost six seats in 1973, despite having increased its own proportion of first preferences.

Central Office Growth. Economic management, gerrymandering, and the encouragement of partisan as opposed to candidate-centered voting are time-honored techniques of vote management, none of which really involved the active intervention of the parties' central offices. The past ten years, however, and particularly the elections of 1981 and 1982, have witnessed a quite unprecedented growth of the parties' central offices and, thereby, a greater role for the national party organizations in the mobilization of the vote. In particular, in the past ten years the parties have developed a much greater awareness of the need to produce attractive and comprehensive policy proposals to win over a doubting public.

This trend is easily evidenced. Reference has already been made to Fianna Fáil's decision in 1977 to issue a formal manifesto for the first time in the postwar period, a change of style that was itself a party-prompted reaction to the coalition parties' joint "statement of intent" in 1973. Following the coalition victory in that year, Fianna Fáil established a wide-ranging policy backup service, headed by a full-time research director and eventually leading to the 1977 manifesto itself, a brightly presented forty-seven-page document listing Fianna Fáil's policy proposals in each area of government activity. As a result of the perceived impact of this program,[25] the party produced a glossy sixty-eight-page booklet entitled *Our Programme for the 80s*, for the 1981 election. In turn, Fine Gael countered with *A Better Future*, equally glossy, shorter (thirty-one pages), but also very comprehensive. Pressure of time on the one hand and the continuing validity of earlier proposals on the other meant that the parties did not issue new and elaborate programs for the 1982 elections. Nevertheless, the actual emphasis on competing policy programs has been a relatively new phenomenon in the past decade of Irish politics. The recent regular alternation in government between Fianna Fáil and the coalition has meant that election outcomes are now uncertain and that voters are aware of the existence of a choice of governments. In this sense the parties are now required to state their intentions at the same time as they appeal for votes. Although the politics of the manifesto are a new phenomenon in Irish politics, they are likely to persist.

Central party activity at the policy level is not concerned simply with the production and distribution of the manifesto. In 1981, for instance, Fianna Fáil headquarters distributed 5,000 posters featuring the party leader to each of the constituencies, 2.75 million election addresses, and some 25,000 *Notes for Speakers*, that is, a list of points and topics suitable for public speeches. In February 1982 the central office distributed some half a million posters, one and a half million leaflets, and the same number of election addresses as before.

Fine Gael headquarters involved itself in much the same way. In 1981 the office was responsible for distributing almost 200,000 posters of the party leader and 750,000 copies of a special election issue of the party newspaper. In February 1982 headquarters issued over 150,000 posters of various types,

Table 4.2 Declared central office expenditure of Irish political
parties, 1976–1982, in constant (1975) prices (in pounds)

	Fianna Fáil	Fine Gael	Labour
1982	164,500	154,800	43,100
1981	192,100	126,900	39,300
1980	165,300	146,900	59,400
1979	125,300	127,800	48,800
1978	118,300	94,200	34,900
1977	140,800	58,500	28,500
1976	131,100	44,900	23,800

Source: Figures published by the parties.

almost 3 million leaflets, 20,000 car stickers, and around 1 million other stickers and badges.

Labour's efforts in this regard were of much smaller scale, of course. In 1981 the party's central office distributed almost 50,000 posters, 250,000 leaflets, and 200,000 copies of a special election newspaper, as well as some 250,000 election addresses. The pattern in 1982 was somewhat similar. Perhaps one indication of the party's poor organization, however, is that in February 1982 it used a substantial amount of campaign material that had been prepared for, but not actually distributed in, the 1981 election.

These activities may seem relatively minor. Nevertheless, including the newspaper advertising commissioned by the parties (in 1981, for instance, Fianna Fáil spent an estimated £400,000 on advertising and Fine Gael £300,000),[26] central party headquarters obviously produces the vast bulk of party campaign material. In *party* terms, the main issues and voter appeals are national, even if local concerns may prevail in certain areas. Moreover, because the central offices increasingly employ the services of speech writers to supply local candidates, much of what voters also hear at the local level may emanate from the national party. In short, the various party headquarters appear to be establishing a greater and greater role in the conduct of election campaigns and the mobilization of voter support. Election campaigns are increasingly national, even if the basic footwork remains with the local organizations.

The growth of the parties' central offices is indeed one of the major features of recent Irish politics, as is evident, for instance, in the growth of central office expenditure. As can be seen in table 4.2, at constant (1975) prices, Fianna Fáil's central office expenditure rose from £131,100 in 1976 to £164,500 in 1982, an increase of over 25 percent (even allowing for the decrease in 1982 relative to 1981). Fine Gael's expenditure in the same period rose from £44,900 to £154,800, an extraordinary increase of almost 250 percent, while Labour's figure rose from £23,800 to £43,100 in 1981, an increase of over 81 percent.

Part of these increases are traceable to additional staff recruitment in the parties' central offices. In 1966, for instance, Fianna Fáil had a full-time staff of six, employed for a total salary bill of just £5,000 per year. In 1973 the party added a full-time research director and a press officer. By 1977 there was a full-time staff of ten, for a total salary bill of almost £40,000, while by 1982 there were thirteen full-time workers in party headquarters, including a new youth officer, with another five or six full-time people—either press officers or researchers—in the parties' offices in the Dáil. In addition, since 1969 the party has maintained a permanent fund-raising committee with a salaried secretary.[27]

The same pattern holds true for Fine Gael. As recently as 1974 the party was staffed only by a general secretary and seven secretarial assistants. In addition, and at least from the early 1960s, Fine Gael has also employed two fund collectors-organizers, whose duties kept them occupied entirely outside the head office and within the local constituency parties. In 1977 and 1978, however, a press officer was appointed as well as an assistant organizer with specific responsibility for the youth section of the party. In 1982 a research officer was also appointed.

Labour constitutes something of an exception here because its minimal budget prevents it from employing a full complement of administrative, research, and publicity staff. In 1982, for instance, the head office was staffed by only a general secretary and two secretarial assistants, though other people have occasionally been recruited to work in the party offices at Leinster House.

The number of full-time party workers obviously increases at election times. In the case of Fianna Fáil, for instance, some seventy-five people worked full time during the February 1982 election, including the election committee itself. In the Fine Gael case, the party office had some thirty full-time workers in 1981, and some forty in February 1982, while Labour had nine full-time people working in both elections.

Organizational Reform. Attempts to centralize party control over local organizations and to revitalize the organizational structure in general have accompanied the expansion of party headquarters. Again, these developments have been most marked in the case of Fine Gael, which, initially at any rate, was organizationally the least cohesive of the three main parties.[28] But both Fianna Fáil and Labour also needed to develop a more coherent and efficient organizational network and electoral strategy. In 1976, for instance, some 100 Fianna Fáil cumainn (branches) were closed down in an effort to achieve what the new general secretary referred to as a more "fair and widespread distribution."[29] These closings in fact represented an attempt to curtail the formation of paper branches: that is, branches that exist in name only, established to further the organizational resources of local notables. More recently, in the wake of its very poor performance in the November 1982 election, Fianna Fáil has made similar attempts to reform its branch structure in the Dublin City area.

In the case of Labour a recent Administrative Council decision has stipulated that, from 1980 onward, to participate in candidate selection conventions, branches must have a certain minimum of members registered at the head office, must have participated in the party's national collection and paid the relevant affiliation fees, and must have been registered for at least six months.

It is in Fine Gael, however, that attempts at organizational revitalization have been most evident, though admittedly Fine Gael is also the party that, in terms of organizational difficulties, faced the most uphill struggle. As late as 1978 the honorary secretaries reported to the Árd-Fheis that some two-thirds of the branches were not affiliated, while only one-third of the constituency executives had responded to requests for information on the number of branches and their financial situation. By 1980, however, not only were the vast majority of branches affiliated with the head office, but also they were believed to be real, active branches. In other words, by 1980 Fine Gael could claim to have centralized its organization and to have eliminated the problem of paper branches as well. In contrast to the relatively dismal picture presented in 1978, the 1980 honorary secretaries' report stated that "we have continued the process of weeding out ineffective branches and are now confident that the 1,849 branches which affiliated for 1979 really exist and are largely effective."[30]

The tightening up of Fine Gael's branch organization was a relatively rapid process, the first stage of which took the form of appointing voluntary public relations officers and organizers in each of the constituencies. Branches were later told that to affiliate and take part in selection conferences and so on, not only must they pay their registration fee, but also they must take part in the Fine Gael National Collection, supply details of their annual accounts to the head office, and have a minimum of nine paid-up members. Ever since the central register of party members became effective for the first time in 1978, these reforms enabled the central office of the party to exert full control over its branch network, tying local parties into a centralized and apparently cohesive organization.

Like both Fianna Fáil and Labour, however, Fine Gael suffered from a proliferation of paper branches. Although the rules concerning participation in the National Coalition, the furnishing of annual accounts to the head office, and, in particular, the need to have a minimum of nine paid-up and centrally registered members combined to make it more difficult to establish and maintain paper branches, in and of themselves these reforms did not solve the problem completely.

In an effort to tackle this difficulty the party therefore introduced what is called a new "model system" for annual general meetings of branches and constituencies and for the conventions held to select candidates for local authority and general elections. Under the new Fine Gael scheme, power accrues to branches according to the number of *electors* for which the branch has responsibility. Each constituency executive allocates a section of the constituency to each branch, notifying party headquarters of the number of members in the branch and the section of the electoral register for which that branch has responsibility. Each branch responsible for up to five hundred electors is then entitled to send three delegates to every constituency convention, with another delegate for every additional 250 electors. A further proviso states that a branch may not send more than one-third of its membership as delegates to any convention, so that a nine-member branch with a brief for one thousand electors may still be represented by only three delegates. These rules apply to branches outside Dublin and Cork Cities. In these latter areas, with a more densely concentrated population and fewer branches, responsibility for up to a thousand electors entitles a branch to three delegates, with one additional delegate for every additional five hundred electors.

Although this reform does not entirely eliminate the possibility of paper branches (a branch may still claim nine members and be allocated responsibility for a certain number of electors and yet exist in name only), it does make it more likely that the affiliated branches are genuine. In the first place, by associating each branch with a certain number of electors, the reform discourages the proliferation of branches in one small area. In the second place, by giving each branch such a specific organizational remit, the party ensures the existence of an external check on the activities of each branch: the absence of organizational activity in an area can be traced to the branch responsible for that area. The final advantage of the scheme is that it encourages the reasonably proportionate representation of all areas in a given constituency. If new branches can be established at will and where sufficient power accrues to the branches to encourage their proliferation, a constituency may be imbalanced in terms of the vast overrepresentation of certain areas where local party notables have established their base. The Fianna Fáil organization in Donegal North-East, which has been most ably described and analyzed by Paul Sacks, provides an example of this situation.[31] At the time of Sacks's study in 1969, sixty-seven Fianna Fáil cumainn in the Donegal North-East area served a total electorate of 37,371. Of these, as many as twenty-five (37 percent) were concentrated in the Milford area of the constituency, which included only 8,691 electors (23 percent) but was at the same time the home base of Neil Blaney, the senior Fianna Fáil politician in the area. As Sacks points out, these cumainn constituted the largest single block in the constituency. Moreover, because intraparty power resided with the cumainn, Blaney's control over the Milford cumainn allowed him control over all county council nominations in the Milford Comhairle Ceanntair, as well as control over the block of Milford delegates at all constituency conventions.[32] The new model scheme of Fine Gael, however, by distributing power to branches according to the number of electors they serve, weakens the possibility for such local intra-constituency hegemony.

Marginal Constituencies. To expand a party's organization to make it more cohesive is one thing; to make campaigning actually more effective is another. One of the first steps toward that end is to decide in which constituencies it is possible to win an extra seat. Among the most crucial tasks facing the national party organizations is therefore the identification of marginal constituencies, which, given the STV electoral system and multimember constituencies, is particularly difficult in the Irish case. The actual mechanics of assessing the degree of marginality in any constituency need not concern us here; suffice it to say that all major parties now appear to agree that the essential element is the "last effective count,"[33] which is calculated by adding to a party's first-preference vote in the preceding election the number of transfers it gained from candidates from other parties and subtracting from this total the number of transfers that "leaked" away from its own candidates to candidates from other parties. Using just such a calculation in 1977, for instance, Fianna Fáil identified twenty-eight constituencies, in twenty of which the party could hope to gain a seat and in eight of which it stood to lose a seat; in all cases the relevant range of vote change was between 0.5 percent and 5.9 percent.[34] In some cases, of course, the calculations are not so precise. In 1981, for instance, the national director of elections for Fianna Fáil stated that all the three-seat and five-seat constituencies could be considered marginal.[35] In August 1982, however, Fine Gael used a technique similar to Fianna Fáil's in 1977 to identify twenty constituencies where, depending on the magnitude of the swing, it was possible in the forthcoming election for the party to win extra seats.[36]

However the index of marginality is estimated, some system of identification of winnable seats is necessary if the parties are to employ their scarce campaign resources in the most effective way. Marginal constituencies are normally accorded priority in the party leader's national tour and receive favored treatment in the distribution of leaflets, posters, and other forms of party propaganda. In some cases the extra campaign effort in marginal seats even involves the elaboration of specific policy proposals for the area concerned or promises of future state aid. In 1981, for instance, conscious of its electoral potential in Dublin, Fine Gael published a special environmental policy package for the Dublin region.[37] At the same time, conscious of his party's vulnerability in Cork, the Fianna Fáil leader promised a Cork audience that the local oil refinery would be retained by the government despite threats of closure, that the national research unit for the microelectronics industry would be located at University College Cork, and that An Foras Forbartha—the national physical and planning research body—would be transferred there from Dublin.[38]

National Control of Local Strategy?

The initial identification of marginal constituencies, the channeling of additional organizational resources to the local campaigns in these constituencies, and the development of specific policies designed to appeal to voters in these areas represent a critical link between vote management strategies at the national and the local levels. In and of themselves, however, they do not challenge the autonomy of the local parties vis-à-vis the central offices, but rather simply supplement the activities of constituency campaigners. In this sense, actual electoral campaigns seem to have remained primarily in local hands even though the center of gravity in Irish parties has shifted noticeably toward the central offices and voters in marginal as indeed in other constituencies therefore increasingly confront *nationally* generated party appeals. Since 1977, however, even at the level of the local campaign, the rule of the national party is ever more evident.

Local parties in Ireland are principally the parties of local notables. As we have seen, most TDs owe their election to party voters, although at the same time most local parties owe their electoral success to the personal appeal of their individual TDs. Parties and candidates exist in a symbiotic relationship, the local party knowing that without certain candidates its appeal would be limited and the local candidate knowing that, in many cases, the party label is necessary to secure election.

At the same time, however, most incumbent TDs realize that a significant challenge to their chances of reelection comes from within the party as well as from outside it. While the ebb and flow of votes from one party to another is generally out of an individual TD's control, depending as it does on national party policy and the like, the shift *within* a party from one candidate to another is in many cases relatively susceptible to control by the individual TD. Much of this intraparty shift derives from the capacity of the individual candidate or TD to service particularistic interests.

In general, the individual incumbent TD will be extremely reluctant to accept a running mate who might challenge his own basis of support. If a party has two safe seats in a constituency, for instance, the two TDs tend to carve out their own bailiwicks, neither encroaching on the other.[39] With only one safe seat, the incumbent will try to ensure that he is not accompanied by a strong running mate who might displace him. Alternatively, with two safe seats, both incumbents will try to prevent the emergence of a strong third candidate. The danger to incumbents is a real one: between 1951 and 1977, for instance, of the 191 TDs who defended and then lost their seats, as many as fifty-eight (30 percent) were displaced by intraparty rivals.[40]

To prevent the emergence of candidates who might challenge their seats, TDs attempt to control the party's nomination conventions. Votes at these conventions are cast on the basis of local party branches, each branch traditionally having an equal number of votes. Thus the more branches loyal to a particular TD, the more likely he is to determine the outcome of the nomination convention. It is for this reason that, as noted above, all three parties have been consistently plagued with the problem of paper branches, the formation of which has given local notables extra votes at selection conferences.

Although the parties' national executives traditionally reserve the right to appoint the chairman of the local selection conferences and although they also reserve the right to determine the number of candidates and the power to ratify those chosen, real control over the candidate list has customarily resided in the hands of the local parties.[41] In the Irish case, this means that the list has, to a great extent, remained within the power of local notables. General party interests on the one hand, however, and the interests of specific notables on the other need not coincide. Although the party may wish to see the nomination of a strong third candidate in a constituency with two safe seats in the hope that a third seat might be gained, the two existing incumbent TDs would probably be unwilling to take the risk. If the third candidate were elected, then of course no individual would suffer and the party would be better off. But if only two seats were retained despite the nomination of three candidates, then there is no guarantee that it would be the two incumbent TDs who were successful. Rather, the third candidate might well displace one of the incumbent TDs. Thus, while the party's position would remain the same, the individual TD in question would lose out. Potentially at any rate, there is thus a permanent play-off between party ambitions on the one hand and incumbent insecurity on the other; and as long as the local procedures remained in the hands of local notables, the outcome of this play-off was likely to come down on the side of caution.

Significantly, however, in line with an increasing competitiveness, the past four election campaigns have also witnessed major attempts by the parties, and particularly by Fianna Fáil and Fine Gael, to circumvent local control of the selection processes and thereby to follow a strategy more favorable toward the interests of party than toward the individual incumbents. In some cases this has involved simply the imposition of extra candidates in individual constituencies. In 1977, for instance, the Fianna Fáil party leader imposed additional candidates in sixteen constituencies, in five of which the imposed candidate was successful. Since then, this practice has also been adopted by Fine Gael. More significantly, however, the new model system of branch organization adopted by Fine Gael has caused a significant decline in the number of paper branches in the party. More importantly, branches no longer enjoy equal voting rights regardless of size, but now have political weight according to their area of responsibility. In this sense the party has made major strides in curtailing powers previously wielded by local notables, powers that, in many cases, have probably acted against the interests of the party as a whole. In effect, through the reorganization of its branch network, Fine Gael has laid the ground for the active involvement of the national party in local affairs.

Also of interest is that the proportion of incumbents defeated by intraparty rivals has also risen significantly since 1977. Taken as a whole, the four elections between 1977 and 1982 saw the defeat of thirty-four incumbents by their running mates: that is, 42 percent of all incumbent losses occurred as a result of intraparty displacement. Conversely, between 1951 and 1973, only 28 percent of incumbent losses resulted from intraparty displacement.[42] Although it is impossible to prove categorically that the increase in intraparty seat turnover results from the intervention of the parties' national executives in the local candidate selection processes, nevertheless it is likely that some relation between the two does exist. In 1977, for instance, two of the five imposed Fianna Fáil candidates who were elected actually displaced incumbent Fianna Fáil TDs.

Particularly interesting, however, is that this development represents a fusion of national and local vote management strategies. Until quite recently there appeared to be two distinct arenas. To be sure, the national arena appears increasingly predominant, as the parties have become more and more aware of the need to set the national political agenda and as they have perceived an increased voter awareness of national political issues. Yet even then, the local organizations preserved their political autonomy. Since 1977, however, and particularly since the November 1982 election, the parties have recognized that this national strategy must also involve a planned and coordinated *local* party strategy, one that ensures that candidates are selected in the interests of the party rather than of the local notables.

Fine Gael is perhaps the first of the parties to realize fully the potential involved in such a coordinated and controlled local strategy. Moreover, the success of this strategy in the November 1982 election is also likely to ensure that the other parties, and particularly Fianna Fáil, will quickly follow suit. As such, it is probably useful at this point to look more closely at the Fine Gael strategy at that election, a strategy that, to some extent at least, was responsible for its winning a higher proportion of Dáil seats than at any other election in the history of the state. This strategy is also interesting as it represents a major attempt at a national *seat-maximizing* strategy as opposed to simply a national *vote-maximizing* strategy.

The Fine Gael Strategy in November 1982. The successful strategy adopted by Fine Gael in the November 1982 election was the culmination of a process that had begun following the defeat of the coalition in 1977, the election of Garret FitzGerald as party leader, and the appointment of a number of new party bureaucrats and strategists at the head office. Part of this strategy has been described already—the emphasis on organizational growth and revitalization, the reform of the very haphazardly organized branch network, and so on. Most significant in the context of this discussion, however, is the emphasis placed by the party on the need for a strategy of seat maximization, which, in this case, involved control of local vote management and of candidate selection processes.

The party's capacity to influence the outcome of local selection conferences stemmed from three factors: first, the reserved right of the national executive to determine the number of candidates to be selected as well as to impose additional candidates; second, the new model system of branch organization that substantially curtailed the power of local notables; and third, the simple authority of the party leadership.

Following the results of the February 1982 election and the defeat of the coalition government, Fine Gael established a new Constituency Review Committee, which met for the first time on 18 April. Between that date and August 1982, when it presented its preliminary report, the committee met on ten occasions and visited twelve of the twenty constituencies it had been asked to investigate.[43] The twenty constituencies involved were those where the party estimated it could win an additional seat, and the brief of the committee was to investigate how the list of candidates selected might be modified to best ensure both a maximization of votes as well as a maximal return on seats.

In most cases the strategy involved attempting to balance a limited number of candidates on the one hand, with a reasonable geographic representation on the other. Although in this sense the party acted no differently from the normal practice adopted by all parties in selecting candidates, Fine Gael sought a balance that did not necessarily take into account the specific individual needs of local notables. As a former general secretary stated, the strategy therefore involved "encouraging someone who was reluctant or convincing the constituency organisation to accept someone they didn't want."[44] In Kildare, for instance, the committee felt that the interests of the party would best be served by dividing the Fine Gael vote between just two candidates, rather than dispersing it among three, a plan that required the third candidate in 1981 and

February 1982 not to offer herself for reselection in November 1982. In Kildare, a five-seat constituency, Fine Gael hoped to win two seats. In February 1982 three candidates had been nominated, between them winning 32 percent of the vote. Despite this reasonably good performance, only one Fine Gael TD was then elected, the last seat in the constituency being taken by a Fianna Fáil candidate, whose vote exceeded that of the remaining two Fine Gael candidates by just 172 votes.

In November 1982, however, with just two candidates, the Fine Gael vote rose to 36.5 percent, which together with a relatively even distribution between both candidates resulted in the election of both on the first and second counts respectively. Yet, although the new strategy was therefore deemed very successful, even if three candidates had been nominated, the party would likely still have won two seats. A third candidate certainly would not have *reduced* the overall number of first-preference votes and, to the extent that the lower-preference transfers remained within Fine Gael, then the party's increased proportion of the poll should have guaranteed the second seat. In 1981, for instance, Fine Gael had also won two seats, despite running three candidates.

The Kildare case is therefore ambiguous, because the increase in first preferences seems to have obviated the need to reduce the number of candidates. In Wexford, on the contrary, Fine Gael's strategy appears unambiguously successful. At the February election this five-seat constituency had given Fianna Fáil three seats and Fine Gael two. Fianna Fáil had taken the third seat from Labour in that election, and it was likely that Labour's vote would continue to slip in November. In a sense, therefore, Fine Gael was trying to win a Labour seat from Fianna Fáil. Because both Fine Gael TDs came from the north and center of the constituency, the committee recommended that a third candidate be nominated from the southern end, the area that included the towns of Wexford (where 18,000 voters were registered) and New Ross (where 8,000 voters were registered). With a reasonably strong potential candidate from this area, Avril Doyle, the first lady mayor of Wexford town, the party believed that her nomination and a more judicious division of first preferences between the two incumbents could give the party a third seat. The strategy worked perfectly. Although Fine Gael's overall vote share rose, the number of first preferences won by the two incumbent TDs fell slightly, as intended. Both had sufficient votes to ensure their own election, but the reduction in their total gave Doyle sufficient first preferences to remain ahead of the Labour candidate. Because Labour's transfers were likely to go predominantly to Fine Gael (as would Fine Gael's go to Labour in similar circumstances), Doyle's consistent plurality over the Labour candidate meant that she would benefit from his earlier elimination. This followed the fourth count, when Doyle had accumulated 6,160 votes against 5,481 for the Labour candidate.

After his elimination, 4,364 lower-preference votes passed to Fine Gael, a transfer sufficient to push the two incumbents past the quota while at the same time placing Doyle close enough to be assured of election. Perhaps the most telling evidence of the effectiveness of the strategy is to note that, despite an increase in the party's first preferences of only 3.7 percentage points (from 37.7 to 41.4), the last effective count for Fine Gael showed an increase of 18 points (from 34.3 to 52.3).

The Wexford strategy illustrates very clearly the two specific components of the Fine Gael approach: first, the geographical division, more or less common to all parties; and second, the attempt to distribute first-preference votes between the candidates in such a way as to gain most benefit from transfers, a practice adopted in most of the twenty marginal constituencies. Electors in the constituency of Dublin South-Central, for instance, were provided with official party leaflets suggesting that if they lived in certain areas they should rank the candidates in one way, while in other areas the ranking should be different. The strategy worked well, Fine Gael picking up a second seat from Fianna Fáil. In Galway West, where Fine Gael hoped to pick up a second seat at the expense of Labour's Michael D. Higgins, a third candidate was selected on the basis of locality: that is, he was not from the same area of the constituency as Higgins, that is, in Galway City itself. The idea was that the single Fine Gael candidate from the city area would monopolize all Fine Gael first preferences there, so maintaining a plurality over Higgins. Moreover, when the third candidate was eliminated, as would inevitably happen, most of his lower-preference votes would transfer within party, because his geographical distance from Higgins's base would militate against cross-party transferring. As it happened, the Fine Gael candidate from Galway City did maintain a plurality over Higgins, also receiving the bulk of the transfers from the eliminated third candidate. Higgins was defeated, and Fine Gael took its hoped-for second seat.

Occasionally, however, the strategy backfired, although at less cost to the party than to individual incumbents. In Dublin South-East, for instance, where a careful division of the first-preference vote was expected to give Fine Gael an extra seat at the expense of Labour, a sitting Fine Gael TD lost his seat to a new intraparty rival. In Louth, where the nomination of a strong candidate from the southern end of the constituency was expected to give Fine Gael a second seat, a growth in Labour first preferences thwarted the strategy: while Fine Gael managed to retain its single seat, the incumbent was defeated and a new Fine Gael TD elected.

In most cases, however, the Fine Gael strategy worked as intended, with extra seats won at the expense of both Fianna Fáil and, perhaps ironically, at the expense of Fine Gael's coalition partner, Labour. In some cases the growth in the party's first-preference votes probably meant success regardless of the new nomination strategy, while in other instances the strategy failed because of an unexpected increase in the support of one of the other parties. Only in one or two instances did the party, or, more properly, individual incumbents, suffer as a result of the Constituency Review Committee's misreading of the local situation—the outcome in Dublin South-East is a case in point.

Much of the success of the strategy depended upon the agreement of individual incumbents to place the overall interests of the party before their own interests. In Wexford, for instance, the chances of a third seat depended explicitly on the agreement of the two incumbents not to try to maximize their individual support, but to allow the third candidate to amass sufficient first preferences to remain ahead of the Labour candidate. As we have seen, the strategy worked. It is also conceivable, however, that it might have backfired and that an incumbent's agreement to curtail his own level of support could have resulted in his own displacement by the third candidate. Such was the fate of two incumbent Fine Gael TDs in Dublin South-East and Louth.

In other words, by pursuing this new strategy, the party is asking its incumbent TDs to take a risk with their own careers in the interests of overall party growth. Whether the individual incumbents will be willing to accept such a risk in the future is debatable. To be sure, there are compensations. Those TDs who did accept the party's recommendations were rewarded with senior positions when the new Fine Gael-Labour government came to office in November. But if an individual incumbent does not expect the party to be successful nor to be able to repay loyalty with jobs after the election and if he believes his own seat to be insecure anyway given the flow of opinion away from his party, then it is unlikely that he will rank the party interest before his own. A party may be more successful if it can persuade its notables to be more altruistic. Altruism itself is really only an attractive option, however, when the party is likely to be successful in the first place. When the electoral chips are down, it may be a case of every incumbent for himself.

Conclusions

1. Irish voters are party voters. Because the STV electoral system also allows Irish voters to be candidate voters, however, the real question is which comes first. For the bulk of *partisan* voters—that is, those voters who give the entire party ticket their highest preferences—it seems that party preference comes first and candidate preference second. This is certainly the case for those voters defined as pure partisans and issue-oriented conditional partisans. For a third group of voters, though, the particularistic conditional partisans,

the candidate comes first, and they support the party because it is the candidate's party rather than vice versa.

2. For those voters who choose party first, national as opposed to local concerns seem to be growing in importance. Certainly, the increased competitiveness of recent Irish elections has also seen a major increase in the organizational resources and activities of the parties at the national level. In addition, it is becoming evident that an ever-growing proportion of the party propaganda emanates from the parties at the national level.

3. For those partisans who choose the candidate first, the strategies adopted at the local level are clearly more important, because nomination strategies and candidate selection remain largely in local hands.

4. What is of more general interest, however, is that even these apparently local-level strategies increasingly tend to be controlled by the parties at the national level, with the fusion of both local and national campaigns. In other words, the parties' central offices not only are accumulating more resources, but also are exerting more influence in what has traditionally been the exclusive preserve of the constituency organizations. While this is particularly true in the case of Fine Gael, there are also indications of the development of a similar approach in Fianna Fáil.[45] Indeed, Fianna Fáil first employed these techniques with the imposition of sixteen additional candidates in 1977, while Labour attempted to exert a similar type of control in 1969 when, following an annual conference decision in 1967, the Administrative Council of the party ruled that all outgoing TDs should take at least one running mate. As it happened, two Labour TDs defied the ruling, while a third refused to defend his seat under these conditions. These refusals, together with the unhappy experience of those who accepted the ruling, led to the repeal of the strategy in 1972.[46]

5. The final point to consider is the possible threat posed to the parties by this new strategy of national control over local organizations. To the extent that national control is in the interest of the party and runs counter to the perceived self-interest of individual candidates or incumbents, then attempts to enforce such control may lead to individual resignations, personalized factional splits, and the like. If the party is likely to increase its support or win government, then there is a greater incentive for the individual candidate or incumbent to be altruistic. If the party is itself under threat of defeat, however, it is unlikely that the individuals within it will be willing to put their personal needs in second place. The seemingly inexorable rise in Fine Gael in 1981 and 1982 thus afforded the national party considerable strength in dealing with its local organizations. In the case of Fianna Fáil, however, the party's apparent decline, particularly in the Dublin region, suggests that it will experience considerably more difficulty in attempting to exert its national authority in a similar way.

Notes

1. Irish Marketing Surveys, *Political Opinion Poll June 7-8, 1981* (Dublin: IMS, 1981), table 30.
2. Basil Chubb, "'Going About Persecuting Civil Servants': The Role of the Irish Parliamentary Representative," *Political Studies* 11, no. 3 (1963): 272-86.
3. R. K. Carty, *Party and Parish Pump: Electoral Politics in Ireland* (Waterloo, Ontario: Wilfrid Laurier University Press, 1981), p. 62.
4. Ibid., p. 68.
5. Ole Borre and Daniel Katz, "Party Identification and Its Motivational Base in a Multiparty System: A Study of the Danish General Election of 1971," *Scandinavian Political Studies* 8 (1973): 69-111.
6. Philip E. Converse, "Of Time and Partisan Stability," *Comparative Political Studies* 2, no. 2 (1969): 139-71.
7. Irish Marketing Surveys, *RTE "Survey"-Politics* (Dublin: IMS, 1976), tables 27 and 28; and *A Survey of Public Opinion* (Dublin: IMS, 1977), tables 3 and 4.
8. John Coakley, "The Referendum and Popular Participation in the Irish Political System" (ECPR Joint Sessions: University of Lancaster, 1981), p. 26.
9. Calculated from data in table 1 of Michael Gallagher, "Party Solidarity, Exclusivity and Inter-Party Relationships in Ireland, 1922-77: The Evidence of Transfers," *Economic and Social Review* 11, no. 1 (1978): 19-32.
10. Carty, *Party and Parish Pump*, p. 120.
11. See Michael Marsh, "Localism, Candidate Selection and Electoral Preferences in Ireland: The General Election of 1977," *Economic and Social Review* 12, no. 4 (1981): 267-86; A. J. Parker, "The 'Friends and Neighbours' Voting Effect in the Galway West Constituency," *Political Geography Quarterly* 1, no. 3 (1982): 243-62.
12. Overnomination (when the number of candidates nominated by a party is significantly greater than the number of seats it hopes to win) has long been regarded by the parties as a serious strategic error. For a political science discussion of the strategy, see Arend Lijphart and Galen Irwin, "Nomination Strategies in the Irish STV System: The Dáil Elections of 1969," *British Journal of Political Science* 9, no. 3 (1979): 362-69; Richard S. Katz, "But How Many Candidates Should We Have in Donegal? Numbers of Nominees and Electoral Efficiency in Ireland," *British Journal of Political Science* 11, no. 1 (1981): 117-22.
13. Parker, "'Friends and Neighbours.'"
14. Marsh, "Localism," p. 285.
15. See Michael Gallagher, *Electoral Support for Irish Political Parties 1927-1973* (Beverly Hills: Sage, 1976), pp. 63-69.
16. See Peter Mair, "Analysis of the Results," in Ted Nealon and Seamus Brennan, eds., *Nealon's Guide to the 22nd Dáil and Seanad Election '81* (Dublin: Platform Press, 1981), pp. 150-54.
17. See Stefano Bartolini and Peter Mair, "The Class Cleavage in Historical Perspective: An Analytical Reconstruction and Empirical Test" (Paper prepared for a conference, DVWP Fachtagung, University of Mannheim, 1983), table 1.
18. See Peter Mair, "Analysis," and "Muffling the Swing: STV and the Irish General Election of 1981," *West European Politics* 5, no. 1 (1982): 76-91.
19. Interview with the author, 11 November 1980.
20. Quoted in Kathleen Joan Kenny, "The Political System of the Irish Republic: Two and a Half Parties in a Developing Nation (Ph.D. diss., Syracuse University, 1972), p. 403.
21. See Barry Desmond, "Submission to the Administrative Council's Sub-Committee," mimeographed (Report prepared for the Labour party's Administrative Council, 1966), pp. 8-9.
22. See, for example, Michael Gallagher, *The Irish Labour Party in Transition 1957-82* (Dublin: Gill and Macmillan, 1982), pp. 31-32.

23. See Peter Mair, "Distracting Choices under the Single Transferable Vote," in Bernard Grofman and Arend Lijphart, eds., *Electoral Laws and Their Political Consequences* (New York: Agathon Press, 1985).

24. A. S. Cohan, R. D. McKinlay, and Anthony Mughan, "The Used Vote and Electoral Outcomes: The Irish General Election of 1973," *British Journal of Political Science* 5, no. 4 (1975): 363–83.

25. A private poll commissioned by Fine Gael showed that 76 percent of respondents were aware of its publication, as against 62 percent awareness of the much more sober coalition program.

26. *Irish Times*, 11 June 1981.

27. This as well as other information, unless otherwise stated, is drawn from interviews with various party officials.

28. See Peter Mair, *The Changing Irish Party System* (London: Frances Printer, forthcoming).

29. Interview with the author, 3 November 1978.

30. Honorary Secretaries' Report to the 1980 *Árd-Fheis*, p. 2.

31. See Paul Sacks, *The Donegal Mafia* (New Haven, Conn.: Yale University Press, 1976).

32. Ibid., p. 109.

33. Compare Vincent Browne, ed., *The Magill Book of Irish Politics* (Dublin: Magill Publications, 1981), p. 5.

34. It is interesting to note in passing that, probably as a result of the increased campaign effort in these constituencies, the more marginal the constituency, the higher was the level of turnout (r = .58) and, to a lesser extent, the Fianna Fáil vote (r = .36).

35. Interview with the author, 10 June 1981.

36. The list of constituencies is shown in an internal Fine Gael document entitled *Interim Report from the Constituency Review Committee* (August 1982).

37. Fine Gael, *A New Deal for Dubliners* (Dublin: Fine Gael, 1981).

38. *Irish Times*, 10 June 1981.

39. See the superbly analyzed example in Sacks, *The Donegal Mafia*, chapter 7.

40. Carty, *Party and Parish Pump*, table 6.2, p. 115.

41. Michael Gallagher, "Candidate Selection in Ireland: The Impact of Localism and the Electoral System," *British Journal of Political Science* 10, no. 4 (1980): 489–503.

42. The 1951–77 figures come from Carty, *Party and Parish Pump*, p. 115. The later figures are calculated from the official results published by the stationery office.

43. This and subsequent information comes from the Fine Gael document entitled *Interim Report from the Constituency Review Committee* (August 1982); see also Peter Murtagh, "Refined FG Strategy Paid Off," *Irish Times*, 29 November 1982; Vincent Browne, "How the Fine Gael Whiz-Kids Sold Us a Taoiseach," *Magill*, December 1982, 4–16.

44. Murtagh, "Refined FG Strategy."

45. See the report in the *Irish Times*, 24 March 1983.

46. See Michael Gallagher, *The Irish Labour Party*, p. 102.

5 Government Formation and Ministerial Selection

BRIAN FARRELL

————The governments of the Irish political system have customarily emerged from clear-cut choices registered in general elections; for long periods of time parties have alternated little in office. A Taoiseach (prime minister) has begun with a popular mandate and with a reasonable expectation of being able to determine the time and circumstances of the next dissolution so as to anticipate a further term. The Taoiseach has chosen a cabinet to accommodate various strands of opinion and to cooperate without undue internal dissension and with broad-based support from parliamentary and constituency parties. These cozy conventions were shattered in the crowded five years after the 1977 general election.

It can no longer be assumed that Irish general elections will give simple answers to the question, who forms government? The relationships between government and Dáil, between party leader and deputies, and between different parties in postelectoral periods that had seemed set in the formal processes of the inherited Westminster model were strained by the circumstances created by the three elections of 1981–82. The responses and reactions of politicians to those events seemed to breach hitherto accepted standards of behavior.

So many changes in such a short time make it doubtful that the system will ever revert to its earlier, more relaxed, and slow-moving mode of ministerial and government replacement. Serious considerations must therefore be given to issues of government formation, ministerial selection and deployment, and executive leadership.

Government Formation

Under the Irish constitution it is the function of the Dáil to nominate the Taoiseach and approve the nomination of the members of the government.[1] The Taoiseach holds office until he either resigns or ceases to retain the support of a majority in the Dáil. But the exercise of these powers has invariably been formal. In the period 1922–77 there were nineteen general elections. On only one occasion, in 1948, was a postelection negotiation between parties required to ensure the formation of a government; in all other cases the Dáil votes merely ratified the outcome of elections. Similarly there were only two occasions, in 1938 and 1944, when a Taoiseach failed to retain the support of a Dáil majority. In both cases the Taoiseach was de Valera; he sought and obtained a dissolution and returned with an overall majority. In the whole period only two incumbent heads of government resigned: in 1959, on his election as president, de Valera stepped down and the Dáil nominated his chosen successor, Sean Lemass; on the resignation of the latter in 1966, the Dáil confirmed the newly elected leader of Fianna Fáil, Jack Lynch, as Taoiseach. On no occasion did the Dáil replace one government with another without the intervention of a general election. Remarkably, throughout the period, the electoral system used was the single transferable vote (STV) system of proportional representation.

The record seems typical of competitive two-party systems, with simple plurality voting. In theory such a working model produces single-party majority governments and contributes to, if it is not responsible for, a stable political system. At first glance, Ireland fits the model. A summary of Irish electoral history and government formation indicates five distinct periods: a decade, 1922–32, in which Fine Gael's predecessor (Cumann na nGaedheal) was in government; sixteen years, 1932–48, of Fianna Fáil government; an uncertain decade, 1948–57, in which a fragile coalition replaced Fianna Fáil in two of four elections; a further sixteen-year dominance of Fianna Fáil, 1957–73; and most recently, in 1973, a National Coalition served a four-year term and then was replaced by a Fianna Fáil majority government. Overall, then, forty-five years of single-party administrations were punctuated by three coalitions totaling ten years in office.

In the light of that experience it is easy to explain the evident hegemony of the executive in the Irish system. Despite the operation of the single transferable vote system of proportional representation, a small number of highly disciplined parties dominate. Despite the constitutional provisions, the Dáil is reduced to a highly formal role in the formation of government, merely registering in its parliamentary liturgy the choice already made by the electorate. There has been no apparent need to develop any machinery or conventions to ease government formation.

This summary obscures, however, other complex features of the Irish system. In particular it ignores the fact that single-party governments have often been in a minority position, depending on the support of deputies outside their ranks, and have often had recourse to prematurely early elections to enhance their parliamentary support. As table 5.1 indicates, single-party majority

Table 5.1 Irish governments, September 1922–December 1982

		Nature of government and duration		
Government	Date of appointment	One party with majority of own supporters	One party without majority of own supporters	Coalition
Pro-treaty[a]	September 1922	1 year[f]		
Cumann na nGaedheal	September 1923	3 yrs., 9 mos.[f]		
Cumann na nGaedheal	June 1927		4 mos.	
Cumann na nGaedheal	October 1927		4 yrs., 5 mos.[g]	
Fianna Fáil	March 1932		11 mos.	
Fianna Fáil	February 1933	4 yrs., 5 mos.		
Fianna Fáil	July 1937		11 mos.	
Fianna Fáil	June 1938	5 yrs.		
Fianna Fáil	July 1943		11 mos.	
Fianna Fáil	June 1944	3 yrs., 8 mos.		
Inter-Party[b]	February 1948			3 yrs., 4 mos.
Fianna Fáil	June 1951		3 yrs.	
Inter-Party[c]	June 1954			2 yrs., 10 mos.
Fianna Fáil	March 1957	4 yrs., 7 mos.		
Fianna Fáil	October 1961		3 yrs., 6 mos.	
Fianna Fáil[d]	April 1965	4 yrs., 3 mos.		
Fianna Fáil	July 1969	3 yrs., 8 mos.		
National Coalition[e]	March 1973			4 yrs., 4 mos.
Fianna Fáil	July 1977	4 yrs., 4 mos.		
Coalition[e]	June 1981			8 mos.
Fianna Fáil	March 1982		9 mos.	
Total		34 yrs., 8 mos.	14 yrs., 9 mos.	11 yrs., 2 mos.
Coalition[e]	December 1982			

Sources: Basil Chubb, *Cabinet Government in Ireland* (Dublin: Institute of Public Administration, 1974), and additional material by author.
a. From spring 1923 called Cumann na nGaedheal.
b. A coalition of all parties except Fianna Fáil. It also included independents.
c. A coalition of Fine Gael, the Labour party, and Clann na Talmhan.
d. Fianna Fáil won exactly half the seats.
e. A coalition of Fine Gael and the Labour party.
f. Government majority due to the fact that Fianna Fáil, the biggest opposition party, did not take their seats.
g. The government had the support of the Farmers' party, which, however, ceased to operate as a party; its members for all intents and purposes became members of Cumann na nGaedheal. In 1930 the government resigned after a parliamentary defeat but immediately renominated.

Table 5.2 Fianna Fáil share of first-preference vote, 1932-1944

Election	Percentage share
1932	44.5
1933	49.7
1937	45.2
1938	51.9
1943	41.9
1944	48.9

Source: Ted Nealon and Seamus Brennan, eds., *Nealon's Guide to the 22nd Dáil and Seanad Election '81* (Dublin: Platform Press, 1981).

governments in Ireland have been less frequent than has been supposed. They have also been more often subject to internal tensions or protected by particular circumstances than had been supposed. It is only against this record that the problems of the most recent Irish single-party government, the Haughey administration of 1979-81, can be understood.

Single-Party Majority Government. The Cosgrave administration of 1923-27 suffered two major internal upheavals. In 1924 the army crisis led to the resignation of two ministers from government; nine deputies resigned their seats and precipitated a mini-general election.[2] The premature disclosure of the Boundary Commission report precipitated a further ministerial resignation in 1925.[3] More importantly, the government's Dáil majority was entirely due to the parliamentary abstention of Sinn Féin (subsequently Fianna Fáil).

In the first three cases of majority government under de Valera there were no serious internal tensions. That achievement has often been attributed to the charismatic leadership exercised by "the Chief,"[4] but there were also special circumstances helping to maintain that majority consensus. Each case was inaugurated by a general election taking place within eleven months of the last election, increasing Fianna Fáil's share of the first-preference vote in successive pairs of general elections as shown in table 5.2.

Between 1933 and 1937 Fianna Fáil was intent on implementing a relatively radical program that included a new constitution; it was a time for the party to stay united in fulfilling the aims for which it was founded. The pressure of international circumstances helped to sustain the unity and discipline of the only Irish government to serve its full term, 1938-43. The de Valera government of 1944-48 saw an erosion of the party support, as evidenced in the vote for an independent republican candidate in the presidential election of 1945 and the subsequent by-election successes of the new Clann na Poblachta;[5] it was not a climate to encourage internal dissent.

There was a change of party and government leader in each of the next two majority governments: 1957-61, 1965-69. Significantly, on each occasion the new leader (Lemass in 1959, Lynch in 1966) made only minimal changes in ministerial personnel—symbolic recognition by experienced senior politicians of the need for careful and cautious management.[6] Lynch's majority government of 1969-73 was severely shaken by the revelations of the arms crisis in 1970, the sudden dismissal of two senior ministers, and the resignation of two others. The reverberations of the affair were to disturb the latest majority administration formed after the 1977 general election.

As the scale of the 1977 election victory unfolded on the night of the count, party leader Jack Lynch commented on television that he anticipated problems. A greatly enlarged back bench and an influx of new deputies were certain to intensify internal party competition. As discussed below, Lynch's ministerial selection was cautious, conservative, and careful to encompass all who might be reasonably considered as alternative leaders. That list included Charles Haughey, dismissed from office by Lynch seven years earlier. The inclusion of so many potential successors and the exclusion of so many newer deputies did not appear to affect Lynch's control of government. It did strain his control of the party, contributed to a division between the front and back benches of the parliamentary party, and encouraged some division between party activists and parliamentarians.

The cracks in party unity and discipline evident during the arms crisis reappeared as individual deputies put forward their own views on Northern Ireland, security, and economic issues. Behind the facade of loyalty, the criticism of Lynch's leadership was converting into an unspoken challenge. Tensions grew as the Lynch government found it increasingly difficult to cope with industrial relations, was forced to reverse a controversial farm levy, provoked a negative response from workers aggrieved by the pay-as-you-earn (PAYE) taxation system, and experienced escalating electoral decline in local and European elections and by-elections. These tensions did not force Lynch's resignation; any grumbling that did appear was far from a putsch. But they did contribute to Lynch's decision to move forward the date of his resignation announcement.

The tensions also contributed to the bitter leadership contest that developed. Fianna Fáil had no previous experience of managing such acute internal divisions. On de Valera's resignation in 1959, Lemass had succeeded without any contest; even the doubtful were ready to close ranks and prepare to fight the next election as a united party. On Lemass's resignation in 1966, a number of contenders appeared, including Charles Haughey, George Colley, and Neil Blaney; none had a clear majority. When Lynch emerged as the clearly acceptable candidate, only George Colley persisted. The vote was decisive: Lynch, 51; Colley, 19.

Circumstances were different in 1979.[7] There were only two candidates,

Haughey and Colley. Each claimed to be able to command a majority. Indeed there is some evidence to suggest that Lynch would have persisted in the leadership had he not been assured that Colley's camp had such a majority.[8] In fact, there was no clear consensus within the parliamentary party. The contest was to be sharp and extremely divisive.

Colley had the support of the party establishment: an overwhelming majority of the cabinet, the leader of the Senate, the former general secretary of the party and the senior members of its national executive, and Lynch's tacit backing. Haughey had used the period of his political exile in the early 1970s to develop a dense network of contacts with local constituency parties and their activists. With a hard core of loyal supporters inside the parliamentary party, he could offer new horizons for backbenchers fearful of electoral defeat as well as greater opportunities for those ready for office.

Since the two men had contested the leadership in 1966, they had come to represent distinct elements within Fianna Fáil. That was reflected in a difference of style, tone, and image. Colley was the mature moderate, committed to the party's ideals, emphasizing its cultural and moral values, its prudence, caution, and balance. Haughey was the rebel—activist, ambitious, adventurous; he used the party's republican rhetoric and was identified with its thrusting economic pragmatism. Beneath these differences were basic, little noticed similarities: they came from comparable social backgrounds, attended the same school, acknowledged a common partisanship, and were contemporaries who had experienced professional success in the 1950s and political promotion in the 1960s.

Both differences and similarities encouraged an emphasis on personality rather than on political issues. Each side's zealous crusade for its own man reflected a deep distrust for the opponent—a rift that would not be easily healed. There was considerable pressure brought on deputies to win votes and rumors of tactics that went beyond acceptable limits. The flow of information and misinformation encouraged speculation that senior deputies had been promised ministerial advancement in return for support; that, too, would fuel future disharmony. But more than anything else, the closeness of the vote fostered disunity. Haughey's 44 to 38 margin over Colley in the parliamentary party was too close for comfort.

Haughey's selection of ministers, discussed below, was necessarily circumscribed. It was necessary to find room for newer deputies and reasonable to promote those who had supported his candidacy. But dismissing four ministers to the back benches was a danger. Haughey's authority was also weakened by an enforced agreement giving Colley, reappointed as Tanaiste (deputy prime minister), a virtual veto on nominations of the two key security ministries, Justice and Defence. That represented a withholding of trust in a secret understanding that quickly became public. The Tanaiste went further in a carefully phrased speech that condemned earlier open criticism of Lynch's leadership, alleged that this had altered the conventions of party discipline, and distinguished his own professed loyalty to the new Taoiseach from what was interpreted as only qualified loyalty to the party leader.[9] In effect it was a challenge. In earlier times it would have been inconceivable; its occurrence would have merited dismissal. That no action was taken reveals something of the new uncertainties about the nature of political authority, the extra pressures created for a challenged Taoiseach, and the new strains imposed on single-party majority government as Ireland entered the 1980s. The implications for the exercise of executive leadership in a cabinet government will be discussed in the last section of this chapter.

It is sufficient here to note that the uncertainties, the pressures, and the strains were responsible for Haughey's decision, apparently made soon after his election, to secure a personal mandate from the electorate. He had inherited a historic parliamentary majority; it was evident, with the more balanced constituency revision, that victory on such a scale could not be repeated. That parliamentary majority, however, had been sharply divided; it was important for the Taoiseach to secure his own majority, however slight. He had also inherited a deteriorating economic situation in which existing expansionist policies were inappropriate. The policy changes now required would be severe and unpopular; it seemed reasonable to hold an election and secure a new mandate before embarking on such a course. The decision to call an election in 1981 did not produce majority single-party governments. It did expose new problems for coalition and minority governments.

Coalition and Minority Government. In its first sixty years Ireland had experienced three periods of coalition government.[10] The first, the Inter-Party government (1948–51), was the product of pragmatic political necessity rather than any coherent theory of sharing executive power. It was formed as the only way of forcing Fianna Fáil out of office after sixteen years in government. It embraced the full spectrum of Irish parliamentary opinion: five separate parties and a heterogeneous collection of independents were required to surpass the majority party. None of these groups had campaigned on a proposed coalition alternative to single-party government. This was the first occasion on which it could be said that the formation of government was totally divorced from the explicit choices offered to the electorate. It was determined by private negotiation among senior political leaders.

Perhaps because of its evolution this first Inter-Party government deviated from some of the established cabinet norms maintained by single-party governments. There was some weakening of the strict conventions of collective responsibility. The authority of the Taoiseach—the last post filled in postelectoral negotiation between the parties—was significantly curtailed. While individual ministers scored some notable policy successes, there was a diminution of coherence and control that contributed to the downfall of this first Inter-Party administration.

Yet, once this loose alliance had been formed, it was accepted as offering an alternative to single-party government. In the next three elections the parties campaigned separately on their own programs but with a declared willingness to share executive power. The second Inter-Party government (1954–57), though encompassing a smaller spread of parties, was essentially a direct descendant of its predecessor; eight of the thirteen members, including Taoiseach and Tanaiste, had served in the earlier administration. That ministerial experience, the more compact coalition grouping of just three parties, and the enhanced authority of a Taoiseach in office for the second time, made it easier to maintain the discipline and established cabinet conventions in this second Inter-Party government.

Defeat in 1957 and an analysis of a new Labour leadership disenchanted with the coalition experience cleared the way for a series of Fianna Fáil successes. In turn, these prompted a reappraisal and the search for a new coalition understanding, both of which had progressed further than generally recognized when the 1973 election was called. Fine Gael and Labour were able to conclude a formal preelection pact. They offered themselves to the electorate as the National Coalition, with an agreed-upon fourteen-point "Statement of Intent." [11]

This third coalition was more compact and cohesive than the earlier examples; in Brian Chubb's words, "much less a government of parties." [12] The enhanced degree of group loyalty in the cabinet was revealed in two difficult situations: when the Taoiseach and another minister voted against the government's Family Planning Bill and subsequently when intemperate remarks by the minister for defense led to the resignation of the president. These were more than just political embarrassments; they raised fundamental constitutional and ideological questions. But the coalition held. There were no resignations.

That constancy in government was mirrored in the loyalty of the parliamentary parties. Among party voters, however, a clear divergence was revealed in the analysis of the 1977 general election results. [13] An examination shows that, where the opportunity arose, 72 percent of Fine Gael supporters allotted their lower-order preferences to Labour, marginally more than in 1933. Comparable Labour transfers to Fine Gael fell from 71 percent in 1973 to 59 percent in 1977.

The results renewed the debate on coalition especially within Labour, as discussed in the first chapter. The outcome was a more cautious approach and an innovation in the hitherto simple arrangements for coalition government formation between party leaders: the introduction of a postelection special delegate conference to determine whether or not the Labour party should agree to participate in any proposed coalition. While this was in some measure a response to a desire among party activists to restrict the power of the leader and parliamentary party, it could also be argued that it strengthened the leader's hand in conducting negotiations with the more powerful coalition partner.

The experience of 1981 suggests that it had no appreciable effect on either side. Michael O'Leary, newly elected leader of the parliamentary party, was committed to the view that Labour should participate in government and confident that this reflected the view of the electorate. Garret FitzGerald, prospective Taoiseach and advocate of a social-democratic emphasis in Fine Gael, was ready to meet any reasonable demands. The two men had served as ministers in the previous National Coalition. Negotiations between them, although judiciously managed to suggest some hard bargaining, were amicable and easy. The subsequent Labour special delegate conference provided an opportunity to air anticoalition rhetoric and express reservations about the vagueness of the arrangement. The majority of delegates were ready enough to endorse the agreement made by the leader. It was evident that, under these circumstances, the special delegate conference was largely confined to a liturgical function; it had no effective role in government formation.

Similarly the special meeting of the Fine Gael parliamentary party to endorse the agreement, held on the same day, was entirely formal. But other problems remained to be solved before a government could be formed. A Dáil majority had to be secured.

In a number of earlier Irish minority governments the dominant party had resorted to a variety of devices to ensure support. After the September 1927 election the leader of the Farmers' party had been appointed as one of five parliamentary secretaries; the party virtually ceased to exist as a national organization and was, in effect, swallowed up by the government party it had consistently supported.[14] In 1932 de Valera undertook to consult with the Labour leadership on future legislation as the price of its support in the division lobbies.[15] It was not a successful venture. Neither then nor subsequently, however, did Fianna Fáil deviate from its rejection of any formal coalition arrangement. Typically, de Valera preferred to resolve the doubts and uncertainties of minority government by having recourse to an early general election. On three occasions (1933, 1938, 1944), this resort to premature dissolution was rewarded by overall parliamentary majorities.

The election of 1948, unique in so many ways, created a coalition stretched across the whole Irish political spectrum. It was less surprising that such a fragile combination should be dissolved by internal dissent than that it should ever have been formed and maintained. "It was nothing more than an extreme form of coalition, put together by party leaders after the election results were known, and based on a statement of future policy which represented a highest common factor of agreement."[16]

In 1951–54 and again in 1961–65, de Valera and Lemass each found themselves forming minority single-party governments.[17] Although there were suggestions that the support of independent deputies had been secured by promises of political favor, particularly on the latter occasion, the evidence suggests that in both cases the fear of an early dissolution was sufficient incentive to keep votes on the government side. Certainly, independent deputies supporting this latter government had considerable ease of access to ministers and, it can be assumed, had a more privileged status than party backbenchers. While these independents benefited in terms of ensuring enhanced capacity to satisfy their own constituents, there is no evidence to suggest that they had any influence either on the general direction of government policy or on the control of parliamentary dissolution.

New Pressures in the 1980s. These conventions, too, were breached in the minority governments of the 1980s. The first FitzGerald coalition of 1981 came to power with the critical support of an independent deputy; Jim Kemmy, in voting, made it clear that he recognized unpopular decisions lay ahead and undertook to support the new government for a reasonable period of time. The discipline of that support, his acknowledged preference for Fitz-Gerald over Haughey, and their shared commitment to a pluralist approach on constitutional issues may have lulled coalition ministers and managers into complacent neglect of the care needed to sustain minority government. In essence, it was Kemmy's vote on the budget that defeated this government. That fact, combined with Kemmy's successful reelection, warned Irish governments that the old rule that independents never provoked dissolutions no longer obtained.

Following the indecisive outcome of the February 1982 general election, the position of the independent and smaller party deputies was again crucial to the formation of government. As discussed in a previous essay,[18] the tactical decision of the three Workers' party deputies not to reveal their intentions inflated the value of independent deputy Tony Gregory's vote. As a result, he was able to negotiate an unprecedented bargain of specific undertakings for his constituents. This did more than underline the fragile parliamentary base of the Haughey minority government. It also increased the traditional competitive constituency pressures on all deputies to promote and secure local issues and demands as their primary function. The fact that both major party leaders had been prepared to make a deal put each under pressure from deputies in their own parties to tailor national policies to local exigencies. It also exposed them to external pressure groups that could threaten to wean voters from traditional partisan allegiances if their demands were not met.

If the Gregory deal dented the relative autonomy of government control of public policy, the failure to formalize the relationship of the Haughey minority government and the Workers' party created another problem. Since there was no agreement, there was no way of predicting how these critical parliamentary votes could be guaranteed; every division became a test of government survival. That uncertainty fed a more general sense of instability. When it appeared to suit the Workers' party, in November 1982, they switched sides and brought down the government. The weapon of parliamentary dissolution had been effectively removed from the government's armory.

The outcome of the election once again left government formation in the hands of the party leaders. Neither Fianna Fáil nor Fine Gael were in a position to form an administration without Labour support. Within the Labour party, the internal debate on coalition was unresolved and remained divisive. In theory, Labour could refuse to support either major party and either force a "good alliance" or, more realistically, precipitate yet another general election; Labour could support one or the other as a minority government; it could join one or other in another coalition. In practice, Fianna Fáil's adamant refusal to consider coalition and the perceived popular rejection of any further period of government instability reduced the option to a single choice: another Fine Gael-Labour coalition.

The results of the November 1982 election brought Fine Gael to a historic high point where it could credibly challenge the fifty-year-old hegemony of Fianna Fáil. It could not form another government without Labour backing. FitzGerald appreciated the strength of anticoalition feeling within the Labour party and understood that the new Labour leader would need to appear to strike a hard bargain. The negotiations between FitzGerald and Dick Spring were again marked by judicious leaks about the difficulties of concluding agreement and stories of Spring's insistence on promoting Labour policies. The eventually agreed-upon *Programme for Government*, as noted earlier,[19] was a carefully couched document designed to maximize support within Labour. Once again the party leaders had managed to translate the electoral outcome into a team for government.

The experience of these three general elections indicates both the enduring strengths and the new challenges to the established conventions affecting government formation in the Irish system. The historical record traced above shows that the apparent dominance of the single-party majority government model is misleading. Present electoral arrangements and the narrow ideological and social cleavage between the major parties suggest that variations of the coalition and minority models are more likely in the future. The intervention of independent and smaller-party deputies in close parliamentary divisions and the continuing local and pressure-group influence point to the need for more definite procedures (perhaps drawing on the European experience of coalition formation)[20] and possibly for more time (between dissolution and the summoning of a new Dáil) to permit government formation. In particular, it seems likely that Fianna Fáil will be forced to reconsider its traditional opposition to coalition. Any general consideration of government formation in the Irish system must also examine and affect the selection and deployment of ministerial personnel.

Ministerial Selection

In the small world of Irish politics few parliamentarians have achieved government office. Even fewer have ascended the greasy pole to become head of government (either as president of the Executive Council or as Taoiseach). The senior echelons of the Irish political elite, sheltered by low rates of turnover, have remained small; a relatively closed world, predominantly male, middle-class, and middle-aged. Once appointed, ministers have typically enjoyed extended periods in office. Resignations, retirements, demotions, and dismissals have been rare. There has not been much room for newcomers. This changed in the 1980s.

The change was most marked at the top of the ministerial ladder. In the first half-century of the independent state, 1922 to the 1973 general election, only five men had headed Irish government (William T. Cosgrave, Eamon de Valera, John A. Costello, Sean Lemass, and Jack Lynch). Within the next decade, 1973–82, three new names were added to the list (Liam Cosgrave, Charles J. Haughey, and Garret FitzGerald). Inevitably such rapid and frequent changes in leadership led to a much more extensive turnover among the rest of the ministerial elite (see table 5.3).

Over the first quarter-century of the state's existence from 1922 to the 1948 general election, only thirty men, evenly divided across the basic cleavage, held office. Over the next decade, from that election to the retirement of de Valera as Taoiseach in 1959, a further twenty-five were recruited. In the following twenty years under Lemass, Lynch, and Cosgrave as successive Taoisigh, thirty-six new ministers were appointed. But the pace of recruitment quickened in the troubled world of Irish politics in the 1980s; a total of twenty-six new ministers were appointed in the three years from Haughey's first government in 1979 to FitzGerald's second coalition in 1982.

This represented a considerable change from the earlier Irish pattern of long ministerial service and aging cabinets documented by Chubb.[21] It marked a less cautious approach to ministerial selection, whether prompted by a Taoiseach's need to respond to the professional ambitions of newer backbenchers or by his desire to form administrations closer to his own perspective within the party. There is a marked difference between the evident effort made by Lynch and Cosgrave to choose ministers across the whole spectrum of their

Table 5.3 Recruitment of ministers to Irish governments, 1922–1982

Period in office	Taoiseach	Size of original government	New ministers	Replace-ments and new appoint-ments	Total number of new ministers
September 1922– September 1923	W. T. Cosgrave	10[a]	10[a]	—	10
September 1923– June 1927	"	11[b]	1	3	4
June 1927– October 1927	"	10	—	—	—
October 1927– April 1930	"	10	1	—	1
April 1930– March 1932	"	10	—	—	—
Total new appointments under	W. T. Cosgrave				15
March 1932– February 1933	E. de Valera	10	10[c]	—	10
February 1933– July 1937	"	10	1	1	2
July1937– June 1938	"	10	—	—	—
June 1938– July 1943	"	10	—	—	—
(Reorganization, September 1939)	"	10	1	—	1
July 1943– May 1944	"	11	1	—	1
May 1944– February 1948	"	11	—	1	1
February 1948– June 1951	J. A. Costello	13	11	1	12
June 1951– June 1954	E. de Valera	12	2	—	2
June 1954– March 1957	J. A. Costello	13	5	1	6
Total new appointments under	J. A. Costello				18
March 1957– June 1959	E. de Valera	11	3	2	5

Table 5.3 *(continued)*

Period in office	Taoiseach	Size of original government	New ministers	Replacements and new appointments	Total number of new ministers
Total new appointments under	E. de Valera				22
June 1959– October 1961	S. Lemass	13	2	1	3
October 1961– April 1965	"	14	1	1	2
April 1965– November 1966	"	14	3	1	4
Total new appointments under	S. Lemass				9
November 1966– July 1969	J. Lynch	14	—	1	1
July 1969– March 1973	"	14	2	1	3
(Reorganization May 1970)	"	14	4	—	4
March 1973– July 1977	L. Cosgrave	15	13	1	14
Total new appointments under	L. Cosgrave				14
July 1977– December 1979	J. Lynch	15	5	—	5
Total new appointments under	J. Lynch				13
December 1979– June 1981	C. J. Haughey	15	5	2	7
June 1981– March 1982	G. FitzGerald	15	9[d]	—	9
March 1982– December 1982	C. J. Haughey	15	3	1	4
December 1982	G. FitzGerald	15	6	1	7
Total new appointments to date under	C. J. Haughey				11

Table 5.3 *(continued)*

Period in office	Taoiseach	Size of original government	New ministers	Replacements and new appointments	Total number of new ministers
Total new appointments to date under	G. FitzGerald				16
Total ministerial appointments, 1922–82					118

Source: Compiled by the author.
a. Includes Cosgrave and three "extern" (see Basil Chubb, *Cabinet Government in Ireland* [Dublin: Institute of Public Administration, 1974], pp. 23–24); though for our purposes all are listed as "new ministers." Cosgrave and three others (MacNeill, McGrath, Hogan) had been members of the seven-man provisional government established by Collins in January 1922.
b. Includes Cosgrave and four "extern" ministers.
c. Includes de Valera, who had been head of the Dáil Éireann governments, 1919–22.
d. Includes James Dooge, technically appointed only on taking his seat in the Senate.

parliamentary parties and the selections made by Haughey and FitzGerald. The change in the age structure of more recent cabinets has, however, been less dramatic than might have been expected (table 5.4). These data support more general findings of age levels of Dáil deputies that indicate the tendency for candidates to establish a professional or business career before seeking election.[22] A separate examination of the new entrants into the last four governments reveals that the later ministers are typically in their early forties when appointed (table 5.5).

Other changes are also evident. The familial relationships that have marked both parliamentary and governmental elite appear less often among the most recent generation of ministers. Only three of the eleven new ministers appointed under Haughey are close relatives of former politicians; two of these appointments were made subsequent to the formation of government. In FitzGerald's case the change is even more marked: while four of his fifteen new ministers are related to former politicians, all are nominees of the Labour party. This is a further indicator of the extent to which, under FitzGerald, Fine Gael has become a "new" party under an old label.

In all stable, competitive parliamentary systems the freedom of the head of government to appoint ministers must of course be balanced by considerations of politics and prudence. Cabinets should reflect the generational, ideological, and sometimes regional range of the party's representatives. Rivals have to be accommodated and critics assuaged. Earlier Irish Taoisigh were

Table 5.4 Average age of ministers for selected governments, 1965–1982

Taoiseach/ government	Date	Party	Average age
Lemass/ last government	April 1965	Fianna Fáil	49
Cosgrave	March 1973	Fine Gael & Labour	48
Lynch/ last government	July 1977	Fianna Fáil	50
Haughey/ first government	December 1979	Fianna Fáil	46.5
FitzGerald/ first government	June 1981	Fine Gael & Labour	48
Haughey/ second government	March 1982	Fianna Fáil	47
FitzGerald/ second government	December 1982	Fine Gael & Labour	44

Sources: Basil Chubb, *Cabinet Government in Ireland* (Dublin: Institute of Public Administration, 1974), p. 85; author's calculations from data in Ted Nealon, ed., *Ireland: A Parliamentary Directory*, for the years 1965–82.

Table 5.5 Average age of new ministers, 1979–1982

Taoiseach/government	Number of ministers	Average age
Haughey/first government	5	42
FitzGerald/first government	9	43
Haughey/second government	3	41
FitzGerald/second government	6	43

Sources: Author's calculations from data in the series of *Nealon's Guides*.

prepared to operate within these limitations. They were ready to continue or renew ministers in office long after their competence or usefulness would justify, rather than risk internal upheaval. They worked with the ministers they inherited rather than indulging their personal preferences. They were also less subject to pressure for promotion from backbenchers.

The criteria for ministerial selection and deployment in the Irish political system have yet to be probed systematically.[23] Capacity has not appeared to be the critical priority. Instead, parliamentary seniority, geographical location in relation to party electoral advantage, and closeness and personal loyalty to the leader have all been mentioned as significant.

The evidence of the last three general elections suggests that seniority is no longer a dominant consideration; it had already been on the wane. Six of the fifteen members of the National Coalition, 1973–77, had only served a single parliamentary term. Only one of the five new men appointed to Lynch's last government had served two full terms, and one (Martin O'Donoghue) was nominated on his first day in the Dáil (table 5.6).

Reduced emphasis on seniority is also evident in the choices made by the two most recent Taoisigh. Their cabinets have tended to have a considerably lower accumulation of parliamentary experience, even when service in the Senate is included, than earlier Irish administrations. There has been greater willingness to nominate newer deputies and an evident desire by each Taoiseach to select within their party colleagues who share their own distinctive philosophies. Neither man, however, has had a free hand. Internal party tensions and the requirements of coalition have restricted both Haughey and FitzGerald in their exercise of the Taoiseach's prerogative to form government.

As noted earlier, Haughey faced considerable internal opposition in creating his first administration in 1979.[24] Given the close outcome of the leadership election, there was a risk that some members of the parliamentary party might refuse to vote for his confirmation by the Dáil. Rarely has a prospective Taoiseach experienced such determined restrictions in his government formation. After protracted negotiations to ensure the support of former cabinet colleagues, Haughey only secured the services of his old rival, George Colley, by agreeing that he would be given an economic ministry and have a virtual veto on the ministerial appointments to the departments of Justice and Defence. On the other hand, Haughey dropped four of the cabinet ministers from Lynch's last government. The five new ministers nominated in the formation of this government and two subsequently appointed were all identified as loyal supporters in Haughey's leadership bid.

Table 5.6 Parliamentary experience of ministers of new Irish governments, 1979–1983

Taoiseach/government	Earliest date of election								
	1954	1957	1961	1965	1969	1973	1977	1981	1982
Haughey/ first government		3	1	3	4	2	2		
FitzGerald/ first government	1		1	4	4	1	3	1	
Haughey/ second government		2		2	3	3	5		
FitzGerald/ second government				2	5		4	3	1

Source: Author's calculations from data in Ted Nealon, ed., *Ireland: A Parliamentary Directory*, for the years 1979–83.

Note: Experience is counted from earliest election to either Dáil or Senate. By-elections are included within the life of each Dáil.

Haughey experienced further difficulties in forming his second administration but was able to reward loyalty and secure a team closer to his own wishes. Colley declined a cabinet post when Haughey refused to reinstate him as Tanaiste because of his open participation in the recent abortive leadership challenge. Instead, Haughey nominated a close and loyal supporter since the time of the arms crisis as both Tanaiste and minister of finance. Three other loyal lieutenants, initially nominated as ministers of state in the first Haughey administration, were now promoted to full cabinet rank. In all, eight of his fourteen ministers had been first nominated to the cabinet by Haughey. In this, too, there was a perceptible weakening of the seniority principle: three of the four new ministers to this short-lived government had only entered the Dáil at the 1977 general election.

The circumstances of coalition circumscribed FitzGerald's freedom in forming government; he had no say in the choice of Labour ministers. He experienced few restraints, however, in selecting the Fine Gael members. In 1981 he ignored the seniority claims of three former ministers of the Cosgrave coalition, allotted the major portfolio of Agriculture to a newly elected deputy, and entrusted the Department of Foreign Affairs to a close confidant who was appointed to the Senate as a nominee of the Taoiseach.[25] Three of his new Fine Gael ministers had only served a single parliamentary term. The selection of the team was tilted toward FitzGerald's own image of Fine Gael as a modern or "new" party; it was not designed to please the longer-serving conservative wing of the "old" parliamentary party.

In his second experience of government formation during December 1982, FitzGerald again exercised his personal judgment in choosing the ten Fine Gael nominees. He did not, on this occasion, exercise the Taoiseach's constitutional right to nominate ministers from the Senate; his previous experiment had generated considerable criticism on the back benches. He had already arranged for one senior former minister to become Ceann Comhairle (chairman of the Dáil), and another former minister had opted for the freedom to criticize from the back benches. Of the three replacements only one (Austin Deasy, named to Agriculture) was identified as an internal party critic of FitzGerald; the other two new ministers belonged to the "new" Fine Gael— one first elected in the 1981 election, the other in the February 1982 election. In an even more striking exercise of the Taoiseach's right to name and allocate ministerial duties, FitzGerald arranged that only one of the seven Fine Gael ministers renominated from the former coalition was given the same portfolio. There had been no comparable cabinet reshuffle since de Valera's reorganization of the government at the outset of World War II in 1939.[26] Such an extensive redeployment of ministerial talent suggests that the Taoiseach had either considerably revised his initial assessments of his team's individual abilities or wished to distance himself from controversial decisions associated with

Table 5.7 Regional distribution of ministers in recent Irish cabinets, 1973–1982

Cabinet	Dublin	Rest of Leinster	Munster	Connacht	Ulster	Total
Cosgrave, 1973	8	4	2	—	I	15
Lynch, 1977	4	2	6	2	I	15
Haughey, 1979	4	3	5	2	I	15
FitzGerald, 1981	6ᵃ	5	2	I	I	15
Haughey, 1982	5	2	4	3	I	15
FitzGerald, 1982	5	6	3	I	—	15

Source: Author's calculations from data in Ted Nealon, ed., *Ireland: A Parliamentary Directory*, for the years 1973–82.
a. Includes Senator James Dooge.

particular ministers in his first team. It could scarcely be expected that such an extensive redistribution of ministerial resources after such a very short period in office would enhance the working efficiency and administrative control of the new government. On the other hand, it did exhibit the central power and influence of the Taoiseach.

This examination of ministerial selection by the two most recent Taoisigh suggests that personal loyalty has become an increasingly important criterion. What of regional electoral considerations in affecting choice? Although it is part of popular mythology that a Taoiseach's choice is strongly swayed by "the need to strengthen the party in a vital area by giving a post to someone from that area,"[27] the evidence on this point in regard to cabinet positions is not persuasive (table 5.7). Geographical considerations do not appear to have influenced the earliest leaders. In his last cabinet Lemass selected two ministers representing the same Dublin constituency, and both Donegal and Mayo were given two ministers each; only three ministers were appointed from the whole of Munster, two of them representing urban constituencies.[28]

In Lynch's case the cabinet seemed to tilt south and west in regional composition. Two of the three new ministers appointed at the time of the arms crisis in 1970 were from Munster, the other from Connacht. Only four of the fifteen members of his last cabinet represented Dublin constituencies. By comparison, eight of the fifteen members of the Cosgrave coalition (including three of the five Labour ministers) were Dublin-based; no member of that government came from Connacht, only one from an Ulster constituency.

The change from Lynch to Haughey redressed the regional balance. In both the cabinets formed by Haughey there was an evident concern to achieve some even geographical spread and a sensitivity to constituency reactions. Undoubtedly some changes were based on the desire to reward loyalty and penalize internal opponents. But on two occasions, in 1979 and 1982, when dropping western-based ministers Haughey was careful to substitute deputies from the same constituencies to his cabinets.[29] In both cabinets the distribution of posts avoids any undue favoring of the heavily populated Dublin and eastern regions and gives symbolic recognition to traditional sources of Fianna Fáil support in the west and south. Donegal, however, was not represented—probably in deference to the strength of Haughey's former colleague, "Independent Fianna Fáil," Neil Blaney. The "Ulster seat" was awarded to the critical five-seat constituency of Davan-Monoghan.[30]

FitzGerald's two cabinets fly in the face of the received wisdom on the need for geographical spread and regional balance. There is a preponderance of members from the Dublin and Leinster regions and a marked absence of western- and northern-based ministers. The selection has been subject to newspaper and popular criticism on the score that the Taoiseach prefers to surround himself with a "Donnybrook set" in government. Donnybrook is a desirable residential area in the south Dublin suburbs and the charge suggests a clique drawn from a professional, fashionable, and economically privileged class. Supporters claim the ministerial selection reveals a willingness to concentrate on competence rather than on electoral advantage. It is perhaps noteworthy that FitzGerald's sole "Ulster seat" initially maintained a ministerial presence in the Cavan-Monoghan constituency; subsequently the nomination of the minister as Ceann Comhairle (chairman) effectively converted this into a four-seat constituency.[31] But the evidence certainly suggests FitzGerald's virtual indifference to location as a significant criterion for selecting government ministers.

The same thing cannot be said for the distribution of junior ministerial appointments. The office of minister of state was instituted in 1978 to replace the former position of parliamentary secretary. At the same time the number of posts was increased from seven to ten; an additional five positions were created in legislation introduced by Haughey. These junior ministers, who are not members of the cabinet, only have access to the government through the minister in whose department they are located. In all Irish governments two junior ministers fulfill the functions of chief whip and responsibility for the Board of Works; other responsibilities are allocated depending on the particular burdens of government and the wishes of individual Taoisigh and ministers.

In the past, leaders have often seen the junior appointments as a form of governmental apprenticeship as well as a means of stiffening local electoral support.[32] Technically the appointments are a function of the government as a whole; in practice they are part of the parliamentary patronage at the disposal of the Taoiseach (table 5.8).

More recent Taoisigh have been more open in the exercise of that patronage and in their nominations have been apparently more concerned about combining rewards for personal loyalty with party electoral advantage. In 1979

Table 5.8 Regional distribution of junior ministers
in recent Irish administrations, 1973–1982

Administration	Dublin	Rest of Leinster	Munster	Connacht	Ulster	Total
Cosgrave, 1973	2	1	3	1	—	7
Lynch, 1977	3	1	1	2	—	7
Haughey, 1979–80[a]	3	4	1	7	—	15
FitzGerald, 1981	4	4	4	1	1	14
Haughey, 1982[b]	2	3	2	3	—	10
FitzGerald, 1982	5	3	4	3	—	15

Sources: Author's calculations from data in the series of *Nealon's Guides* and *Magill Books of Irish Politics*.
a. Combines the initial ten appointments in December 1979 and five further appointments in March 1980, following new legislation.
b. Appointments made, March–June 1982. There were five vacant offices when the 23rd Dáil recessed in July 1982.

Haughey dropped four of the ministers of state appointed under Lynch (three others were promoted to cabinet rank) and promoted seven backbenchers who had been prominently associated with his leadership bid. He also ensured a wide geographical spread and reinforced this with five further junior appointments in March 1980. The distribution indicated a sensitivity to satisfying constituencies (Carlow-Kilkenny, Galway West, Mayo West) that had lost ministers in the transition from Lynch; local party agitation was responsible for the reinstatement of Denis Gallagher, dropped from the cabinet, as minister of state. It was also noted that in a number of cases Haughey rewarded constituencies with second appointments (Clare, Galway West, Mayo West), and these were seen as efforts to promote deputies who had supported his candidacy. In forming his 1982 administration Haughey dropped three of his former junior nominees and demoted two cabinet ministers to ministers of state. He also left five vacancies, a decision alternately interpreted as an economy measure or as a way of exercising control over his parliamentary party by withholding rewards.[33] The ten appointed, however, were again judiciously scattered throughout all regions.

FitzGerald's selection of junior ministers in 1981 was less evenly spread geographically. Of the fourteen, two were newly elected and three others had served a single parliamentary term. While the selection could be seen as an effort to ensure a ministerial presence in key constituencies, it was generally seen as reinforcing FitzGerald's determination to promote those who shared his own vision of Fine Gael. On his return to power in 1982, he appointed the full complement of fifteen ministers of state; eight of these were new appointments. Five former Fine Gael ministers of state were dropped; four had been first nominated by FitzGerald the previous year, and the other was the sole junior minister surviving from the Cosgrave coalition of 1973-77. Four of the six new ministers appointed had less than a year's parliamentary service. The selection of this second team suggested some concern for geographical spread (although considerably tilted toward the eastern regions) but more significantly rewarded a high proportion of the new Fine Gael parliamentarians.

It seems clear that the somewhat cynical view of ministerial selection as primarily a calculation of appointments designed to maximize electoral support does not survive scrutiny. On the other hand, the search for talent is guided by criteria other than simple professional capacity and competence. In particular, recent Taoisigh seem to have placed more emphasis on promoting members who share their own views rather than necessarily accommodating the whole spectrum of party opinion. This may be a further indication of a subtle but decisive change in the role of Taoiseach in the Irish political system.

Executive Leadership

The office of Taoiseach is at the critical center of public decision making in Ireland. The incumbent is easily the most powerful figure on the Irish political stage. Traditionally, the role has been seen as that of chairman rather than of chief. Many factors have all combined to limit the exercise of executive leadership: the constitution and the legal system, the processes of cabinet government and civil service procedures, the familiar and ambiguous public attitudes to authority, the pressures of party colleagues and supporters, and the patterns and practices established by predecessors. Other considerations have focused increasing attention on the persona of the leader: inherited campaigning methods and modern marketing techniques alike make this individual the symbol of the party. Domestically, the Taoiseach is the arbiter of internal bureaucratic and political wrangles; internationally, the spokesman of the nation and its representatives at bilateral and European Community "summits." The media and public opinion polling have both accepted and abetted these emphases; there is constant pressure to play the role of chief.

Neither of the most recent holders of the office has successfully resolved these conflicting tensions. Each may be said to have contributed to them. Haughey's own persona has been perceived as a central issue within and between parties. FitzGerald has effectively created a new and larger Fine Gael around what was once little more than a faction. Each man has attempted to put a personal stamp on the formation, style, and direction of government. Both have suffered failures and have been blamed for electoral defeats. The contrast and conflict between Haughey and FitzGerald have been central to Irish electoral politics in the 1980s.

There have been some less obvious similarities in the contributions of both men to the development of the Irish executive tradition. Under both the size and influence of the Taoiseach's department within the public service have grown far beyond the model of the small private office that seemed sufficient for earlier leaders. This, coupled with frequent changes of minister, may well have contributed to a decline in the authority of the Department of Finance; it may also have increased the tendency of other departments and ministers to refer relatively minor but contentious issues to the Taoiseach in cabinet as final arbiter. Certainly, the expansion of the press relations function as well as the trend toward centralized decision making has reinforced a presidential tendency in the role of Taoiseach. To some extent, this may be seen as an inevitable consequence of developments in the European Community as basic decision making has shifted from the formal institutions established under the Treaty of Rome to the regular meetings of heads of government. This mirrors the movement toward summitry as a means of resolving Anglo-Irish tensions. It also is the outcome of a concentrated phase of continuous electioneering.

Whatever the causes, there is a significant shift toward elevating the role of Taoiseach. Implicit in that movement is a reshaping of the relationship between Taoiseach and government ministers, manifest to date in a more frequent change of ministers. In the future more frequent change at the top may be demanded.

In the early 1970s it was possible to stress the importance of stability in a small liberal-democratic state system. In the 1980s more dynamic forces come into play for an Ireland struggling to maintain and raise living standards for a rapidly growing population in a small open economy buffeted by a worldwide recession induced by successive oil crises. The result has been to increase the load of government decision making. External forces restrict the range of choices. At the same time domestic constraints (a relatively underdeveloped economy, a narrow tax base, small home market) and inflated expectations— in part fueled by past political promises and rhetoric—intensify pressures. In such a situation the head of government is virtually thrust into the role of chief, a style of executive leadership that imposes strains on the existing framework of governmental administration. Such strains are likely to demand considerable structural adjustments; they are also likely to impose greater penalties for political failure.

Notes

1. The standard account is Basil Chubb, *Cabinet Government in Ireland* (Dublin: Institute of Public Administration, 1974).
2. Maryann Gialanella Valiulis, *Almost a Rebellion: The Irish Army Mutiny of 1924* (Cork: Tower Books, 1985).
3. Geoffrey Hand, "MacNeill and the Boundary Commission," in Francis X. Martin and Fran-

cis J. Byrne, eds., *The Scholar Revolutionary* (Shannon: Irish University Press, 1973), pp. 199ff.

4.   Cf. Brian Farrell, "De Valera: Unique Dictator or Charismatic Chairman?" in John P. O'Carroll and John A. Murphy, eds., *De Valera and His Times* (Cork: University Press, 1983), pp. 35ff.

5.   Cf. Maurice Manning, *Irish Political Parties* (Dublin: Gill and Macmillan, 1972), pp. 102–3.

6.   For Lemass's view see Brian Farrell, *Sean Lemass* (Dublin: Gill and Macmillan, 1983), pp. 101ff.

7.   A detailed account of the background is given in Vincent Browne, "The Making of a Taoiseach," *Magill*, January 1980.

8.   Personal information. Lynch's preference was for a younger successor, Desmond O'Malley, but the latter was unwilling to split the opposition to Haughey.

9.   The text of Colley's speech is given in the *Irish Times*, 21 December 1979.

10.   For a recent discussion and fuller references see Brian Farrell, "Coalitions and Political Institutions," in Vernon Bogdanor, ed., *Coalition Government in Western Europe* (London: Policy Studies Institute, 1983).

11.   Text of "Statement of Intent," in Ted Nealon, ed., *Ireland: A Parliamentary Directory, 1973–74* (Dublin: Institute of Public Administration, 1974), pp. 68–69. On the formation of the National Coalition, see Maurice Manning, "The Political Parties," in Howard R. Penniman, ed., *Ireland at the Polls: The Dáil Election of 1977* (Washington, D.C.: American Enterprise Institute, 1978), pp. 91–92.

12.   Basil Chubb, *The Government and Politics of Ireland*, 2d ed. (London: Longman, 1982), p. 195.

13.   See Richard Sinnott, "The Electorate," in Penniman, *Ireland at the Polls*, p. 63.

14.   On the Farmers' party, see Manning, *Irish Political Parties*; Warren Moss, *Political Parties in the Irish Free State* (New York: Columbia University Press, 1933).

15.   On Labour involvement, see Brian Farrell, *Chairman or Chief? The Role of Taoiseach in Irish Government* (Dublin: Gill and Macmillan, 1971), pp. 36–37.

16.   Chubb, *Cabinet Government*, p. 41.

17.   See Farrell, *Sean Lemass*, pp. 120–21.

18.   Brian Farrell, "The Context of Three Elections," chap. 1 of this volume.

19.   Ibid.

20.   For a recent discussion, see Bogdanor, *Coalition Government*.

21.   Cf. Chubb, *Cabinet Government*, pp. 82ff.

22.   David M. Farrell, "Irish Parliamentary Representation: A Socioeconomic Study of Dáil Eireann" (Master's thesis, University College, Dublin, 1980); see appendix. For a useful summary, see David M. Farrell, "Age, Education and Occupational Backgrounds of TDs and 'Routes' to the Dáil: The Effects of Localism in the 1980s," *Administration* 32, no. 3 (Autumn 1984).

23.   For preliminary discussion, see Brian Farrell, *Chairman or Chief?* pp. 9ff, and Basil Chubb, *Government and Politics*, pp. 186ff.

24.   Farrell, "Context of the Three Elections."

25.   Under the British constitution, the Taoiseach nominates eleven members of the sixty-strong Seanad (Senate). The constitution also provides that no more than two members of the government (excluding Taoiseach, Tanaiste, and minister for finance) may be nominated from the Seanad. Only one such senatorial minister had been appointed, in de Valera's last cabinet, 1957. For a discussion of the issue, see Farrell, *Chairman or Chief?* pp. 15–16.

26.   For details and discussion of this government reorganization, see Farrell, *Lemass*, pp. 53–55.

27.   Chubb, *Cabinet Government*, p. 87. Cf. Farrell, *Chairman or Chief?* pp. 10–11. More colloquially this aspect is discussed in terms of "distributing Mercs" (the state-supplied cars

and drivers regarded as an important symbol of ministerial power and influence). The view has been promoted in journalism by John Healy (formerly "Backbencher") in the *Irish Times*. He is also responsible for the term "half-car" applied to junior ministerial appointments discussed below.

28. Farrell, *Chairman or Chief?* p. 11, lists only two Munster ministers because of the erroneous omission of Dr. P. J. Hillery of Clare.

29. In 1979 Maire Geoghegan-Quinn replaced fellow Galway West deputy Bobby Molloy. In 1982 two Clare deputies, Prendan Daly and Sylvester Barrett, exchanged status; the former promoted from minister of state to government minister, the latter demoted.

30. There is no consciously established convention that a cabinet seat be located in one of the three Ulster counties in the republic, though they have often been favored. Indeed, between 1922 and 1954 every cabinet included at least one minister born in Northern Ireland. Insofar as sensitivity to northern representation is a relevant criterion, the Louth constituency (often favored in ministerial selection) might be included.

31. Tom Fitzpatrick became Ceann Comhairle of the Twenty-fourth Dáil. Since the outgoing Ceann Comhairle is automatically deemed to be reelected, there are now only four contested seats in Cavan-Monoghan.

32. Farrell, *Chairman or Chief?* pp. 14-15.

33. Cf. comment by Denis Coughlan, "Haughey May Leave Junior Posts Unfilled," *Irish Times*, 31 August 1982.

6 Women and the Elections

MAURICE MANNING

Background: 1922–1977

As far as the role and participation of women in politics were concerned, the years after the achievement of Irish independence were disappointing. At one level, the absence of women in politics was surprising because the new state had begun its life in 1922 with universal suffrage and firm guarantees against any discrimination on the ground of sex. Moreover, women had been actively and prominently involved in the Sinn Féin movement. In fact, one of the leading women of the time, Countess Markievicz, had been appointed minister for labour in the first republican government in 1919. At another, perhaps more realistic level, however, the political culture of the new state—authoritarian, conservative, and male-dominated—was hardly promising for women. Those who had come to prominence during the independence period, surely atypical of the majority of Irish women, were almost certainly better suited to the flamboyance of a revolutionary period than to the dull realities of politics in postindependence Ireland. Nor was the low level of women's political participation after the initial burst particularly strange. Duverger has pointed out that it was not unusual for women to be very involved in significant numbers immediately after the gaining of suffrage, but to lapse into apathy afterwards.[1]

The decades after independence justified this observation and belied earlier expectations that women would be active and numerous in political life. In 1952, thirty years after independence, fewer women were in elected politics than had been the case in 1922, and their impact and effectiveness were undoubtedly less than in the early stages. In the Dáil of 1923, for example, there were five women members, the highest number elected to the Dáil until the election of 1977, when six were returned. Moreover, it was not until 1977 that a woman was appointed minister of state (junior minister), while the first woman was not actually appointed to the cabinet until 1979.

From 1922 to 1977, of the 650 elected to the Dáil, only 24 were women—
just 4 percent. Moreover, of these women in elected politics during the first
fifty years of the state, almost all had one thing in common—they were in
some way related to dead male TDs or were connected to national figures
either as a widow, sister, or daughter. Only five of the twenty-four could be
said to have succeeded in politics on their own, and of these five, only one
served more than one term of office.

Nor is the picture radically different from the situation in the upper house,
the Senate. During the life of the first Senate (1922–36), six women were
elected at different stages to the sixty-member chamber. Unlike the position in
the Dáil, however, some of these were women of outstanding quality whose
political promotion was entirely based on their own merits. In the second
version of the Senate, that established under the 1937 constitution, nineteen
women in all were elected in the period between 1938 and 1977—that is,
nineteen women over a total of thirteen Senate elections. Two aspects of this
low level of women's representation in the Senate are striking. First is the fact
that eleven of the Senate seats after each election are nominated directly by the
Taoiseach, who could, if he so wished, have used this device to redress the
obvious imbalance in representation. No Taoiseach, however, used this power
to this end or even adverted to it as something that needed to be done. The
second surprising aspect is that even after the 1977 election, only three women
had been elected from the university panels. The country's university graduates elect six of the Senate's seats, and presumably here the women's movement should have been making breakthroughs at an earlier stage. Indications
were, though, that the issue of increased women's representation was becoming
significant.

At the regional level, the failure of fifteen of the country's twenty-six
counties ever to elect a woman TD in the period up to 1977 highlights the
underrepresentation of women in national politics even further. In fact, the
number of women candidates available to the electorate has always been very
small. In addition to the twenty-four successful candidates, only sixty-five
women have ever stood for the Dáil in nineteen general elections, with over
half of that number standing for minor parties or as independents. In other
words, most women who aspire to election did not even pass the first hurdle,
that of getting past the party delegates and party organizations. In its own way,
that is a cruel indication of how the party activists assessed the importance of
women in politics and their realistic chances of electoral success.

One further background point needs to be made about the position of
women in Irish politics after independence. The traditional routes of entry to
Irish politics have been involvement in the "national" movement, relationship
to a sitting TD or membership of a political family, prominence in sporting, or,
more recently, public or media activity and involvement in local politics. Re-

cently, involvement in local politics has been the most usual and most effective method of entry.

County councils and city corporations are especially useful to candidates who wish to build up a political profile and provide the constituency service on which to base their attempts at Dáil election. Women's position at the local level was not much better, however. In the local elections of 1934, thirteen women were elected over a total of twenty-seven local councils. Thirty-three years later, in 1967, the situation had hardly improved at all. In the county council elections of that year, twenty women were elected out of a total of 687 councillors. In the subsequent local elections in 1974, attention was paid to women's issues, and women's pressure groups attempted to promote their own candidates. In addition, by 1974 all parties were committed, at least in principle, to the idea of having more women in politics. The electorate was well admonished as to its duty in this regard. This pressure, however, had little effect. Of the twenty-seven county councils, eight still had no woman councillor, and in all, only twenty-seven women councillors were elected—just seven more than in 1967. In overall terms in 1974, this represented about 5.7 percent of the total number of seats held at all levels throughout the country.[2]

Thus, in the half century after independence, the impact of women on Irish politics in both numerical representation and quality of that representation has been slight. Indeed, it is difficult to ignore the judgment of one leading feminist and historian, Dr. Margaret McCurtain, who wrote in 1978: "Irish women in post revolutionary Ireland did not make the political traditions; they inherited them from fathers, husbands and brothers."[3]

Developments after 1977

This lack of electoral success tended to obscure significant developments in other areas. As in many other countries, the media increasingly focused on the role of women and on the activities of women's organizations. Programs specifically devoted to women's issues, forcefully presented, and often radical in content, became a regular feature of Irish radio and television. This was true too of the national newspapers, though with differing degrees of emphasis. In addition, a number of publications exclusively designed to cater to what was seen as the new mood and needs appeared. In general terms, the 1970s saw the emergence of a confident, articulate, at times aggressive, if not always coherent, lobby, whose differing views were very easily subsumed into what was broadly labeled the women's movement. Some of these women quickly established themselves as national figures. Issues such as contraception, divorce, and sexual discrimination in many areas, and other topics that had previously been all but ignored now featured regularly, undoubtedly creating a new awareness.

This new interest was reflected in the increase in the number of women's organizations from eighteen national voluntary groups in 1970 to fifty-five such groups in 1981. From a political point of view, perhaps the most significant was the establishment in 1971 of the Women's Political Association (WPA), a nonpartisan organization that focused its attention on the need for greater involvement of women in the decision-making process. What made it different from other such groups was its concentration on educational and practical support for women candidates in their attempts to gain positions of influence in the different political parties and in seeking nomination for elective office. The WPA, however, was only one in this new proliferation of women's organizations, which ranged from moderate organizations aiming for legislative changes, equality legislation, and better social services, to radical groups that concentrated their attentions more on such major but still deeply sensitive issues as contraception, divorce, and abortion.

As in other countries, the impact of the women's movement was felt in two particular ways; it helped to politicize women's issues and bring them to public attention, while it also created public personalities of some of the women who came to be closely identified with particular causes. This politicization process, while attracting attention, was still confined to a small proportion of the total female population. Nonetheless, there was both impact and response. In 1979 the government awarded the Council for the Status of Women consultative status. The new leader of Fine Gael, Garret FitzGerald, set out specifically to win the support of women voters and to attract able and active women candidates. The number of women in trade union politics increased, as did the visibility of leading women party members. Women's groups formed within the major political parties. Legislation too reflected this trend, with laws enacted for equal pay, the establishment of an Equality Employment Agency, and the introduction in 1979 of an (admittedly restrictive) contraception act.

The European parliamentary elections and local elections of 1979 provided an ideal opportunity to test whether this progress had been real and effective, or merely illusory. In the European elections, of forty-six candidates, five were women, and after the ballots were counted, women had won two of the fifteen seats. What is significant, however, is that Garret FitzGerald chose to use the elections to introduce a new type of woman candidate—women who had no party political background, but who were recognized "stars" of the women's movement. Two such, Nuala Fennell and Monica Barnes, made their debut for Fine Gael. In spite of reservations and at times hostility from traditional elements in their new party, each performed well, though not actually winning seats.

Whether their presence and the new interest of all parties in women's issues decided many voters, outweighing traditional issues and loyalties, is difficult to say. Their presence, however, clearly helped draw women's organi-

Table 6.1 Women candidates elected in the 1979 local elections

Councils	Fianna Fáil	Fine Gael	Labour	Others
County Councils 698 Seats	9	19	4	2
Boro' Councils 108 Seats	4	4	2	3
Total 806 Seats	13	23	6	5

Source: Department of the Environment, Franchise Section.

zations that had tended to avoid partisan politics into the electoral debate. The two women elected, however, were from the traditional mold: Sile de Valera, twenty-four-year-old granddaughter of Eamon de Valera, was elected for Fianna Fáil in Dublin, and Eileen Desmond, who first came into politics in 1965 as a widow, but who had since established a solid personal reputation, was elected in Munster for Labour.

The woman's issue was less obvious in the local elections, though here again, the Fine Gael party, in the process of rebuilding itself after the traumatic defeat of 1977, consciously sought out new women candidates. As an opposition party whose own internal structures were undergoing transformation, apparently Fine Gael had greater flexibility in this regard than Fianna Fáil had. The overall results reflected this flexibility. Overall then, the local elections of 1979, coming after a decade of publicity and organization by various sections of the women's movement, could hardly be seen as a significant advance or breakthrough (see table 6.1). The only point of difference between this and earlier elections was the high number of new women councillors with obvious Dáil potential and ambition. Almost half the women candidates elected were from Fine Gael, which won twenty-three seats as against thirteen for Fianna Fáil, six for Labour, and five others (see table 6.1). Overall, however, the gains made were slight. Still only forty-seven councillors out of a total of 806—just over 6 percent—were women, a fractional improvement on the situation five years earlier. Nor was there any real advance in the major urban centers. Thirteen of the 108 seats in the four main cities were won by women—four each to Fianna Fáil and Fine Gael, two to Labour, and three to others.

The June Election of 1981

Fine Gael took the initiative in seeking women's votes in the June election in two ways: first, by running more candidates than any other party (sixteen, as against ten for Fianna Fáil and ten for Labour) and also by some of its policy proposals (see table 6.2). Of the thirty-six candidates nominated by the major parties, only five were outgoing—three from Fianna Fáil and one each from Fine Gael and Labour. What distinguished the Fine Gael list from the other parties was the continuation of the party's policy of running "name" candidates from the women's movement, a tactic that the party first attempted in the European parliamentary elections. One result of this, however, was the heightening of tension and the creation of opposition in many constituencies where the new candidates were seen as having been imposed to the exclusion of long-serving local members.

The second aspect of Fine Gael's approach that attracted attention was the controversial proposal to pay £9.60 per week to wives working at home as part of a transfer from their husbands' tax credit. This scheme, which was never implemented, became a major talking point, arousing a great deal of skepticism and not a little opposition. It was also seen as an earnest statement (if a somewhat gimmicky one) of Fine Gael's intention to push the women's issue high up on the agenda for the election debate.

In the election, the only winning candidate from the women's movement was Nuala Fennell for Fine Gael in Dublin South. What was more significant was the composition of the eleven new TDs, seven of whom were elected for the first time. Although five of the eleven were of the traditional mold, with strong family backgrounds in politics, the remaining six had no such ties. For the first time the majority of women elected had broken from the traditional mold, and now, as with their male colleagues, four of the six owed their election in a large part to their participation in local government.

FitzGerald's first administration formed after the election had a woman, Eileen Desmond, in the senior Ministry of Health and Social Welfare and also saw the appointment of a junior woman minister to that same department. In the Senate election that followed, nine of the sixty members elected were women—the highest total ever. The party breakdown here was: Fine Gael five; Fianna Fáil two; Labour one; Independents one. Of that nine, only two could be said to have come from a politically active background. Perhaps most significant, though, was the appointment by Garret FitzGerald of Gemma

Table 6.2 Women candidates, per party, June election 1981

Parties	Candidates per party	Candidates elected
Fianna Fáil	10	4
Fine Gael	16	6
Labour	10	1
Others	5	0
Total	41	11

Source: Department of the Environment, Franchise Section.

Table 6.3 Women candidates, per party, February election 1982

Parties	Candidates per party	Candidates elected
Fianna Fáil	11	2
Fine Gael	11	5
Labour	5	1
Others	8	0
Total	35	8

Source: Department of the Environment, Franchise Section.

Hussey as Leader of the House, with a wide-ranging mandate to increase its workload and update its procedures.

In spite of this, however, women's issues never really achieved primacy in the short lifetime of the first FitzGerald administration, which was dominated by, and subsequently fell on, economic issues. The £9.60 proposal had not been fully implemented by the time the government fell. Indeed, when serious questions were raised about its feasibility, no subsequent attempt was made to revive it.

The February Election of 1982

The February 1982 election, precipitated by the government's budget defeat, was fought almost entirely on the larger question of the management of the economy, and the question of women's issues figured less than in the previous election. Fianna Fáil, now in opposition, somewhat surprisingly made no attempt to match Fine Gael in attracting star candidates, and when the list of candidates was published, there were no real surprises (see table 6.3).

Four of the outgoing women TDs lost their seats. Of these, three — Madeleine Taylor of Fine Gael, and Carrie Acheson and Eileen Lemass of Fianna Fáil — lost to male colleagues of their own party, while the conservative Alice Glenn of Fine Gael, who incidentally had been hostile to many aspects of the women's movement, lost her seat to the Independent, Tony Gregory. The only gain among women candidates was in Fine Gael, where Gemma Hussey, Senate leader and one of the most prominently identified members of the moderate section of the women's movement, won a seat in the highly marginal Wicklow constituency.

Little changed in the overall level of representation in the Senate. With one woman senator less than in the previous election, Fine Gael remained the largest party with four seats, Fianna Fáil had two, Labour one, and one (nominated) Independent. The circumstances surrounding Charles Haughey's return to power left little room for detailed discussion of women's issues, and the eight months from then until his government's defeat in November were domi-

163

nated by the Gregory deal, the change in economic policy, and internal party dissension in Fianna Fáil.

The cabinet was once again exclusively male, with the demotion of Maire Geoghegan Quinn to junior minister status. In the Senate, Charles Haughey did nominate one woman member, Camilla Hannon, leader of the Irish Countrywomen's Association, and supported the nomination of Tras Honan as the Speaker of that body, the first time the position had been held by a woman.

The November Election of 1982

Although the second election of 1982 was once again a crisis election, by now candidates and support patterns in various constituencies had become fairly well established. The only new woman candidate of significance to emerge was Lady Valerie Goulding, nominated by Fianna Fáil in Dun Laoghaire. Lady Valerie, a widely respected and well-known worker in medical rehabilitation, had been nominated to the Senate in 1977 by Jack Lynch. Fianna Fáil strategists saw her as somebody who could counter the appeal of Monica Barnes in Dun Laoghaire. Otherwise, parties had a clear idea where gains could be made. The candidate list, which was much less speculative than in previous elections, reflected this certainty. This time, just thirty-two women candidates appeared on the list, though it was significant that only twenty-three of these were nominated by the three main parties, as against thirty-six women candidates in the June election of 1981. Clearly the parties now knew where gains could be made and were unwilling to run superfluous or "no hope" candidates.

In this third election with fewer women candidates than in either of the previous elections, the number of women elected reached an all-time high of fourteen (see table 6.4). Among the fourteen elected were three who had lost their seats eight months earlier, while the three new women TDs, Mary O'Rourke of Fianna Fáil and Monica Barnes and Avril Doyle of Fine Gael, were all of ministerial caliber. What was also significant was the route of entry to politics of the fourteen women members with the emphasis now moving strongly from the traditional family or inherited seat to other means of entry:

Table 6.4 Women candidates, per party, November election 1982

Parties	Candidates per party	Candidates elected
Fianna Fáil	7	4
Fine Gael	11	9
Labour	5	1
Others	9	0
Total	32	14

Source: Department of the Environment, Franchise Section.

Table 6.5 Age, marital status, and educational levels of
women elected to the Dáil and the Senate, November 1982

	Dáil	Senate
Age		
Under 30	2	0
30–40	5	2
40–50	4	3
50–60	3	1
Over 60	0	0
Marital status		
Married	10	6
Unmarried	2	0
Widowed	2	0
Educational level		
First only	0	0
Second	5	2
Third	9	4

Source: Ted Nealon, ed., *Nealon's Guide to the 24th Dáil and Seanad: 2nd Election '82* (Dublin: Platform Press, 1983).

Table 6.6 Women members of national parliaments and
European Parliament in the European Community

	National			European		
Country	Seats	Women	Percent	Seats	Women	Percent
Belgium	212	16	7.5	24	2	8.3
Denmark	179	42	23.4	16	5	31.2
France	491	21	4.3	81	18	22.2
Great Britain	635	23	3.8	81	11	13.6
Greece	300	14	4.7	24	2	8.3
Ireland	166	14	9.0	15	2	13.3
Italy	630	51	8.1	81	11	13.6
Luxembourg	59	8	13.5	6	2	33.3
The Netherlands	150	22	14.6	25	6	24.0
West Germany	498	52	10.4	81	12	14.8
Total	3,320	263	7.9	434	71	16.4

Source: Information supplied by European Parliament office, Dublin 1984.

five of the women came from a political background, six came from local government, and three came from the women's movement. These gains were not continued in the Senate election that followed, in part because the leading women senators had gained Dáil election. There were now six women senators as against nine after the June election of 1981. The six included Brid Rodgers of the Northern Ireland Social Democratic and Labour party (SDLP), who had been nominated by the Taoiseach. Otherwise, Fine Gael and Fianna Fáil won one seat each, Labour won two, and one went to an Independent senator.

Garret FitzGerald continued the pattern he established in his first administration by filling a senior position in the cabinet with a woman, appointing Gemma Hussey minister for education. In addition, he created a new junior ministry in his own department with special responsibility for women's affairs, a position filled by Nuala Fennell.

Table 6.5 gives a profile of women members elected to the Irish parliament in November 1982. The woman elected to the Dáil will, on average, be younger than her male counterpart, is likely to be better educated or to be educated above the general Dáil average, and, perhaps surprisingly, is likely to combine a full-time political career with family responsibilities.

Conclusion

With a total representation of 8.3 percent, Irish women are not far out of line with the general level of representation in other European Community countries (see table 6.6). Nor is the level of women's representation at ministerial levels all that much different in Ireland, as table 6.7 makes clear.

Nonetheless, a rise of merely eight Dáil members from the six of 1977 to the fourteen of 1982 with no real increase in Senate representation can hardly be seen either as comforting or as a breakthrough. The efforts of the various women's organizations in arousing consciousness and attempting to mobilize a

Table 6.7 Position of women in the governments of the member states of the European Community

Country	Number of ministers	Women ministers	Percent	Number of secretaries of state	Women secretaries of state	Percent
Belgium	15	1	6.66	10	3	30.00
Denmark	21	4	19.04	—	—	—
France	23	3	13.04	19	3	15.78
Great Britain	21	1	4.76	26	1	3.84
Greece	22	1	4.54	28	2	7.14
Ireland	15	1	6.66	15	1	6.66
Italy	30	1	3.33	59	2	3.38
Luxembourg	9	1	11.11	2	0	0
The Netherlands	15	2	13.33	15	3	20.00
West Germany	16	1	6.25	49	1	2.04
Total	187	16	8.55	223	16	7.17

Source: Information supplied by Office of the European Parliament, Dublin.

women's vote has not met with any overwhelming success and certainly not been matched by any dramatic increase in the level of representations. The years 1977–82, however, may well be seen as a watershed period as far as women in Irish politics are concerned, for two main reasons: first, the breaking of the traditional mold whereby virtually the only route of entry to Irish politics open to a woman was through family connections, and, secondly, the emergence of high-quality politicians among the women elected and their ability to show that they are much more than one-issue politicians and beyond any possible charge of tokenism. In the process, this new breed of woman politician has shown an ability to work through and adapt to the party processes in a way that will surely be emulated in years to come.

Notes

1.   Maurice Duverger, "The Political Role of Women," (UNESCO, 1955).
2.   Maurice Manning, "Women in Irish National and Local Politics 1922–1977," in Margaret McCurtain, ed., *Women in Irish Society 1922–1977* (Dublin: Arlen House, 1978).
3.   McCurtain, ed., *Women in Irish Society.*

7 Media Coverage of the Irish Elections of 1981–1982

JOHN BOWMAN

Introduction

Despite some misgivings within their own ranks and criticism from all points in the political spectrum, the Irish media served voters better in the three elections between June 1981 and November 1982 than they had previously done.[1] Coverage of these elections—if not always comprehensive—was voluminous, reflecting the considerable demand for political news and comment from readers, listeners, and viewers. The mass circulation newspapers especially deserve credit for avoiding the trivialization, sensationalism, and apathy prevalent in such papers elsewhere.

In their election coverage, Irish reporters, news editors, special correspondents, broadcasters, and even cartoonists can be classified as belonging to the so-called "sacerdotal style" of election reporting, thinking of themselves as "providing a service" and of an election as "an intrinsically important event" entitled to "substantial coverage as of right." In contrast, the pragmatic school of communicators are to be found editing the front pages and the radio and television news bulletins, their belief being that the election "must fight its way in on its own merits."[2] But even when an election fails to win top news billing in Ireland, the prominence of election news is affected but not its contents or length.

The Press. Every morning the national newspapers—each a newspaper of record—give extensive coverage to the campaign. Indeed, in the three elections here considered other news rarely pushed the election off the front pages. Of 162 election editions of the *Irish Times*, the *Irish Press*, and the *Irish Independent*, no fewer than 141 led with an election topic.[3] The same papers also published approximately one editorial a day—occasionally none and in some editions two. Each morning the readers of these papers could expect

Table 7.1 Editorial coverage of elections,
1969 and 1981–1982 (column inches per issue)

Newspaper	June 1969 election	Average of 1981–82 elections
Irish Independent	381	559
Irish Press	447	587
Irish Times	477	575
Evening Press	n.a.	134
Evening Herald	n.a.	284
Sunday Independent	610	627
Sunday Press	615	624
Sunday World	not published	143
*Sunday Tribune*ᵃ	not published	732
Sunday Journal	not published	285

Source: Tabulated from F. X. Carty, *Elections '82* (Dublin: Able Press, 1983), p. 10. Carty gives separate figures for each election in 1981–82. My figure is an average of Carty's three averages.
Note: n.a. = not available.
a. This newspaper was not published during November 1982 election.

almost 600 column inches of election material. The more serious Sunday papers offered even more; only the evening papers and the popular tabloids, the *Sunday World* and *Sunday Journal*, obliged the election to compete with more sensational material (see table 7.1).

The Irish newspapers have national circulations.[4] The exception is the *Cork Examiner*, whose 70,000 readers are predominatly in the Munster region (see table 7.2). But, like the Dublin-based papers and Radio Telefís Éireann (RTE), it treats election news on a national level. Those who follow an election closely through the media—and Irish voters increasingly get their information that way—read, hear, and see a national debate with the same themes recurring in most media on any given day.

The press is private and Irish-owned, largely serious, and relatively nonpartisan. The *Irish Press* group, which publishes the *Sunday Press* and the *Evening Press* along with the morning *Irish Press*, was founded by Eamon de Valera, the founding father and guru of Fianna Fáil. Although the paper was once jeered at as the "kept paper" of Fianna Fáil, its news coverage has won a reputation for fairness, and its expression of loyalty to the founder's party is now more likely to cause annoyance within Fianna Fáil than in other parties.[5]

The *Irish Independent* group publishes the *Sunday Independent* and the *Evening Herald* along with the daily *Irish Independent*, which is the largest-circulation daily in the country. Although it is sometimes criticized for an increasingly brash style and sense of news values, it seems to take elections more seriously than some other news.

The *Cork Examiner* relies on its Munster base for 90 percent of its circulation. Like the *Independent* group, it leans toward Fine Gael.

The *Irish Times* is formally the paper of record—an independent liberal paper, always willing to give minorities their say, that is read by the intelligentsia. Whereas at a British election press conference some journalists and politicians might be carrying the *Guardian* and others the *Times* or *Daily Telegraph*, at such a gathering in Ireland the *Irish Times* would invariably be the choice.

The *Sunday Tribune*, which flourished for the first two of these elections, enjoyed a circulation similar to that of the *Irish Times* but with greater penetration of the rural community. The brash *Sunday World*, a tabloid, gave less space to the election, and the short-lived *Sunday Journal* enjoyed little credibility because its editor was seconded to the Fianna Fáil press office for the duration of the election.

The fifty or so provincial papers are important sources, widely read in their own localities, but they too—most markedly in their editorials—increasingly take a national view of the election, in addition to giving details of candidates' speeches and analyzing local constituencies.

Table 7.2 Adult readership of the principal morning daily, evening, and Sunday newspapers, by region and community, 1979-1980 (percent)

| | | Region | | | | Community | |
| | | | Rest of | | Connacht and | | |
Newspaper	All	Dublin	Leinster	Munster	Ulster	Urban	Rural
Irish Independent	30	31	39	22	28	30	29
Irish Press	15	10	18	16	20	15	16
Irish Times	12	25	9	6	5	17	4
Cork Examiner	12	1	1	38	0	10	14
Evening Press	27	53	25	15	10	36	15
Evening Herald	20	43	22	4	6	29	7
Cork Evening Echo	6	0	0	21	0	9	2
Sunday Press	55	45	55	59	62	48	63
Sunday Independent	51	55	57	48	43	53	49
Sunday World	47	44	50	50	44	49	45

Source: Basil Chubb, *The Government and Politics of Ireland* (Stanford, Calif.: Stanford University Press, 1982), p. 68.
Note: Adult means age fifteen and over. Ulster refers to the three Ulster counties in the Republic.

Broadcasting. RTE, a state-appointed corporation, enjoys a monopoly in public service broadcasting in the Republic.[6] Two qualifications should be added: half the population—those along the east coast—can receive all four British television channels; and RTE's monopoly in radio has in recent years been effectively broken by the proliferation of illegal local stations, the "pirates." The pirates played a marginal role in these elections because of their access to the youth vote; tempted by this factor, the parties bought advertising space and participated in the election coverage offered on the pirates. Since the transmissions were illegal and political advertising is banned on RTE, the anomalies of these arrangements resulted in their being discontinued.[7]

Considerable efforts are made to honor RTE's code of impartiality during election periods. Although politicians are inevitably sensitive at such a period, there is general agreement that RTE achieves its objective of being fair. It must be admitted that it falls short of the standard achieved by radio before the advent of television in 1962. Then absolute impartiality was easily achieved by offering—aside from party political broadcasts—no coverage of the election campaign at all: the era, one might say, of silent radio.

Since the 1960s increasingly comprehensive coverage has been offered on both radio and television. Each program sector originates its own material, but the senior producers and department heads participate in an overall General Election Steering Group under the chairmanship of the deputy director general. This group monitors all coverage, the better to comply with the statutory requirement of balance. The importance of meeting this requirement during election campaigns is evident, and considerable care is taken to ensure that time is allocated according to the proportional strength of the parties. Balance within each program is the ideal, but this is in conflict with program requirements, as in RTE's desire to broadcast a one-to-one debate between the rivals for Taoiseach. Instead, balance between the parties is achieved over a series of programs.

Political advertising is not permitted by law: instead party political broadcasts are allocated according to party strength in the outgoing Dáil and also to groups fielding at least seven candidates. The parties decide the form and contents of these broadcasts, RTE being merely the publisher.

Some of RTE's best coverage of these campaigns was based on the speed of response possible in broadcasting. Between two editions of a daily newspaper, at least five current affairs programs would be broadcast: "Day by Day" at 11 A.M., "The News at 1:30," "The News at 6:30"—all on radio—followed on television by the news at 9 P.M. and an extended election edition of "Today Tonight." All these forums, along with the evening papers, could publish responses to, or rebuttals of, positions first announced in the morning papers.

In news bulletins and in the important News Features segment of the "News at 1:30" and "News at 6:30," election material must compete with the news of the day. Other programs often become election forums during the campaign, emphasizing the major issues and accelerating the tendency for the election to become national in character.

Toward a Presidential-style Campaign

The most pronounced change in media coverage of these elections was the increasing emphasis on the two rivals for the office of Taoiseach. A trend toward a more presidential style of campaigning, already evident in the 1970s, was significantly greater in these elections, for a number of reasons.[8] Both the men who would be Taoiseach, Charles Haughey and Garret FitzGerald, were contesting their first campaigns as party leaders in the June 1981 election; both were more charismatic than their predecessors; both sought a high media profile and were considered good performers on television by their camps when this series of elections opened. Opinions on this score were to change in the course of the elections.

Moreover, the two felt intense rivalry and antipathy for each other's style and brand of politics. All of this, along with conscious efforts by both parties in their campaign strategies to emphasize their party leaders, resulted in three elections that were more presidential in style than any that preceded them.

Given this new style of politics, the poor press that Haughey, the Fianna Fáil leader, received throughout proved a liability to his party. Going into the first election, his party managers presumed that what one commentator described as "the cult of Mr. Haughey" would prove an electoral asset. "The party intends to pursue a 'regal' style campaign, comparable in many ways to American presidential elections, where the party leader, rather than the party itself, will be used as the main lure for those all-important votes."[9] Haughey himself was hurt and annoyed by his treatment by the media. At a press conference during the third election campaign, he complained that he was "sick and tired of seeing his party being the victim" and being cast in the role of "bad boys."[10] The previous February the *Cork Examiner*'s political correspondent had written of "a virulent media campaign" against Haughey, especially evident at press conferences, where an "almost truculent attitude" was adopted by an influential section of the Dublin media.[11]

In that election Haughey had claimed that there was a "carefully concentrated and orchestrated campaign" against him in the press.[12] Commenting on such complaints in an editorial, the *Irish Times* urged its readers to remember that the opinion polls, not the newspapers, put FitzGerald "first twenty and then thirty points ahead of Mr. Haughey, thus setting off something of a personality contest in this electoral campaign." Pointing out that Haughey had "always had the name of being especially conscious of the value of good public and/or press relations—the image, as we now say," the editorial stated that he may have placed "too much reliance on favourable notice." Nevertheless, the editorial accepted that FitzGerald was "the darling of the newspapers for the time being" and that "a considerable amount of antipathy" was evident in press reporting of Haughey. It added: "He may complain, but some of this reaction is certainly fuelled by members of his own party. Even in mid-election there were dissidents around him."[13]

Fianna Fáil strategists felt considerable alarm at Haughey's bad showing in the polls and in the press. That he was an electoral liability was covertly admitted to journalists by the most senior members of the party. One senior Fianna Fáil politician—who supported Haughey during all the leadership crisis in Fianna Fáil[14]—confided to this writer on the eve of the February 1982 poll that "without our friend of course we'd be walking away with the election."[15]

Journalists who reflected this pessimism were often accused of bias: even to question Haughey on his poor showing in the opinion polls vis-à-vis Fitz-Gerald—as on radio's "Day by Day" in February 1982—promoted an irascible refusal to discuss the election in terms of "a talent contest."[16] Yet there was ample evidence that the electorate considered credibility as Taoiseach important in their voting preferences. Moreover, for a Fianna Fáil leader to object to such a question seemed inappropriate since his party's electoral slogans had always emphasized the party leaders: "Up Dev!," "Let Lemass Lead On," "Let's Back Jack," and—under Haughey—the campaign song "Arise and Follow Charlie." Haughey's dismissal of the opinion polls when they bore such bad news for the party and especially for him seemed at odds with the fact that, during his early months as leader, the party had commissioned private polls and heartened by his initial popularity, had focused their campaign on him.

In contrast, FitzGerald, the Fine Gael leader, received a good press. RTE's experienced political correspondent, Sean Duignan, in a discussion of the political coverage, described FitzGerald as "enormously appealing to the media—his is open and responsive, he knows the requirements in the press and because of his own background he knows people in the media on a personal basis."[17] FitzGerald was also more accessible to journalists than Haughey; he traveled on his party's press coach. Haughey traveled through the country in helicopters with the press in pursuit; when not in his helicopter, he preferred to travel by car ahead of the Fianna Fáil bus.

Haughey's great professionalism was often acknowledged, but on the hustings FitzGerald's approach had its own appeal. Mary Holland noted in the *Sunday Tribune* how he

> treats everybody who questions him with infinite courtesy. He explains the details of the Government's Youth Employment Agency to a nervous

teenager, for example, as carefully as he might to a journalist on television. This takes time and it's doubtful whether most people, blinded by television lights and buffeted by the crowd, can take in the fine print of what he is saying. It drives his aides, who are always wanting to push him onto the next stop, out of their minds.

It was a cliché of Irish politics, Holland noted, that FitzGerald was not "good on the hustings, that he lacks the common touch, is always late, does not have Charlie Haughey's easy way with a glad hand. It is true that FitzGerald is not at his best being photographed with a gaggle of adoring girls and that, for a confirmed family man, he seems distinctly ill at ease holding a baby." [18]

FitzGerald's accessibility was extended to the foreign media. Party managers can be reluctant to facilitate the interests of foreign media on the grounds that time is scarce and no votes are to be won through granting their requests for exclusive interviews. The British print and broadcasting media, however, have significant audiences in the Republic. They showed a marked antipathy toward Haughey and a warmth toward FitzGerald. Niall Kiely, on the campaign trail with FitzGerald, reported that foreign journalists "take to Garret like ducks to water. He is quotable, talkative, approachable. Within minutes he is into it, his overcoat rolled in a ball and bundled on a shelf. Deficits, budget strategies, psephological minutiae—the favoured topics on which he is versed to perfection: the patter never slick, indeed tongue tripping over bundles of phrases." [19]

Peter Dunn's report in June 1981 in the London *Sunday Times*—which enjoys a significant readership in the Republic—was typical of Fleet Street's image of FitzGerald. Dunn introduced him as "the world's most numerate politician." FitzGerald was "kind and (*everyone* says so) transparently honest, but his distracted academic manner is often taken for aloofness. Haughey kisses babies and even more enthusiastically, their mothers. FitzGerald shakes babies by the hand." [20]

This point, thought Conor Cruise O'Brien, was intended to suggest that FitzGerald was "unfit for the hurly-burly of the hustings and perhaps, more generally, for the rough world of politics." According to O'Brien—a cabinet colleague of FitzGerald's in 1973-77—this would be a mistaken judgment: "As far as the election is concerned, it would be quite wrong for Garret to try to compete with Charlie Haughey in the application of bogus bonhomie; Charlie has inexhaustible supplies of that stuff from a great factory of his in Kinsealy [Haughey's home]. Garret is right to appear in his own character, which is *genuinely* bonhomous, but not smarmy." FitzGerald however, seen close up in the cabinet, was "*not* too nice for this rough world." He was, wrote O'Brien, "about as nice as you can be" if you get ahead in politics, "but no nicer. There is steel under all that pretty wool." [21] Bruce Arnold in the *Irish*

Independent suggested that FitzGerald "could never be described as a one hundred per cent politician. He neither orchestrates, nor manipulates. But he is very much more politically shrewd, than the loquacious, professorial exterior might suggest." [22]

While advising the voters to ignore personalities and vote on issues, the print media throughout these elections emphasized the increasingly presidential style of campaigning and were themselves among the main expressions of this change. One index of the change is the extent to which photographs of the main party leaders have increased: in the 1969 election, photographs of the Fianna Fáil leader Jack Lynch totaled twenty-six in the three Dublin dailies; Haughey's total in November 1982 was eighty-eight. For Fine Gael, Liam Cosgrave was featured fourteen times in 1969, FitzGerald seventy-six in November 1982. [23]

That Haughey got a bad press is clear from the most casual perusal of the newspaper files on these elections. Whether the criticism was justified is another question. His friend Anthony Cronin, invited to come to his defense in the *Independent* toward the end of the third campaign, concluded that there was "something wrong" when FitzGerald's qualities were "bruited from the housetops" while Haughey's were "caricatured, concealed and distorted to a degree unprecedented in our public life." [24] Haughey himself believed that he was receiving unfair treatment. He alternated between shrugging it off and complaining in private, or sometimes in public, about it. When the question of a smear campaign against him came up at a press conference in February 1982, Albert Reynolds, his director of elections and ministerial colleague, handled the issue: "Most of you have a fair idea about what is going on." Denis Coghlan in the *Irish Times* reported Reynold's chronicling of the Fine Gael whispering campaign. "Then, with his Fianna Fáil dander up, he identified the hotbeds of this sedition—pubs." This is how Fine Gael was spreading the lies about Haughey. "And Mr. Reynold's offer as proof of the falsity of such whispers: could any journalist present point to a single fault of Mr. Haughey's handling of a single situation?" [25]

Bruce Arnold was one of Haughey's principal critics and one of those most often attacked by Fianna Fáil—it was later revealed that Haughey's minister for justice had Arnold's telephone tapped during Fianna Fáil's short term in government in 1982. [26] Arnold noted toward the end of the third campaign that at every press conference Haughey had complained of "a campaign of vilification." When asked to be more specific, he had described the campaign "as 'orchestrated,' as emanating from Fine Gael, and from Fine Gael sympathisers within the media," and he especially identified the *Irish Independent*. "Beyond saying 'We will know who we mean,' he has not spelt out the nature of the vilification, nor its sources." Defining "vilify" as "to dishonour, depreciate, disparage, defame," Arnold suggested that Haughey had spent the election campaign vilifying FitzGerald by accusing him variously "of being untrustworthy on the Pro-Life Amendment (on abortion), of 'stealing' documents, of secret collusion over the Northern Ireland Assembly with James Prior, and of collaboration with the British." It would, concluded Arnold, "be hard to find a more textbook set of examples of vilification" in the Irish political culture.

Although Haughey had been unfairly treated in a number of instances, Arnold wrote, there was "no evidence" of a campaign. Instead the record suggested "a form of self-vilification" on Haughey's part, which journalists had properly reported. Haughey could be faulted for his judgment of people, for his handling of the confidence motion on his leadership, and on policy areas such as Northern Ireland and the economy: his behavior on these fronts had been "so erratic, contradictory and perverse, as to represent a serious assault by Mr. Haughey on himself." [27]

Haughey's wife, Maureen, was asked in the *Irish Press* if she believed there was a media conspiracy against her husband. She replied: "Yes. I didn't at first. But now I am convinced that it is inspired by Britain. Haugheybashing is popular with the Brits." The Irish media could be "blatantly unfair"; even the *Irish Press* group had "gone like the others"; it was "no longer Dev's paper." [28]

The previous day the *Irish Press* had complimented Haughey for his "fighting form" at a grueling seventy-five-minute press conference.

> And no matter how tough the going gets, he remains unfailingly courteous and he keeps his sense of humour. It is important that this be remembered. There have been many harsh things said about Mr. Haughey and usually they have been justified. But there is a side to the man—a quality that goes beyond the simplistic beauty contest of media images — which even his opponents must admire.

The *Press* added: "Unfortunately the same cannot be said for many of those who are closest to him." [29]

The June 1981 Campaign

Fianna Fáil has traditionally been the best organized and most professional of the Irish parties. In no sphere has this been more evident than in election campaigns, where its press and publicity work has outclassed that of all other parties. By 1981, when the first of these elections was called, the Fine Gael machine, for the first time in the party's history, was reputedly as professional.

This professionalism was immediately demonstrated by the surprise announcement of a whistle-stop tour by FitzGerald in a specially fitted press train. Dublin-based reporters joined the train, which held a series of press conferences for the provincial papers throughout the first weekend of the campaign. Party supporters were encouraged to meet the train in each provincial town, and newspaper editors, reporters, and photographers from the catchment area were invited. All this provided excellent footage for Fine Gael political broadcasts and also—as the party managers well knew—irresistible visual material for the press photographers and television cameras. "Garret's train" was a considerable media coup by Fine Gael. It was a moot point whether it was more effective than Fianna Fáil's use of a helicopter to carry Haughey around the country in his "meet the people" tour. Both parties also used campaign buses.

The sophistication of the publicity machines of the main parties—Labour lacked the resources to compete at this level—was evident in May 1981. It was expected to be "the greatest press, public relations and publicity campaign ever mounted" in the country. Michael Brophy reported that public relations and advertising executives were "making a determined effort to turn election '81 into their own vehicle of ideas, razz-a-matazz, and projection," all costing one million Irish pounds. Fianna Fáil would be spending the most and would employ three advertising agencies to help focus on specific targets in the electorate, notably first-time voters.[30]

Such an approach can persuade journalists to reflect the election fever in a greater allocation of editorial space. Moreover, party strategists were increasingly aware of how to generate copy that would find its way into the news. Realizing the media's hunger for election material, they anticipated the news editors' needs, punctuating each day with press conferences, briefings, interviews, speeches, and scripts. The opinion polls, especially those in the *Irish Times* and the *Irish Independent*, along with the special formats of broadcast debates, originated on the media side.

Another change first evident in the 1981 election was the significant move away from the traditional stenographer role of Irish journalists. The number of column inches given to scripts and speeches was down since 1969.[31] The *Irish Times*, in an editorial entitled "And May the Best Showman Win," did not regret the passing of the "script factories" based on party headquarters and manned by ghostwriters. "Gone are the speech marathons. The scripts which are issued are not always the scripts of speeches actually delivered. They are political fodder for the newspapers, the radio and television news." Instead of "relentless oratorical combat," the parties had

> all decided that entertainment of the people is their job. Or at least that a message comes across best in the guise of entertainment.
> So we have the T-shirts, so we have the pop tunes, so we have the

Christian-name posters and slogans: "Garret is good for you," "Chase me Charlie . . ." The caravans roll across the country and bread and circuses are brought to the people.

Such an approach, added the paper, should ensure that the politicians would not complain "that the media are trivializing and distorting: they are doing it themselves. Is this frivolous? Vulgar? Detrimental to our culture? Yes, but America more or less devised this sort of show and does not seem to have suffered all that much." Fortunately, the editorial concluded, "there is some substance under the froth."[32]

The substantive issues in the campaign as identified by the politicians, the media, and the public—when polled—were the economic questions. Here the media were, if anything, ahead of the parties. The need to curb foreign borrowing and to get the public finances into a healthier state had been emphasized in print before the election was called.[33] To some extent the media forced this aspect of the economy to the forefront; the *Irish Independent*, for instance, argued that "nasty medicine" was needed.[34]

Too many shallowly researched constituency profiles were published in print and in the electronic media during this campaign. With multiseat constituencies and considerable rivalry within as well as between parties, Dublin-based journalists found it difficult to report accurately on the complexity of each constituency given the constraints of time and resources.

The political correspondents abandoned their traditional approach of "reading" the election by keeping their "ears close to the ground." They had been proved so wrong by the opinion polls, public and private, during the 1977 election that they learned their lesson and demonstrated considerable caution on this occasion. More opinion polls were published than in any previous election, and there is little need to doubt their accuracy. The poll results were eagerly awaited and, although party strategists attempted to minimize any bad news, were given considerable credence by all interested parties.

Broadcast coverage of the election in current affairs programs often took the form of live debates between spokespersons of the main parties on the major issues. Live debates were considered better than other formats for a number of reasons: in a fast-moving election they could take account of the latest developments; the audiences and, probably, the politicians preferred them; and they had considerable advantages for the broadcasters in a context as sensitive as an election campaign. A live studio debate places less onus on the broadcaster to ensure final balance since the politicians may be presumed to some extent to look after themselves. Program formats offering edited recorded interviews place a greater burden on the production team, which is likely to be charged with bias no matter how the material is edited. For instance, if John Kelly's statement on "Today Tonight" at the beginning of the

Figure 7.1   Martyn Turner cartoon, *Irish Times*, 6 June 1981

campaign that he would prefer a Fine Gael government "uncontaminated by any form of alliance or coalition" had been made in a filmed interview, the producer would have had to decide what prominence to give to this choice of words, whose tone—once they were uttered—Kelly regretted.[35]

Broadcast coverage of Irish elections had never included a one-to-one debate between the rivals for the office of Taoiseach. In the 1981 campaign RTE program makers suggested a number of such debates: "Day by Day" invited both leaders to a radio debate for the first Monday of the campaign; "This Week," also on radio, invited them for the last Sunday; but the most significant negotiations turned on the possibility of a "Today Tonight" television debate, abandoned by RTE's election committee after two weeks' negotiations because of the "mutually irreconcilable" positions of the parties.[36] Haughey, while "prepared to debate with anyone, anywhere, anytime," thought that the Labour leader, Frank Cluskey, was entitled to join the debate.[37] FitzGerald then offered both a three-way and a two-way debate and accused Haughey of being shy: "[RTE] can't lasso him and drag him into the studio."[38] The *Independent*'s headline was partisan: "Haughey Dodges Trial by TV." Editorially the paper regretted the failure to reach agreement: in debate Haughey and FitzGerald "could have provided the country with more insight into their respective parties' thoughts on the future of this country than a couple of tons of scripts would do." [39]

The compromise formula for the major television event of the election was a program offering three "Meet the Press"-style sessions with the same team of four journalists questioning each party leader in turn. By common consent the formula was not successful; also by common agreement Haughey fared best. Chris Glennon in the *Independent* believed he had "clearly outperformed his opposition rivals." [40] Tom McGurk, television critic of the *Sunday Tribune*, concluded that Haughey "came, stooped and conquered." [41] James Downey, reviewing the entire campaign in the *Irish Times*, suggested that in Haughey his party had found a "secret weapon." He

> appeared relaxed, rested, bland and completely at ease in answering the attacks made on his handling of the economy. His advisers had persuaded him to spend a leisurely weekend, and it was obviously good advice: of signs of tiredness and short temper there were none.
>
> On Tuesday Fianna Fáil claimed that his performance had been worth three Dáil seats to them. But Cluskey, in rebuke to a reporter who said that performance was what mattered on television, said: "Yes—in a play." [42]

Among the least impressed by the party leaders' interviews were the four journalists chosen to put the questions: Paul Tansey, Bruce Arnold, Michael Mills, and the ubiquitous Vincent Browne. Haughey they found competent, cool, buoyant, and excellently prepared: Arnold believed he " 'performed' best and 'defeated' us." Arnold thought FitzGerald

> "performed" more honestly, which led him into the much more real territory of argument and discussion, but made him, at the same time, more vulnerable. Frank Cluskey "performed" dogmatically and with a stubborn determination to exploit his best political assets: this, again, made for a debating stalemate but one which he seemed to turn to his advantage at the end.

To Tansey, Haughey's recourse to statistics was selective, which left the panel in a difficult position: "To challenge each statistic produced would have been extremely tedious in what was already a fairly technical debate. To pursue the matter to its conclusion would have appeared overly aggressive and would have created the impression that a bunch of unelected journalists were insulting the Taoiseach."

Mills shared this view, finding it impossible "to interrupt the flow of words . . . without appearing rude, aggressive or politically biassed." His piece, entitled "How We Bored the Nation: The TV Debate," is a telling piece of evidence of how unpredictable live television can be and of how difficult it is to elicit answers from politicians unwilling to impart the information sought. Mills wrote:

> At one stage Bruce Arnold asked a three-part question of Dr. FitzGerald which he proceeded to answer in twelve parts. Half way through I had lost the entire drift; I knew I had a question to ask, arising out of an earlier part of his reply, but by the end of his reply I could not be sure if he had answered my question at some stage and in any case I had forgotten the question.[43]

Identifying the key issues, asking the right questions, was not enough: did the media fail in the 1981 election to communicate to the voters the extent of the problem in the public finances whose scale was soon to be widely accepted? Retrospectively Browne believed that the campaign had "exposed some critical inadequacies on the part of the media, which led to an unsatisfactory campaign and a confused decision on the part of the electorate." Collectively the communicators had failed to persuade the politicians of all parties to face some of the contradictions in their own manifestoes. Such failures, in Browne's view, rendered the election "meaningless—the electorate was voting for a chimera, either because the Fianna Fáil record was not presented to it or because the alternative offered was entirely unrealistic."[44]

The February 1982 Campaign

The collapse of the Fine Gael-Labour coalition government on the harsh budget they felt obliged to introduce in February 1982 precipitated the second of this series of Irish elections. In *Magill*, Browne suggested that the media should ponder its earlier failures. "The responsibility for ensuring that this election is not another piece of codology rests largely with the media. If we don't force the politicians to face up to the real issues in this campaign and give straight answers to the questions that arise, then nobody will." He also suggested "some kind of joint effort" at the campaign press conferences, whose traditional pattern he criticized as "too diffused."[45]

At the opening press conference of the election, Browne and others pursued the question of foreign borrowing with Haughey, who repeatedly accused the outgoing government and the media of being "mesmerised" by the issue. Annoyed by the persistent questioning, Haughey protested that the press conference should not be "a cross-examination." One journalist asked, "What else is it?" The limitations of the press conference format are manifest, especially where the politician can ignore a supplementary question by turning to those eager to raise a fresh issue. In fact, at the Fine Gael press conference the following day, the chairman, Jim Dooge, invoked fairness to other journalists as a criterion for breaking off a particular line of questioning. Nevertheless, the campaign press conferences were a considerable improvement on those of the 1970s and earlier.

Browne also provided the major scoop of the election with the publication of a Finance Department document that, it was suggested in *Magill*, revealed "the extent of Haughey's misrepresentation of public finances."[46] Browne himself almost became an issue in the election. The *Sunday Tribune* reported the response within Fianna Fáil. "The man in Fianna Fáil headquarters spoke slowly, picking his words deliberately. 'We think Vincent Browne is somewhat insane. He's on a constant ego trip. He promotes gutter journalism and is a totally discredited journalist.' "[47]

The *Irish Times* declared from the outset that the election would prove "some sort of watershed"; it criticized "the spendthrift fashion of recent years" and emphasized the need for leadership, complimenting the outgoing coalition government for attempting to provide it. "They may have fumbled, mumbled, and bumbled from time to time, but at least they made an effort." The paper suggested that if the voters "placed any value on the virtues of tenacity and honesty and on their own future, they would return the Coalition parties to government with a thumping majority."[48] Although the paper's editorials remained broadly procoalition, they did not offer such explicit advice to voters for the rest of the campaign.

The *Irish Times* was critical of Haughey's dismissal of the media's concern with foreign borrowing. If the Fianna Fáil leader "tries to ease us into a relaxed mood, with his talk of hypnotism, he deserves rejection at the polls." The country needed "a rescue job." The parties should "talk facts and figures." They, along "with our style of politics," were on trial; "above all—no lullabies."[49] The paper remained critical of Fianna Fáil, describing a picture of Haughey and a senior minister "with thumbs up" as looking like "nothing so much as Astaire and Crosby bursting into a reprise with 'a couple of song-and-dance men.' "[50]

This note was typical of the media's reporting of this election, whether in editorials or in questioning at press conferences or in broadcast interviews. The budget and fiscal issues were central. RTE's political correspondent, Sean Duignan, believed that the media "came down decisively on one side on these issues," supporting the outgoing coalition government's analysis and having a "very considerable" influence with the electorate.

Maurice Manning of Fine Gael believed that the economists and the media had profoundly changed the voters' perceptions between the elections. "You had women on doorsteps worried about the current budget deficit, for God's sake." Michael D. Higgins, Labour's chairman and a leading left-winger, was critical of the media's initial emphasis on the budget and their delay in perceiving that the issue most relevant to the electorate was unemployment. "The fact is that the media reflects the dominant political forces of society and the concerns of these forces alone." Manning thought there was "a certain arrogance in saying that the media should dictate the issues of a campaign." In his experience the party machines were "highly sensitive" to the electorate's preoccupations, and it was the voters who determined the issues. He believed the media should "try to broaden out debate" but had "no right to try to dictate what the issues should be."

The view that the media were preoccupied with Haughey and that much of their tone was unfair had considerable support. Geraldine Kennedy, then political correspondent of the *Sunday Tribune*, accepted that the media were biased against Fianna Fáil but, she thought, "for quite good reasons." They were, she argued, in a position to judge Haughey, the divisions within Fianna Fáil, and the party's capacity to "implement a clear and consistent policy in government." The media "made its collective mind up on these issues as it had a right to do but more importantly, the media reported on these issues for the benefit of the electorate, as it had a duty to do." Apart from these conclusions, she allowed that "there was a lot of personal sniping against Charlie Haughey that was unfair. It could just as equally have been done on Garret FitzGerald, and it wasn't."[51] Tony Gregory, the Dublin Independent deputy, went so far as to suggest that Fianna Fáil would have achieved an "overall majority government—there is no question about it—but for the campaign against Haughey, which demeans and brings him down, and it has the automatic effect of doing the same thing right around the country to the name of the Fianna Fáil organization."[52]

The role of broadcasting in this election was curtailed both by a work-to-rule dispute by film editors and by the financial crisis facing the corporation. RTE found itself "in an impossible situation"; it was "financially impoverished" yet eager to offer the public "comprehensive and full coverage of a unique election."[53] Financial borrowing was the selected solution, and coverage was on a scale similar to that in June 1981, although considerable limitations were imposed by the film editors' dispute.

The television coverage emphasized constituency profiles less than hitherto: broadcasters had increasing misgivings that such reports, expensive in money and manpower, posed difficulties because of the Irish system of multiseat proportional representation. Moreover, their audience appeal was limited to electors in the constituencies concerned and those addicts of election coverage who appreciate the minutiae about every marginal constituency. In the event, the film editors' dispute prevented the five constituency profiles that had been filmed for "Today Tonight" from being transmitted.

Radio covered fewer constituencies than usual, emphasizing the critical marginals. Some policy debates on television were set in constituencies where the issue was of special significance. This brought the coverage outside Dublin while maintaining a wide appeal and a more relevant format for a national communications system. On radio, "This Week," "Day by Day," "Saturday View," "Women Today," specialist programs, Irish language programs, Radio 2's "Kenny Report," and the regular "News at 1:30" and "News at 6:30" all combined to give a comprehensive service. Indeed, some listeners complained that there was no escape from the election.

At the early press conferences the question of a television debate between the alternative leaders was mooted. The usual skirmishing followed, with party managers anxious to achieve the optimum setting for any encounter without appearing publicly reluctant to participate. Labour again claimed the right to join the debate, but eventually the Labour leader, Michael O'Leary, accepted a separate interview. Given the complex preplanning that such a debate demands, either contestant can usually veto participation on grounds that are plausible at least to his own supporters. This time both parties presumed they had something to gain from a debate, and so—for the first time in Irish electoral history—it was agreed.

The newspapers noted the limitations of such a program as a guide to who would best govern the country, but they also overexaggerated its importance, ensuring a very wide audience and general acceptance by the electorate, the press, and the politicians that it might prove the climax of the campaign. Aengus Fanning in the *Independent* emphasized that success in the television debate depended "more on vague general impressions gained by viewers than on either leader's mastery of the art of political debate, or knowledge of the state of the economy." It was, he added, FitzGerald's "misfortune that his blinding command of statistics, and his incredible memory which enabled him to rattle off figures with impressive accuracy, are of little advantage on television." In fact, research had shown that FitzGerald's "wizardry with figures" in the previous election had proved "a distinct liability."[54]

Viewers of the debate differed on whether FitzGerald's preoccupation with the small print of policy was a fault or a virtue. The general consensus was that Haughey's better performance was of greater benefit to him since his low rating in the polls ensured that he could only move up. John Healy thought it all "came perilously close to being the yawn of the election."[55]

Magill was again dissatisfied: the media's role "was not prominent enough and . . . a great number of significant issues in the campaign were ignored or not teased out adequately." *Magill* did not exclude its own performance from this criticism. It suggested that the function of journalists was to inform the electorate so that they could arrive at "a meaningful decision." Consequently it was not sufficient for the media to report the "sayings and doings of politicians": rather, it was their duty to be investigative and analytical, exposing "inconsistencies and contradictions where they arise." In *Magill*'s view, the media "did this hardly at all in this past campaign." Instead of such "tough reportage," there was a surfeit of "color reporting." And television, admittedly constrained by the film editors' work-to-rule dispute, "made little attempt to do anything other than to present talking heads each night debating the issues —something which radio was doing very adequately anyway."

Magill concluded that journalists should "examine what it is we are supposed to be about and are not distracted from that by wails, especially from Fianna Fáil, that we overstepped our role." The basic criticism was not that the media had exceeded their responsibility but that they had "inadequately fulfilled it."[56]

The November 1982 Campaign

The election of November 1982, being the third campaign within eighteen months, found all the parties financially weak. Expenditure on the campaign was a fraction of what it had been in June 1981, the most obvious change being the cuts in newspaper advertising.[57] Consequently there was greater reliance on the editorial pages to communicate with the voters.

The polls again showed that economic issues were the major preoccupation of the electorate, and the media's concern with public finances continued. As in February the politicians were anxious to assure journalists that they were making no promises entailing further capital expenditure. The polls also showed Fianna Fáil trailing the coalition's total support. Fine Gael strategists were content to fight the election on credibility and the economic questions; Fianna Fáil seemed anxious to seek new issues that might bring them increased support.

An early attempt by Fianna Fáil to make the proposed antiabortion amendment to the Constitution an election issue failed.[58] A week before polling day, Fianna Fáil accused FitzGerald of collaboration with the British on policy toward Northern Ireland, citing as part of its evidence a meeting in London between FitzGerald and the duke of Norfolk. Casting the aging Norfolk as a British spy may have been credible to Fianna Fáil supporters, but the press corps thought it a joke or perhaps a measure of the party's desperation.[59] Then FitzGerald's suggested North-South cross-border police force—whatever its merits, a proposal ill suited to an election campaign—gave Fianna Fáil the opening it was seeking. Playing down the Norfolk case, it brought this controversy to the center of the campaign in its closing stages.[60]

Here were issues that the editorial writers could pronounce on, and they were decisive and divergent in their views. The *Irish Independent* was critical of Haughey's charge of collaboration against FitzGerald. It was "so patently incorrect" that the paper concluded that "the campaign barrel has been scraped and has yielded a red herring in the shape of the North." It was exceeding the rules of political debate "when one side accuses the other of 'secret collabora-

tion' with a third party, especially when the facts do not sustain the allegation."[61] The *Irish Press* criticized what it termed FitzGerald's "ludicrous"
proposal for an all-Ireland police force. It was "dismaying to many of his
supporters," who fear that he may have "snatched defeat from the jaws of
victory."[62] The *Press* believed Haughey to be the more competent politician,
criticizing FitzGerald's "political naivety,"[63] and seemed to support Fianna
Fáil's criticism that the Fine Gael leader was not sufficiently independent of
British policy on Northern Ireland: to the *Press* it looked as if "the general
thrust of the 'Garret the Goodie' as opposed to 'Charlie the Baddie' image of
the two political leaders fostered in the British media has at last broken through
the Irish election campaign, with obvious implications for Irish sovereignty
and the future of Northern Ireland."[64]

Broadcast coverage of this campaign was affected by the financial difficulties of RTE. Constituency profiles were again reduced in number, and live
debates between front-bench spokespersons on radio and television constituted
the main staple of election coverage.

Some controversy surrounded a film made for a Fine Gael party political
broadcast. Tom O'Dea, television critic of the *Irish Press*, wrote that Fine
Gael had "peopled its film with characters taken from the front bench of
Fianna Fáil—most of them caught in shifty poses. . . . Had the film been
made for an RTE comedy show there would have been hell to pay." After it
"the wall-eyed, traditional, straight-to-camera productions looked very old-
fashioned and unskilled."[65]

Although Fine Gael's broadcasts were bitterly attacked by Haughey, their
professionalism was acknowledged. Behind them was one of the party's key
publicity strategists, Bill O'Herlihy, a former television reporter who had
switched to public relations. Another of the party broadcasts showed a citizen
walking along the street reading a succession of Fianna Fáil policy documents
and eventually falling down a manhole. They were considered "tough and
very slick," reminiscent of "the best American political commercials—perhaps
those devised by Bob Haldeman for the Nixon campaign in 1968."[66]

Again in this campaign haggling, brinkmanship, and gamesmanship sur-
rounded the issue of a one-to-one television debate between the rival leaders.
This time it appeared that Fine Gael was wary of a contest, in contrast to
FitzGerald's initial challenge in the first of these elections in June 1981.
Haughey, however, said he would "relish the chance of a television debate."[67]
Since it can be fairly claimed that the challenger is usually keenest for such a
confrontation, the enthusiasm of Fianna Fáil was a measure not only of its
confidence in Haughey's performance the previous February, but also of its
awareness that it was far from confident of winning the election, despite its
press conference bravado. The *Irish Independent* felt that FitzGerald was
"right to be cautious about such a programme because, with all his experience,

he is still a hesitant debater on the box, too careful about getting his statistics right to have time for the cut and thrust of instant controversy. Mr. Haughey shows more zest for such things."[68]

The *Irish Press*, among other papers, put considerable pressure on Fine Gael to agree to a debate. Its headline on 16 November was "TV Showdown Put in Jeopardy: Fine Gael Quibbles over Terms for Big Debate." The paper's editorial stated that voters had come to expect such debates and that although FitzGerald had "little to gain from facing Mr. Haughey on television," he would "lose a lot of respect if he refuses."[69]

Eventually terms were agreed between the party managers, and the debate took place. It was generally accepted as the most significant media event of the election. Newspaper coverage was exhaustive. Even FitzGerald's late refusal to attend a photo call became a major talking point in the press. The *Irish Press* reported that an "irate" FitzGerald, "obviously angered" by Haughey's recent "personal attacks," refused a handshake, which the editorial writer thought "a pity."[70] What was clear was that Fine Gael strategists, hoping that the bitterness of Haughey's attacks in recent days would swing votes in their direction, did not wish to confuse the party leaders' images by a widely publicized handshake. Such attention to detail, the pervasive print coverage of the debate, and the attention given to it here are all symptomatic of the extent to which television has accelerated a tendency toward a presidential style in Irish politics.

Haughey's failure to repeat some of the accusations against FitzGerald that had marked his recent press conferences aroused much comment. Haughey's advisers explained that they did not want "a slanging match": hence his reluctance to repeat the charge that FitzGerald had been "a collaborator" with the British over policy toward Northern Ireland.[71] Although the *Irish Press* pronounced the result "a draw . . . the general verdict of both viewers and experts," the *Irish Independent* reflected a more widespread view in its headline: "Buoyant FitzGerald Wins the TV Debate." Its political correspondent concluded that FitzGerald had "put behind him the disaster" of the February performance and had shown "a convincing demonstration of debating superiority."[72]

What FitzGerald had in fact shown was a new willingness to accept his party strategists' advice to avoid his usual detailed statistical arguments and to accept the limitations of a television debate of this kind. He was well rehearsed, anticipated many of Haughey's points, and performed more effectively. And having scored in the gamesmanship stakes by refusing the handshake photograph, FitzGerald minimized whatever debits there were on this score by explaining that his reason for declining was lest it would all "look like the beginning of a prize fight." He did not want the debate "to be seen as something to do with pugilism."[73]

Figure 7.2   Martyn Turner cartoon, *Irish Times*, 9 June 1981

That such misgivings were well founded could be shown by Sean Egan's report in the *Independent* on the morning after the debate: "They changed corners, came out fighting and this time the title changed hands too." It was a "superb recovery" by FitzGerald, who "knew he had won. . . . This time he had kept his head in cool, clinical fashion. Maybe it was all due to his hair-dresser. For the first time in political memory his hair was actually brushed down."[74] The boxing metaphor was even used by Fine Gael strategists, who privately were annoyed that the program was allowed to run over to complete the agreed topics: "With our man so far ahead on points after an hour, no wonder we wanted it concluded on time."[75]

Vincent Browne concluded that "as coached," FitzGerald "never used a statistic throughout the debate and used a technical economic term (GNP) only once." This reflected an election campaign that "was all about credibility and professionalism."[76]

Conclusion

Although only two television debates between the candidates for Taoiseach have taken place, they have created a general expectation that a debate should be the climax of an election campaign. Thus they replace the two rival eve-of-poll rallies in the center of Dublin that once concluded an Irish campaign. This change may even be considered an advance since the rallies were exclusively an opportunity of preaching to the converted and the television debates place a premium on converting those identified in the polls as "Don't knows," whose preference could decide the election. The fascination of the print media with the event symbolized broadcasting's erosion of their earlier predominance in political communication. But because of the widespread and mainly non-partisan coverage of politics in all printed media in Ireland, broadcasting has not assumed as important a role as it has in other countries.

Neither electors nor politicians—nor journalists for that matter—could quibble at the extent of the media's coverage; what may provide grounds for dissent is the content. Politicians have their complaints but have no experience and little knowledge of the less satisfactory communications structures in other countries. Voters—if readership and audience figures are a guide—seem content with the current Irish structure, although some interest groups would welcome a different emphasis and greater direct access to the politicians would be welcome. Radio seems the most promising medium for such access.

Meanwhile the professional communicators are becoming increasingly skeptical of their own performance: more investigation and analysis are prescribed by those who believe that the media have a critical contribution to make in determining the agenda for the election; others believe that the voters, politicians, and media form a competitive marketplace in which the free play of market forces yields the best results. Whatever the outcome of this debate, the canvas supplied by Irish newspaper publishers and by RTE is a generous one, partly because of voters' interest in what is seen as a national spectator sport.

Notes

1.   Given the extent of the coverage, the paucity of media analysis in Ireland, and the need to cover three elections in one chapter, I have had to adopt a relatively subjective approach, and it should be emphasized that this chapter is not based on a content analysis of the total

media coverage of these elections. I have made an effort to include the views of others, whether politicians or communicators, who have commented on the media coverage. If I have emphasized personalities rather than issues, tone rather than content, it is because other chapters have covered these campaigns and the policy issues.

I participated in the coverage of all three elections as presenter/moderator of the daily hour-long radio current affairs program "Day by Day" and was also one of the presenters on the television program "Today Tonight" for the third election. I attended press conferences throughout all campaigns and anchored radio coverage of the results for each election.

2. Adapted from Jay G. Blumer, "Producers' Attitudes towards Television Coverage of an Election Campaign: A Case Study," in Jeremy Tunstall, ed., *Media Sociology* (London: Constable, 1970), pp. 411–38.

3. Based on F. X. Carty, *Elections '82: What the Papers Said* (Dublin: Able Press, 1983), table 7, p. 11.

4. Basil Chubb, *The Government and Politics of Ireland* (Stanford, Calif.: Stanford University Press, 1982), pp. 57–69.

5. Throughout 1983, for instance, the *Irish Press* thought the proposed antiabortion amendment to the Constitution unnecessary, a stance opposed to official Fianna Fáil policy.

6. Chubb, *Government and Politics*, pp. 70–79.

7. *Irish Times*, 5 June 1981; John Healy, "Battle of the Air," ibid., 15 February 1982.

8. See for instance, Michael Mills, "Campaign to be Held under Unique Conditions," *Irish Press*, 22 May 1981; editorial, "Personalities Overshadow Real Issues in Election," *Sunday Independent*, 7 June 1981.

9. Gerard O'Regan, "Charlie Begins 'Presidential' Run in Fine Gael Heartland," *Irish Independent*, 23 May 1981.

10. *Irish Independent*, 6 November 1982.

11. Fianna Fáil Press Office, "Why All the Haughey Bashing?" *Magill*, February 1982.

12. RTE Radio, "This Week," 21 February 1982.

13. *Irish Times*, 11 February 1982.

14. Haughey survived three challenges to his leadership in the twelve months beginning in February 1982. Much media coverage of these challenges was resented by Haughey supporters: there was a tendency to blame the media for the divisions within the party. Before these demonstrations of dissent Haughey claimed in June 1981 that "the idea of a split in Fianna Fáil was a journalistic myth." Annette Blackwell, "Haughey: My Political Future on Line in Campaign," *Irish Independent*, 8 June 1981.

15. Confidential source.

16. RTE Radio, "Day by Day," 9 February 1982.

17. *Magill*, March 1982.

18. Mary Holland, "Garret is Good for Who?" *Sunday Tribune*, 7 February

19. *Irish Times*, 10 February 1982.

20. Peter Dunn, "The Other Fella," *Sunday Times*, 7 June 1981.

21. Conor Cruise O'Brien, "Babies, Wild Dogs and Coalition," *Magill*, June 1981.

22. *Irish Independent*, 3 June 1981.

23. Based on Carty, *Elections '82*, tables 20–21, p. 15.

24. Anthony Cronin, "Haughey, the Man and the Legend," *Irish Independent*, 17 November 1982.

25. *Irish Times*, 9 February 1982.

26. The tap was authorized on the grounds that leaks to Arnold from members of Haughey's own cabinet could have endangered national security. The telephone of Geraldine Kennedy, then political correspondent of the *Sunday Tribune*, was also tapped. For coverage of the

scandal, see national newspapers, 19–27 January 1983; for results of Fianna Fáil's inquiry, *Irish Times*, 17 February 1983.

27. Bruce Arnold, "The Campaign of Vilification," *Irish Independent*, 20 November 1982.
28. "How Charlie Stands Up to the Pressure—by Maureen Haughey," *Irish Press*, 18 November 1982.
29. *Irish Press*, 17 November 1982.
30. Michael Brophy, "It's the Day of the Image Makers," *Irish Independent*, 22 May 1981.
31. F. X. Carty, *Press Coverage of the 1981 General Election* (Dublin: Able Press, 1981), p. 4.
32. *Irish Times*, 28 May 1981.
33. See, for instance, the debate between economists "Whom God Would Destroy He First Makes Mad," *Magill*, May 1981; see also articles by Brendan Walsh and Colm McCarthy, *Irish Times*, 29–30 September 1980. FitzGerald claimed during this election that the media had underestimated the public's willingness to support tough economic measures ("This Week," RTE Radio, 14 February 1982).
34. *Irish Independent*, 28 May 1981.
35. See *Irish Times*, 27 May 1981.
36. *Irish Press*, 5 June 1981.
37. *Irish Times*, 4 June 1981.
38. *Irish Press*, 5 June 1981.
39. *Irish Independent*, 4 June 1981.
40. Ibid., 9 June 1981.
41. *Sunday Tribune*, 14 June 1981.
42. *Irish Times*, 11 June 1981.
43. "How We Bored the Nation," *Magill*, June 1981.
44. *Magill*, February 1982.
45. Ibid.
46. Vincent Browne, "How Haughey Cooked the Books in 1981," *Magill*, February 1982.
47. Joe Carroll, "Who Is This Man and Why Is He Saying These Things about Me?" *Sunday Tribune*, 7 February 1982.
48. *Irish Times*, 28 January 1982.
49. Ibid., 29 January 1982.
50. Ibid., 30 January 1982.
51. *Magill*, March 1982.
52. *Success*, October 1982.
53. Bob Collins, "1982 Election," *Irish Broadcasting Review*, no. 14 (Summer 1982).
54. Aengus Fanning, "Trial by TV: How the Party Leaders Can Lose Out," *Irish Independent*, 11 February 1982.
55. *Irish Times*, 17 February 1982.
56. *Magill*, March 1982.
57. Denis Doghlan, "Big Parties Tighten Belts in Campaign," *Irish Times*, 6 November 1982; and Carty, *Elections '82*, pp. 16–17.
58. *Irish Times*, 6 November 1982.
59. David McKittrick, "Collusion Allegations Ridiculous, Says Duke," *Irish Times*, 23 November 1982.
60. For text of FitzGerald's proposal, see *Irish Times*, 19 November 1982.
61. *Irish Independent*, 18 November 1982.
62. *Irish Press*, 20 November 1982.
63. Ibid., 22 November 1982.
64. Ibid., 18 November 1982.

65. Ibid., 20 November 1982.
66. *Magill*, December 1982.
67. *Irish Independent*, 8 November 1982.
68. Ibid., 16 November 1982.
69. *Irish Press*, 16 November 1982.
70. Ibid., 23 November 1982.
71. *Irish Independent*, 23 November 1982.
72. Ibid.; *Irish Press*, 23 November 1982.
73. *Irish Independent*, 24 November 1982.
74. Ibid., 23 November 1982.
75. Confidential source.
76. *Magill*, December 1982.

8   The Senate Elections

Composition of the Senate

The relative lack of public and scholarly interest in elections to the Irish Senate reflects the clearly subordinate role of the upper chamber in the legislative process, the predictability of the outcome in any Senate election results, and the extent to which the selection of the Senate is overshadowed by the co-inciding general election to the Dáil.[1] The near-absence of analytical studies of Senate elections is unfortunate.[2] The Irish Senate is a very unusual example of an upper house in which the dominant basis of representation is vocational or functional, by contrast with the more common territorial basis of selection. No other national parliament includes a house constituted along these lines, but in the Federal Republic of Germany, one *Land*, Bavaria, has a sixty-member Senate comprising representatives of ten vocational groups. This essay will examine the three most recent Irish Senate elections, which provide adequate material for analysis of the Irish experience of vocational representation.

The life span of the Irish Senate is tied to that of the lower house: an election must take place within ninety days of a dissolution of the Dáil. Senators are chosen through three channels: (1) forty-three are elected by an electoral college from five panels representing certain vocational interests; (2) six are elected by graduates of the country's two universities (three from each); and (3) eleven are nominated by the Taoiseach at his own discretion. Since the first of these channels accounts for five-sevenths of the entire membership of sixty, it will be the primary focus of this chapter.

Legal provisions for election to the five vocational panels contrast sharply with those governing Dáil elections. In the first place, the electorate is highly restricted. It consists of members of county and county-borough councils, out-going senators, and incoming Dáil deputies, subject to the proviso that an elector may cast only one vote even if he holds more than one qualifying position (deputies, for instance, are entitled to only one vote, although most are also county or county-borough councillors). Every elector may, however, vote on each of the five panels.

Second, the nomination process is restricted. Each panel is divided into two "provisional subpanels," to which candidates are nominated. Each candidate must be proposed to the Oireachtas subpanels by four deputies or senators, none of whom may nominate more than one candidate. On the Nominating Bodies subpanels, each candidate is to be nominated by an organization registered for this purpose. The number of such organizations in 1981 and the number of candidates that each was entitled to nominate are indicated in table 8.1. These organizations vary enormously in composition and in orientation, including ones as diverse as the Royal Irish Academy of Music, the Federated Union of Employers, and the Irish Wheelchair Association. They propose candidates in accordance with their own internal procedures, except in the case of the General Council of County Councils and the Association of Municipal Authorities of Ireland, which are required to poll their members on the matter. The law also stipulates that each subpanel is entitled to a certain minimum representation; this minimum is shown in table 8.1.

Third, each candidate must be qualified for the panel to which he is nominated. He must possess, to the satisfaction of the returning officer, "knowledge and practical experience" of designated areas of activity with which that panel is associated.

Fourth, polling is by mail and is governed by regulations designed to prevent corrupt practices. Electors must vote in the presence of an authorized person,[3] who verifies a declaration of identity, and must forward their ballot papers to the returning officer (the clerk of the Senate) by registered mail.

The final contrast with Dáil election procedures relates to the rules for

Table 8.1 Distribution of seats and nominating bodies among Senate vocational panels, 1981

Panel	Number of seats	Minimum required from each subpanel	Number of nominating bodies	Number of nominations allowed to each body
Culture and education	5	2	22	1
Agriculture	11	4	8	2
Labour	11	4	2	7
Industry and commerce	9	3	32	1
Administration	7	3	8	1
Total	43	16	72	—

Source: Seanad Éireann, *Seanad General Election, August 1981, and Bye-elections to 1977–81 Seanad* (Dublin: Stationery Office, 1982).

counting votes. Although the single transferable vote system of proportional representation is used in elections to both chambers, the rules for counting votes in Senate panel elections incorporate a modification of the Dáil rules. The procedure for distributing surplus votes in Dáil elections introduces a random element in certain circumstances in that the number of ballot papers available for transfer may exceed the number to which continuing candidates are entitled. The number of papers transferred is, in effect, reduced by a random method, but this is usually of little consequence when the number of ballot papers is large. Because of the much smaller size of the Senate panel electorate, each ballot paper is treated as if it had the value 1,000, but when a surplus distribution of the kind instanced above arises, *all* of the ballot papers in question are transferred physically, but at reduced value. The random element is thus reduced to insignificance.[4]

Furthermore, extra rules have been introduced into the Senate electoral law to ensure that a balance is maintained between the two subpanels in the case of each panel. These rules prevent the elimination of candidates from a subpanel when it would result in that subpanel failing to attain its minimum share of seats and provide for the elimination of candidates of a subpanel that has already won its maximum number of seats. It is thus possible for a candidate to be eliminated even though he has more votes than other, continuing candidates.[5]

University senators are also elected by postal ballot. There are two constituencies, the National University of Ireland and Dublin University (Trinity College), each of which returns three senators. A candidate must be proposed by two registered Senate electors, with the assent of eight others. The electorate comprises all graduates who are Irish citizens and have registered as electors. The rules for counting votes are the same as those used in Dáil elections. The Constitution places no restriction on the Taoiseach's choice of the remaining eleven senators; he must, of course, secure the assent of the persons concerned.

Panel Candidates and the Campaign

Nominations. The three Senate general elections held as a consequence of the three Dáil dissolutions took place in August 1981, April 1982, and January 1983. Each election was governed by a similar timetable. The first step is the nomination of candidates by registered bodies, which takes place after the assembly of the new Dáil. The nominating bodies put forward seventy-nine candidates in 1981, out of a possible total entitlement of ninety-two. In 1982 this number dropped to seventy-four, and in January 1983 seventy-three candidates were proposed. These candidates consisted overwhelmingly of people who were identified with one of the three main parties. Only two independent candidates were nominated in 1981 and 1982; three were nominated in 1983.

Oireachtas nominations close just over a week later. In theory, members
of the Oireachtas can nominate up to fifty-six candidates. In practice, the
maximum possible number tends to be less, since the effective membership of
the Oireachtas generally falls below its full number of 226 owing to the election
of some outgoing senators to the new Dáil. There is nevertheless a tendency
for each party to make its full share of nominations. Thus, in the three elections the Fianna Fáil parliamentary party nominated twenty-six, twenty-two,
and eighteen candidates, respectively; Fine Gael put forward nineteen in 1981
and 1982 and twenty-one in 1983; and the Labour party named four in the
first two elections and five in 1983. In this year, too, a Workers' party candidate
who had been defeated in the Dáil election was nominated. One independent
candidate was proposed in 1981 and another in 1983, though the latter was
associated with Neil Blaney's Independent Fianna Fáil party.

It should be pointed out that these figures do not include other nominations that were rejected by the returning officer when he completed the
panels a week after the close of nominations. In 1981, for example, one Nominating Bodies candidate on the Industrial and Commercial Panel was disquali-
fied, on the grounds that there was no evidence of "knowledge and practical
experience" on his part of the relevant area; another, proposed by separate
nominating bodies for both the Cultural and Educational Panel and the Labour
Panel, was forced to choose between them, and selected the latter; and the
Labour party's Oireachtas nominee on the Cultural and Educational Panel
was disallowed, on the grounds that its candidate had already been proposed
by a nominating body.

Little effort was made to disguise the partisan nature of nominations to
both types of subpanel. In 1981, for instance, all but three candidates were
identified with one of the three main parties; all but twenty-five had been
previously active in electoral politics at the local or national level; twenty-six
had been candidates in the June 1981 Dáil election; and eleven were unsuccessful outgoing Dáil deputies. It was presumably because of the overwhelming
party political dominance of the elections that many nominating bodies agreed
to propose the candidacy of individuals prominently associated with political
parties rather than nominating independent candidates of their own. Others,
however, have followed a consistent tendency to favor one particular party; the
most outstanding example was the Irish Congress of Trade Unions, which is
closely linked to the Labour party.

The Oireachtas nominations were even more frankly political; each parliamentary party released details of the slate of candidates it had selected as a
party list. The collective party nature of this selection may be illustrated by the
instance of the Fine Gael list in 1981. An examination of the names of the
proposers of each candidate shows a clear alphabetical pattern: the party's
nominees on the Industrial and Commercial Panel were proposed by deputies

whose names began with letters B and C, moving to C–D on the Cultural and Educational Panel, E–K on the Labour Panel, and M–R on the Administrative Panel, with the remaining deputies and senators proposing the candidates on the Agricultural Panel. While the parties may informally solicit the opinion of the returning officer as to the acceptability of the qualifications of the proposed candidates, it is clear that the expression "knowledge and practical experience" is interpreted in a broad sense; it is party sponsorship that matters. A number of candidates had previously contested Senate elections on panels other than the one for which they were nominated in 1981, for example; in one case a candidate on the Labour Panel had previously been elected on the Agricultural and Administrative Panels.

The Campaign. Senate election campaigns differ in a number of significant respects from Dáil campaigns, and the recent elections were no exception. In the first place, conflict between parties and between candidates tended to find little public expression. This tranquility arose in part because the issues had already been thrashed out at length in the Dáil election campaign. It also reflected a perception that the outcome of the election was not crucial. Given the Taoiseach's right to nominate eleven senators, the opposition would find it difficult to capture control of the second chamber and, even were such an event to take place, it could in no way negate the government's control of the Dáil. That the pursuit of extra votes is far from ruthless may be seen from a consideration of the extent of double qualifications. Most deputies had a second qualification as county councillors, which was "wasted"; yet deputies were not put under any pressure to resign council seats with a view to maximizing the party vote by co-opting a replacement councillor of the same party. The gain to individual deputies from the dual local and national mandates was clearly seen to be greater than the gain to the parties from any possible expansion in their number of electoral college voters.

A further reason for the subdued nature of the campaign may be attributed to its second distinctive feature. Senate election campaigns tend to be individual rather than collective, and party headquarters play little role. After giving its imprimatur to a slate of candidates, the central party organization retires from the campaign until polling takes place. While electors vote in the presence of an "authorized person," the two larger parties in particular attempt to maximize turnout and to promote strict party voting. In 1981, for instance, Fianna Fáil appointed in each county and county borough a convenor whose duty it was to summon local electors to a central meeting preceding the completion of ballot papers. Fine Gael appointed thirty voting supervisors, whose areas of jurisdiction corresponded in general with administrative counties but occasionally with Dáil constituencies. The supervisors were to assist electors in filling in five specimen ballot papers—one for each panel—in order of choice for Fine Gael candidates, with preferences continuing for Labour candidates, for later transcription onto the official ballot papers in secret but in the presence of the authorized person. The Labour party, with fewer electors and a smaller number of candidates, did not find so much organization necessary. It nevertheless circulated to its electors a list of party candidates, requesting that, after casting top preferences for these candidates, other pro-government candidates be supported. Even Sinn Féin the Workers' party that had no candidates of its own, offered advice to its electors on candidates deemed worthy of support. Similar arrangements were made by the parties in 1982 and 1983, though by then the positions of the Labour party and of the Workers' party were slightly different.

The third distinctive feature of Senate campaigns is the role played by individual candidates. The importance of each vote in a small electorate and the large number of candidates pursuing the same party vote encourage an intense form of personal canvassing. The fact that the electorate is dispersed throughout the country makes a large amount of traveling necessary, contrasting sharply with the door-to-door canvass characteristic of Dáil elections, though no less exhausting. The absence of a "floating vote," aside from a small number of nonaligned electors, encourages intraparty rivalry and leaves nonparty politicians with little prospect of success.

The Results

The Vocational Panels. Since the composition of the Senate electorate is known (it is published as a supplement to the state gazette),[6] the strength of the parties can be gauged in advance of the election. The distribution of the electorate in 1981 is indicated in table 8.2. It had changed little since 1977: Fianna Fáil and Fine Gael were slightly stronger, the Labour party and others slightly weaker. The outcome of the election could be predicted with reasonable accuracy on the assumption that the first preference vote on each panel would reflect accurately the party political composition of the electorate, that the nonparty electors would not support an independent candidate or one of the three major parties *en bloc*, and that votes would transfer strictly within parties and between Fine Gael and Labour. Given its electoral alliance with Fine Gael, the Labour party could expect to win a single seat on each panel, with the two larger parties dividing the remainder evenly between them. In the event, this is precisely what happened. Labour ended up with five seats and Fianna Fáil and Fine Gael with nineteen each, matching one another equally on each panel.

The actual vote on each panel is summarized in table 8.2. The valid polling, ranging between 882 and 884, represented 98 percent of the electorate. The high degree of party voting is clear; much of the variation from one panel

Table 8.2 Distribution of electorate and of
votes in Senate panel elections, 1981, by party

Panel	Fianna Fáil	Fine Gael	Labour party	Others	Total
			Parties		
Culture and education	434	349	99	—	882
(N)	(13)	(9)	(1)	(0)	(23)
Agriculture	422	358	83	19	882
(N)	(12)	(14)	(2)	(1)	(29)
Labour	422	346	116	—	884
(N)	(8)	(7)	(6)	(0)	(21)
Industry and commerce	427	374	81	—	882
(N)	(17)	(19)	(1)	(2)	(39)
Administration	427	362	94	—	883
(N)	(8)	(8)	(1)	(0)	(17)
Electorate	404	335	82	82	903
(Total candidates)	(58)	(57)	(11)	(3)	(129)

Sources: Seanad Éireann, *Seanad General Election, August 1981, and Bye-elections to 1977–81 Seanad* (Dublin: Stationery Office, 1982), and information supplied by the political parties and by the Department of the Environment.
Note: Figures in parentheses refer to numbers of candidates.

to another may be explained in terms of variation in the behavior of the non-aligned vote. Fianna Fáil won between eighteen and thirty votes more than its strict party maximum (of 404, if all Fianna Fáil electors voted); Fine Gael won between eleven and thirty-nine above its party maximum (335); and the Labour vote ranged from one below to thirty-four above its number of electoral college votes (82). Not surprisingly, nonparty candidates fared poorly: the Oireachtas nominee on the Agricultural Panel won nineteen votes, but neither of the independent Nominating Bodies candidates on the Industrial and Commercial Panel won any.

This result was broadly reproduced in 1982 and 1983, when the level of turnout was similarly high. The composition of the electorate had changed little, except that in 1982 the parties of the outgoing coalition government were in a marginally better position. Despite this, however, Fine Gael lost a seat on the Administrative Panel to Fianna Fáil for reasons that will be seen below. With this exception, where Fianna Fáil won four seats to Fine Gael's two, the result on each panel in 1982 and 1983 was as in 1981: Labour won one seat, with the remainder being evenly divided between Fianna Fáil and Fine Gael. Independent and other candidates fared little better than before, those from the Nominating Bodies subpanels received almost no votes.

As has been observed, Oireachtas nominees tend to perform better in Senate elections than candidates proposed by nominating bodies.[7] Since the introduction of the present electoral rules in 1947 the Nominating Bodies candidates have almost never won more than the minimum number of seats they are guaranteed. Before 1981 the only exceptions were on two panels in 1948 and on one in 1951, when the Nominating Bodies candidates won a single seat more than the minimum number. The normal outcome, then, has been sixteen seats for Nominating Bodies and twenty-seven for Oireachtas candidates. It will be seen from table 8.3 that this tendency has been dramatically reversed in the three most recent elections. In 1981, Nominating Bodies candidates won two seats more than the minimum number, and in 1982 and 1983 this increased to five. So strong was this movement, indeed, that the rules for counting votes had to be invoked in several cases to ensure that the Oireachtas subpanel would receive due representation; in the past these rules had been used only to protect Nominating Bodies candidates. The most dramatic instance was in the case of the Administrative Panel in 1982, when the Fine Gael candidate who had led his party in terms of first preference votes was excluded along with other Nominating Bodies candidates to prevent that subpanel being overrepresented. Although Fine Gael's share of the poll should have entitled it to two additional seats, there was only one continuing Fine Gael candidate on the Oireachtas subpanel to whom its votes could transfer; Fianna Fáil thus won an extra seat at Fine Gael's expense.

Despite this reversal of the traditional bias, Oireachtas nominees tend on average to win more votes than their Nominating Bodies counterparts; in many cases, the better *aggregate* position of the latter arises simply because there are more candidates. One obvious explanation of the advantage enjoyed by Oireachtas nominees is that strong candidates with impeccable party cre-

Table 8.3 Distribution of seats by subpanel, Senate panel elections, 1981–1983

Panel	August 1981 subpanel Nominating bodies	Oireachtas	April 1982 subpanel Nominating bodies	Oireachtas	January 1983 subpanel Nominating bodies	Oireachtas
Culture and education	3	2	3	2	2	3
Agriculture	5	6	6	5	6	5
Labour	4	7	4	7	4	7
Industry and commerce	3	6	4	5	5	4
Administration	3	4	4	3	4	3
Total	18	25	21	22	21	22

Sources: Seanad Éireann, *Seanad General Election, August 1981, and Bye-elections to 1977–81 Seanad* (Dublin: Stationery Office, 1982); ibid., 1982; ibid., 1983.

dentials find it easier to secure an Oireachtas nomination. If so, might not the stronger electoral showing of Oireachtas nominees be due to their greater individual popularity, rather than to the recommendations of a political elite? This issue may be examined further by contrasting the characteristics of nominees to either subpanel. Candidates may be grouped into a number of categories, using the extent of their exposure to the Senate electorate as the primary criterion. In the case of the 1981 candidates, four groups were identified:

1. Outgoing deputies and senators, who had been in public eye for at least four years and had extensive opportunities for self-publicity (this group numbered forty-two, of whom eleven were former deputies).

2. Other persons involved in the national electoral process, who had had some media exposure, but where this was either not recent or not continuous (thirty-seven in number, including former deputies, former senators and candidates in Dáil elections or in the 1979 elections to the European Parliament).

3. Persons involved in politics at the local level only, whose reputations were confined to particular regions (twenty-four, comprising county and county borough councillors and candidates in the 1979 local elections).

4. Persons without any electoral involvement, who had to rely on a reputation for achievements, if any, in other areas (twenty-six in number).

This unidimensional yardstick of the strength of a candidate's profile has obvious drawbacks, and there are difficulties in assembling fully accurate information. Nevertheless, the absence of any alternative quantifiable criterion leaves little choice if an attempt is to be made to control for candidate type in assessing electoral attitudes toward the two subpanels.

The distribution of these four types of candidates between the two subpanels may be seen in table 8.4. It will be clear that the stronger the profile of the candidate, the greater the likelihood that he is an Oireachtas nominee. It will also be apparent, however, that Oireachtas nominees tend, on average, to win more votes, regardless of the type of group in question. Finally, the obvious point is confirmed that the higher the profile of the candidate the larger his average vote, regardless of the subpanel in question. The conclusion, then, appears to be that two factors contribute to a candidate's share of the vote: the strength of his public image and the subpanel to which he is nominated. It should be noted that the data on which table 8.4 is based have been weighted to control for differences in the numbers of candidates contesting each panel. The individual votes on each panel have been multiplied by a weighting factor (number of candidates on the panel concerned divided by mean number of candidates per panel) so that the mean adjusted vote per candidate is the same in each panel.

Another consideration that may affect a candidate's popularity with the Senate electorate is the likelihood of his subsequently winning a Dáil seat. If a

Table 8.4 Mean adjusted vote for selected groups
of candidates, Senate panel elections, 1981

Candidate type	Subpanel		
	Nominating bodies	Oireachtas	Total
Outgoing deputy or senator	42	51	47
(N)	(18)	(24)	(42)
Other national involvement[a]	33	36	34
(N)	(22)	(15)	(37)
Local electoral involvement[b]	28	37	31
(N)	(16)	(8)	(24)
No electoral involvement	15	28	17
(N)	(23)	(3)	(26)
Total	29	43	34
(N)	(79)	(50)	(129)

Sources: Calculated from data in Seanad Éireann, *Seanad General Election, August 1981, and bye-elections to 1977–81 Seanad* (Dublin: Stationery Office, 1982), and from data obtained from other sources.

Note: Figures in parentheses refer to numbers of candidates. The first preference vote won by each candidate has been adjusted to take account of variation in competitiveness across the panels (as measured by number of candidates per panel): it has been multiplied by the ratio of the number of candidates contesting the panel in question to the mean number of candidates per panel (which is 129/5, or 25.8).

a. Former deputy or senator, candidate in Dáil elections of 1981 or earlier, or in European elections of 1979.

b. Candidate in 1979 county or county-borough elections.

candidate has been narrowly defeated for a marginal seat in a Dáil election, for instance, party strategists may calculate that the party's interests would best be served by ensuring him the publicity attendant on a term in the Senate, thus improving the chances of winning an extra Dáil seat at the next general election. On the other hand, such a candidate may be seen as a threat by sitting deputies. Certain deputies are believed to make a practice of undermining potential rival power bases within their own local parties by promoting Senate candidates who have little prospect of a Dáil seat but who might provide invaluable assistance within the constituency. It has not been possible to take account of this factor in table 8.4 because of difficulties of measurement, but it may help to explain the pronounced electoral popularity of outgoing deputies and senators.

The University Constituencies. The elections for the two three-member university constituencies predictably contrasted with the panel elections. In the first place, the electorates, and consequently the numbers of voters, were much larger. The Dublin University electorate numbered nine thousand, of whom

62 percent cast valid votes in 1981, 64 percent in 1982, and 73 percent in 1983. In the National University fifty thousand electors were registered, and the valid turnout in the three elections was somewhat lower, at 48, 45, and 47 percent, respectively, in the three elections. Second, the grip of the political parties was considerably weaker; although several candidates had party connections, these were in general played down, with candidates tending to project themselves as independents or as individuals who had, at most, merely a leaning in the direction of a particular party. Third, and perhaps as a consequence of these two factors, popular interest in the university elections was a good deal higher than in the panel elections, with public meetings and debates taking place.

The tone of the campaign also varied from one university to the other. In neither case could it be said that a central issue dominated. Candidates in the National University constituency consisted of a mixture of those who stood for general policies and those defending positions on specific issues such as (in 1981) the poor, prisoners rights, Northern Ireland, and educational policy. One of the two specifically political candidates who had stood in the Dáil election, Gemma Hussey (later to become a Fine Gael deputy and government minister), was elected, but her Labour party colleague was defeated. On Hussey's election to the Dáil in 1982 her Senate seat was taken by party colleague James Dooge, former minister for foreign affairs. Dooge was joined in the Senate in 1983 by another former deputy, Michael D. Higgins, chairman of the Labour party, who took the seat held since 1977 by Professor John A. Murphy of Cork. The third seat was won in 1981 and held in the two subsequent elections by a candidate who represented the Simon Community, a voluntary social service organization.

The Trinity College candidates were similarly divided into those offering policies of a general nature and those defending particular interests. Only one party political candidate, who had contested the 1981 Dáil election on behalf of the Labour party, was returned in all three elections. A second seat was won in 1981 and subsequently held by another independent who was known for his strong views on the Northern Ireland issue, while the third seat alternated between two independents.

The Taoiseach's Nominees. In each case, the new Taoiseach was able to secure his government's position in the Senate by means of his eleven nominees. In 1981 Garret FitzGerald renominated an independent senator first nominated by Jack Lynch in 1977. This was T. K. Whitaker, a public servant who had been prominently involved in the country's industrial development policies since the 1950s. As part of the coalition government arrangements, four Labour party supporters were nominated on the proposal of the party leader, Michael O'Leary, while the remaining six members were Fine Gael supporters. One

Table 8.5 Party composition of Senate after general elections, 1981–1983

Section	Party	August 1981	April 1982	January 1983
Vocational panels	Fianna Fáil	19	20	19
(43)	Fine Gael	19	18	19
	Labour party	5	5	5
Universities	Fine Gael	1	1	1
(6)	Labour party	1	1	2
	Independents	4	4	3
Taoiseach's nominees	Fianna Fáil	—	8	—
(11)	Fine Gael	6	—	5
	Labour party	4	—	3
	Independents	1	3	3
Total	Fianna Fáil	19	28	19
(60)	Fine Gael	26	19	25
	Labour party	10	6	10
	Independents	5	7	6

Sources: Ted Nealon and Seamus Brennan, *Nealon's Guide to the 22nd Dáil and Seanad Election '81* (Dublin: Platform Press, 1981); *Nealon's Guide to the 23rd Dáil and Seanad: Election '82* (Dublin: Platform Press, 1982); and *Nealon's Guide to the 24th Dáil and Seanad: 2nd Election '82* (Dublin: Platform Press, 1983).

appointment was consequent on the Taoiseach's decision to nominate one government minister from outside the Dáil: James Dooge, the minister-designate for foreign affairs.

Charles Haughey dropped Whitaker in 1982 but, despite his weak position in the house in view of the results of the panel elections, two of his appointees were from Northern Ireland and were not members of Fianna Fáil: John Robb, a prominent Protestant of broadly nationalist views, and Seamus Mallon, deputy leader of the Social Democratic and Labour party (SDLP). A third nominee was a supporter of Neil Blaney's Independent Fianna Fáil party in Donegal, being thus disposed to be favorable to the new government.

In 1983 Garret FitzGerald went further, appointing three senators from Northern Ireland. In addition to renominating Robb and replacing Mallon by SDLP General Secretary Brid Rodgers, he also appointed a well-known northern trade unionist, Stephen McGonagle. This left only five seats for Fine Gael nominees and three for the Labour party, a balance that once again reflected interparty arrangements within the government.

Conclusion

The overall party political composition of the three Senates is indicated in table 8.5. It will be seen that in 1981 Fine Gael won a plurality (twenty) of the forty-nine elective seats, and the coalition parties had a clear position of dominance. This dominance was consolidated by the Taoiseach's appointees, which left the coalition with almost a two-to-one majority over Fianna Fáil. With thirty-six seats, the Fine Gael and Labour parties had the clearest lead they had ever enjoyed in the Senate since at least the 1950s (in 1977 they had twenty-four seats to Fianna Fáil's twenty-nine, and in 1973, when again there was a Fine Gael Taoiseach, thirty-five to Fianna Fáil's eighteen). This pattern was reproduced in 1983 (though Fine Gael lost one seat and Independents gained one), but was, of course, reversed in the intervening election. What is rather surprising about the 1982 case is that Charles Haughey, who after the Senate elections needed eleven more supporters to command a majority, chose to appoint only eight senators who were members of Fianna Fáil. This decision not to pursue an overall majority in the Senate again underlines the extent to which that chamber is seen as playing a subsidiary political role.

The elections did little to change the Senate's image as "a place for grooming new Dáil candidates and as a political resting place for defeated deputies."[8] In 1981 twenty-three senators had sought election to the Dáil, and in all, twenty-eight candidates defeated in the Dáil election (ten of them outgoing deputies) contested the Senate election in August. This tendency of the Senate to play the role of antechamber to the Dáil was reflected in its high turnover rate. In 1981 only twenty-four senators had been members of the outgoing body, and the corresponding figures in 1982 and 1983 were thirty and thirty-two.

The recent Senate elections have given no hint that the party political mold in which the selection process has been set is likely to crack, still less to be replaced by the vocational mold envisaged in the Constitution. To what extent does this pattern reflect the nature of Irish political culture, or how far is it a function of electoral law and technical provisions? It would be difficult to argue that the five groups of interests from which senators are elected (including the university representatives under the cultural and educational umbrella) correspond to five discrete segments of the Irish population. The area represented by the panels overlap, permitting individuals to be associated simultaneously with more than one panel. While Irish society, like industrial societies in general, is clearly patterned along class lines, it lacks the deep vertical segmentation into separate corporate entities that is a prerequisite to genuine vocational representation. For such representation, some source of division capable of challenging the dominance of the party political cleavage would be needed.

The electoral law, while it permits vocational representation and perhaps (by providing for Nominating Bodies candidates) even encourages it, does little to ensure that such representation will come about in so infertile a soil. There is nothing comparable with the strong voice given to vocational organizations in the selection of the Bavarian Senate. The rules that secure the election of a minimum number of Nominating Bodies candidates on each panel, regardless of the number of votes they have won, could be used to effect the return of candidates strongly committed to vocational interests rather than to political parties. This outcome would, however, require agreement among the Nominating Bodies that only such candidates would be put forward, an unlikely prospect in view of the diverse nature of the organizations registered on each panel.

Lacking such an arrangement, effective vocational representation will probably be procured only by nomination of *senators* (and not merely of candidates) by registered organizations, on the lines of the selection of the National Economic and Social Council. The council, an advisory body to the government, has succeeded in retaining as its basis a vocational principle of representation, while the Senate has failed. It consists of ten representatives each of industry, the trade union movement, and farming organizations, together with sixteen government nominees.

The three recent Senate elections confirmed, then, that the Irish experiment at the establishment of a vocationally oriented second chamber has foundered on the rock of the country's relatively homogeneous political culture; electoral law has been unable to assert an alternative set of political fault lines across the preexisting party political ones.

Notes

1. On the Senate in general, see Thomas Garvin, *The Irish Senate* (Dublin: Institute of Public Administration, 1969); and John MacG. Smyth, *The Theory and Practice of the Irish Senate* (Dublin: Institute of Public Administration, 1972).
2. The 1977 Senate election was the first to be the subject of extensive analysis; see Maurice Manning, "The Senate Election," in Howard R. Penniman, ed., *Ireland at the Polls: The Dáil Elections of 1977* (Washington, D.C.: American Enterprise Institute, 1978), pp. 165–73; and John Coakley, "The Irish Senate Election of 1977: Voting in a Small Electorate," *Parliamentary Affairs* 33, no. 3 (1980): 322–31.
3. Persons authorized to verify this procedure include the Senate returning officer, the clerk of the Dáil and certain local officials.
4. This difficulty is discussed in John Coakley and Gerald O'Neill, "Chance in Preferential Voting Systems: An Unacceptable Element in Irish Electoral Law," *Economic and Social Review* 16, no. 1 (1984): 1–18.
5. On Senate electoral law, see Garvin, *Senate*, pp. 24–39; and Smyth, *Senate*, pp. 27–43.
6. Supplement to *Iris Oifigiuil*, no. 57, 17 July 1981; ibid., no. 24, 23 March 1982; ibid., no. 104, 28 December 1982.
7. Garvin, *Senate*, p. 32.
8. Manning, "Senate Election," p. 167.

9 Prospects for Democratic Politics in Ireland
BASIL CHUBB

Political Climate

In the early 1980s the political climate in the Republic of Ireland was distinctly unsettled. The unprecedented succession of three general elections exacerbated, though it did not create, that unease. The elections of June 1981 and February 1982 were widely reckoned to be unsatisfactory because they produced "hung" (without safe government majorities) parliaments. Many deplored the fact that after both elections a few uncommitted and radically inclined deputies held the balance of power with consequential opportunities to exploit that position. The dissatisfaction was the greater because this period of Dála (assemblies) with no stable majorities and spancelled governments coincided with the low point of an economic recession sparked off by the second world oil crisis and with a growing recognition of the need, too long deferred, to adjust inflationary public spending policies to a more austere economic regime.

Nor did the advent of a government with a majority after the November 1982 election dispel the unease. Apart from the fact that, economically, things had to get worse before they could get better, the performance of the coalition government did not inspire confidence: evidence from polls in the summer and autumn of 1983 suggested that a majority wished to see yet another change of government. Besides, during the eighteen-month period of virtually continuous election fever, the electorate had been told much and had learned much about abuses of power by those in office, about "low standards in high places," about the factional fighting in the parties, and about the performance of its parliamentary representatives.

All this produced a malaise, a sense that the political system was working badly and a feeling that things must change. Social scientists with a longer perspective also contributed to this climate of opinion.[1] Perhaps many believed that Ireland had reached the end of an era politically, as it so evidently had economically.

Even with this growing unease and dissatisfaction, the elections themselves did not provide much, if any, evidence that fundamental changes in party and electoral politics had occurred or were likely to do so. The succession of three elections in a row, though unprecedented, was not the result of important shifts in electoral opinion, although these might have been expected given the considerable social changes of the past two decades. Nor had the politicians or political parties changed much except for the growing professionalism of the party machines. The basic structure of Irish electoral politics remained as yet unaltered.

What these elections brought home to people was rather the irrelevance of the Oireachtas to the solution of the fundamental problems facing the community. A growing recognition of the ineffectiveness of the Dáil in making policy led to growing criticism and, lately, proposals for and attempts at reform. More seriously, an increasing number of Irish people, like people in other modern democracies, are beginning to doubt whether electoral politics or parliaments have or can have the central relevance in some areas of policy that democratic theory prescribes and that those who talk and write about elections often seem to assume. In Ireland, as elsewhere, there have been efforts to conduct public business on tripartite or corporatist lines and to devise appropriate structures for the purpose. If they developed, these would effect an even more comprehensive removal of the Oireachtas to the governmental sidelines, as the experiences of the 1970s showed.

At a yet more fundamental level, Irish government, like government elsewhere, is showing signs of "overload" leading to "ungovernability," to use the terminology of the political scientist. So far, these signs are more indicative than substantial. Nevertheless, although Ireland is still a parliamentary democracy, there are no grounds for complacency about its prospects for remaining so. The democratic mainspring, its representative institutions, does not function well.

The 1981–1982 Campaigns

Although three general elections in quick succession led people to feel that something had changed and changed for the worse, on the contrary, very little had changed. These elections confirmed that the basic framework of Irish electoral politics stood almost as rigid and intact as ever. It did not require any fundamental shift of electoral opinion to produce a "hung" Dáil or "unstable" governments. This was a real possibility at many elections for a half-century, and occasionally it occurred. The results of the June 1981 and the February 1982 elections were not unlike those of February 1948. In the past, governments relied upon independents on a number of occasions. Although admittedly some of those so-called independents were virtually camp followers,

Table 9.1 Combined strength of the three major parties, Fianna Fáil,
Fine Gael, and Labour, at general elections, 1961–1982 (percent)

Election	First-preference votes	Seats won
1961	88	92
1965	97	98
1969	97	99
1973	95	99
1977	93	97
1981	92	95
1982 February	94	96
1982 November	94	97

Source: Calculated by author from election returns.

they could and did exact a price for their support, albeit their price was nothing like as high as that exacted by deputy Tony Gregory in 1982.

During almost the whole history of the state, the three major parties have dominated elections and politics generally. In these three elections, they together won between 92 percent and 94 percent of the total first-preference vote and between 95 percent and 97 percent of the seats. These proportions are within the range of their experience over the past half-century and, more precisely, within the narrower range typical of the past two decades (see table 9.1). Again, the support that each attracted was of the same order as usual. This was true even though, on the one hand, Fine Gael continued its steady growth winning its biggest ever share of the first-preference vote and of seats at the November 1982 election and, on the other, the Labour party continued its steady reversion to the level of support (9 percent) it had twenty-five years before. Significant though these shifts might have been, they did not upset the basic fact of Irish electoral arithmetic, namely that Fianna Fáil was still attracting the same general level of support that it had had over the previous half-century, sufficient to allow it to hope realistically for near enough to a majority of votes at any election to enable it to win a majority of seats and to form a government independent of all others.

In those circumstances—and, to repeat, they obtained during the whole of the previous half-century—governments were either Fianna Fáil, as they were for nearly forty out of the fifty years between 1932 and 1981, or anti-Fianna Fáil coalitions, as they were during the remaining ten years. The governments that emerged from the three elections of 1981–82 continued that pattern. If these elections showed evidence of changes, they were of the straws-in-the-wind variety: none of these were "realigning" elections.

Not surprisingly, there was no change in party strategies, nor did the electorate change its perception about the choices offered. These elections boiled down, as usual, to a choice between Fianna Fáil and a Fine Gael-Labour coalition. Fianna Fáil, appropriately to its level of electoral support, had always been and remained on these occasions, a strictly competitive party. On the other side, Fine Gael and Labour again pursued a coalition electoral strategy and, despite the hesitations and equivocations of Labour and the open hostility of some of its dissident minority, the public perceived them as the alternative to Fianna Fáil.

The incidence of three elections in quick succession was due to the activities in the Dáil of supporters of small parties and independents who had sufficient seats to hold the balance between the two major groups. Neither their members, however, nor the need of political leaders to attract some support from that quarter to secure a majority were of themselves anything new. What was new perhaps was that most of the small-party representatives and Independents were of a more independent and fissiparous breed than many of those in the past, as they showed by their willingness to bring down the governments that they had been instrumental in getting into office.

Not only did the *volume* of support for the three major parties remain consistent enough to preserve the essential foundations of Irish electoral politics, but also the *pattern* of that support, according to survey evidence. Table 9.2 shows the social composition of the vote for the major parties in 1969, 1977, and just before each of the three elections of 1981–82. On the basis of the 1969 Gallup survey, John Whyte characterized Irish politics as "politics without social bases,"[2] while R. K. Carty, reviewing the findings of an Irish Marketing Surveys poll in 1970, confirmed this: "The support bases of Irish parties do not rest upon distinctive social groups." He thought that by "comparative standards Irish parties have very broadly based support."[3] Both referred to the two biggest parties in particular, for they both recognized that to an extent the Labour party presented a different picture. The data in table 9.2 suggest that the same is still true. Likewise, Whyte's observation that Fianna Fáil "draws support fairly evenly from all social categories" was as true in 1982 as it was in 1969. So, too, Fine Gael: in 1969 it drew support from all categories, though not so evenly as Fianna Fáil. By 1981–82 its support more closely mirrored the community. Labour also has not altered much. If anything, it, like Fine Gael, has become more heterogeneous.

The same stability, relatively speaking, is evident in other measurable characteristics of the vote, for example, region, community type, or age. Certainly, there have been changes, even swings of a sort and generational changes, but these have not been major, permanent movements of a kind that might have caused a *fundamental* change in the pattern of electoral support. On the contrary, most writers remark upon the stability of the vote. In the whole of the country's electoral history, only the elections of the early 1940s have been generally identified as marking a "crucial" turning point sufficient to justify the use by some of the term "a realigning" election.[4]

Table 9.2 Social composition of major party vote, 1969–1982 (percent)

	1969	1977	1981	February 1982	November 1982
Fianna Fáil					
Nonmanual	32	20	27	25	25
Skilled manual	13	23	25	20	22
Unskilled manual	33	32	29	34	30
Farmers: 50 or more acres[a]	13	9	7	7	8
Farmers: Fewer than 50 acres[b]	9	16	13	14	15
Representatives[c]	7	10	7	12	9
Fine Gael					
Nonmanual	34	31	31	33	35
Skilled manual	12	14	21	22	18
Unskilled manual	19	16	21	22	23
Farmers: 50 or more acres[a]	28	16	15	15	13
Farmers: Fewer than 50 acres[b]	7	23	13	9	11
Representatives[c]	33	40	21	23	22
Labour					
Nonmanual	23	16	26	25	23
Skilled manual	21	28	23	19	25
Unskilled manual	52	53	44	44	45
Farmers: 50 or more acres[a]	2	1	4	4	5
Farmers: Fewer than 50 acres[b]	2	1	3	7	1
Representatives[c]	51	63	32	27	39
All respondents					
Nonmanual	30	24	28	27	28
Skilled manual	14	21	24	21	21
Unskilled manual	33	29	28	31	30
Farmers: 50 or more acres[a]	15	10	9	10	9
Farmers: Fewer than 50 acres[b]	7	16	11	11	12

Source: Michael Marsh, "Electoral Volatility in the Republic of Ireland, 1948–1983," in Ivor Crewe and David Denver, eds., *Electoral Volatility in Western Democracies* (Beckenham, Kent: Croom-Helm, 1985). Marsh's data derived from Social Surveys (Gallup Poll) for 1969 and from material made available by Irish Marketing Surveys Ltd.
a. In 1969, farmers with over 30 acres.
b. In 1969, farmers with under 30 acres.
c. Representativeness calculated by summing differences between party and whole-sample profiles.

Given the patterns of party support in Ireland, a major political change might be brought about if the electorate become more volatile, that is, if party support oscillated or swung more violently than it had in the past. Journalists and others have sought for, and occasionally found, signs that more people than hitherto change their allegiances, or that at this or that recent election there was a swing of the "farmer vote" or the "youth vote." It is said, for example, that the loss of office by the coalition government in the 1977 election occurred partly because the government had alienated the farm vote in the east. Just as the evidence of the composition of party support suggests, however, that no *large-scale* change in electoral opinion has occurred, according to Michael Marsh, neither do the various measures of elector volatility. On the contrary, using Pedersen's "volatility index," he found that "at five of the six elections between 1948 and 1965 net volatility was higher than at any of the six subsequent elections."[5] In addition, survey evidence of voting intentions, measured regularly between 1974 and 1982, indicates that since late 1979 fluctuations were much *less* pronounced than during the earlier period. Finally, analysis of survey evidence about how people had voted as well as their future voting intentions led Marsh to conclude that a large proportion of voters do not change their party preferences between two consecutive elections. All in all he concluded that "volatility had not increased."[6]

The political campaigns of these three elections also displayed considerable continuity with the past. Generalizing about the elections of the 1960s and 1970s, Michael Gallagher commented that

> even though the subjects of political debate were now social and economic, the issues remained as unclear as ever. It was practically impossible to discern genuine differences between the major parties. Both agreed that unemployment and inflation were undesirable, and claimed to be entirely pragmatic in their approach to these problems. . . . Both claimed to be non-ideological parties and both proclaimed the virtues of pragmatism. . . . [Labour's] left-wing rhetoric generally had a rather hollow and unreal ring about it because everyone knew that the party could attain power only as part of a coalition which would be at most slightly left of centre [7]

He thought that from the 1950s onward, elections were fought over issues like the competence and credibility of governments and the personalities and styles of party leaders.

Gallagher's generalizations would serve well to characterize the 1981–82 campaigns. It would be necessary to add only that these campaigns were notorious for an even greater element than before of "Dutch auction" politics: that is, promises and undertakings at both national and local levels designed to attract support regardless of their social or economic consequences or of general party policy.

Parties and Factions

The experience of the elections of 1981 and 1982 suggests that the foundations of Irish politics remained intact and that the considerable rigidity of the party system persisted. If there are to be major changes, they would have to be of a kind that undermines these foundations. What in recent experience suggests that such changes are in train?

First and most obvious is the persistence of the factions that arose within Fianna Fáil in the late 1960s. The intensification of these rivalries to the point that, in the very shadow of elections, some attempted to remove Charles Haughey from the leadership seems to be of great potential significance. The critical size of the electoral support for Fianna Fáil is a major governor of the structure and working of Irish politics. The ability of the party to maintain the level of that support election after election has contributed powerfully to keeping the whole system unchanged. If that support were to be permanently eroded, Irish politics might change considerably.

The persistence of these factions with periodic eruptions into challenges to the leadership almost certainly prevented the party from winning a majority at each of the 1981–82 elections. The "Haughey factor," people said, lost these elections for Fianna Fáil. Certainly, the remarkable events in the party in the years 1979–83 centered largely upon him—the manner of his accession, his style of leadership, his conduct of affairs, and his friends. All were unprecedented. Unprecedented, too, was the unhappiness of some of the middle-class supporters of the party at the activities and demeanor of some of Haughey's closest colleagues. Although he eventually won a decisive victory confirming his leadership, in 1983 few viewed him as the unequivocally accepted leader of a unified party.

Probably Fianna Fáil will never again be the loyal, unified "movement" that it once was, but it would be premature to forecast a radical change on account of the "Haughey factor" and the factional fighting of recent years. On the contrary, it is the resilience of the party during those years that is noteworthy. Split apart as it was, it could still win 45.3 percent of first-preference votes at the first of this series of elections, 47.3 percent at the second, and 45.2 percent at the third, all well above its lowest totals in the past. Assailed as Haughey was by powerful colleagues and handicapped by the antics of some of his friends and by his image as an electoral liability, he retained the support of that critical segment of the party that had put him into the leadership, namely backbenchers "with stronger links to local politics, to the activist organisation and, perhaps, to local opinion generally, particularly in small town, rural and working-class areas."[8] These are the critical people in the engine room of Fianna Fáil; it is they who above all are the key to Fianna Fáil's retention of its core support. This segment, together with those who in turn support them, yearn for the old days of a united movement whose leaders are ordinarily the government of the day. Never again will they have the leadership of a messianic kind like de Valera nor an apostolic successor like Lemass, but they will coalesce behind any leader who can win general elections. That is the touchstone. Many of these—more than is now admitted—wondered if Haughey was an electoral liability in 1981–82, as the opinion polls indicated he was, and it was on this account that they contemplated his removal. When the party faces the next election, much will depend on its assessment of him as an electoral winner. His recent success in asserting his leadership and the rise in his popularity rating probably mean that the question of replacing him will not even arise.

Fianna Fáil, which for so long had no succession problems, certainly has yet to learn how to handle them without doing itself harm. It is premature, however, to see a permanent erosion of its support arising from a leadership struggle. Party splits are the less likely because no obvious constitutional, ideological, or socioeconomic issues divide the party or cleave the electorate as a whole in such a way that a significant section of Fianna Fáil's heterogeneous support is sliced off.

It has been argued, though, that demographic changes might critically erode Fianna Fáil's parliamentary position. A study of regional patterns of voting has led Peter Mair to suggest that the shift of population and hence of parliamentary representation from the constituencies of the west, with their loyal and unwavering Fianna Fáil majorities, to Dublin and the east, with their more volatile electorate prone to swing from election to election, has upset an important, perhaps critical, stabilizer of Irish electoral politics.[9] In the past, he argues, Fianna Fáil's core strength in the west was solid enough to cushion the pendulumlike swing of the east and usually to allow the party to retain power, particularly if aided by the failure of Fine Gael and Labour party supporters to transfer their lower-preference votes within the coalition. Today, though, the steadily changing demographic profile no longer allows this to happen, and Ireland now has an "available electorate," that is, one that is more susceptible to wooing and more likely to register larger swings than before.[10] Because the government practice of manipulating constituency sizes and boundaries to its own advantage has lately given way to adjustments by nonpartisan electoral commissions, these demographic changes will no longer be hindered by gerrymandering in favor of the west. Although the precise effect of the changes that Mair identifies is problematic, its direction is clear: it makes life harder for Fianna Fáil, and just might harm it enough to alter fundamentally the pattern of party support.

This discussion of the possibilities of major changes in Irish politics has so far centered upon Fianna Fáil. On the other side, the continued rise in the support for Fine Gael has raised speculation over whether that party, after November 1982 within five seats of Fianna Fáil, is now poised to challenge Fianna Fáil as the alternative government in an essentially two-major-party system. The two principal factors behind the sharp increase in support for Fine Gael were Garret FitzGerald's personal popularity and the moderniza-

Table 9.3   Strength of the major parties at elections, 1932–1982 (percent)

Party	First-preference votes				Seats			
	1932–77 Min. Max.	1981	1982 (Feb.)	1982 (Nov.)	1932–77 Min. Max.	1981	1982 (Feb.)	1982 (Nov.)
Fianna Fáil	42 52	45	47	45	44 57	47	49	45
Fine Gael	20 35	36	37	39	21 38	39	39	42
Labour	8 17	10	9	9	5 15	9	9	10

Source: Calculated by author from election returns.

tion that transformed it into a much more efficient organization than it had ever been. It is now plausible to argue against the traditional view that the main parties enjoy fundamentally different levels of support (see table 9.3).

In the early 1980s some in Fine Gael claimed that the party was now a *parti a vocation majoritaire*, to use Duverger's term, that is, a party that has a parliamentary majority or thinks and acts as though it is likely to be able to command one. This stance would lead it to pursue a strictly competitive strategy. No doubt many of its local activists and some of its leaders would do this happily, for they can hardly abide coalition with Labour. Paradoxically, however, if Fine Gael acted in this way, it would lose a sizable proportion of Labour party supporters' transfers, which in the past were the votes that helped to win the extra few seats to bring it to its present position. This would make a formidable task the more difficult.

Indeed, an element of euphoria runs through Fine Gael's aspirations, certainly in the short term. The hardships due to recession will not have disappeared before the next election, even if that were delayed to the last possible moment. Nor will the more deep-rooted economic problems have been solved. The task will be made more difficult because of doubts about FitzGerald's ability to lead the party or the coalition government with sufficient guile or muscle. His handling of the abortion referendum issue in 1983 increased these doubts considerably. At that time and after, the ambivalence toward him of some deputies of his own party and of some party activists was very evident. For Fine Gael, too, has internal dissensions. Like the other parties, these result from its failure more than a decade ago to solve problems of modernization, epitomized in the controversy sparked off by the publication of *A Just Society*, the manifesto of a progressive younger element in the party who were attempting to revise its social aims and program.

An alternation of power between Fianna Fáil and Fine Gael, each realistically able to hope for a majority, is an unlikely development: still less, an entirely new left-versus-right alignment of Irish politics advocated by a few on the far left and the far right. Fianna Fáil and Fine Gael have together never won more than 85 percent of first preferences. It is hard to envisage a situation where they will virtually monopolize the vote or, given proportional representation, the seats. If the present situation changes fundamentally at all, it is likely to be because the parties become more evenly matched at a level where allies are needed to attain office. Fine Gael has always been in this position: Fianna Fáil has recently had to contemplate it. Already, in the 1981–82 elections, Fianna Fáil took a step in this direction when Haughey engaged in talks with the smaller parties and Independents.

If the formation of coalitions were only a matter of agreement on policies to be pursued in office, it could be convincingly argued that coalition—whether of Fine Gael and Labour, Fianna Fáil and Labour, or even of Fianna Fáil and Fine Gael in what would be almost a "grand coalition"—should not be too difficult to arrange. In a comparative study of the policy stances of parties in national party systems and of party members inside parties, Ronald Inglehart and Hans Klingemann found that, when judged by reference to attitudes on socioeconomic issues, Irish parties were closer together than the parties in any other European Community country (see figure 9.1). Much the same might be said in relation to other issues. Paradoxically, coalition might be easier because, as Inglehart and Klingemann also found, *inside* each of the three main Irish parties members had more disparate views on socioeconomic issues than had the members of any other community party. If successful coalitions were only or mainly a matter of "policy distance," they should be easier to make and sustain in Ireland than elsewhere. The experience of Fine Gael and Labour also might seem to support this. If the newly installed Oireachtas committee system works, it might well promote more bipartisan attitudes on policy issues.

There is, however, more to the successful practice of coalition politics than considerable agreement on policy issues. The style of politics in a country becomes a way of life for those who practice the art. In Ireland, party politics have usually been, above all, adversary politics. There are good historical reasons for this, and though to a great extent these no longer obtain, ingrained attitudes and traditional practices persist. Fianna Fáil in particular has always been the very epitome of a party that practices strictly competitive politics. For periods during two decades (1948–57 and 1973 to date), Fine Gael and Labour have formed and sustained coalitions, but many in those parties regard them as an unpalatable necessity to keep Fianna Fáil out.

Here perhaps distinctions need to be drawn between leaders, other party activists and members, and supporters. No doubt "elite accommodation," that is, agreement and compromise among leaders who desire to get and hold onto office, are relatively easy as the experience of the Fine Gael-Labour coalition shows. It is not too difficult to envisage even Fianna Fáil leaders making such accommodation. Undoubtedly, too, parties can persuade their supporters in the electorate to transfer lower preferences to the party's advantage. It is a

Figure 9.1   Location of political parties on a left-right dimension (numbers indicate the specific political parties as given in the key alongside)

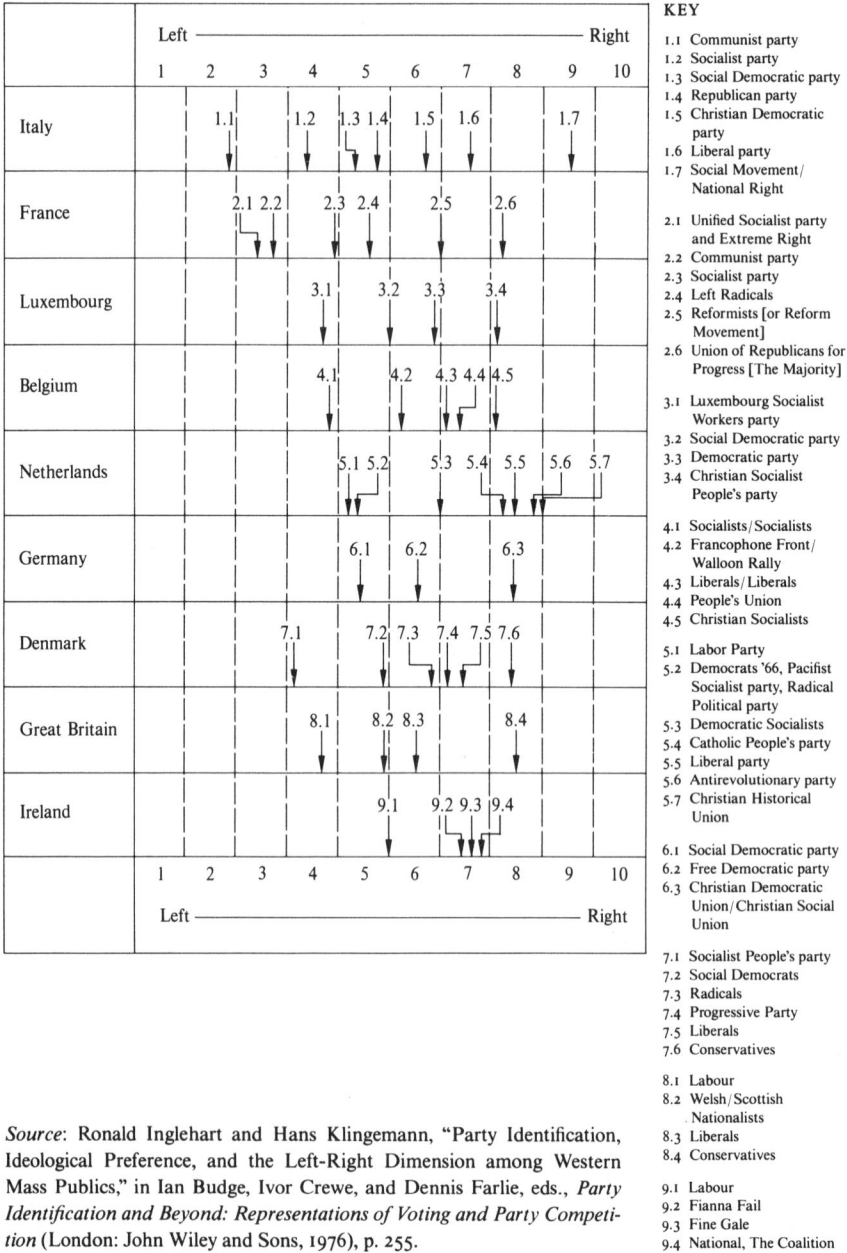

	Left ———————————— Right	
	1 2 3 4 5 6 7 8 9 10	
Italy	1.1 1.2 1.3 1.4 1.5 1.6 1.7	
France	2.1 2.2 2.3 2.4 2.5 2.6	
Luxembourg	3.1 3.2 3.3 3.4	
Belgium	4.1 4.2 4.3 4.4 4.5	
Netherlands	5.1 5.2 5.3 5.4 5.5 5.6 5.7	
Germany	6.1 6.2 6.3	
Denmark	7.1 7.2 7.3 7.4 7.5 7.6	
Great Britain	8.1 8.2 8.3 8.4	
Ireland	9.1 9.2 9.3 9.4	
	1 2 3 4 5 6 7 8 9 10	
	Left ———————————— Right	

KEY

1.1 Communist party
1.2 Socialist party
1.3 Social Democratic party
1.4 Republican party
1.5 Christian Democratic party
1.6 Liberal party
1.7 Social Movement/National Right

2.1 Unified Socialist party and Extreme Right
2.2 Communist party
2.3 Socialist party
2.4 Left Radicals
2.5 Reformists [or Reform Movement]
2.6 Union of Republicans for Progress [The Majority]

3.1 Luxembourg Socialist Workers party
3.2 Social Democratic party
3.3 Democratic party
3.4 Christian Socialist People's party

4.1 Socialists/Socialists
4.2 Francophone Front/Walloon Rally
4.3 Liberals/Liberals
4.4 People's Union
4.5 Christian Socialists

5.1 Labor Party
5.2 Democrats '66, Pacifist Socialist party, Radical Political party
5.3 Democratic Socialists
5.4 Catholic People's party
5.5 Liberal party
5.6 Antirevolutionary party
5.7 Christian Historical Union

6.1 Social Democratic party
6.2 Free Democratic party
6.3 Christian Democratic Union/Christian Social Union

7.1 Socialist People's party
7.2 Social Democrats
7.3 Radicals
7.4 Progressive Party
7.5 Liberals
7.6 Conservatives

8.1 Labour
8.2 Welsh/Scottish Nationalists
8.3 Liberals
8.4 Conservatives

9.1 Labour
9.2 Fianna Fail
9.3 Fine Gale
9.4 National, The Coalition

Source: Ronald Inglehart and Hans Klingemann, "Party Identification, Ideological Preference, and the Left-Right Dimension among Western Mass Publics," in Ian Budge, Ivor Crewe, and Dennis Farlie, eds., *Party Identification and Beyond: Representations of Voting and Party Competition* (London: John Wiley and Sons, 1976), p. 255.

different matter for the party rank and file at constituency and local levels: they above all are uneasy in coalition situations. Nor do the deputies adapt well to genuine coalition practice. Irish parliamentary practice contrasts greatly with the consensus politics of those European countries where coalition politics are the norm. It also differs from the practice of the European Parliament. Irish members of that parliament, all of whom are, or have been, members of the Oireachtas, tell of having to adapt to a wholly different style of operation from that to which they were accustomed at home.

In spite of the experience of Fine Gael and Labour, the practices and demeanor of active participants in parliamentary, electoral, and constituency levels reflect the Irish tradition of adversary politics. Those who engage in it, above all in Fianna Fáil, will not easily abandon the habits of a lifetime. Although the political situation might seem to require coalition politics, and leaders within a hand's grasp of winning power are likely to make coalition pacts, genuine coalition politics with all parties willing to be involved might be some way off.

Stability and Local Politics

This analysis has suggested that the considerable stability of Irish politics to which attention has so often been drawn persisted into the early 1980s. Further, it is far from certain that anything like radical changes in the party system or electoral politics are impending, despite the general unease and, as survey evidence indicates, higher levels of dissatisfaction with all governments. Over the years, the system has accommodated or withstood the decline of the constitutional issues on which it was based; the departure of the "revolutionary generation" of leaders who founded it; the subsequent resurgence in worsened form of the Northern Ireland problem; a quarter of a century of rapid industrial and economic change that transformed the country from an agricultural, rural society into an urban, industrial one; and considerable though hesitant changes in the culture of the community.

On the contrary, one basic feature of the system, its clientelist and localist character, has seemingly strengthened (many political scientists would have hypothesized the reverse). Writing of the early 1970s, R. K. Carty identified this feature as still a governing factor in Irish electoral politics, which left the parties "with neither the will nor the capacity to develop an effective policy-making machinery."[11] Similarly, Tom Garvin's study of Haughey's accession to the leadership in 1979 led him to conclude that "Fianna Fáil's central motor is its network of localist connections."[12] The same could be said of the other parties. More generally, reviewing the experience of the past quarter of a century, Garvin concluded that "the primacy of the politics of local representation over the politics of government . . . is as strong in 1982 as it was in 1957—

perhaps stronger . . . political life is still a matter of the parish pump writ large at national level." [13]

There was ample evidence of this in 1981–82. Leaders seeking to scrape up enough support in the Dáil to be elected Taoiseach, as well as governments with insecure majorities, paid considerable attention to constituencies with marginal seats and to individual deputies who might be wooed. The period was particularly marked—disfigured some would say—by the greater attention than usual paid to satisfying many constituency and local demands and interests; by the wheeling and dealing of leaders and local activists alike to "deliver" a seat, or better still, an extra seat; by the appeasing of regional ambitions for a minister or a minister of state or at least a senator from the area, the better to look after it, of course. There appeared to be a growth of the well-known Irish phenomenon of the local "bailiwick," that is, of identifying an individual deputy, despite the electoral system of proportional representation in multimember constituencies, with a particular area within his constituency. This area, regarded as his territory where he is seen as the sole source of patronage, is free from penetration by his fellow deputies of the same party. He also would expect to be consulted by ministers or shadow ministers on the interests of this region. Admittedly, in recent elections evidence has also pointed in the other direction. The central organizations of the parties have on occasion tried to break down the bailiwick system in certain constituencies. "Vote management," that is, cooperation between candidates of a party in a constituency to get their supporters to vote in such a way as to maximize the impact of the party vote, has been practiced in a few constituencies in recent elections. The strong instinct of territoriality, however, which is deeply bred into members and followers alike, will not be changed easily by leaders at headquarters.

In these circumstances, elections tend to focus much more on electing local public persons to office and keeping them there than on elucidating the general direction that the public desires the government to take. As a consequence, the role of the party system and of the Oireachtas in making policy is meager. In Ireland the significance of elections and electoral politics as an influence upon public policy is arguably small. They do not play the central role that some democratic theories propose and many people imagine. Except for the admittedly important function of producing governments and offering the possibility of changing one set of leaders for another, they are not, literally, decisive events. Perhaps the constitutionalist view that the heart of political decision making lies in the interaction between government and an Oireachtas that mirrors public opinion needs to be modified in present-day Ireland. Evidence suggests an increasing recognition of this fact, as well as attempts to remedy the situation. There have also evolved alternative procedures for policy making that bypass the ordinary constitutional channels. More generally, some signs point to a breakdown of the whole system.

The Oireachtas and Policy Making

It cannot by any stretch of the imagination be said that the Dáil deputies returned at any of the trio of elections had received coherent instructions from their electorates, not least because those electorates were not asked coherent questions. Although the campaign debates in each case featured the problems most in the mind of the public, they either took place on a highly generalized plane or concentrated on bickering over marginal issues like the size of the current budget deficit. To a considerable extent they were not about issues at all, but about capacity—who would make the better Taoiseach? Of course, the party appeals were also loaded with election "goodies"—favorable decisions on local matters and promises of attractive benefits on a regional or national level.

The mandates that each incoming government received in these circumstances can at best be described as imprecise. Perhaps it is too much to expect more. Do incoming governments and representative assemblies anywhere ever get precise instructions except in unusual circumstances? Perhaps not, but that does not prevent the parliamentarians of some countries from playing a positive role in the formation of policy. No doubt the practice of all countries falls short of the liberal-democratic ideal to some degree. It falls very short indeed in the case of Dáil Éireann.

The Irish adopted the British parliamentary system at a time when the British parliament was strongly dominated by the cabinet, which had acquired a monopoly of initiative in proposing policy and legislation. The Dáil has never broken out of this tradition, and for purposes of retaining their seats, deputies do not need to break out of it, given the election system and highly developed clientelist practices. The long survival of this type of politics and even its intensification recently have not encouraged deputies to assume a more active role in policy formation or surveillance.

An increasing number of deputies, however, recognize this problem. A Fine Gael policy document published in 1980 and largely the work of John Bruton, one of the younger generation of deputies, was unequivocal on the subject: "In practice it [the Dáil] plays practically no effective part in either making the laws or even the expert criticism of them."[14] It is the government that introduces virtually all policy proposals and legislative changes, and it is the members of the government on the one side and a small group of opposition leaders on the other—the so-called shadow cabinet or shadow spokesmen —who have the lion's share of debating these proposals. Furthermore, because

Irish parliamentarians from the beginning adopted a strictly gladiatorial style of behavior, the opposition either does not want to play a constructive role or is not permitted to do so.

In these circumstances, the contribution of the Dáil to making policy is small: the Seanad's is even smaller. Even where members do have a lively interest, as for example in health or social services, it is more often than not from the point of view of their constituents as individual consumers, or in the case of agriculture, as local producers. When it comes to public expenditure, their contribution has been cursory; in the case of defense and foreign affairs, it has been negligible. In the 1960s and 1970s, major policy developments in such areas as economic planning and incomes policy occurred without the prior approval of the Dáil and, in fact, without much Dáil discussion at any time.

All this is not to say that governments can ignore entirely the expression by deputies of the desires and reactions of their constituents. This is, however, essentially a negative influence, consisting of advice about what "they" will not accept "down the country," west of the Shannon, or wherever. What it does mean is that within this constraint, and always provided that ministers ensure that enough regard is paid in their departments to deputies representations, governments have considerable freedom for maneuver and deputies, as one of them, Barry Desmond, so cruelly put it a few years ago, are "political favour peddlers, consumer representatives, and clerical messenger boys on behalf of constituents." [15]

In recent years, this state of affairs began to evoke criticism from some of the politicians involved, which the Fine Gael document reflected. Perhaps it was caused by the influx of larger numbers of deputies with third-level education and of more young professional people. Paradoxically, it occurred during a period when the amount of constituency work and the ferocity of competition among deputies to engage in it were increasing and when more and more ministers were employing growing numbers of people in their departmental secretariats at state expense to handle constituency matters. The Fine Gael *Policy on Reform* evoked enough support, at least at leader level in the coalition, to set a reform movement in motion. In 1981 a government discussion document entitled *A Better Way to Plan the Nation's Finances* proposed a much greater involvement of deputies in deciding and scrutinizing state spending. Previously, after years of desultory advocacy by both Fianna Fáil and the coalition when out of office, a committee to examine the reports and accounts and overall operating results of state-owned enterprises had been set up in the late 1970s. In 1983, by agreement between the parties, a number of committees either of the Dáil or of the two houses (joint committees) were instituted. The intention was to increase the role of the public representativeness in policy formation and the control of expenditure and to improve their ability to scrutinize the conduct of the government. Some of these committees are potentially of great significance, for their activities could alter the role of parliamentary representatives and the relationship between the Oireachtas and the government.

Traditionally, the Oireachtas has not operated through committees to any great extent, and the reports of those committees that have sat have usually not been debated or followed up in any systematic way. Nothing like the powerful committees found in Congress or in the state legislatures of the United States has ever existed in Ireland. Such powerful committees as those are the product of a very different, more potent, concept of the role of parliament as "the legislature" and parliamentary representatives as "legislators."

Among the committees instituted in 1983, however, the activities of at least two could radically alter the relationship between governments and the Oireachtas, if they work as intended. It is precisely this that the minister responsible, John Bruton, said he did intend: "Changes which I will be seeking to introduce will, I hope, have the effect of restoring the balance in favour of democratically elected representatives and restoring their primary role in the formulation of our legislation and in the granting of money paid in taxes by our people. This is why representatives are elected." [16] (We can perhaps forgive him the use of the word "restoring.") One of these potentially significant committees is the Dáil Committee on Public Expenditure, which, among other things, "will be concerned with the examination of the policy behind longer term Government spending programmes in any area it chooses." The purpose is "to involve Dáil Deputies to a much greater extent in examining *the effectiveness of and justification for ongoing programmes* of public expenditure." [17]

Another committee, the Joint Committee on Legislation, is more radical in concept—radical at least in an Irish context—for it

> will be empowered to invite views in writing and orally from interested persons or groups on the subject matter of Bills or other legislative proposals which are referred to it. . . . The intention is that the Committee . . . will then publish a record of their proceedings before the second stage of the Bill is ordered or, in fact, before the legislation is finally drafted, as appropriate.[18]

The evident influence of U.S. practice is as striking as is the break from traditional Irish practice based on the early twentieth-century British pattern.

Through the establishment of these and other committees, the minister, John Bruton, "hoped that both the role of the Houses of the Oireachtas and of the individual members can be enhanced." [19] If they do establish themselves and operate as he appeared to envisage, it will indeed. It is a big "if," involving as it does changes in long-established attitudes, priorities, and working practices of ministers, higher civil servants, and, above all, rank-and-file deputies. Will capacity and zeal at this kind of activity pay dividends at the ballot box? That might be the crucial question.

Toward a Corporatist State?

Introducing his proposals for Oireachtas reform, John Bruton suggested a second reason why the relevance of public representatives, and hence of elections, to policy making has been increasingly called in question recently: "While the Oireachtas is the constitutional body responsible for the enactment of legislation, modern society has given rise to powerful pressure groups which have found it more beneficial to lobby Governments directly because the Government is seen to be the controlling power of the State apparatus."[20] It is, of course, in the very nature of pressure groups to seek to make their representations and apply their pressure directly to those who have the power to make the decisions that they desire to influence. Nor is there necessarily anything undesirable about this from the point of view of democracy: on the contrary, according to pluralist theories of democracy. Increasingly, however, pluralist theories have come to be seen as inaccurate or overoptimistic. In particular, critics point to the development in many countries of political structures and practices involving ministers, public servants, and the spokesmen of major pressure groups to decide policy and conduct administration by agreement among themselves. A decade ago, Philippe Schmitter dubbed these developments "societal corporatism," and it appeared to him that they were "the concomitant, if not the ineluctable, component of the post-liberal, advanced capitalist, organized democratic welfare state."[21]

Developments of this kind have taken place in Ireland in recent years. Some of them at least appear to have cut new channels of political activity effectively bypassing the admittedly silted up parliamentary channels that the constitution prescribes. It is this type of development that threatens the relevance of the Oireachtas more than the simple lobbying activities to which John Bruton referred.

The practice of associating representatives of pressure groups with policy making and administration in a more positive way than by merely making representations is of long standing. By the middle of this century, interest spokesmen were to be found not only on advisory and consultative bodies but also on the boards of administrative agencies and state enterprises, together usually called "state-sponsored bodies" in Ireland. Sometimes the relevant industry, employer body, trade union, or professional association acquired formally or de facto the right to nominate their representative. Such membership means that a pressure group is directly involved in government in an area in which it has an interest. The Oireachtas, or at least the nonofficial members of the two houses, have little influence, direct or otherwise, on the policies of these bodies or over their conduct of business. It is only recently with the reports of the Joint Committee on State-Sponsored Bodies that the Oireachtas has even been put in possession of systematic information and then only about one group of these bodies, the commercial or public enterprise group.

From the 1950s new patterns of decision making emerged for dealing with industrial development, prices, wages, and economic and social planning generally. Their characteristic feature was the tripartite membership of the bodies set up to deal with these matters. The Capital Investment Advisory Committee and the Committee on Industrial Organization set up to deal with problems of adapting Irish industry to membership of the European Communities were among the first. By the 1960s the normal pattern had become a tripartite arrangement (government, management, and labor), with much of the work being done by professional staffs and officers. In 1963 the National Industrial Economic Council (NIEC), created to study and advise on the development of the economy, was composed largely of public servants, representatives of the Irish Congress of Trade Unions, and employer bodies. Its enlarged successor from 1973, the National Economic and Social Council (NESC), which included spokesmen for agriculture as well as the NIEC troika, was designed to be "a forum for discussion of the principles relating to the efficient development of the national economy and the achievement of social justice and to advise . . . on their application."[22] Its remit covered almost every aspect of economic policy and many social and developmental problems.

Although NIEC and NESC were essentially advisory bodies, they were clearly at the heart of state economic planning, for their membership included the state's planners and their reports obviously influenced policymakers and thus policy. As important, their deliberations created a climate of opinion among a small group of key people in the community. The very kind of planning attempted, what had come to be known as "indicative planning," required "the introduction into policy responsibility of those persons and institutions who had most influence in the economy,"[23] and what success it achieved was due to this. Reviewing this period, the historian J. J. Lee thought that these bodies "began the integration of management and trade unions into the formulation of public policy" and that "a subtle shift in the nature of public decision making" had taken place.[24] This was "tripartism," as defined by Grant, a system in which major economic decisions are discussed and agreed upon between the state and the major employer and trade union bodies.[25]

The experience of the Employer-Labour Conference in the making and monitoring of national wage agreements from 1970 onward illustrates how easily further steps were taken down the same road. By this time it was coming to be recognized that without some certainty about the direction and pace of wage changes and some degree of control over them, economic planning and even short-term budgeting were hazardous exercises. For their part, employer organizations were coming to recognize that wage movements were inextricably tied up with state decisions of such matters as tax and changes in social welfare contributions and benefits. By the early 1970s the Federated Union of Employers advocated more state involvement and "argued the case for effective tripartite negotiations."[26]

In this area, it appeared, the state had perforce to seek, while employers and unions had to assume, the role of "social partners" making and attempting to fulfill "social contracts," that is, mutually agreed-on arrangements to which, when made, all three parties were bound to conform and which they had to enforce so far as they could. Although national wage agreements were voluntary agreements, they were adopted as state policy, were binding on the public sector, and were enforced in the private sector so far as the parties, including the state, could manage. A small steering committee, which met frequently and regularly for more than a decade, became a potent instrument for interpreting, monitoring, and enforcing the agreements. On occasions, the state legislated to enforce agreements. Thus, national wage agreements came to have, in the words of the historian of Irish trade unionism, "something of the character of public law."[27] In 1979 the national wage agreement was incorporated in a wider agreement, the National Understanding for Economic and Social Development, which, besides pay, covered taxation, industrial development, employment, industrial relations, social welfare, and health. A similar "understanding" was agreed on in 1980.

Thus by the end of the decade the major umbrella organizations in the industrial sector were directly involved in making policy, which the state was committed to implementing and to which they, in turn, were committed to trying to get their members' consent and subsequent compliance. Increasingly, they had become "agencies of mobilization and social control for the state vis-à-vis their members,"[28] and Ireland was exhibiting another of the distinguishing characteristics of corporatist politics. Although the 1980 National Understanding was not followed by another and the system of national wage agreements was abandoned—both victims of the second world oil crisis—in 1982 Lalor was able to say with some justification that Ireland still had a wage policy by "climate of opinion." Moreover, in 1983 the Federated Union of Employers chided the government for not having taken up its proposal for what it called a "sensible" national pay policy integrated with modest changes in taxation.

Similar relationships are evident elsewhere. In the agricultural sector the government and the umbrella organizations have close working relationships that are the more necessary because in this sector many decisions are made in Brussels and not Dublin, where, to some extent, they both operate as pressure groups in tandem. In 1977 Mark Clinton, a former minister for agriculture, said that "Ministers for Agriculture have become Ministers for Farmers": reciprocally, the Irish Farmers' Association now has "to be regarding . . . [itself]

as in a kind of partnership with the Government."[29] Similarly, some discern a symbiotic though unformalized relationship between the Roman Catholic Church and the state in respect to education and perhaps some aspects of other social services, though, as John Whyte showed conclusively in his *Church and State in Modern Ireland 1923-1979* (Dublin, 1980), it is necessary to be very cautious making generalizations in this area.

It has been a notable feature of tripartite or corporatist activities that they have been carried on in private, as is so much of the business of policy making in any case. Policies made by the process described above hardly, if at all, involved the Oireachtas at any stage, even in ex post facto legitimation. As far as the Oireachtas was concerned, the reports of NIEC and NESC might never have been written. Ireland's economic plans, coyly known as "programmes," were not formally submitted to the Oireachtas nor were successive wage agreements and national understandings.

These developments have contributed to the growing divorce of parliamentary, party, and electoral politics from policy making and administration in some areas of public business. In his contribution to the Institute of Public Administration's twenty-five-year survey of Irish society and government, T. J. Barrington summed it up thus: "Strategic decisions about the society have been reached with the 'social partners' or with the great vocational and corporate interests, not with the legislature. One wonders how the democratic system can maintain itself when its central institution is content to be largely irrelevant to such major decision-making."[30] Although it is possible that Ireland will not go farther down the road to corporatism in the immediate future, Lalor concluded from his study of Irish developments that "the trend towards the integration of the central interest groups into the decision making processes of the state . . . seems certain to persist."[31] It is clear that governments need the close cooperation of the major pressure groups and that they, or their leaders at least, see great advantages in this cooperation also. Whatever the forms that cooperation takes—and it does not have to be highly institutionalized in formal organizations or mandatory procedures and behavior—it will inevitably involve close relationships between a small number of politicians in power, senior public servants, and pressure group officers and spokesmen. As S. E. Finer once remarked, "A close relationship tends to become a *closed* one."[32] Ireland's experience in recent years bears testimony to the truth of Finer's aphorism.

Although these developments have certainly closed policy making and administration to the Oireachtas in the relevant areas, a more sanguine view is possible with a wider democratic perspective. In the past, most writers on this subject have viewed corporatist phenomena as a threat to democracy. More recently, however, others have noted that at least some of these developments involve considerable participation or representation of those affected.

This was precisely a feature of the procedures adopted by both employers and unions in Ireland in making the national wage agreements. It was the practice of the Irish Congress of Trade Unions to seek a mandate from a delegate conference both to open negotiations and, subsequently, to ratify a draft agreement. Delegates to these conferences numbered between four and five hundred: in addition, many constituent unions submitted the draft agreements to a ballot of their members to mandate their delegates. On the employers' side, negotiations on behalf of the major umbrella organization, the Federated Union of Employers, operated under the guidance of its General Council, which comprised 250 members. Draft agreements were submitted not only to this body for approval but also to sectoral and regional representative bodies as well. By procedures of this sort, leaders of corporate groups can, in Alan Cawson's words, "derive their legitimacy from popular involvement," and Robert Dahl's term "corporate pluralism" might seem to apply. By contrast, the government was conspicuous by its failure to consult its representative institutions.[33]

The Problem of Ungovernability

T. J. Barrington wrote of "the hastening drift of ungovernability"[34] in his survey of Irish politics during the last quarter of a century, which, significantly, he entitled, "Whatever Became of Irish Government?" The development of tripartism was itself in part a response by government to a growing problem of getting the consent and compliance necessary for the successful conduct of economic policy. Similar phenomena have been remarked upon in other democratic countries. Some writers have discerned a general tendency to what they term "overload" and "ungovernability."

Richard Rose, defining ungovernability as "the problems thrown up by challenges to the authority of fully legitimate governments,"[35] pointed out that these problems are not concerned wholly with consent and compliance but also with effectiveness. Effectiveness suffers when governments become overloaded, whether in financial matters or in their ability to cope with their public services. The need for consent and compliance on the one hand is related to a need for effectiveness on the other, and in some democracies today that relationship might be, and some writers say is, a malignant one. Many economists and political scientists and some politicians would argue that most democracies are clearly overloaded, with public expenditure and public sector wage costs outstripping available resources and with clear signs of overcomplex, overstrained political and administrative organizations failing to administer or enforce the law in some areas. Many politicians, however, particularly those in office or aspiring to it, some political scientists, and a few economists recognize that electorates long used to rising levels of prosperity will not tolerate

227

Table 9.4 Expenditure of public authorities
in Ireland, 1961–1980 (percent of GNP)

	1961	1971	1980
Total public expenditure	33.7	43.5	66.0
Social expenditure (education, health, housing, social welfare)	13.9	20.4	27.1

Source: Derived from K. A. Kennedy, "The Fiscal Framework," in *Ireland in the Year 2000: Towards a National Strategy—Issues and Perspectives* (Dublin: An Foras Forbartha, 1983), p. 63.

Table 9.5 Total general government expenditure in the countries of the
European Community as a percentage of gross domestic product, 1960–1981

	1960	1973	1981
Belgium	30.53	39.36	58.96
Denmark	26.40	42.73	59.65
Greece	23.77	28.90	39.82
France	34.49	38.46	48.92
Ireland	26.71	38.99	58.05
Italy	30.13	37.77	50.81
Luxembourg	29.32	35.66	59.64
Netherlands	33.20	49.35	59.29
United Kingdom	33.95	41.09	45.39
West Germany	32.40	40.34	49.31

Source: Douglas Todd, *The Growth of Public Expenditure in the EEC Countries 1960–1981: Some Reflections*, Economic Papers No. 29 (Brussels: Directorate-General for Economic and Financial Affairs, Commission of the European Communities, 1983).

lower levels of services or lower living standards. On the contrary, they demand that these be continuously improved, at least for their own particular social group. The syndrome is particularly evident in recession: it does not follow that electorates can be persuaded to abate their demands appropriately.

Contemporary Ireland exhibits the signs and symptoms that make up this syndrome and seems to be in the early stages of the disease. To begin with, public expenditure is at a level that cannot long be sustained in present, and perhaps any, circumstances. As Irish politicians, like others, discovered when periods of fast economic growth came to an end, what Richard Rose called "the juggernaut of incrementalism" rolled remorselessly on.[36] By 1980 total public expenditure reached two-thirds of gross national product (see table 9.4). Ireland's experience has evidently been much the same as that of the European Community countries. In fact as table 9.5 indicates, both the level of public expenditure and the rate of its growth have been comparatively high. If Rose and others are right, this is a cul-de-sac, and the end of the road is quite near.

If, as is the case in Ireland, growth is insufficient to cover the annual increment of public expenditure (and borrowing can be only a temporary expedient), cuts must take place in real private earnings, earnings already diminished by higher taxes as governments strain to pay the rising public sector bill. Either that, or public expenditure itself must be cut. In Ireland, recourse to either course of action triggered other symptoms of the syndrome, namely rising demands on politicians to exempt this, that, or the other sector, backed by direct action such as the marches of protest against the pay-as-you-earn tax system from 1979 onward and the threats in early 1983 to withhold pay-related social insurance contributions. Rising unemployment, which is likely to continue, might well provoke other direct action in the future.

The turbulence of the eighteen-month period of these three elections was caused partly by politicians, both those who attempted to face up to problems of economic overload and those who decided to continue fudging them. It was worsened by the ineptness or unpalatability of the remedial measures proposed. It would, however, be wrong to assume that stability is ensured by having a majority government in office, as was the case after the November 1982 election. The public opinion survey figures for dissatisfaction remain high —and that dissatisfaction is caused by mere corrective touches on the tiller. The reversal of long-term trends and the solution of deep-seated problems demand more. Consequently, on present indications, Ireland probably faces a prolonged period during which the outward and visible signs of ungovernability will increase.

The administration of public services presents a similar picture. Barrington summarized the position thus: "in the legislative bodies, institutional paralysis; in the popularly elected local bodies, institutional decay; and in the rest, institutional proliferation—proliferation within the institutions and proliferation between them." [37] The shortcomings of the Oireachtas have already been noted. Local government, a keystone to democracy, "has been so chipped away and the local representation system has been treated with such apparent contempt that . . . at least part of our government edifice is in danger of collapse." [38]

Barrington is right. There can be no doubt that our representative institutions both national and local have been neglected and ignored. As a result, they are now incapable of effectively monitoring the activities of the administrative authorities, which in theory they control, the less so as these have become more complex.

Complexity, however, not only has made administrative bodies harder to control (in itself one form of ungovernability) but also has sometimes led to inefficiency, to unmet legal requirements, and to unperformed public services, (other forms of ungovernability). At times, such powerful groups as those in agriculture and the professions have an interest in thwarting state policy or even the law, creating yet another form of ungovernability.

Examples of administrative breakdown abound: the campaigns to eradicate bovine tuberculosis, the control of water pollution, fire prevention and fire services, the housing of itinerants, "the belated and disastrous introduction of automatic data processing in the Department of Social Welfare," to cite but a few.[39] It is possible, also, to point to more general failures as, for example, in physical planning and the protection of the environment; in transport policy; in telecommunication services; in failure to collect taxes or to reform the system. These failures—and there are many of them—have sometimes resulted from specific noncooperation or defiance. Farmers, fishermen, veterinarians, industrial workers, and some classes of taxpayers are among those who have at times made the law inoperable, occasionally even by violence as did salmon fishermen in the summer of 1983. Just as surely, though less overtly, the wholesale ignoring by both private sector management and even some state boards of the guidelines in the economic programs of the 1960s and early 1970s or the insistence of some work groups in demanding, and the willingness of some managements to pay, "over-the-odds" pay rises have shown up the impotence of government. Governments themselves have caved in and ignored their own guidelines on occasion.

All this is symptomatic of the failure of the institutions of government and in particular of representative institutions. The growing propensity to take direct action in order to insist on, or to prevent, a particular outcome might well arise from the observed weakness of government or from contempt for those who operate it so inefficiently. Sometimes, too, outside-the-system activities can be more effective. Such action itself, however, further weakens the system. It is a vicious spiral.

If, as is possible, the Northern Ireland conflict spreads into the Republic, some will, quite certainly, take direct action, that is, on-the-street and paramilitary activities. A continuous trickle of armed robberies by the Irish Republican Army (IRA) and the Irish National Liberation Army (INLA) and an occasional murder or other violent incident suggest the possibility of ungovernability of yet another kind that would make the activities of a few fishermen, strikers, or farmers look very minor by comparison.

As yet, although Ireland is still recognizably a democracy, its democratic institutions are not working well. They have not developed sufficiently to cope with the demands now made upon them. Some regard this deficiency as demonstration of a need to modernize and adjust the parliamentary and administrative machinery. Some, often practical people in office both in the public and the private sectors, have been drawn to tripartite or corporatist institutions that bypass normal constitutional channels, a tendency that others believe contributes to the irrelevance of representative institutions and threatens democracy. A few see Ireland, like other modern democratic states, heading down a governmental cul-de-sac. If those who doubt the very governability of democracies are correct, fundamental questions arise about the prospects for democratic government.

Notes

1. This is epitomized in the Institute of Public Administration's review of the last quarter of a century, Frank Litton, ed., *Unequal Achievement: The Irish Experience 1957-1982* (Dublin: 1982).
2. In Richard Rose, ed., *Electoral Behavior: A Comparative Handbook* (New York: Collier Macmillan, 1974), p. 619.
3. R. Kenneth Carty, *Party and Parish Pump: Electoral Politics in Ireland* (Waterloo, Ontario: Wilfrid Laurier University Press, 1981), pp. 83, 72.
4. See, for example, Michael Gallagher, *Electoral Support for Irish Political Parties 1927-1973* (Beverly Hills, Calif.: Sage, 1976), pp. 23ff; Richard Sinnott, "The Electorate," in Howard R. Penniman, ed., *Ireland at the Polls: The Dáil Election of 1977* (Washington, D.C.: American Enterprise Institute, 1978), p. 42.
5. Michael Marsh, "Electoral Volatility in the Republic of Ireland, 1948-1983," in Ivor Crewe and David Denver, eds., *Electoral Volatility in Western Democracies* (Beckenham, Kent: Croom-Helm, 1985).
6. Ibid.
7. Michael Gallagher, "Societal Change and Party Adaptation in the Republic of Ireland, 1960-1981," *European Journal of Political Research* 9 (1981): 273.
8. Tom Garvin, "The Growth of Faction in the Fianna Fáil Party, 1966-80," in *Parliamentary Affairs* 34 (Winter 1981): 119.
9. Peter Mair, "Analysis of Results (Dáil General Election 1981)," in Ted Nealon and Seamus Brennan, eds., *Nealon's Guide to the 22nd Dáil and Seanad Election '81* (Dublin: Platform Press, 1981), pp. 150-54.
10. Ibid.
11. Carty, *Party and Parish Pump*, p. 141.
12. Garvin, "The Growth Faction in the Fianna Fáil Party," p. 121.
13. In Litton, ed., *Unequal Achievement*, pp. 23, 37.
14. *Reform of the Dáil: Fine Gael Policy of Reform of the Dáil, January 1980* (Dublin, 1980), p. 3.
15. Barry Desmond, *The Houses of the Oireachtas: A Plea for Reform, a Memorandum to the Government* (Dublin, 1975), p. 4.
16. Press release issued by the Government Information Services, 27 May 1983, p. 12.
17. Ibid., p. 2 (author's italics).
18. Ibid., p. 5.
19. Ibid., p. 10.
20. Ibid., p. 4.
21. Philippe C. Schmitter, "Still the Century of Corporatism?" in Philippe C. Schmitter and Gerhard Lehmbruch, eds., *Trends towards Corporatist Intermediation* (Beverly Hills, Calif.: Sage, 1979), pp. 20, 22.
22. Terms of reference quoted in Stephen Lalor, "Corporatism in Ireland," in *Administration* 30, no. 4 (1982): 82.

23. Ibid.
24. Joseph J. Lee, ed., *Ireland 1945-70* (Dublin: Gill and Macmillan, 1979), p. 20.
25. Denis Kavanagh and Richard Rose, eds., *New Trends in British Politics: Issues for Research* (Beverly Hills, Calif.: Sage, 1977), p. 172.
26. Director General of the Federated Union of Employers, Daniel J. McAuley, "New Relations between Government and Management (OECD: Paris, 1976), p. 20.
27. Charles McCarthy, *Decade in Upheaval: Irish Trade Unions in the Sixties* (Dublin: Institute of Public Administration, 1973), p. 197.
28. Leo Panitch, "The Development of Corporatism in Liberal Democracies," *Comparative Political Studies* 10 (1977): 66.
29. *Irish Times*, 10 February 1977.
30. In Litton, ed., *Unequal Achievement*, p. 103.
31. Stephen Lalor, "Corporatism in Ireland," p. 86. See also Eugene McCarthy, "Collective Bargaining and Economic Policies—Dialogue and Consensus" (Paper delivered at OECD Conference, 18-20 July 1983) (Dublin: Federated Union of Employers, 1983).
32. Samuel E. Finer, *Anonymous Empire*, 2d ed. (London: Pall Mall Press, 1966), p. 38.
33. Alan Cawson, in Graeme Duncan, ed., *Democratic Theory and Practice* (Cambridge: Cambridge University Press, 1983), p. 183; Robert A. Dahl, *Dilemmas of Pluralist Democracy: Autonomy vs. Control* (New Haven and London: Yale University Press, 1982), p. 68.
34. Litton, ed., *Unequal Achievement*, p. 104.
35. Richard Rose, *Governing and 'Ungovernability'*, Studies in Public Policy No. 1 (Glasgow: Centre for the Study of Public Policy, University of Strathclyde, 1977), p. 3.
36. Richard Rose, *The Juggernaut of Incrementalism: A Comparative Perspective on the Growth of Public Policy*, Studies in Public Policy No. 24 (Glasgow: Centre for the Study of Public Policy, University of Strathclyde, 1978).
37. Litton, ed., *Unequal Achievement*, pp. 97-98.
38. Ibid., p. 103.
39. Ibid., p. 100.

10   The General Election of 1987

BRIAN FARRELL AND DAVID M. FARRELL

Background

The three general elections of 1981–82 and the major political events surrounding them (the New Ireland Forum, the challenges to Haughey's leadership of Fianna Fáil, the abortion referendum) had posed searching questions
for Irish democracy.[1] The campaigns had concentrated public and media
attention on the difficulties of economic management and on the need to contain the burden of state expenditure and national debt repayment; they had
uncovered some knotty aspects of achieving sensitive social policy change that
would balance the values of an older generation against the demands of a
rapidly growing younger one; they had revealed a high degree of political
uncertainty and a growing tendency toward voter volatility. The vulnerability
of the political system had been exposed and the need for effective executive
leadership, parliamentary restraint among opposing parties, and some new
consensus among competing interest groups clearly identified. But as the
eighties progressed, there was little sign of positive response.

Northern Ireland remained an issue high on the political agenda. The
New Ireland Forum had been designed to manufacture and articulate a new
constitutional-nationalist consensus. The diversion of time and effort seemed
justified when, after twelve months of deliberations, an agreed report was
signed by the leaders of all the participating political parties on 2 May 1984.
That same evening a sharp divergence on the interpretation of the report
emerged.

All agreed on the analysis of the problem, accepted the need to accommodate Unionist attitudes, and identified three possible resolutions (a unitary
state, a federal/confederal state, some form of joint authority) while remaining
"open to discuss other views which may contribute to political development."[2]
However, Haughey insisted that the report endorsed the unitary state ideal

and that this should continue to be the exclusive basis of Irish government policy. That view was rejected by the other party leaders and led, in turn, to a renewal of internal dissension within Fianna Fáil.

The Haughey interpretation of the Forum Report was challenged by Desmond O'Malley, who was also critical of the party's opposition to a more liberal contraceptive bill proposed by the government. Eventually (after the withdrawal of the party whip and his subsequent formal expulsion) O'Malley established a new political party, the Progressive Democrats (PD), in December 1985. Although in terms of leadership a breakaway from Fianna Fáil, the PD quickly drew disproportionate support from Fine Gael. Its claim to break the mold of Irish party politics, which had been set in the civil war of 1922–23, was soon translated into the image of a populist right-of-center party committed to less government expenditure, significant tax reform, and a liberal line on social reform issues. The middle class had secured a new political vehicle.

In the meantime, the coalition government's attempt to launch a new economic program, "Building on Reality," in October 1984 fell victim to the continuing recession. Despite severe measures to curb public expenditure, the current budgetary deficit was difficult to control. Unemployment rose and emigration—an old touchstone of Irish economic activity—rose with it. Insistent demands for special treatment by organized interest groups and a series of major company closures did nothing to improve the industrial relations climate. Attempts to curb public service pay claims led to confrontations with teachers and complaints that the health services were being dismantled. Within the cabinet there was a growing rift between those whose first priority was a commitment to fiscal rectitude and those seeking to soften the impact of harsh measures; there was also disagreement in regard to the role of public and private enterprise. In time these disagreements would harden into a partisan division that would split the coalition.

However, on the diplomatic front, the coalition scored a considerable triumph. Since Lynch's time as Taoiseach in the 1970s, there had been a series of Anglo-Irish summits in an attempt to resolve the Northern crisis. The Haughey-Thatcher summit of 8 December 1980 had promised a consideration of the "totality of relationships within these islands" but progress had been frustrated by premature claims from Dublin about possible new constitutional arrangements. However, talks between officials on both sides had continued. After the New Ireland Forum, FitzGerald restored the political dialogue with Thatcher and, building on understandings already achieved between officials, achieved a new Anglo-Irish agreement at Hillsborough on 15 November 1985.[3] This recognizes that the present (carefully undefined) status of Northern Ireland cannot be changed without the consent of a majority, recognizes the nationalist aspiration to unity, and provides for an Intergovernmental Council, which gives a Dublin minister an input into British policy toward Northern Ireland. The Hillsborough Agreement was welcomed by all sides in Britain, by most constitutional nationalist parties on both sides of the Irish border, and by senior politicians sympathetic to Ireland in North America and Europe. Haughey and Fianna Fáil were critical and expressed reservations about the constitutionality of the measure. It was also immediately (and, since then, constantly) denounced by all brands of Unionist opinion and by Sinn Féin. Polls have indicated a very broad acceptance of the agreement by Irish public opinion (including Fianna Fáil respondents).

If this response indicated a willingness to accept change, it was only on a narrow front. As part of the "constitutional crusade," FitzGerald was committed to amending the Irish constitution, which expressly provides that "no law shall be enacted providing for the grant of a dissolution of marriage."[4] This was also part of the Labour party program. Public opinion polls through the mid-eighties indicated growing support for a severely restricted divorce jurisdiction. Despite the ambiguities revealed in the abortion referendum campaign and the known, openly expressed opposition of Roman Catholic Church leaders to any change in the constitutional ban on divorce, the coalition decided to embark on another constitutional referendum. The extent of marital breakdown had already been acknowledged in an all-party parliamentary report. However, Fianna Fáil was reluctant to press for change. The amendment proposed by the government would admit some form of divorce but was attacked as the thin edge of the wedge; issues of land inheritance and public morality were raised. The combination of ecclesiastical and political opposition and popular suspicion overwhelmed FitzGerald's crusade for a pluralist Ireland. On 26 June 1986 the amendment was rejected by 63 percent of those voting.

By this time, the coalition government was seen to be approaching a terminal stage. In February 1986 FitzGerald had attempted to give his administration a new face and reduce its internal tensions by a major ministerial reshuffle. The effort was frustrated by the refusal of a Labour minister to relinquish the health portfolio as well as by the failure to introduce any new blood. In the event, whatever the Taoiseach's intentions, a switch of Fine Gael ministers in the pivotal Department of Finance was regarded as a determination by the senior party in government to pursue a more rigorous policy of fiscal rectitude.

From June 1986, following defections from both Fine Gael and Labour, the government was in a minority position in the Dáil. There were further rumblings in the backbenches as preparation of the annual estimates was undertaken and the Labour leader publicly signaled his intention to recommend his party not to participate in a future coalition. By mid-October 1986 the internal cabinet division on the general targets for the 1987 budget and estimates ran along party lines and a coalition breakup was only a matter of time.[5] In parliament, despite considerable ministerial efforts to placate disgruntled backbenchers, the government became dependent on the casting vote of the Ceann Comhairle (speaker) for survival right up to the Christmas recess. The Twenty-fourth Dáil never reconvened. On 20 January 1987 the Labour ministers withdrew from government. Fine Gael, as a minority government, announced its proposed budget and promptly sought a dissolution. The 1987 general election campaign was under way.

The circumstances in which the coalition dissolved, the emergence of the Progressive Democrats, the continued opposition of Fianna Fáil to all Fine Gael policy initiatives, and the determination of smaller political groups to contest the election raised the prospect of some new ideologically based choice for the Irish electorate. Voter volatility had already been exhibited in the 1981–82 campaigns. Since that time the pressures of recession, despondency regarding control of public finances, resistance to cuts in social services or increases in taxation, and depression in the face of growing trends in unemployment and emigration had weakened support for the major parties and the first public opinion polls revealed a high level of "don't know" respondents.

Fine Gael, badly limping in the polls and damaged by supporters defecting to the Progressive Democrats, attempted to recover ground by forcing a long campaign. They needed time to distance themselves from their former coalition partners in Labour, to force Fianna Fáil to reveal its policy proposals in some detail, to prove to the electorate that the Fine Gael budget (in effect, the party's campaign manifesto) represented the right way to tackle the nation's problems, and to head off the new challenge to its traditional middle-class support from the Progressive Democrats.

Fianna Fáil appeared comfortably ahead when the "don't knows" were distributed in the polls. It was affected by the defection of four deputies to the Progressive Democrats and refused to be drawn into the Fine Gael strategy. Fianna Fáil's central argument was that coalition had once again failed and that only strong, unified, single-party government could tackle Ireland's problems. They were slow to start the campaign and reluctant to spell out specific policies.

The Progressive Democrats were the new, unpredictable element in this election. They had drawn sitting deputies from the two main parties who were likely to retain seats; they were challenging for support. To some they seemed to offer the prospect of an alternative coalition. But the PD claimed to break the established mold.

On the left, the Labour party and the Workers' party jousted for support. Both proposed increased state intervention to counter the failure of private enterprise to provide employment and advocated a wider tax base. On the fringe, a variety of smaller groups and independents increased the total num-

ber of candidates to 466; these included the Green Alliance and Provisional
Sinn Féin competing, for the first time, to take seats in the Dáil.

The Campaign

The last decade has seen Irish political parties following a trend evident among
most West European parties. Fianna Fáil, since 1977, and Fine Gael, since
1981, have been running increasingly professional campaigns, making greater
use of private agencies to market themselves, and concentrating their attention
more on national media strategies.[6] In terms of expertise both parties are now
evenly matched; each started the serious business of national campaign organization in autumn 1986. They were in competition with the Progressive
Democrats, whose national organizers had been drawing up plans since summer. By the time the election was called, all three had their campaign machinery ready for action.

Private public opinion polls had been commissioned (Fine Gael also
commissioned qualitative research) to identify target votes, ideal issues, and
appropriate campaign slogans and to help in designing constituency vote-
management strategies. New logos had been created for the parties; posters,
election literature, and merchandising items were produced and distributed,
billboards booked. Advertising agencies were ready to produce copy for
national and local newspapers. Public relations agencies and sophisticated
recording studios were engaged to produce slick television election broadcasts.
Media experts were employed to grill party spokespeople in television practice
sessions. All that remained by New Year's was for the election to be called.

The smaller parties—largely due to financial constraints—continued to
focus their attention on the local campaigns, concentrating their efforts on
those constituencies where they were running candidates. For Labour and the
Workers' party, national campaigning had developed little from the use of a
press officer and the extensive use of posters (though Labour did use an advertising agency). In all, according to one estimate, Labour spent £175,000 on
their national campaign and between £1,500 and £9,000 in each of the thirty-
three constituencies in which they were campaigning. The Workers' party spent
a total of £8,000. Expenditure for the three main parties was as follows: Fianna
Fáil, £2 million; Fine Gael, £800,000 by national headquarters and between
£5,000 and £15,000 in each of the forty-one constituencies; the Progressive
Democrats spent a total of £780,000.[7]

Fianna Fáil and Fine Gael once again gave some attention to vote-
management strategies. For Fine Gael the strategy this time was less one of
electoral gains and more one of minimizing losses. In general, the careful
strategy of November 1982 (described by Mair above)[8] was not repeated as

deputies scrambled over one another to hold onto their seats. Fianna Fáil appeared to have done little better, with few strategically inspired surprises.

Fine Gael started the campaign with support at rock bottom. The government's unpopularity, the worsening economic crisis, and the party's tough, hair-shirt budgetary proposals did not augur well for electoral victory. The indications were that Fianna Fáil would win quite comfortably. This appeared to be confirmed by the first opinion poll, published in the second week, which gave Fianna Fáil 52 percent of the vote.[9]

The day after the Dáil was dissolved, Fine Gael released its manifesto, which proposed, among other things, to reduce public spending, cut borrowing, reform the tax system, sell off shares in a selection of public companies, and introduce a scheme whereby young people could start work with lower levels of pay than usually accepted by the unions. This latter proposal was a favorite of FitzGerald's and he had received a positive feedback when testing it in front of several audiences prior to the campaign. The Progressive Democrats had already released position papers some months before, proposing to cut public expenditure, reform the tax system, and sell off shares in public companies. Clearly, there was a close similarity between the two parties. Fine Gael now put pressure on Fianna Fáil to specify their economic proposals.

Fianna Fáil refused to play ball. Haughey was determined to let Fine Gael do all the running, hoping that somewhere on the campaign trail the party would slip up.[10] One week after the release of the Fine Gael program, the Fianna Fáil party produced its manifesto, which also proposed public expenditure cuts and tax reform and placed great emphasis on the need to "go for growth." The manifesto was everything but specific.[11] In retrospect, this strategy backfired. The impression is that voters viewed the muzzled Fianna Fáil with some suspicion. Support for the party slipped in successive opinion polls. By the end of the campaign, a poll published on the last Sunday showed the party's support had dropped to 45 percent. The difference between Fianna Fáil and a possible Fine Gael–Progressive Democratic combination had shrunk from 14 points at the start of the campaign to just 2 points.

Another factor in the Fianna Fáil vote slippage was FitzGerald's victory in a live television debate with Haughey toward the end of the campaign, which was given extensive coverage in all media. Fine Gael morale picked up and for the first time in the campaign the party looked as if it had a chance of at least spoiling a Fianna Fáil victory. On the last Saturday of the campaign FitzGerald advised Fine Gael voters to transfer their votes to Progressive Democrat candidates. Some behind-the-scenes discussions had been taking place between the two parties. Fine Gael was anxious to make an arrangement with the Progressive Democrats whereby a speech by FitzGerald recommending interparty transfers would receive, at worst, a muted negative response from Desmond O'Malley. Accounts differ: Fine Gael strategists claim a tacit agreement was made; Progressive Democrat strategists claim that Fine Gael overtures were rebuffed. In any event, O'Malley made a strong speech in response, stressing his party's independence from either of the two major parties and rejecting any arrangement with Fine Gael.

The Results

The results were unsurprising (see table 10.1). Fianna Fáil won a plurality of the votes, but their vote had dropped 1 percent and they failed to get an overall majority. This was the party's worst result since 1961. The Fine Gael vote plummeted 12 percent to a level below their 1977 disaster. They had not had a result like that since 1957. For Labour, the vote was the lowest in the party's history, more than 3 points down from November 1982. Two parties made gains. The Workers' party vote rose by a modest half percent. The Progressive Democrats won 11.9 percent of the vote, an impressive result for a party barely one year old.

The translation of votes into seats proved beneficial for the established parties. Proportionality is measured in table 10.1 according to an index calculated by dividing the party's percentage of seats by its percentage of votes. Where the index is above 100 this indicates a bonus of seats, which was the case for Fianna Fáil and Fine Gael, and particularly fortuitously, for Labour. An index of less than 100 reflects, certainly in the case of the Workers' party,

Table 10.1   Results of the 1987 election

	Votes number	Votes percent	Nov. 1982 percent of votes	Seats number[a]	Seats percent	Index of proportionality
Fianna Fáil	784,547	44.2	(45.2)	81	49.1	111
Fine Gael	483,647	27.2	(39.2)	50	30.3	111
Progressive Democrats	210,583	11.9	—	14	8.5	71
Labour	112,031	6.3	(9.4)	12	7.3	116
Workers' party	67,273	3.8	(3.3)	4	2.4	63
Other	119,084	6.7	(2.9)	4	2.4	36
Total	1,777,165			165		
Total electorate	2,455,515					
Turnout	72.7%					

Sources: Department of the Environment, Dublin. The November 1982 figures are from *Nealon's Guide to the 24th Dáil and Seanad* (Dublin: Platform Press, 1983).
a. Excluding the seat of the Ceann Comhairle (chairman) of the outgoing Dáil, Tom Fitzpatrick (Fine Gael), who was automatically reelected.

Table 10.2 Regional percentage of the 1987 vote
(November 1982 percentages in parentheses)

	Fianna Fáil	(Nov. 1982)	Fine Gael	(Nov. 1982)	Progressive Democrats	Labour	(Nov. 1982)	Others	(Nov. 1982)
Dublin region	40.5	(38.3)	23.7	(41.1)	13.6	7.1	(10.5)	15.2	(10.1)
Rest of Leinster	45.7	(46.2)	27.3	(38.8)	11.0	9.5	(11.8)	6.5	(3.2)
Munster	42.7	(46.1)	26.9	(36.2)	15.0	6.8	(11.3)	8.6	(6.4)
Connaught/ Ulster	49.7	(51.8)	31.8	(41.7)	5.6	1.2	(2.3)	11.6	(4.2)

Source: Shane Kenny and Fergal Keane, *Irish Politics Now* (Dingle, County Kerry: Brandon and RTE, 1987).

the disproportionality of STV for smaller parties and for the Progressive Democrats bad vote management and weak local party structure.

In table 10.2 the result is broken down in terms of European Parliament constituencies, giving a good impression of regional variations. It can be seen that whereas Fianna Fáil dropped overall, the one area where it rose was the Dublin region (by almost 2 percent), replacing Fine Gael as the largest party in the capital. Fianna Fáil's worst result was in Munster, the area where the PD made its greatest gains. Fine Gael lost right across the board, but particularly in Dublin where its vote was almost halved. Most of this went to the Progressive Democrats, but there were also gains by Fianna Fáil, the Workers' party, and independents. The Fine Gael predicament was best summarized in Dublin Central, where the party had lost its two sitting deputies prior to the election due to defections. The local party organization was unable to mount a credible campaign due to internal faction fighting and as a result the party won no seats (the Fine Gael vote dropped by two-thirds). Labour's vote dropped most heavily in Dublin and Munster, going to the Progressive Democrats and, in Dublin especially, to the Workers' party, which with 7.5 percent was now stronger in Dublin than Labour (7.1 percent).

The occupational class voting trends in table 10.3 provide some support for the argument that the emergence of the Progressive Democrats either reflects or has caused something of a realignment in Irish politics, prompting one political scientist to suggest that there are now "some" social bases to Irish party politics.[12] The biggest gains for the Progressive Democrats were among the middle classes and the larger farmers. In contrast, Fianna Fáil has continued to lose its catchall edge, making modest gains among the working classes and losing most votes among the middle classes and large farmers.

Table 10.3   1987 vote by occupational class
(November 1982 figures in parentheses)

	All classes	Middle class	Skilled working class	Unskilled working class	Farmers (50 acres or more)	Farmers (50 acres or less)
Fianna Fáil	38 (40)	30 (37)	45 (42)	41 (40)	30 (37)	48 (51)
Fine Gael	25 (37)	27 (46)	23 (31)	15 (28)	45 (54)	35 (35)
Progressive Democrats	11 (—)	18 (—)	9 (—)	9 (—)	10 (—)	2 (—)
Labour	4 (9)	4 (7)	4 (11)	7 (14)	1 (6)	2 (1)
Others / don't know	21 (13)	21 (10)	18 (16)	28 (18)	13 (3)	14 (14)

Source: *IMS/Sunday Independent* poll, 15 February 1987 ($N = 1,052$). November 1982 figures are from table 3.4 in this volume.

Labour and Fine Gael votes dropped among all classes, with the sole exception of small farmers. Fine Gael's biggest losses were among the middle classes and unskilled workers.

Transfer patterns mirror the recent political developments. In 1987 Fianna Fáil voters continued to vote predominantly for all Fianna Fáil candidates and, to a large degree, for nobody else (for comparisons, see Sinnott above).[13] The big change was over interparty transfers. With the breakup of the Fine Gael–Labour coalition the transfers from Fine Gael to Labour dropped to less than 40 percent, and from Labour to Fine Gael less than 33 percent. Labour voters transferred all over the place. Fine Gael voters followed their leader's advice and more than 60 percent of them (in some cases more than 70 percent) transferred to the Progressive Democrats. There were similarly high interparty transfers from the Progressive Democrats to Fine Gael (almost 54 percent). This was probably less a case of Progressive Democrat voters ignoring their leader's rejection of the Fine Gael offer and more one of the traditional Fine Gael supporters giving a lower preference to the home team.

Government Formation and Ministerial Selection

Although the outcome of the election was indecisive, there were no frenzied efforts as in 1981–82 to manufacture a parliamentary majority.[14] The prospects for a Fine Gael–Progressive Democrat coalition had been reduced by failure to orchestrate transfers; besides, the two parties were twenty seats short of a majority. Efforts to form an "alliance of the left" were, at best, concerned with coordinating opposition and were unsuccessful. Any prospect of a majority coalition or "national government" required a change of leadership in Fianna Fáil. That was not a realistic option, nor were deals to gain support. Haughey, once again deprived of outright victory, had to wait for the opening day of the Twenty-fifth Dáil. On 10 March 1987, after a tied Dáil vote of 82–82 (with independent deputy Gregory abstaining), Haughey became Taoiseach with the casting vote of the Ceann Comhairle.

There were few surprises in his cabinet selection. Only four newcomers were appointed. The indifference to geographical spread, already noticed,[15] was again evident; two were chosen from constituencies already represented in cabinet. Neither age nor previous parliamentary experience were considered as major criteria. Only one new minister was in his thirties; the average age of newly appointed ministers was 47.5 years and the overall age of the cabinet was 51. Only one woman was appointed.

The PD defections had resolved any issues of internal party loyalty and Haughey showed some concern about filling senior and sensitive portfolios with experienced ministers. Finance, foreign affairs, and justice were all allocated to men who had served in these departments. He also made some structural changes. At cabinet level, responsibility for the public service was returned to the minister for finance and a new minister for marine affairs was appointed. At junior ministerial level, new men were appointed to special responsibilities for science and technology, food, horticulture, and marketing and constituted a new, higher tier of ministers of state.

But within two days of taking office, the new Haughey administration acknowledged that the condition of the public finances left little scope for initiative. No special funds were made available in the areas newly allocated to ministers. On 31 March the new government introduced a budget that was even more severe than that proposed by Fine Gael: expenditure targets were tighter and severe cutbacks were announced in health and education services and in building grants. Fianna Fáil, which had withstood the pressure to spell out policy details during the campaign, was now committed to a package of measures broadly similar to those advocated by Fine Gael.

Predictably, this strategy was attacked by parties and deputies on the left of the parliamentary spectrum. But both Fine Gael and Progressive Democrats were broadly supportive. There were early signs that Haughey's slender hold on power was more likely to be challenged by Fianna Fáil backbenchers, fearful of the local consequences of expenditure cuts, than by the formal opposition. It was also clear that a broad public consensus existed for necessary remedial action. This was put to the test in early May when a proposed three-day strike by electrical power workers collapsed in the face of concentrated media criticism, trade union opposition, and public hostility.

In the meantime, the resignation of Dr. Garret FitzGerald as leader of Fine Gael on 11 March marked a major change in Irish political life.[16] He had built up his party's organizational and electoral appeal in the 1970s and withdrew before any damaging postmortem on its 1987 performance. The contest for the party leadership was brisk, businesslike, and singularly lacking in acrimony. Out of a field of three former ministers, the parliamentary party chose forty-two-year-old Alan Dukes, former minister for agriculture, finance, and education.

Prospects

A decision of the Supreme Court created a new dilemma for Ireland by striking down the Single European Act (a measure to expand the area of political cooperation within the European Community). It thrust the country into another constitutional referendum and raised questions about the operational definition of a separation of powers doctrine in the Irish system. In any event, the Irish people approved the Dáil's act by more than a two to one margin.

It was only the latest manifestation of the need for a thorough overhaul. No one surveying the Irish political scene can ignore the evidence of strain and government overload, which was analyzed in an earlier essay by Basil Chubb.[17] The system has shown a remarkable resilience in the face of economic, demographic, and political pressures and an extraordinary record of stability. Now the case for structural reform is manifest at a variety of levels: administrative, parliamentary, and executive. The effective, automatic implementation of policy can no longer be taken for granted; failure in tax collection, for instance, has become a political embarrassment. Deputies on all sides are frustrated by their restricted role and concerned about playing an active part in the initiation and scrutiny of legislation. But as an Irish cabinet once again confronts the daily tasks of crisis management, there seems little likelihood that it will find the time, energy, and political will to tackle structural reform. Indeed, it can scarcely do so without some intensive examination of its own procedures. That might best be accomplished within a broad consideration of the whole constitution. After fifty years, a document designed by a different generation for a different Ireland requires reexamination. A new constitution would represent not a break but a continuance of the strongly entrenched Irish liberal-democratic tradition.

Notes

1. For fuller treatment, see Brian Farrell, "The Context of Three Elections," chapter 1 of this volume.
2. New Ireland Forum, *Report* (Dublin: Stationery Office, 1984), p. 30.
3. For background to the Hillsborough Agreement, see Brian Farrell, foreword to C. J. N. Townshend, ed., *Consensus in Ireland: Approaches and Recessions* (forthcoming).

4. Article 41.3.2. For the "constitutional crusade," see Farrell, "Context of Three Elections."

5. For a detailed account of the background to the breakup, see "The Phoney War," in Shane Kenny and Fergal Keane, *Irish Politics Now: 'This Week' Guide to the 25th Dáil* (Dingle, County Kerry: Brandon and RTE, 1987).

6. David M. Farrell and Martin Wortmann, "Party Strategies in the Electoral Market: Political Marketing in West Germany, Britain, and Ireland," *European Journal of Political Research* (forthcoming 1987).

7. "The Handlers and the Handled," in Kenny and Keane, *Irish Politics Now*, p. 30.

8. See Peter Mair, "Party Organization, Vote Management, and Candidate Selection," chapter 4 of this volume.

9. Richard Sinnott has made the point that the poll reports exaggerated Fianna Fáil's true position because they did not allow for an unusually high number of "don't knows," a large proportion of which were inclined to vote Fine Gael. In reality, he argues, Fianna Fáil's support in the polls suggested right from the beginning of the campaign that the party would fail to win an overall majority. See Richard Sinnott, "The 1987 Election in the Republic of Ireland," in Tom Garvin and Michael Laver, eds., *Irish Political Studies*, vol. 2 (forthcoming).

10. Sam Smyth, "The Emperor Strikes Back," *In Dublin*, 5-18 March 1987, is a journalist's account from inside Fianna Fáil headquarters.

11. For further discussion, see "Fianna Fáil's Commitments," in Brian Trench, ed., *Magill Book of Irish Politics: Election February '87*, (Dublin: Magill Publications, 1987), pp. 18-19.

12. Michael Laver, "Measuring Patterns of Party Support in Ireland," *Economic and Social Review* 18, no. 2 (1987).

13. These figures are from Michael Gallagher, "The Transfer Pattern," in Trench, *Magill Book of Irish Politics*, pp. 10-13.

14. For a detailed discussion of the events after the election, see "Irish Politics Now," in Kenny and Keane, *Irish Politics Now*, pp. 55ff.

15. See Brian Farrell, "Government Formation and Ministerial Selection," chapter 5 of this volume.

16. For a fuller account of FitzGerald, see "Irish Politics Now," pp. 62-70.

17. See Basil Chubb, "Prospects for Democratic Politics in Ireland," chapter 9 of this volume.

Appendix A
Procedures for Voting and
Counting the Votes in Force in 1981–1982

BASIL CHUBB

The conduct of elections in each constituency is in the hands of a "returning officer" who is county registrar (in the case of Dublin or Cork, city or county sheriff) and on whom statutory duties are placed.[1] Polling takes place on a day fixed by the minister of the environment, but it must fall between dates fixed by statute by reference to the dissolution of the previous Dáil. In the case of islands where there is the possibility of delay due to the weather, the returning officer has the discretion to fix a day before the appointed polling day. Polling day is not a legal holiday and in practice it has always been an ordinary weekday.

Voters cast their ballots at polling stations, often schools, near their homes. Each elector is notified by post of a prescribed polling station and may vote only in that station. By law, the polls are required to be open for a period of at least twelve hours fixed by the minister for the environment between 8:30 A.M. and 10:30 P.M. Postal voting is confined to members of the defense forces and the Garda Siochana (police).

Ballot paper lists the names of the candidates in alphabetical order. The highest number of candidates in any constituency was fifteen; the highest where three seats were contested was thirteen. The ballot paper contains the following information on each candidate: full name, address, occupation, and party (if any); candidates may choose to use either Irish or English in presenting all or part of this information. A candidate does not have complete freedom to designate party affiliation. The law provides for the establishment and maintenance of a Register of Political Parties. To be registered a party must be a genuine political party and be organized to contest elections. The name of a party will not be registered if it is identical with the name of a party already registered or if it might be confused with one. Only those candidates accepted officially by registered parties are entitled to include the party name on the ballot paper; other candidates may, if they wish, have the term "nonparty" inserted after their name.

The elector casts a single-transferable vote, that is, a vote which, in the words of

---

1. The principal acts governing voting and counting the votes are the Electoral Act, 1923 (no. 12) and the Electoral Act, 1963 (no. 19).

the statute, is "capable of being given so as to indicate the voter's preference for the candidates in order." In other words, the voter rank orders as many of the candidates as he desires. Voting machines are not used, the ballot papers are not machine readable, and no use is made of computers.

The rules for counting the votes and ascertaining who has been elected are precise and detailed. The first stage in the count in each constituency is to scrutinize all papers and to reject invalid votes. A vote is invalid if it does not bear the figure "1" or some mark such as X or a check mark standing alone, when only one choice is made, if it contains "1" more than once, or if anything is written on the paper by which the voter may be identified. The valid papers are sorted into parcels according to the first preferences and the parcels are counted. Each candidate is credited with the number of votes in his parcel and the total of the valid votes is ascertained.

At this point the returning officer is able to calculate and declare the "quota," the number of votes necessary to secure the election of a candidate. The quota used in Irish elections is the "Droop quota," the smallest number of votes that suffices to elect the requisite number of candidates while being just big enough to prevent any more being elected. It is expressed in the formula:

$$\text{Quota} = \frac{\text{the number of valid votes}}{\text{the number of seats} + 1} + 1$$

Any candidate who obtains a quota or more is declared elected. In these three elections two-thirds of all quotas were between 7,000 and 8,000 votes; the highest quota was 11,441 and the lowest was 6,317.

If the number elected at this, the first, count is less than the number of places to be filled, as it usually is, the counters begin to transfer votes. First, any surplus votes of candidates declared elected at the first count are transferred to other candidates, the biggest surplus first. A surplus is "the number of votes by which the total number of votes credited to a candidate exceeds the quota." To distribute the surplus of a candidate elected on the first count, the officials re-sort all of that candidate's votes and arrange them in parcels according to next available preferences shown on them. Candidates who receive such preferences have transferred to them a proportionate number of the appropriate parcel. This number is calculated by means of the following formula:

No. of candidate A's votes to be transferred to candidate B		No. of candidate A's surplus votes / No. of votes transferable from candidate A to all other candidates		No. of papers in candidate B's parcel of votes transferable from candidate A
	+		×	

Thus the elected candidate is left with a quota, and the other candidates have passed on to them appropriate additions to their parcels of votes. Whenever in the later stages of a count a candidate is elected with more than the bare quota, this process of transferring votes is continued, but instead of re-sorting all the candidate's votes, only the last parcel is taken and re-sorted.

Ballot Paper in Use, 1981–1982.
This ballot is reprinted from the Electoral (Amendment) Act, 1972.

FORM OF BALLOT PAPER
(Front of Paper)

Counterfoil	Marcáil ord do	
No.	rogha sna-spáis	
	seo síos.	Marc Oifigiúil. →
	Mark order of	Official Mark.
	preference in	
	spaces below.	

DOYLE—WORKERS PARTY.
(James Doyle, of 10 High Street, Builder.)

LYNCH—DEMOCRATS.
(Jane Ellen Lynch, of 12 Main Street, Grocer.)

O'BRIAIN—CUMANN NA SAORÁNACH.
(Séamus O'Briain, ó 10 An tSráid Ard, Oide
Scoile.)

O'BRIEN, EAMON (BARRISTER)—NON-PARTY.
(Eamon O'Brien, of 22 Wellclose Place,
Barrister.)

O'BRIEN, EAMON (SOLICITOR)—YOUNG IRELAND.
(Eamon O'Brien, of 102 Eaton Brae,
Ranelagh, Solicitor.)

O'CONNOR—NATIONAL LEAGUE.
(Charles O'Connor, of 7 Green Street,
Gentleman.)

THOMPSON—FARMERS PARTY.
(William Henry Thompson, of Dereen Park,
Farmer.)

TREORACHA.

I. Féach chuige go bhfuil an marc
oifigiúil ar an bpáipéar.

II. Scríobh an figiúr 1 le hais ainm an
chéad iarrthóra is rogha leat, an
figiúr 2 le hais do dhara rogha, agus
mar sin de.

III. Fill an páipéar ionas nach bhfeicfear
do vóta. Taispeáin *cúl an pháipéir*
don oifigeach ceannais, agus cuir sa
bhosca ballóide é.

INSTRUCTIONS.

I. See that the official mark is on the
paper.

II. Write 1 beside the name of the
candidate of your first choice, 2
beside your second choice, and so
on.

III. Fold the paper to conceal your
vote. Show *the back of the paper* to
the presiding officer and put it in
the ballot box.

When in the course of a count there are no surpluses to be transferred and seats still remain to be filled, the candidate with the lowest number of votes is declared eliminated from the contest and those votes are transferred to the next available preference shown on the ballot papers. This process of transferring surpluses and the votes of eliminated candidates to continuing candidates goes on until either the necessary number of seats is filled or, as often happens, only two candidates are left in, neither with a quota. In this case, the candidate with the higher number of votes credited is declared elected "without reaching the quota." The numbers of candidates so elected in these three elections were 42 (1981), 29 (1982a), and 19 (1982b) of the total 166 deputies returned; in each case the Ceann Comhairle (speaker) was deemed to be returned without contesting. The number of extended counts was much reduced; only 18 of the total 123 contests went to ten or more counts, all in larger constituencies.

Appendix B
Irish Parliamentary Election Results: 1981,
February 1982, November 1982, and February 1987

COMPILED BY RICHARD M. SCAMMON

Dáil Election, 1981: First-preference Votes and Final Distribution of Seats

Constituency	Total	Fianna Fáil	Fine Gael	Labour	Other[a]
Carlow-Kilkenny	56,435	26,468	20,821	7,269	1,877
Percent of total		46.90	36.89	12.88	3.33
Number of seats	5	2	2	1	—
Cavan-Monaghan	60,411	26,501	24,789	—	9,121
Percent of total		43.87	41.03	—	15.10
Number of seats	5	2	2	—	1
Clare	45,329	26,590	13,902	2,471	2,366
Percent of total		58.66	30.67	5.45	5.22
Number of seats	4	3	1	—	—
Cork East	42,861	16,324	19,422	724	6,391
Percent of total		38.09	45.31	1.69	14.91
Number of seats	4	1	2	—	1
Cork North-Central	45,452	17,248	15,465	7,163	5,576
Percent of total		37.95	34.02	15.76	12.27
Number of seats	5	2	2	1	—
Cork North-West	33,947	15,621	14,278	4,048	—
Percent of total		46.02	42.06	11.92	—
Number of seats	3	1	2	—	—
Cork South-Central	49,934	21,517	21,098	6,961	358
Percent of total		43.09	42.25	13.94	0.72
Number of seats	5	2	2	1	—
Cork South-West	33,764	14,143	15,280	3,244	1,097
Percent of total		41.89	45.26	9.61	3.25
Number of seats	3	1	2	—	—

Dáil Election, 1981: (*Continued*)

Constituency	Total	Fianna Fáil	Fine Gael	Labour	Other[a]
Donegal North-East	32,287	12,394	11,503	470	7,920
Percent of total		38.39	35.63	1.46	24.53
Number of seats	3	1	1	—	1
Donegal South-West	34,716	15,774	13,316	—	5,626
Percent of total		45.44	38.36	—	16.21
Number of seats	3	2	1	—	—
Dublin Central	46,529	20,020	13,409	8,146	4,954
Percent of total		43.03	28.82	17.51	10.65
Number of seats	5	2	2	1	—
Dublin North	27,062	12,555	10,190	4,317	—
Percent of total		46.39	37.65	15.95	—
Number of seats	3	1	2	—	—
Dublin North-Central	40,581	20,664	10,341	1,823	7,753
Percent of total		50.92	25.48	4.49	19.10
Number of seats	4	2	1	—	1
Dublin North-East	32,411	14,095	9,126	2,852	6,338
Percent of total		43.49	28.16	8.80	19.56
Number of seats	4	2	1	—	1
Dublin North-West	32,419	14,484	10,635	4,022	3,278
Percent of total		44.68	32.80	12.41	10.11
Number of seats	4	2	2	—	—
Dublin South	50,806	21,513	23,369	4,973	951
Percent of total		42.34	46.00	9.79	1.87
Number of seats	5	2	3	—	—
Dublin South-Central	48,949	16,815	14,283	5,884	11,967
Percent of total		34.35	29.18	12.02	24.45
Number of seats	5	2	2	—	1
Dublin South-East	40,815	15,702	17,542	4,993	2,578
Percent of total		38.47	42.98	12.23	6.32
Number of seats	4	2	2	—	—
Dublin South-West	36,167	14,419	13,810	6,419	1,519
Percent of total		39.87	38.18	17.75	4.20
Number of seats	4	2	1	1	—
Dublin West	46,758	18,076	19,679	3,694	5,309
Percent of total		38.66	42.09	7.90	11.35
Number of seats	5	2	3	—	—

Dáil Election, 1981: (*Continued*)

Constituency	Total	Fianna Fáil	Fine Gael	Labour	Other[a]
Dun Laoghaire	48,170	18,030	20,916	7,722	1,502
Percent of total		37.43	43.42	16.03	3.12
Number of seats	5	2	2	1	—
Galway East	33,090	17,509	15,581	—	—
Percent of total		52.91	47.09	—	—
Number of seats	3	2	1	—	—
Galway West	50,840	27,999	15,250	6,226	1,365
Percent of total		55.07	30.00	12.25	2.68
Number of seats	5	3	1	1	—
Kerry North	34,285	17,476	7,264	5,685	3,860
Percent of total		50.97	21.19	16.58	11.26
Number of seats	3	2	—	1	—
Kerry South	33,593	15,865	7,907	8,221	1,600
Percent of total		47.23	23.54	24.47	4.76
Number of seats	3	1	1	1	—
Kildare	47,060	22,884	14,843	8,635	698
Percent of total		48.63	31.54	18.35	1.48
Number of seats	5	2	2	1	—
Laoighis-Offaly	56,002	27,929	25,287	2,394	392
Percent of total		49.87	45.15	4.27	0.70
Number of seats	5	3	2	—	—
Limerick East	48,590	20,535	16,410	5,745	5,900
Percent of total		42.26	33.77	11.82	12.14
Number of seats	5	2	2	—	1
Limerick West	33,189	21,355	11,834	—	—
Percent of total		64.34	35.66	—	—
Number of seats	3	2	1	—	—
Longford-Westmeath	45,365	21,211	16,362	3,219	4,573
Percent of total		46.76	36.07	7.10	10.08
Number of seats	4	2	2	—	—
Louth[b]	45,763	18,861	13,678	2,861	10,363
Percent of total		41.21	29.89	6.25	22.64
Number of seats	4	2	1	—	1
Mayo East	32,351	17,444	14,907	—	—
Percent of total		53.92	46.08	—	—
Number of seats	3	2	1	—	—

Dáil Election, 1981: (*Continued*)

Constituency	Total	Fianna Fáil	Fine Gael	Labour	Other[a]
Mayo West	32,108	17,356	14,752	—	—
Percent of total		54.06	45.94	—	—
Number of seats	3	2	1	—	—
Meath	50,640	22,364	17,154	8,641	2,481
Percent of total		44.16	33.87	17.06	4.90
Number of seats	5	2	2	1	—
Roscommon	33,153	16,013	13,067	—	4,073
Percent of total		48.30	39.41	—	12.29
Number of seats	3	2	1	—	—
Sligo-Leitrim	47,689	23,787	16,968	361	6,573
Percent of total		49.88	35.58	0.76	13.78
Number of seats	4	2	2	—	—
Tipperary North	32,346	14,769	9,487	7,504	586
Percent of total		45.66	29.33	23.20	1.81
Number of seats	3	1	1	1	—
Tipperary South	41,751	17,291	11,743	8,989	3,728
Percent of total		41.41	28.13	21.53	8.93
Number of seats	4	2	1	1	—
Waterford	43,723	16,953	18,338	1,632	6,800
Percent of total		38.77	41.94	3.73	15.55
Number of seats	4	2	2	—	—
Wexford	49,820	24,027	18,022	6,788	983
Percent of total		48.23	36.17	13.63	1.97
Number of seats	5	2	2	1	—
Wicklow	41,050	17,035	14,348	5,894	3,773
Percent of total		41.50	34.95	14.36	9.19
Number of seats	4	2	1	1	—
Total	1,718,211	777,616	626,376	169,990	144,229
Percent of total		45.26	36.46	9.89	8.39
Number of seats	166	78	65	15	8

Source: *Election Results and Transfer of Votes* (Dublin: Stationery Office, 1981).
a. The total vote under "Other" included 29,561 Sinn Féin the Workers' party (1 elected), 7,107 Socialist Labour (1), 571 Socialist (0), 358 Communist (0), and 106,632 all others, including Non-party (6).
b. The Speaker of the Dáil is automatically reelected and in this election his constituency was Louth.

Dáil Election, February 1982: First-preference
Votes and Final Distribution of Seats

Constituency	Total	Fianna Fáil	Fine Gael	Labour	Other[a]
Carlow-Kilkenny	54,281	26,024	19,258	7,109	1,890
Percent of total		47.94	35.48	13.10	3.48
Number of seats	5	2	2	1	—
Cavan-Monaghan	58,132	28,411	24,763	—	4,958
Percent of total		48.87	42.60	—	8.53
Number of seats	5	3	2	—	—
Clare	43,569	25,875	14,172	1,957	1,565
Percent of total		59.39	32.53	4.49	3.59
Number of seats	4	3	1	—	—
Cork East	41,213	16,411	17,179	946	6,677
Percent of total		39.82	41.68	2.30	16.20
Number of seats	4	1	2	—	1
Cork North-Central	42,577	18,361	15,203	5,629	3,384
Percent of total		43.12	35.71	13.22	7.95
Number of seats	5	2	2	1	—
Cork North-West	33,494	15,888	14,545	3,061	—
Percent of total		47.44	43.43	9.14	—
Number of seats	3	1	2	—	—
Cork South-Central	48,476	20,280	19,209	6,494	2,493
Percent of total		41.84	39.63	13.40	5.14
Number of seats	5	2	2	1	—
Cork South-West	32,821	14,725	15,881	2,215	—
Percent of total		44.86	48.39	6.75	—
Number of seats	3	1	2	—	—
Donegal North-East	29,906	10,075	11,474	493	7,864
Percent of total		33.69	38.37	1.65	26.30
Number of seats	3	1	1	—	1
Donegal South-West	33,107	15,897	11,273	—	5,937
Percent of total		48.02	34.05	—	17.93
Number of seats	3	2	1	—	—
Dublin Central	45,742	19,713	12,994	5,042	7,993
Percent of total		43.10	28.41	11.02	17.47
Number of seats	5	2	1	1	1
Dublin North	27,154	12,631	10,612	3,911	—
Percent of total		46.52	39.08	14.40	—
Number of seats	3	1	2	—	—

Dáil Election, February 1982: (*Continued*)

Constituency	Total	Fianna Fáil	Fine Gael	Labour	Other[a]
Dublin North-Central	40,795	20,872	13,322	2,172	4,429
Percent of total		51.16	32.66	5.32	10.86
Number of seats	4	2	2	—	—
Dublin North-East	31,887	15,674	10,174	2,137	3,902
Percent of total		49.15	31.91	6.70	12.24
Number of seats	4	2	2	—	—
Dublin North-West	31,581	15,176	9,787	2,412	4,206
Percent of total		48.05	30.99	7.64	13.32
Number of seats	4	2	1	—	1
Dublin South	51,454	20,967	25,898	4,589	—
Percent of total		40.75	50.33	8.92	—
Number of seats	5	2	3	—	—
Dublin South-Central[b]	47,082	19,666	17,207	6,600	3,609
Percent of total		41.77	36.55	14.02	7.67
Number of seats	5	2	1	1	1
Dublin South-East	40,151	13,455	18,543	5,402	2,751
Percent of total		33.51	46.18	13.45	6.85
Number of seats	4	1	2	1	—
Dublin South-West	35,698	16,745	11,890	7,063	—
Percent of total		46.91	33.31	19.79	—
Number of seats	4	2	1	1	—
Dublin West	45,234	18,857	19,211	2,617	4,549
Percent of total		41.69	42.47	5.79	10.06
Number of seats	5	2	3	—	—
Dun Laoghaire	48,511	15,820	23,380	7,776	1,535
Percent of total		32.61	48.20	16.03	3.14
Number of seats	5	2	2	1	—
Galway East	32,097	17,697	13,454	946	—
Percent of total		55.14	41.92	2.95	—
Number of seats	3	2	1	—	—
Galway West	48,572	27,840	13,803	5,718	1,211
Percent of total		57.32	28.42	11.77	2.49
Number of seats	5	3	1	1	—
Kerry North	33,110	17,697	5,643	8,552	1,218
Percent of total		53.45	17.04	25.83	3.68
Number of seats	3	2	—	1	—

Dáil Election, February 1982: (*Continued*)

Constituency	Total	Fianna Fáil	Fine Gael	Labour	Other[a]
Kerry South	32,531	16,010	9,342	7,038	141
Percent of total		49.21	28.72	21.63	0.43
Number of seats	3	1	1	1	—
Kildare	46,464	24,079	14,894	7,491	—
Percent of total		51.82	32.05	16.12	—
Number of seats	5	3	1	1	—
Laoighis-Offaly	53,816	27,143	23,941	2,608	124
Percent of total		50.44	44.49	4.85	0.23
Number of seats	5	3	2	—	—
Limerick East	47,336	21,421	14,979	2,684	8,252
Percent of total		45.25	31.64	5.67	17.43
Number of seats	5	2	2	—	1
Limerick West	31,715	20,237	11,478	—	—
Percent of total		63.81	36.19	—	—
Number of seats	3	2	1	—	—
Longford-Westmeath	43,124	22,550	17,496	957	2,121
Percent of total		52.29	40.57	2.22	4.92
Number of seats	4	2	2	—	—
Louth	43,511	20,497	13,239	3,474	6,301
Percent of total		47.11	30.43	7.98	14.48
Number of seats	4	3	1	—	—
Mayo East	31,093	17,411	13,548	—	134
Percent of total		56.00	43.57	—	0.43
Number of seats	3	2	1	—	—
Mayo West	30,623	16,587	13,416	620	—
Percent of total		54.17	43.81	2.02	—
Number of seats	3	2	1	—	—
Meath	49,063	24,970	19,065	3,540	1,488
Percent of total		50.89	38.86	7.22	3.03
Number of seats	5	3	2	—	—
Roscommon	31,785	17,386	14,399	—	—
Percent of total		54.70	45.30	—	—
Number of seats	3	2	1	—	—
Sligo-Leitrim	45,700	24,368	17,126	399	3,807
Percent of total		53.32	37.48	0.87	8.33
Number of seats	4	3	1	—	—

Dáil Election, February 1982: (*Continued*)

Constituency	Total	Fianna Fáil	Fine Gael	Labour	Other[a]
Tipperary North	31,709	15,586	8,185	7,763	175
Percent of total		49.15	25.81	24.48	0.55
Number of seats	3	1	1	1	—
Tipperary South	39,580	19,167	12,497	7,758	158
Percent of total		48.43	31.57	19.60	0.40
Number of seats	4	2	1	1	—
Waterford	41,566	16,443	15,714	1,982	7,427
Percent of total		39.56	37.80	4.77	17.87
Number of seats	4	1	2	—	1
Wexford	48,815	23,721	18,382	4,694	2,018
Percent of total		48.59	37.66	9.62	4.13
Number of seats	5	3	2	—	—
Wicklow	40,058	14,618	14,512	8,026	2,902
Percent of total		36.49	36.23	20.04	7.24
Number of seats	4	1	2	1	—
Total	1,665,133	786,951	621,088	151,875	105,219
Percent of total		47.26	37.30	9.12	6.32
Number of seats	166	81	63	15	7

Source: *Election Results and Transfer of Votes* (Dublin: Stationery Office, 1982).
a. The total vote under "Other" included 36,263 Sinn Féin the Workers' party (3 elected), 2,716 Irish Republican Socialist (0), 462 Communist (0), and 65,778 all others, including Non-party (4).
b. The Speaker of the Dáil is automatically reelected and in this election his constituency was Dublin South-Central.

Dáil Election, November 1982: First-preference
Votes and Final Distribution of Seats

Constituency	Total	Fianna Fáil	Fine Gael	Labour	Other [a]
Carlow-Kilkenny	55,804	24,879	20,139	7,511	3,275
Percent of total		44.58	36.09	13.46	5.87
Number of seats	5	2	2	1	—
Cavan-Monaghan	57,247	31,401	25,703	—	143
Percent of total		54.85	44.90	—	0.25
Number of seats	5	3	2	—	—
Clare	45,250	25,406	14,826	2,344	2,674
Percent of total		56.15	32.76	5.18	5.91
Number of seats	4	2	2	—	—
Cork East	41,567	16,385	17,688	1,191	6,303
Percent of total		39.42	42.55	2.87	15.16
Number of seats	4	2	2	—	—
Cork North-Central	42,767	18,181	15,402	5,623	3,561
Percent of total		42.51	36.01	13.15	8.33
Number of seats	5	2	2	1	—
Cork North-West	33,237	14,775	16,263	2,199	—
Percent of total		44.45	48.93	6.62	—
Number of seats	3	1	2	—	—
Cork South-Central	49,451	19,631	19,765	6,496	3,559
Percent of total		39.70	39.97	13.14	7.20
Number of seats	5	2	2	1	—
Cork South-West	33,019	13,772	16,460	—	2,787
Percent of total		41.71	49.85	—	8.44
Number of seats	3	1	2	—	—
Donegal North-East	30,230	10,488	11,183	562	7,997
Percent of total		34.69	36.99	1.86	26.45
Number of seats	3	1	1	—	1
Donegal South-West	32,199	17,648	12,579	—	1,972
Percent of total		54.81	39.07	—	6.12
Number of seats	3	2	1	—	—
Dublin Central	44,476	18,560	14,181	3,337	8,398
Percent of total		41.73	31.88	7.50	18.88
Number of seats	5	2	2	—	1
Dublin North	27,975	12,706	11,809	3,460	—
Percent of total		45.42	42.21	12.37	—
Number of seats	3	1	2	—	—

Dáil Election, November 1982: (*Continued*)

Constituency	Total	Fianna Fáil	Fine Gael	Labour	Other[a]
Dublin North-Central	40,470	19,727	14,824	3,082	2,837
Percent of total		48.74	36.63	7.62	7.01
Number of seats	4	2	2	—	—
Dublin North-East	32,508	13,912	10,733	3,089	4,774
Percent of total		42.80	33.02	9.50	14.69
Number of seats	4	2	2	—	—
Dublin North-West	31,809	12,778	9,647	2,053	7,331
Percent of total		40.17	30.33	6.45	23.05
Number of seats	4	2	1	—	1
Dublin South	52,400	19,178	27,494	4,299	1,429
Percent of total		36.60	52.47	8.20	2.73
Number of seats	5	2	3	—	—
Dublin South-Central[b]	45,858	17,019	18,142	6,425	4,272
Percent of total		37.11	39.56	14.01	9.32
Number of seats	5	1	2	1	1
Dublin South-East	39,859	12,417	18,894	5,893	2,655
Percent of total		31.15	47.40	14.78	6.66
Number of seats	4	1	2	1	—
Dublin South-West	37,656	13,757	12,602	7,814	3,483
Percent of total		36.53	33.47	20.75	9.25
Number of seats	4	2	1	1	—
Dublin West	46,566	17,046	20,106	1,835	7,579
Percent of total		36.61	43.18	3.94	16.28
Number of seats	5	2	2	—	1
Dun Laoghaire	50,178	15,081	26,358	6,130	2,609
Percent of total		30.06	52.53	12.22	5.20
Number of seats	5	1	3	1	—
Galway East	32,815	16,902	14,823	926	164
Percent of total		51.51	45.17	2.82	0.50
Number of seats	3	2	1	—	—
Galway West	49,323	26,287	16,800	4,449	1,787
Percent of total		53.29	34.06	9.02	3.62
Number of seats	5	3	2	—	—
Kerry North	33,638	17,231	6,683	9,724	—
Percent of total		51.22	19.87	28.91	—
Number of seats	3	2	—	1	—

Dáil Election, November 1982: (*Continued*)

Constituency	Total	Fianna Fáil	Fine Gael	Labour	Other[a]
Kerry South	32,939	15,099	8,414	7,609	1,817
Percent of total		45.84	25.54	23.10	5.52
Number of seats	3	1	1	1	—
Kildare	48,359	23,124	17,651	7,366	218
Percent of total		47.82	36.50	15.23	0.45
Number of seats	5	2	2	1	—
Laoighis-Offaly	54,915	27,604	25,066	2,050	195
Percent of total		50.27	45.65	3.73	0.36
Number of seats	5	3	2	—	—
Limerick East	47,221	21,984	15,997	4,793	4,447
Percent of total		46.56	33.88	10.15	9.42
Number of seats	5	2	2	1	—
Limerick West	31,795	19,780	12,015	—	—
Percent of total		62.21	37.79	—	—
Number of seats	3	2	1	—	—
Longford-Westmeath	43,411	22,997	18,778	1,636	—
Percent of total		52.98	43.26	3.77	—
Number of seats	4	2	2	—	—
Louth	43,677	18,825	14,751	6,435	3,666
Percent of total		43.10	33.77	14.73	8.39
Number of seats	4	2	1	1	—
Mayo East	31,502	16,759	14,292	—	451
Percent of total		53.20	45.37	—	1.43
Number of seats	3	2	1	—	—
Mayo West	30,646	16,218	13,132	1,296	—
Percent of total		52.92	42.85	4.23	—
Number of seats	3	2	1	—	—
Meath	50,997	24,223	18,490	8,284	—
Percent of total		47.50	36.26	16.24	—
Number of seats	5	2	2	1	—
Roscommon	32,804	17,483	15,321	—	—
Percent of total		53.30	46.70	—	—
Number of seats	3	2	1	—	—
Sligo-Leitrim	46,431	24,616	19,241	562	2,012
Percent of total		53.02	41.44	1.21	4.33
Number of seats	4	2	2	—	—

Dáil Election, November 1982: (*Continued*)

Constituency	Total	Fianna Fáil	Fine Gael	Labour	Other[a]
Tipperary North	32,211	15,788	9,234	7,189	—
Percent of total		49.01	28.67	22.32	—
Number of seats	3	1	1	1	—
Tipperary South	40,287	18,710	13,527	8,050	—
Percent of total		46.44	33.58	19.98	—
Number of seats	4	2	1	1	—
Waterford	42,867	16,700	16,971	1,760	7,436
Percent of total		38.96	39.59	4.11	17.35
Number of seats	4	2	2	—	—
Wexford	50,361	23,254	20,862	4,962	1,283
Percent of total		46.17	41.42	9.85	2.55
Number of seats	5	2	3	—	—
Wicklow	41,995	14,982	15,438	7,681	3,894
Percent of total		35.68	36.76	18.29	9.27
Number of seats	4	1	2	1	—
Total	1,688,720	763,313	662,284	158,115	105,008
Percent of total		45.20	39.22	9.36	6.22
Number of seats	166	75	70	16	5

Source: *Election Results and Transfer of Votes* (Dublin: Stationery Office, 1983).
a. The total vote under "Other" included 54,888 the Workers' party (2 elected), 7,012 Democratic Socialist (0), 398 Irish Republican Socialist (0), 259 Communist (0), and 42,451 all others, including Non-party (3).
b. The Speaker of the Dáil is automatically reelected and in this election his constituency was Dublin South-Central.

Dáil Election, February 1987: First-preference Votes and Final Distribution of Seats

Constituency	Total	Fianna Fáil	Fine Gael	Progressive Democrats	Labour	Other[a]
Carlow-Kilkenny	57,485	25,527	14,873	8,063	7,358	1,664
Percent of total		44.41	25.87	14.03	12.80	2.89
Number of seats	5	2	1	1	1	—
Cavan-Monaghan[b]	57,812	31,747	18,927	—	—	7,138
Percent of total		54.91	32.74	—	—	12.35
Number of seats	5	3	2	—	—	—
Clare	47,373	25,022	13,274	5,603	600	2,874
Percent of total		52.82	28.02	11.83	1.27	6.07
Number of seats	4	2	2	—	—	—
Cork East	41,770	16,347	12,739	4,276	888	7,520
Percent of total		39.14	30.50	10.24	2.13	18.00
Number of seats	4	2	1	—	—	1
Cork North-Central	43,343	16,127	11,372	7,245	3,720	4,879
Percent of total		37.21	26.24	16.72	8.58	11.26
Number of seats	5	2	2	1	—	—
Cork North-West	33,404	15,120	14,488	3,796	—	—
Percent of total		45.26	43.37	11.36	—	—
Number of seats	3	1	2	—	—	—
Cork South-Central	56,259	18,460	12,254	14,047	4,862	6,636
Percent of total		32.81	21.78	24.97	8.64	11.80
Number of seats	5	2	1	1	1	—
Cork South-West	33,402	15,132	14,566	3,570	—	134
Percent of total		45.30	43.61	10.69	—	0.40
Number of seats	3	1	2	—	—	—
Donegal North-East	29,420	9,512	8,734	—	393	10,781
Percent of total		32.33	29.69	—	1.34	36.65
Number of seats	3	1	1	—	—	1
Donegal South-West	31,575	18,384	9,403	—	—	3,788
Percent of total		58.22	29.78	—	—	12.00
Number of seats	3	2	1	—	—	—
Dublin Central	47,456	19,993	5,973	6,361	1,399	13,730
Percent of total		42.13	12.59	13.40	2.95	28.93
Number of seats	5	3	—	1	—	1
Dublin North	34,018	16,542	8,878	4,008	3,433	1,157
Percent of total		48.63	26.10	11.78	10.09	3.40
Number of seats	3	2	1	—	—	—

Dáil Election, February 1987 (*Continued*)

Constituency	Total	Fianna Fáil	Fine Gael	Progressive Democrats	Labour	Other[a]
Dublin North-Central	42,924	21,344	10,397	3,582	2,973	4,628
Percent of total		49.73	24.22	8.34	6.93	10.78
Number of seats	4	2	2	—	—	—
Dublin North-East	38,279	19,663	7,243	4,655	2,227	4,491
Percent of total		51.37	18.92	12.16	5.82	11.73
Number of seats	4	2	2	—	—	—
Dublin North-West	34,621	16,737	6,493	—	1,370	10,021
Percent of total		48.34	18.75	—	3.96	28.94
Number of seats	4	2	1	—	—	1
Dublin South	57,331	20,496	17,704	11,957	2,684	4,490
Percent of total		35.75	30.88	20.86	4.68	7.83
Number of seats	5	2	2	1	—	—
Dublin South-Central	51,692	21,149	14,267	5,212	4,701	6,363
Percent of total		40.91	27.60	10.08	9.09	12.31
Number of seats	5	2	2	—	1	—
Dublin South-East	38,270	12,522	12,251	5,961	3,480	4,056
Percent of total		32.72	32.01	15.58	9.09	10.60
Number of seats	4	1	1	1	1	—
Dublin South-West	41,454	16,004	5,250	8,169	5,065	6,966
Percent of total		38.61	12.66	19.71	12.22	16.80
Number of seats	4	2	—	1	1	—
Dublin West	51,712	20,920	11,456	6,014	1,185	12,137
Percent of total		40.45	22.15	11.63	2.29	23.47
Number of seats	5	2	1	1	—	1
Dun Laoghaire	55,702	14,576	17,077	11,023	6,484	6,542
Percent of total		26.17	30.66	19.79	11.64	11.74
Number of seats	5	1	2	1	1	—
Galway East	32,958	17,074	10,416	5,468	—	—
Percent of total		51.81	31.60	16.59	—	—
Number of seats	3	2	1	—	—	—
Galway West	52,762	19,979	9,600	11,360	3,878	7,945
Percent of total		37.87	18.19	21.53	7.35	15.06
Number of seats	5	2	1	1	1	—
Kerry North	34,765	16,712	10,087	—	6,739	1,227
Percent of total		48.07	29.01	—	19.38	3.53
Number of seats	3	1	1	—	1	—

Dáil Election, February 1987 (*Continued*)

Constituency	Total	Fianna Fáil	Fine Gael	Progressive Democrats	Labour	Other[a]
Kerry South	33,211	17,926	5,946	3,215	4,559	1,565
Percent of total		53.98	17.90	9.68	13.73	4.71
Number of seats	3	2	1	—	—	—
Kildare	53,705	22,913	14,124	6,320	7,567	2,781
Percent of total		42.66	26.30	11.77	14.09	5.18
Number of seats	5	2	2	—	1	—
Laoighis-Offaly	56,122	30,204	17,479	5,353	818	2,268
Percent of total		53.82	31.14	9.54	1.46	4.04
Number of seats	5	3	2	—	—	—
Limerick East	49,613	12,633	8,881	18,427	2,201	7,471
Percent of total		25.46	17.90	37.14	4.44	15.06
Number of seats	5	1	1	2	—	1
Limerick West	34,006	17,443	9,464	6,580	519	—
Percent of total		51.29	27.83	19.35	1.53	0.00
Number of seats	3	2	—	1	—	—
Longford-Westmeath	45,152	26,017	12,416	5,401	1,038	280
Percent of total		57.62	27.50	11.96	2.30	0.62
Number of seats	4	3	1	—	—	—
Louth	46,809	18,470	10,820	5,219	6,205	6,095
Percent of total		39.46	23.12	11.15	13.26	13.02
Number of seats	4	2	1	—	1	—
Mayo East	30,920	17,224	13,028	—	—	668
Percent of total		55.71	42.13	—	—	2.16
Number of seats	3	2	1	—	—	—
Mayo West	30,290	17,197	13,093	—	—	—
Percent of total		56.77	43.23	—	—	—
Number of seats	3	2	1	—	—	—
Meath	55,195	27,694	14,172	4,831	3,631	4,867
Percent of total		50.17	25.68	8.75	6.58	8.82
Number of seats	5	3	2	—	—	—
Roscommon	32,416	16,241	12,103	—	—	4,072
Percent of total		50.10	37.34	—	—	12.56
Number of seats	3	2	1	—	—	—
Sligo-Leitrim	45,706	23,574	14,160	2,521	—	5,451
Percent of total		51.58	30.98	5.52	—	11.93
Number of seats	4	3	1	—	—	—

Dáil Election, February 1987 (*Continued*)

Constituency	Total	Fianna Fáil	Fine Gael	Progressive Democrats	Labour	Other[a]
Tipperary North	33,291	17,099	7,859	2,444	4,558	1,331
Percent of total		51.36	23.61	7.34	13.69	4.00
Number of seats	3	2	1	—	—	—
Tipperary South	41,501	17,661	8,480	4,402	3,820	7,138
Percent of total		42.56	20.43	10.61	9.20	17.20
Number of seats	4	2	1	—	—	1
Waterford	44,594	19,000	12,420	5,347	3,358	4,469
Percent of total		42.61	27.85	11.99	7.53	10.02
Number of seats	4	2	1	1	—	—
Wexford	52,922	23,233	16,783	4,708	5,086	3,112
Percent of total		43.90	31.71	8.90	9.61	5.88
Number of seats	5	2	2	—	1	—
Wicklow	46,003	14,988	12,184	5,450	7,754	5,627
Percent of total		32.58	26.49	11.85	16.86	12.23
Number of seats	4	2	1	—	1	—
Total	1,777,288	784,626	481,146	210,593	114,556	186,366
Percent of total		44.15	27.07	11.85	6.45	10.49
Number of seats	166	81	51	14	12	8

Source: Data in these tables were developed from election issues of the *Irish Times* and *Irish Press*; small discrepancies may be found between these figures and those in the final, official canvass results to be published later this year by the Stationery Office in Dublin.

a. Among the eight members elected to the Dáil classified as "Other" were four Workers' Party, one Democratic Socialist, one Independent Fianna Fáil, and two independents.

b. In Cavan-Monaghan the Fine Gael Speaker of the Dáil was deemed to be automatically reelected by virtue of his office.

Glossary

The transliterations in parentheses, prepared by Dr. R. B. Walsh, lecturer in phonetics, University College, Dublin, are intended to represent roughly in English orthographic values the pronunciations used by a majority of Irish people. They do not represent accurate Gaelic pronunciations. Italics in transliterations indicate stressed syllables.

Árd-Fheis (ord-*esh*): literally "the great convention," the annual conference of the political parties.

Bunreacht na hÉireann (bunracht ne *hay*run): "the fundamental law of Ireland," the constitution of Ireland adopted in 1937. This was preceded by the constitution of the Irish Free State, 1922–37, and the constitution of Dáil Éireann, 1919–22.

Ceann Comhairle (kyown *koor*-leh): "president of the council," the chairman of the Dáil. The deputy chairman is *Leas-Cheann Comhairle* (lass kyown *koor*-leh).

Clann na Poblachta (clown ne *pub*lakta): "the people of the republic," a Republican-Socialist party that played an important part in the defeat of Fianna Fáil in 1948.

Clann na Talmhan (clown ne ta*loon*): "the people of the land," a short-lived party mainly representative of smaller farmers in the 1940s and 1950s.

Dáil Éireann (dawl *ay*-run): "the assembly of Ireland," the popularly elected lower house: the chamber of deputies.

Éire (*ay*reh): Ireland, the constitutional name of the state. The genetive form, "Eireann" (*ay*-run), is often attached to other names such as Dáil Éireann, above, and Radio Telefís Éireann, below.

Fianna Fáil (*fee*-an-a *fawl*): "the warriors of destiny," the largest Irish political party, founded by de Valera in 1926.

Fine Gael (fin-a *gale*): "family-group of the Gaels," second largest political party, derived from Cumann na nGaedheal ("the club, or association, or the Gaels"), which accepted the Anglo-Irish Treaty settlement of 1922.

Gaeltacht(a): Irish speaking area(s), now confined to small enclaves along the western seaboard.

Gárda Siochána (gawrda shee-*kaw*-ne): "guardians (of the peace)," the national police force that has maintained the tradition of being unarmed since its inception.

Oireachtas (ih-*rock*-tus or *ih*-ruck-tus): "gathering," the official title of the whole Parliament—president, Dáil, and Seanad.

Radio Telefís Éireann (*rah*-dee-oh *tell*-a-feesh *ay*-run): "the radio and television of Ireland," the national broadcasting service. Customarily abbreviated as RTE.

Seanad Éireann (shanad *ay*-run): the Senate of Ireland, upper house of limited powers; forty-three members elected by members of the Dáil, the outgoing Seanad, and the county and borough councils, six by the graduates of the two universities, and eleven nominated by the Taoiseach.

Sinn Féin (shin *fayn*): "Ourselves," originally a separatist national party established by Arthur Griffith in 1905. The title has been adopted by a variety of political groupings at different stages since that time.

Tanaiste (*taw*-nish-deh): "next-in-line, or heir apparent," the deputy prime minister. Not necessarily right of succession.

Taoiseach (*tee*-shuk) *pl. taoisigh*: "chief or leader," the head of the executive, the prime minister.

Teachta Dála (*tak*-tuh *dawl*-uh): "emissary to the Dáil," or deputy. Customarily abbreviated as TD.

Contributors

HOWARD R. PENNIMAN, general editor of the At the Polls series, is adjunct scholar at the American Enterprise Institute. For thirty years he was a professor of government at Yale University and Georgetown University. He is an election consultant to the American Broadcasting Company and the author of several books on U.S. government and politics. Penniman was a member of the official U.S. observer team for the 1982 and 1984 elections in El Salvador and the 1984 constituent assembly elections in Guatemala.

JOHN BOWMAN (Ph.D., Trinity College, Dublin), a journalist and historian, covers politics and radio and television for RTE. He is the author of *De Valera and the Ulster Question: 1917–1973* (1982).

BASIL CHUBB is professor of political science at Trinity College, Dublin, and author of *The Government and Politics of Ireland, A Source Book of Irish Government, The Government: An Introduction to Cabinet Government in Ireland*, and *The Constitution and Constitutional Change in Ireland*. He is active in public affairs and is at present chairman of the National Employer Labour Conference.

JOHN COAKLEY is a lecturer in politics at the National Institute for Higher Education, Limerick. He has published articles on Irish and comparative politics in a number of journals.

BRIAN FARRELL is associate professor of government and political science at University College, Dublin. He is author of *Chairman or Chief? The Role of Taoiseach, The Founding of Dáil Éireann*, and *Sean Lemass*, and is contributing editor of *The Irish Parliamentary Tradition* and *Communications and Community in Ireland*. He is senior current affairs presenter on RTE television and conducted much of the coverage of the four elections, including the debates between the party leaders.

DAVID M. FARRELL is currently a tutor in the Department of Politics, University College, Dublin; he was formerly a research student at the European University Institute, Florence. He has published articles on the composition of the Dáil and party campaigns.

PETER MAIR is a lecturer in government at the University of Manchester and formerly lectured at the National Institute of Higher Education, Limerick, the University of Strathclyde, Glasgow, and the European University Institute in Florence. He is coeditor of *Western European Party Systems: Continuity and Change* (1983) and of *Party Politics in Contemporary Western Europe* (1984) and is currently completing a book on the postwar Irish party system.

MAURICE MANNING is currently Fine Gael member of the Dáil for Dublin North-East. A lecturer in political science at University College, Dublin, he has written and broadcast extensively on Irish politics.

JOSEPH O'MALLEY has been political correspondent with the *Sunday Independent* since 1973. From 1969 to 1972 he was editor of *This Week* magazine.

RICHARD M. SCAMMON, coauthor of *This U.S.A.* and *The Real Majority*, is director of the Elections Research Center in Washington, D.C. He has edited the biennial series *America Votes* since 1956. He has supplied national election data for all volumes in the At the Polls series.

RICHARD SINNOTT, a lecturer in politics at University College, Dublin, has published work on Irish political attitudes, electoral behavior, and the party system. He holds a Ph.D. from Georgetown University. He spent the academic year 1984-85 as the Jean Monnet Fellow at the European Institute, where he was working on the politics of industrial policy.

Index

40–45, 69, 71, 73, 74–75, 76, 78, 91, 93,
95, 140, 148, 162–63, 180–84, 207–11; of
November 1982, 22–25, 45–49, 69, 71, 72,
73, 76, 85, 91, 95, 96, 141, 163–65, 184–88,
207–11; of February 1987, 232–43. *See
also* Senate
Electorate, 59, 62–63, 79, 81, 94–99, 104–10,
172, 217–19; cleavages, 60–63, 68–73; dissatisfaction of, 4, 15, 19, 53, 66, 68, 84, 85,
206–7, 226–30, 232, 235; and government
formation, 132; occupational structure,
60–61; for Senate, 192–93, 194, 196–203;
transfer patterns, 90–94, 105–10, 126, 138,
210–11, 232, 235, 237, 238–41; turnout,
14, 18–19, 25, 40, 109, 238–40; voting
criteria, 104–10, 127–28, 239–40. *See also*
Opinion polls; Women; Youth
Electoral strategy, 15, 37, 41–42, 79, 104–28,
183, 208–9
Electronic media. *See* Radio broadcasting;
Radio Telefís Éireann
Emigration, 1, 4, 233
Employer-Labour Conference, 223
European Commission, 18, 20
European Economic Community (EEC), 35,
152, 153, 215, 223, 227, 242
European Parliament, 4, 7, 51–52, 68, 75,
135, 159, 161, 200, 217, 239
Evening Herald, 168
Evening Press, 168

Fanning, Aengus, 183
Faulkener, Padraig, 66
Family Planning Bill, 2, 138
Farmers' party, 139
Farrell, Brian, 59
Federated Union of Employers, 224, 226
Federated Workers Union of Ireland (FWUI),
52
Feminist vote. *See* Women
Fennell, Nuala, 159, 161, 165
Fianna Fáil, 1, 10, 11, 12, 18, 24–25, 27, 32,
41, 42, 53, 57, 61, 107, 137–38, 150, 208–9,
214, 215, 232; and abortion, 23–24, 27, 47,
76; by-elections, 6, 18–20, 27, 32, 33, 68,
85; campaign advertising, 39, 115; campaign finances, 22–23, 49–51, 116–17,
236; campaign issues, 32, 35–36, 64, 65,
73–90, 111, 175, 232; campaign strategy,
15, 37, 79, 121–24, 208–9, 236–38; candi-

date selection, 104–10; economic proposals, 32, 33–35, 237; election of 1977; 3–5,
63–66, 91, 95; election of 1981, 7–10,
37–40, 69, 71, 77, 83, 87, 91, 175–80; election of February 1982, 13–14, 40–45, 69,
71, 78, 81, 88, 91, 95, 180–84; election of
November 1982, 22–25, 32, 45–49, 71, 72,
76, 88–89, 91, 141–42, 184–88; election of
February 1987, 232–41; election results,
8–9, 15–17, 25, 40, 90–94, 96, 238–40;
European Parliament, 68, 75; and
government formation, 132; internal
problems, 7, 18, 21, 27, 32–35, 46, 53,
135–37, 147; manifestoes, 35–36, 115, 237;
and media, 168, 169, 171, 172, 174–76, 181,
182, 184–85; Northern Ireland policy, 5,
6–7, 8, 18, 27–28, 34, 35, 47, 81, 203, 232,
233–34; opinion polls, 3, 15, 43, 64–69,
71–99, 209; party reform, 117–19, 207;
public service reform, 3, 237; republican
traditions, 5, 6, 24, 61; Senate representation, 195, 196, 197–98, 203–4; single-party
majority government, 134–37; support,
85–94, 96–99, 104–10, 111, 120–21, 209,
212–13, 237; *The Way Forward*, 21, 23,
32, 45, 46, 81; women and, 160–61,
162–63, 165; youth and, 3, 97. *See also*
Haughey, Charles
Fine Gael, 1, 5, 24–25, 26, 32, 40–41, 53–54,
57, 61, 63, 68, 107, 111, 145, 208–9; and
abortion, 23–24, 28, 47; by-elections, 6–7,
18–20, 32, 68, 85; campaign advertising,
40, 43, 115–16, 185; campaign finances,
11–12, 22–23, 49–50, 51, 116–17, 236;
campaign issues, 7–8, 32, 36, 73–90;
campaign strategy, 37, 79, 121–27, 208–9,
236–38; candidate selection, 104–10, 124;
coalition policy, 8, 9–10, 12, 25–26, 37,
43–44, 78, 79, 89, 92–93, 138–39, 141, 148,
208–9, 214, 215, 220; economic proposals,
32, 237; election of 1977, 2–5, 72, 91, 138;
election of 1981, 7–8, 37–40, 71, 83, 89, 91,
96, 175–80; election of February 1982,
13–14, 40–45, 69, 74, 81, 89, 91, 95, 180–
84; election of November 1982, 22–25,
45–49, 69, 72, 81, 89, 91, 95, 124–27, 141,
184–88; election of February 1987, 234–
40; election results, 8–9, 15–17, 25, 40,
90–94, 238–40; European Parliament, 68;
internal problems, 20–21, 53, 147, 214,

74, 81, 82, 83, 84, 86, 209. *See also*
Opinion polls
Irish National Liberation Army (INLA), 229
Irish Press: campaign coverage, 167, 175,
185, 186; political orientation, 168
Irish Republican Army (IRA), 35, 39, 229
Irish Republican Socialist party, 15
Irish Times: campaign coverage, 35, 167,
171–72, 174, 176–77, 179, 181; opinion
polls, 39, 44, 73–74, 76, 82, 83, 84, 86;
political orientation, 169, 181. *See also*
Opinion polls
Irish Transport and General Workers Union
(ITGWU), 17, 52

Joint Committee on State-Sponsored Bodies,
222
Just Society program, 111–12, 214

Kelly, John, 21, 177–78
Kemmy, Jim, 13, 15, 17, 24, 140
Kennedy, Geraldine, 182
Kiely, Niall, 173
Klingemann, Hans, 215

Labour party, 1, 2, 12, 46, 54, 59, 107, 111,
112–13, 145, 208–9, 234–36; and abortion,
24; by-elections, 18; campaign advertising,
116; campaign finances, 49–50, 51–53,
117, 236; campaign issues, 8, 36, 180–81,
234; campaign strategy, 37, 41–42, 183,
208–9; candidate selection, 104–10; coalition policy, 9–10, 16–17, 21–22, 25–26,
37, 43–44, 52, 89, 92–93, 138–39, 141, 148,
149, 208–9, 214, 215, 234–35; election of
1977, 2–4, 72, 91, 138–39; election of 1981,
8–10, 37–40, 91, 176; election of February
1982, 13–14, 40–45, 69, 74, 91; election of
November 1982, 45–49, 69, 91, 141; election of February 1987, 234–40; election
results, 8–9, 15–17, 24–25, 40, 90–94,
238–40; European Parliament, 8, 51–
52, 68; internal problems, 21–22, 45, 53;
leadership of, 3, 45, 178; manifestoes, 36;
and media, 176, 180, 181–82, 183;
Northern Ireland policy, 8, 78; opinion
polls, 8, 16, 64, 65, 67, 68, 72, 75, 209;
party reform, 117–19; Senate representation, 195, 197, 198, 202–4; support, 21–22,
57, 72–73, 89, 91, 92–94, 104–10, 209,

213; women and, 160–61, 162, 165. *See
also* Cluskey, Frank; National Coalition;
Spring, Dick
Lalor, Patrick J., 224, 225
Lemass, Eileen, 18–19, 162
Lemass, Sean, 111, 132, 135, 140, 142, 149,
212
Lenihan, Brian, 34, 48
Lipset, Seymour Martin, 58–61
Loughnane, Bill, 45
Lynch, Jack, 3, 5, 14, 15, 16, 18, 32, 37, 68,
82–83, 111, 132, 135, 136–37, 142, 147,
149, 151, 163, 174, 202, 233

MacArthur, Malcolm, 20
McCreevy, Charles, 21, 84
McCurtain, Margaret, 158
MacGiolla, Tomas, 19
McGonagle, Stephen, 203
McGurk, Tom, 179
McSharry, Ray, 19, 26
Magill magazine, 42, 51, 180–81, 183–84
Maher, T. J., 4, 69
Mair, Peter, 213, 236
Mallon, Seamus, 203
Manning, Joseph, 107
Manning, Maurice, 181–82
Market Research Bureau of Ireland Ltd.
(MRBI), 28, 43, 47, 75, 76, 82, 85, 86. *See
also* Opinion polls
Markievicz, Countess, 156
Marsh, Michael, 63, 107, 211
Media, 18, 24–25, 26, 39, 44, 48, 50, 53, 152,
158, 167–88, 232, 237. *See also* News-
papers; Radio broadcasting; Radio Telefís
Éireann
Mills, Michael, 179
Mountbatten, Lord Louis, 5
MRBI. *See* Market Research Bureau of
Ireland Ltd.
Murray, John, 49

National Coalition, 37, 65, 118, 132, 138, 139,
146–47
National Development Corporation, 9, 25, 36
National Economic and Social Council
(NESC), 223, 225
National Industrial Economic Council
(NIEC), 223, 225
National Planning Board, 36